NEW DIRECTIONS TEN

Edited by James Laughlin

This is the tenth volume in the series of *New Directions in Prose & Poetry*. All but the book for 1942 are now out print, but the most important material from the complete series was reprinted in 1947 in the anthology *Spearhead*, which is in print.

New Directions

in prose and poetry

AN ANNUAL EXHIBITION GALLERY OF NEW
AND DIVERGENT TRENDS IN LITERATURE

ACKNOWLEDGMENTS

The Publisher wishes to express his thanks for kind permission to reprint the following selections to the editors of—*The Modern Review* for "Existentialism" by Paul Kecskemeti; the London *Daily Telegraph* for "Hollywood is a Term of Disparagement" by Evelyn Waugh; *The Harvard Advocate* for "The Walgh-Vogel" by Richard Wilbur; *The New Mexico Quarterly* for "Time's Rhetoric" by Warren Wirtz; *Partisan Review* for "A Distant Episode" by Paul Bowles; *Commentary* for "America the Beautiful" by Mary McCarthy; *Politics* for "Dedication Day" by James Agee; *Furioso* for "The Amateurs" by Howard Nemerov; *Delta* for poems by Hubert Creekmore; *The Listener* for a poem by Julian Orde; *Horizon* for "Flesh Farewell" by Donald Windham and for a poem by Peter Viereck; and to *Accent* for a story by Jack Jones. Robert Duncan's poem "Heavenly City, Earthly City" was first published by Berne Porter, Berkeley, California.

MANUFACTURED BY DUDLEY B. KIMBALL AT THE BLUE RIDGE MOUNTAIN PRESS, IN PARSIPPANY, NEW JERSEY, U. S. A.

This volume is dedicated
by its editor to

ALFRED and BLANCHE KNOPF

who, over the years of their publishing,
have so greatly enriched American culture
by providing English translations
of significant European books

CONTENTS

NOTES ON CONTRIBUTORS

JAMES AGEE is the film critic for *The Nation* and writes occasional film criticisms for *Time*. Previously he worked for *Fortune*. He is the author of a book of poems, *Permit Me Voyage*, published by the Yale University Press in 1935. *Let Us Now Praise Famous Men*, a book with text by Agee and photographs by Walker Evans, was brought out by Houghton Mifflin in 1941.

LLOYD ALEXANDER was born in Philadelphia in 1924 and now lives in Drexel Hill, Pa. He was discharged from the Army in Paris and was given a scholarship to the Sorbonne by the Ministère des Affaires Etrangères. In Paris he met Paul Eluard and with his help began a translation of his poems. Since then he has done translations of Jean-Paul Sartre's *Le Mur* and *La Nausee* which are to be published by New Directions.

PAUL BOWLES first won recognition as a composer of music in the modern idiom. He wrote the incidental music for *The Glass Menagerie* and his musical settings for Charles Henri Ford's poems have been recorded. He translates from the French and his version of Jean-Paul Sartre's *No Exit* appeared on Broadway. His short stories have been published in the leading literary magazines, and he will soon publish a novel based on his experiences in North Africa, where he has spent enough time to be able to speak Arabic.

RENE CHAR, whose poetry is presently enjoying a great popularity in Paris, is the subject of a recently published book of criticism *Avez-vous lu Char?* In his early forties, Char hails from the south of France, and has been a manufacturer of plaster. He first came to prominence as a follower of Eluard, but his work is in no sense imitative.

ELLIOTT COLEMAN lives in Baltimore where he teaches in the English Department of Johns Hopkins. He is director of

9

the Summer School at Cummington. New Directions will shortly publish his 39 *Night Sonnets.*

ALEX COMFORT has emerged as one of the leaders among
the new English writers who are opposed to war to the extent of
doing something about it. He is a doctor. His novel *The Power
House* and his poems *The Song of Lazarus* have been published
in this country by the Viking Press.

HUBERT CREEKMORE, born in Mississippi, has lived for a
number of years in New York, where he worked for New Directions. He has published four volumes of poems—the last one
being *The Long Reprieve* in 1947—and one novel, *The Fingers of
Night.* A second novel, *The Welcome,* has just been issued. At
present he is teaching at the University of Iowa.

ROBERT DUNCAN is a young California poet who has published two volumes of verse. His most recent, *Heavenly City,
Earthly City,* has won wide critical acclaim.

RICHARD EBERHART lives and works in Cambridge. During the war he served as an officer in the Navy. His early volumes of poetry include *Reading the Spirit, Song and Idea* and
Poems, New and Selected. He has edited with Selden Rodman
an anthology, *War and the Poet,* and last year his most recent
volume appeared under the title of *Burr Oaks.*

PAUL ELUARD is probably the most widely known poet of
the Paris Surrealist movement. He lives in Paris and during the
war was active in the French Resistance. He has published many
volumes of verse, and a book of translations of his early poetry,
Thorns of Thunder appeared in London shortly before the war.
Next year New Directions will bring out a book of his poetry
translated by Lloyd Alexander.

LESLIE FIEDLER has contributed to many literary magazines. He spent almost four years in Navy service in the Pacific
and China, after which he worked at writing on a Rockefeller
Foundation Fellowship. He now teaches at Montana State University. For the Navy he learned to speak Japanese.

PAUL GOODMAN was born in 1911 and educated at City
College, New York, and at the University of Chicago. He now
lives in New York, is married and has two children. He was one
of the *Five Young American Poets* of 1941, and in the same year
published a novel, *The Grand Piano,* and a book of plays, *Stop*

Light. Other published works are *The Facts of Life, Art and Social Nature, The State of Nature* and *Kafka's Prayer.* He says he has about fifteen more books ready for publication.

JULIEN GRACQ is a well-known writer in his native France. His first novel, the post-surrealist, neo-romantic *Chateau D'Argol,* was published in Paris not long before the war and was enthusiastically received. During the war he served in the French Army and was a prisoner in Germany. New Directions is publishing a translation of his second novel, *The Dark Stranger,* in the near future. He is also a playwright and critic.

ELEANOR HESTHAL was born in San Francisco in 1911 and still lives there. She graduated from the University of California and is now teaching English at the California Labor School. Last year she received the Phelan Award for Poetry.

LIZ JACOBSON was born in a small town (Kamenetz-Litowski) in Russia and was brought here by her parents as a little child. She has lived in Cleveland, Ohio ever since and graduated from a grade school, high school and Western Reserve University all in that city. She has worked as correspondent, staff writer and special writer for the *Cleveland Plain Dealer* and has written for many magazines. She once ghost-wrote a book for a prominent Clevelander and "would not do it again for all the money in the world." At present she is at work on a novel.

JACK JONES has lived most of his life in the New York suburbs of Scarsdale and White Plains. He was born in Dallas, Texas, in 1923, and states that he died about 1960 of radio-active poisoning. He attended Swarthmore College for a year, and has since worked in a chemical factory in Queens, in a printing plant in Manhattan and as a reader for Twentieth Century Fox. He has been working for the last year on a novel.

PAUL KECSKEMETI, born in Hungary in 1901, received his Ph. D. in philosophy from the University of Budapest. He has published many articles on philosophical subjects and worked as a correspondent for The United Press in Germany and France. He is now working for the War Department on cultural and political reorientation of occupied areas.

O. KLAUSNER was in school from the ages of six to twenty, and caught in the depression from twenty until World War II. He then served in the Army for three years, during which he fought in most of Europe. A play by him is announced for fall production by "The Poet's Theatre."

SEYMOUR KRIM was born in New York City in 1922 and was educated in the public schools of that city and those of Newark, New Jersey. He attended the University of North Carolina fitfully for a year and a half and then came back to New York where he has been ever since. He is married to Eleanore Goff, the dancer.

IRWIN KROENING is 32 years old and was born in Milwaukee, Wisconsin. Since he completed his education he has worked at an assortment of odd jobs—advertising copy-writer, laboratory assistant, riveter, cocktail-bar pianist, teacher, janitor and night watchman. He studied psychology at the University of Wisconsin with particular interest in schizophrenic speech behavior. When his wife died of rheumatic heart disease in 1946 he left school and has since been roaming around the country.

JAMES LAUGHLIN is the editor of New Directions, and, in another world, an inventive writer on subjects connected with the sport of skiing. A volume of his poems, *Some Natural Things*, was published two years ago by New Directions, and a new one, *A Small Book of Poems*, appeared this summer in Milan in Giovanni Scheiwiller's *Pesce d'Oro* Series.

MARY McCARTHY is well known for her theatrical column in *Partisan Review*. She was born in Seattle, Washington, graduated from Vassar College and has contributed to *The New Republic*, *The Nation* and other periodicals. In 1942 she published a novel, *The Company She Keeps*.

CARSON McCULLERS was born in Columbus, Georgia, in 1917. At the age of seventeen she came to New York with the intention of attending Columbia University, but, having lost all her tuition money on the subway, she attended night school instead and worked at odd jobs in the daytime. Her first published work was a short story in *Story Magazine*, which appeared in 1934. Her first novel, *The Heart Is A Lonely Hunter*, was published by Houghton Mifflin in 1940, and her second, *Reflections In A Golden Eye*, in 1941. Her last book, *A Member Of The Wedding*, appeared last year. She is married and lives in Nyack.

HENRI MICHAUX, of Belgian origin, will make a trip here this year. Michaux has become a Parisian, and, after the publication of some ten books of poetry and prose poetry, ranks with

Eluard as the greatest living French poet. New Directions will bring out *A Barbarian in Asia,* a book which Michaux wrote about the people of India, China, Japan, etc. following a sojourn in those regions. It has been translated by Sylvia Beach. Michaux is also a painter of some renown and a show of his work is to be held this year in one of the New York galleries.

HOWARD NEMEROV was born in New York City in 1920 and graduated from Harvard in 1941. At present, following wartime service in the Air Force and marriage to an English girl, he teaches at Hamilton College. His book of poems, *The Image and the Law,* was published last year. He is an editor of *Furioso.*

JULIAN ORDE'S parents are both painters. She was brought up in London and Paris and was taught to draw at the Chelsea Polytechnic. Later she studied acting at the Royal Academy of Dramatic Art and was on the stage for six years. At present she works as a copy-writer and film manager of a large advertising agency in London. She has published short stories and has had seven short films produced. Her first feature film, *The Small Voice,* is soon to be shown.

ROBERT PAYNE was born in Cornwall, England, in 1911, and was educated at various universities and shipyards; he visited Spain during the Civil War and was an armament officer at Singapore and later a professor in China. He wrote *Forever China, China Awake,* and edited a book of Chinese verse translations, *The White Pony,* but likes most a novel called *The Mountains and the Stars* and his short stories not yet published.

RENATO POGGIOLI, one of the editors of the Italian literary quarterly *Inventario,* is Associate Professor of Slavic and Comparative Literature at Harvard University.

JOHN H. PORTER has written book reviews for the *New York Times, The New Republic* and other publications.

JACQUES PREVERT is best known for his work in the cinema, notably *Les Enfants du Paradis,* but he is also one of the most popular of contemporary French poets. His book *Paroles,* published by Bertelé, has had an enormous sale and been widely influential.

F. T. PRINCE is one of the best contemporary English poets, whose first volume, *Poems,* established his reputation when it was published in London by Faber and Faber. New Directions published his *Selected Poems*.

ISAAC ROSENFELD was born in Chicago in 1918. He studied at the Universty of Chicago where he took an MA in philosophy. Since 1941 he has been living in New York where he has worked in editorial positions on *The New Republic*, the *American Jewish Record* and the *New Leader*. He now teaches night school at New York University and has a Guggenheim Fellowship in creative writing. He has published short stories in leading national magazines and his novel *A Passage from Home* was published by the Dial Press in 1946. He is married and has two children.

GEORGE SEFERIS is one of the leaders in the poetic renaissance in modern Greece. His first collection of poems was published in 1932 and was hailed as a turning point in modern Greek poetry. He was born in Smyrna in 1900, and was educated in Athens and afterwards studied law in Paris. He has lived in England and made a translation of Eliot's *Waste Land* which has had a great influence in Greece. A book of Seferis' poetry, *The King of Asine*, translated by Lawrence Durrell, Bernard Spencer and Nanos Valaoritis, with an excellent introduction by Rex Warner has just been published in England by John Lehmann Ltd.

JOHN SENIOR, after army service and graduation from Columbia University, won the Glasscock Memorial Poetry Award in 1945. Born in 1923, he has contributed articles and reviews to *The Nation* and other periodicals, has written a novel and taught English at Bard College.

PHILIP SIEKEWITZ began to write while in the Army, and "The Petition" is his first published work. He is now a graduate student at the University of California, working toward a Ph. D. in biochemistry.

WILLIAM JAY SMITH was born in Louisiana in 1918 and, being the son of a professional soldier, spent his early years on Army posts. During the war he was naval liaison officer with the French Navy and is now a Rhodes scholar at Oxford. In 1945 he was awarded the Young Poets Prize by *Poetry* and his work has also appeared in *Chimera*, *The New Republic*, *Furioso* and, most recently, in *Horizon*. A first collection, *Poems*, was published last year by the Banyan Press.

RUTH STEPHAN, who makes her home in Westport, Connecticut, is the editor of one of our most original and intriguing Little Magazines, *The Tiger's Eye*. Two years ago she paid a visit to Peru, where she collected the material for her *Little Anthology of Peruvian Poetry*.

PETER VIERECK was born in New York in 1916. He studied at Harvard and at Christ Church, Oxford (as a Henry Fellow). He is one of the only Harvard students to win at the same time the Garrison Medal for the best poetry and the Bowdoin Prize for the best prose. His first book, a psychological and historical analysis warning against the Nazi menace, was published by Knopf in 1941, *Metapolitics: From the Romantics to Hitler*. During the war he served three years overseas as an enlisted man in the African and Italian campaigns and then taught history at the G. I. University at Florence. From 1946 to 1947 he was an Instructor at Harvard and this year has been an Assistant Professor at Smith College.

VERNON WATKINS, like his friend Dylan Thomas, is a Welshman. He publishes with Faber & Faber, under the critical eye of T. S. Eliot, and is rated one of the best of the younger British poets. New Directions recently introduced him to America with a volume of *Selected Poems*, and will follow up next year with a collection of his translations of German.

EVELYN WAUGH, since *Brideshead Revisited*, has written two brilliant short novels, of which *The Loved One* has recently appeared in this country with enormous success. His *A Handful of Dust* is in New Directions "New Classics Series".

WILLIAM WEAVER, a young poet and an experienced translator, is now studying, writing and traveling in Italy.

BROM WEBER was born in New York City in 1917. He had worked at a wide variety of jobs and had contributed to *The Nation, The New Republic, Twice-A-Year* and other publications before reaching full stature with the publication of his *Hart Crane: A Biographical and Critical Study* this year. He is working on a novel and lecturing on modern literature and writing at the City College of New York and the Rand School of Social Science.

RICHARD WILBUR was born in New York City in 1921 and grew up on a New Jersey farm. He attended Amherst College for four years, was in the Army for two years and received an M. A. from Harvard last year where he is now a Junior Fellow of the Society of Fellows. He is married and has a young daughter. His book of poems, *The Beautiful Changes*, was recently published.

TENNESSEE WILLIAMS, since the great success of *A Streetcar Named Desire*, has been compared by critics with Eugene O'Neill: he deserves it, but in the furor over his dramatic writing it should not be overlooked that Williams is also a good poet (see *Five Young American Poets: Series III*) and a fine prose writer (New Directions has just published *One Arm*, a collection of his short stories). Recently Williams has been living in Rome, but returned to the States for the staging of his new play, *Summer & Smoke*. A collection of his short one-act plays is available under the title of 27 *Wagons Full of Cotton*.

DONALD WINDHAM was formerly an editor of *Dance Index*. He has published short stories in the leading literary magazines and collaborated with Tennessee Williams on the Broadway play *You Touched Me*. Recently he has been living in Europe.

WARREN WIRTZ is equally known for his poetry and his music. His poems have appeared in *Kenyon Review* and other literary magazines and he has written a symphony for Dmitri Mitropoulos. He has composed other symphonic and chamber music and has served as assistant to Ernst Krenek at Hamline University in St. Paul. At present he is in Paris on a Woolley Foundation Fellowship.

16

A FEW RANDOM NOTES
FROM THE EDITOR

DURING the greater part of the year while this volume was being
assembled I had the good fortune to be living, working and travelling in Europe—France, Switzerland, Italy, Austria, Germany
and England. My journey was a business trip, with three purposes: most important, to search for inexpensive printers who
could be used for printing the type of high quality but small selling books which the inflation of costs here at home has now made
unpublishable on a business basis; secondly, to work out distribution systems for New Directions books in the European
markets; and finally, to look for new European writers who
might merit translation here.

I'm happy to report that I met with some success on all these
scores. We are now experimenting with the printing of books in
Italy, France, England and Germany. The exhibitions of New
Directions books held in Paris and the cities of Switzerland were
well attended and aroused an eager and intelligent response. A
great many Europeans read English and are hungry for good
American books. While I did not find any extremely promising
new writers in Switzerland and Germany, there are many in
France and Italy. We are now preparing translations of Julien
Gracq, Henri Michaux, the early Sartre, Giuseppe Berto and
Elio Vittorini which will prove that point.

But the internal affairs of New Directions are hardly of interest to many readers. More diverting perhaps are my personal
reactions to the general state of European culture today as it
bears on our own. I had lived several years in Europe before the
War and I returned to it with a rough knowledge of the languages
and a longing to revisit places where I had been so happy in
the days of youth. I am strongly antipathetic to what I call the
visual and aural vulgarities of the USA—things that so constantly offend the eye (the ugly buildings and almost everything that

17

the automobile has brought us) and the ear (what comes out of the radio and juke box). These prejudices were greatly indulged by Europe. Certain elements in each country are busy copying our bad habits, but the price of gasoline (about a dollar a gallon on the average) has so far curtailed their efforts. Except for the bombed and shelled areas, Europe is just as handsome as it ever was. In city or country it is bliss to the eye. And I didn't hear a radio for months at a time. . . .

But the human landscape *has* changed. The people are only superficially the same. As you live with them you realize how much the War has upset their equilibrium. Of course, it is not the same in each country. Switzerland is a state of mind all unto itself. Of the countries hurt by the War (Switzerland was both hurt and helped) Italy seems to me the furthest ahead in her "recovery." (I did not visit Belgium or Holland, which are both reported to be coming back strong.) What struck me most was how almost everyone you meet, regardless of class, would like to emigrate to America. (I did not talk to many farmers; they are probably content—because they are making so much money.) If you live in Europe with one of our green passports it is a very different place than it is for those who know they can't get away if Russia decides to move West to the Atlantic. (In Trieste, where I went to see Joyce's brother, Stanislas, and the family of Italo Svevo, I found out what the Communists do when they come into a bourgeois city. There was a period of about a month between the departure of the Germans and the arrival of our troops, during which the Reds were in control. They were very efficient. They had lists of all the more solid citizens in the city and they marched them out back of town and pushed them into some deep pot-holes in the ground.) It is not a case of war-scare. People here at home are far more jittery than they are there. It is a case of the absence of long-term expectation. All but the Communists, who swallow what they are told to, realize that the disease of Statism is in full fever and not likely to be checked in ten years or even in twenty. American aid can help patch up the broken-down economies but it does not give Europe the moral tools to set up forms of government of a liberal type which can withstand the winds that blow from Moscow. I except from that statement England, which has a very sound and effective democracy, perhaps a better one than our own.

Your typical young European city man, even in the oasis of Switzerland, richest country in the world, unless he has taken down the Stalinist hook, cannot see much future for his life. By that I don't mean the American dream that he will move from a Chevrolet to a Buick to a Cadillac. In Europe it is still possible to be "successful" in terms other than the monetary. What worries the young European is the prospect of perpetual political and social unrest, of never being able to settle down to a decade of work in comparative tranquility. A few writers, of course, thrive on chaos—possibly Sartre is one of them—but most want a more stabilized climate to work in. And certainly publishers and editors *have* to have some sense of security to make any long-term plans. There was a period immediately after the War when book sales boomed in France and Italy. But now the continuing inflation in France has brought on a book crisis. Sales have collapsed, and most of the new houses founded since the War with them. In Italy it is only slightly better.

Everywhere I encountered the obsession of wanting to get to America. And since it is impossible in most countries to get a visa for more than a tourist visit unless you have been on a waiting list for years the dream exists outside the realm of things possible and often takes on the characteristics of other unfulfillable desires. Whence arise some strange distortions. People long for America so hard that they begin to hate it. You will find writers who have obviously been influenced by modern American literature (Hemingway is the great influence in Italy; Steinbeck, Dos Passos, Faulkner, Caldwell et al. in France) righteously attacking our culture. Hollywood, of course, makes a wonderful whipping boy. And so do trash novels like *Forever Amber*, which has been translated into French and sold heavily. French critics probably resent as much as *Amber* the fact that French readers will buy such muck. I'm afraid that there is some serious danger that French reading tastes could be debased in the way that has happened here if the same mass marketing procedures were applied. That is a frightening thought. But it is still in the future. For the present it can be clearly demonstrated that the average European reading taste is far above our deplorable standard.

From our own experience with New Directions books, and from conversations with publishers of Little Magazines, I have come to the conclusion that there are about 25,000 readers in the United States who now and then buy or read a "highbrow" book or magazine. By "highbrow" I mean books on the same level of literary integrity with say—at random—Marianne Moore, Saul Bellow, Carson McCullers, Tennessee Williams. . . . Twenty-five thousand in a population of—what is it now?—a hundred and fifty million? Then turn to a little population such as the French-speaking Swiss, of whom there are perhaps four million in all, and you will find that a book club like the Guilde du Livre has 80,000 members and habitually gives them books which range, on the scale of value set above, from upper-medium to highbrow. The Guilde du Livre in recent years has successfully distributed books by Kafka, Baudelaire, Radiguet, Ramuz, and even Jarry! That is just one example of the higher European taste standard. Many more could be brought forward.

How do you account for it? Better education? Possibly. But that is only part of it. The main thing, I think, is the overall atmosphere—the *respect* for the mind and its pleasures. In Europe a poet is an object of honor, not of derision. And people are not so constantly on the search for ways of diverting themselves that will not require any thought. A writer in Europe can feel that he is part of the community. He does not have to apologize for his occupation—as he does here unless he makes a great deal of money. I don't mean to say that Europeans spend all their leisure with their noses glued to "good" books. Far from that. Many of them are too hard up to buy books. But, whatever their situation in life, they are more likely than not to respect the *idea* of books, and to think of books as being something more consequential than packages of merchandise, and to have an innate taste for the better in preference to the worse.

Perhaps another way of expressing this is to use the word *tradition*. For many centuries good books were held in esteem by the small educated classes, and this veneration filtered through to the uneducated classes. In the last hundred years education has been extended further down the social scale in Europe. But the extension has been very gradual. It has been so gradual that the tradition of quality has never been seriously interrupted.

Here in America I would say that the tradition of quality *has* been interrupted because we leapt in a few generations from the small cultivated élite of the Eastern seaboard to a huge mass of citizens, many of diverse immigrant origin, who have been taught *how* to read, but not *what* to read.

Does that make sense? Or is it too much of a simplification?

At this point, I would urge the reader to take leave of my opaque colloquialisms and read Mary McCarthy's "America The Beautiful" which will be found a few pages further on in this volume. Here he can watch one of our keenest American minds bite into problems related to those we have just been discussing, and in a style so beautifully fashioned as to be a joy in itself.

I accept Miss McCarthy's thesis that Americans are not really materialistic, but with this reservation: most of the "new" Americans (and a lot of the "old" ones, too) certainly do worship the possession of money. But I think they worship it for what it does for them. Europeans are more materialistic than we are in the sense that they would seldom waste the money we do on pleasures that leave no physical trace. Few Europeans could ever bring themselves to blow fifty dollars on an evening in a nightclub. They would buy something of value with it. Hence the number of French who put money "into" fine editions and illustrated books. Could we not say that the "new" American wants money because of the sense of action and importance it yields him, and not because he believes in material possessions?

What *do* Americans believe in anyway? They believe in "being happy"—"the pursuit of happiness," as if you could run and throw salt on its tail. Americans are forever thinking up ways to "be happy," and they feel guilty if they aren't. Europeans have a long inherited history of mostly not being happy and they seem to have developed the habit of enjoying life whether they are "happy" or not.

If our American literary culture is, in its wide extension, debased today, I think it is because two trends, or social situations, coalesced to its detriment. Movement I: "Education" of vast masses so rapidly that the tradition of quality was weakened. Movement II: The drive to "make" money moving into the field of mass production of culture. If our masses had been educated so gradually that the tradition of quality had had time to filter down from the élite, then the merchants of culture would have been obliged to market a quality product. Now that the market for trash has been firmly established it will take a long, long time (if it is possible at all) to improve its quality.

Can we learn anything from Europe that might help us raise our broad standard of literary taste? I doubt it. Well . . . we can learn patience . . . Translating the good European books for publication here is important; it injects some new life into our creative blood stream. But importing them will not materially alter the reading habits of the masses. That can only be achieved with time—through the establishment of a tradition, sponsored by a cultural élite (which can just as well be an élite of working people using public libraries as rich patrons in panelled halls) and through the divorce of high and low culture.

Many readers will bridle at that last statement. I may be wrong, but I don't think you can ever get the whole reading public educated to the point where it can take in *The Golden Bowl*. Even a GPU couldn't manage that. But I don't see why we should not be able to develop in three generations an élite literary taste in 1% of the citizenry. 1% of 150,000,000 is a lot of readers —enough, economically, to support as many really first-rate writers as we are likely to produce at any one time. Then it wouldn't much matter what the gross public read, and the hacks and touts could get as rich as they pleased catering to them.* As things now stand, the intermixture of high and low culture in the book world creates a market confusion which prevents the buying power of the existing élite from being channelled undividedly to the support of the best writers. (To explain, in detail, exactly how that confusion operates would require a considerable essay; I touched briefly on the subject in my editorial notes to this volume last year, and I may likely get back to it next time.)

Yes, I think we can hope to have 1% reading at the level of Henry James in three generations. But it is not going to come about through wishful thinking alone. It will require continuous militant action on the part of all of us who would welcome even so modest a millenium. By militancy I don't mean that you are to take out your shotgun and blow the britches off of You-Know-Whom and his like. Spare yourself the chair and them for a more lingering punishment. Look for more constructive ways of fighting the good fight. Above all look for little things that will support the cause. There are hundreds of ways in which you can take action, but here are a few modest proposals:

1) If you learn from your children that there is a teacher doing enlightened work in their school, one who is instilling a love of good reading, go out of your way to let the teacher know she is appreciated. Teaching is a pretty thankless profession in the USA. Try to give the good teachers support on the social level. Make them feel important.

2) Get your weight behind anyone on the staff of your local public library who shows signs of enlightenment. So much can be done at that level. As a taxpayer, you have some say in what the library buys and displays.

---

* The high point in big-time hackery seems to have been reached last year when a public opinion expert opened a branch of his business to pre-test audience reactions to manuscripts in progress.

(*Continued on page* 510)

AMERICA THE BEAUTIFUL

(*The Humanist In The Bathtub*)

Mary McCarthy

A VISITING EXISTENTIALIST wanted recently to be taken to dinner
at a really American place. This proposal, natural enough in a
tourist, disclosed a situation thoroughly unnatural. Unless the
visiting lady's object was suffering, there was no way of satisfying
her demand. Sukiyaki joints, chop suey joints, Italian table d'-
hote places, French provincial restaurants with the menu written
on a slate, Irish chophouses, and Jewish delicatessens came abun-
dantly to mind, but these were not what the lady wanted.
Schrafft's or the Automat would have answered, yet to take her
there would have been to turn oneself into a tourist and to present America as a spectacle, a *New Yorker* cartoon or a savage
drawing in the *New Masses*. It was the beginning of an evening
of humiliations. The visitor was lively and eager; her mind lay
open and orderly, like a notebook ready for impressions. It was
not long, however, before she shut it up with a snap. We had no
recommendations to make to her. With movies, plays, current
books, it was the same story as with the restaurants—*Open City,
Les Enfants du Paradis*, Oscar Wilde, a reprint of Henry James
were *pâté maison* to this lady who wanted the definitive flap-
jack. She did not believe us when we said that there were no
good Hollywood movies, no good Broadway plays—only curios,
she was merely confirmed in her impression that American intellectuals were "negative."

Yet the irritating thing was that we did not feel negative.
We admired and liked our country; we preferred it to that
imaginary America, land of the *peaux rouges* of Caldwell and
Steinbeck, dumb paradise of violence and the detective story,
which had excited the sensibilities of our visitor and of the up-

23

to-date French literary world. But to found our preference, to locate it materially in some admirable object or institution, such as Chartres, say, or French café life, was for us, that night at any rate, an impossible undertaking. We heard ourselves saying that the real America was elsewhere, in the white frame houses and church spires of New England; yet we knew that we talked foolishly—we were not Granville Hicks and we looked ludicrous in his opinions. The Elevated, half a block away, interrupting us every time a train passed, gave us the lie on schedule, every eight minutes. But if the elm-shaded village green was a false or at least an insufficient address for the *genius loci* we honored, where then was it to be found? Surveyed from the vantage point of Europe, this large continent seemed suddenly deficient in objects of virtue. The Grand Canyon, Yellowstone Park, Jim Hill's mansion in St. Paul, Monticello, the blast furnaces of Pittsburgh, Mount Rainier, the yellow observatory at Amherst, the little-theatre movement in Cleveland, Ohio, a Greek revival house glimpsed from a car window in a lost river-town in New Jersey—these things were too small for the size of the country. Each of them, when pointed to, diminished in interest with the lady's perspective of distance. There was no sight that in itself seemed to justify her crossing of the Atlantic.

If she was interested in "conditions," that was a different matter. There are conditions everywhere; it takes no special genius to produce them. Yet would it be an act of hospitality to invite a visitor to a lynching? Unfortunately, nearly all the "sights" in America fall under the head of conditions. Hollywood, Reno, the share-croppers homes in the South, the mining towns of Pennsylvania, Coney Island, the Chicago stockyards, Macy's, the Dodgers, Harlem, even Congress, the forum of our liberties, are spectacles rather than sights, to use the term in the colloquial sense of "Didn't he make a holy spectacle of himself?" An Englishman of almost any political opinion can show a visitor through the Houses of Parliament with a sense of pride or at least of indulgence toward his national foibles and traditions. The American, if he has a spark of national feeling, will be humiliated by the very prospect of a foreigner's visit to Congress—these, for the most part, illiterate hacks whose fancy vests are spotted with gravy, and whose speeches, hypocritical, unctuous, and slovenly, are spotted also with the gravy of political patronage, these persons are a reflection on the democratic process rather than of it; they expose it in its underwear. In European legislation, we are told, a great deal of shady business goes on in private, behind the scenes. In America, it is just the opposite, anything good, presumably, is accomplished *in camera,* in the committee rooms.

It is so with all our institutions. For the visiting European, a trip through the United States has, almost inevitably, the character of an exposé, and the American, on his side, is tempted by love of his country to lock the inquiring tourist in his hotel room and throw away the key. His contention that the visible and material America is not the real or the only one is more difficult to sustain than was the presumption of the "other" Germany behind the Nazi steel.

To some extent a citizen of any country will feel that the tourist's view of his homeland is a false one. The French will tell you that you have to go into their homes to see what the French people are really like. The intellectuals in the Left Bank cafés are not the real French intellectuals, etc., etc. In Italy, they complain that the tourist must not judge by the *ristorantes;* there one sees only black-market types. But in neither of these cases is the native really disturbed by the tourist's view of his country. If Versailles or Giotto's bell-tower in Florence do not tell the whole story, they are still not incongruous with it; you do not hear a Frenchman or an Italian object when these things are noticed by a visitor. With the American, the contradiction is more serious. He must, if he is to defend his country, repudiate its visible aspect almost entirely. He must say that its parade of phenomenology, its billboards, super-highways, even its sky-scrapers, not only fail to represent the inner essence of his country but in fact contravene it. He may point, if he wishes, to certain beautiful objects, but here too he is in difficulties, for nearly everything that is beautiful and has not been produced by nature belongs to the 18th century, to a past with which he has very little connection, and which his ancestors, in many or most cases, had no part in building. Beacon Street and the Boston Common are very charming in the 18th-century manner, so are the sea captains' houses in the Massachusetts ports, and the ruined plantations of Louisiana, but an American from Brooklyn or the Middle West or the Pacific Coast finds the style of life embodied in them as foreign as Europe; indeed, the first sensation of a Westerner, coming upon Beacon Hill and the gold dome of the State House, is to feel that at last he has traveled "abroad." The American, if he is to speak the highest truth about his country, must refrain from pointing at all. The virtue of American civilization is that it is unmaterialistic.

25

This statement may strike a critic as whimsical or perverse. Everybody knows, it will be said, that America has the most materialistic civilization in the world, that Americans care only about money, they have no time or talent for living; look at radio, look at advertising, look at life insurance, look at the tired business man, at the Frigidaires and the Fords. In answer, the reader is invited first to look into his own heart and inquire whether he personally feels himself to be represented by these things, or whether he does not, on the contrary, feel them to be irrelevant to him, a necessary evil, part of the conditions of life. Other people, he will assume, care about them very much: the man down the street, the entire population of Detroit or Scarsdale, the back-country farmer, the urban poor or the rich. But he accepts these objects as imposed on him by a collective "otherness" of desire, an otherness he has not met directly but whose existence he infers from the number of automobiles, Frigidaires, or television sets he sees around him. Stepping into his new Buick convertible, he knows that he would gladly do without it, but imagines that to his neighbor, who is just backing *his* out of the driveway, this car is the motor of life. More often, however, the otherness is projected farther afield, onto a different class or social group, remote and alien. Thus the rich, who would like nothing better, they think, than for life to be a perpetual fishing trip with the trout grilled by a native guide, look patronizingly upon the whole apparatus of American civilization as a cheap Christmas present to the poor, and city people see the radio and the washing-machine as the farm-wife's solace.

It can be argued, of course, that the subjective view is prevaricating, possession of the Buick being nine-tenths of the social law. But who has ever met, outside of advertisements, a true parishioner of this church of Mammon? A man may take pride in a car, and a housewife in her new sink or wallpaper, but pleasure in new acquisitions is universal and eternal—an Italian man with a new gold tooth, a French bibliophile with a new edition, a woman with a new baby, a philosopher with a new thought, all these people are rejoicing in progress, in man's power to enlarge and improve. Before men showed off new cars, they showed off new horses; it is alleged against modern man that he did not make the car but his grandfather did not make the horse either. What is imputed to Americans is something quite different, an abject dependence on material possessions, an image of happiness as packaged by a manufacturer, content in a can.

26

This view of American life is strongly urged by advertising agencies. We know the "other," of course, because we meet them every week in full force in the *New Yorker* or the *Saturday Evening Post,* those brightly colored families of dedicated consumers, waiting in unison on the porch for the dealer to deliver the new car, gobbling the new cereal ("Gee, Mom, is it good for you too?"), lining up to bank their paycheck, or fearfully anticipating the industrial accident and the insurance-check that will "compensate" for it. We meet them also, more troll-like underground, in the subway placards, in the ferociously complacent One-A-Day family, and we hear their courtiers sing to them on the radio of Ivory or Supersuds. The thing, however, that repels us in these advertisements is their naive falsity to life. Who are these advertising men kidding, besides the European tourist? Between the tired, sad, gentle faces of the strangers around us and these grinning Holy Families, there exists no possibility of even a wishful identification. We take a vitamin pill with the hope of feeling (possibly) a little less tired, but the superstition of buoyant health emblazoned in the bright, ugly pictures has no more power to move us than the blood of St. Januarius.

Familiarity has perhaps bred contempt in us Americans: until you have had a washing machine, you cannot imagine how little difference it will make to you. Europeans still believe that money brings happiness, witness the bought journalist, the bought politician, the bought general, the whole venality of European literary life, inconceivable in this country of the dollar. It is true that America produces and consumes more cars, soap, and bathtubs than any other nation, but we live among these objects rather than by them. Americans build skyscrapers; Le Corbusier worships them. Ehrenburg, our Soviet critic, fell in love with the Check-O-Mat in American railway stations, writing home paragraphs of song to this gadget—while deploring American materialism. When an American heiress wants to buy a man, she at once crosses the Atlantic. The only really materialistic people I have ever met have been Europeans.

The strongest argument for the un-materialistic character of American life is the fact that we tolerate conditions that are, from a materialistic point of view, intolerable. What the foreigner finds most objectionable in American life is its lack of basic comfort. No nation with any sense of material well-being would endure the food we eat, the cramped apartments we live in, the noise, the traffic, the crowded subways and buses. American life, in large cities, at any rate, is a perpetual assault on the senses and the nerves; it is out of asceticism, out of unworldliness, precisely, that we bear it.

This republic was founded on an unworldly assumption, a denial of "the facts of life." It is manifestly untrue that all men are created equal; interpreted in worldly terms, this doctrine has resulted in a pseudo-equality, that is, in standardization, in an equality of things rather than of persons. The inalienable rights to life, liberty, and the pursuit of happiness appear, in practice, to have become the inalienable right to a bathtub, a flush toilet, and a can of Spam. Left-wing critics of America attribute this result to the intrusion of capitalism; right-wing critics see it as the logical dead end of democracy. Capitalism has certainly played its part, mass production in itself demanding large-scale distribution of uniform goods, till the consumer today is the victim of the manufacturer who launches on him a regiment of products for which he must make house-room in his soul. The buying impulse, in its original force and purity, was not nearly so crass, however, or so meanly acquisitive as many radical critics suppose. The purchase of a bathtub was the exercise of a spiritual right. The immigrant or the poor native American bought a bathtub, not because he wanted to take a bath, but because he wanted to be in a *position* to do so. This remains true in many fields today; possessions, when they are desired, are not wanted for their own sakes but as tokens of an ideal state of freedom, fraternity, and franchise. "Keeping up with the Joneses" is a vulgarization of Jefferson's concept, but it too is a declaration of the rights of man, and decidedly unfeasible and visionary. Where for a European, a fact is a fact, for us Americans, the real, if it is relevant at all, is simply symbolic appearance. We are a nation of twenty million bathrooms, with a humanist in very tub. One such humanist I used to hear of on Cape Cod had, on growing rich, installed two toilets side by side in his marble bathroom, on the model of the two-seater of his youth. He was a clear case of Americanism, hospitable, gregarious, and impractical, a theorist of perfection. Was his dream of the conquest of poverty a vulgar dream or a noble one, a material demand or a spiritual insistence? It is hard to think of him as a happy man, and in this too he is characteristically American, for the parity of the radio, the movies, and the washing machine has made Americans sad, reminding them of another parity of which these things were to be but emblems.

28

The American does not enjoy his possessions because sensory enjoyment was not his object, and he lives sparely and thinly among them, in the monastic discipline of Scarsdale or the barracks of Stuyvesant Town. Only among certain groups where franchise, socially speaking, has not been achieved, do pleasure and material splendor constitute a life-object and an occupation. Among the outcasts—Jews, Negroes, Catholics, and homosexuals —excluded from the communion of ascetics, the love of fabrics, gaudy show, and rich possessions still anachronistically flaunts itself. Once a norm has been reached, differing in the different classes, financial ambition itself seems to fade away. The self-made man finds, to his anger, his son uninterested in money; you have shirtsleeves to shirtsleeves in three generations. The great financial empires are a thing of the past. Recent immigrants —movie magnates and gangsters particularly—retain their acquisitiveness, but how long is it since anyone in the general public has murmured, wonderingly, "as rich as Rockefeller"?

If the dream of American fraternity had ended simply in this, the value of humanistic and egalitarian strivings would be seriously called into question. Jefferson, the Adamses, Franklin, Madison, would be in the position of Dostoevsky's Grand Inquisitor, who, desiring to make the Kingdom of God incarnate on earth, inaugurated the kingdom of the devil. If the nature of matter is such that the earthly paradise, once realized, becomes always the paradise of the earthly, and a spiritual conquest of matter becomes always an enslavement of spirit (conquered Gaul conquered Rome), then the atomic bomb is, as has been argued, the logical result of the Enlightenment, and the land of opportunity is, precisely, the land of death. This position, however, is a strictly materialist one, for it asserts the Fact of the bomb as the one tremendous truth: subjective attitudes are irrelevant; it does not matter what we think or feel; possession again in this case is nine-tenths of the law.

It must be admitted that there is a great similarity between the nation with its new bomb and the consumer with his new Buick. In both cases, there is a disinclination to use the product, stronger naturally in the case of the bomb, but somebody has manufactured the thing, and there seems to be no way *not* to use it, especially when everybody else will be doing so. Here again the argument of the "others" is invoked to justify our own procedures—if we had not invented the bomb, the Germans would have; the Soviet Union will have it in a year, etc., etc. This is keeping up with the Joneses indeed, our national propagandists playing the role of the advertising men in persuading us of the "others" intentions.

It seems likely at this moment that we will find no way of not using the bomb, yet those who argue theoretically that this machine is the true expression of our society leave us, in practice, with no means of opposing it. We must differentiate ourselves from the bomb if we are to avoid using it, and in private thought we do, distinguishing the bomb sharply from our daily concerns and sentiments, feeling it as an otherness that waits outside to descend on us, an otherness already destructive of normal life, since it prevents us from planning or hoping by depriving us of a future. And this inner refusal of the bomb is also a legacy of our past; it is a denial of the given, of the power of circumstances to shape us in their mold. Unfortunately, the whole asceticism of our national character, our habit of living in but not through an environment, our alienation from objects, prepare us to endure the bomb but not to confront it.

Passivity and not aggressiveness is the dominant trait of the American character. The movies, the radio, the super-highway have softened us up for the atom bomb; we have lived with them without pleasure, feeling them as a coercion on our natures, a coercion coming seemingly from nowhere and expressing nobody's will. The new coercion finds us without the habit of protest; we are dissident but apart.

The very "negativeness," then, of American intellectuals is not a mark of their separation from our society, but a true expression of its separation from itself. We too are dissident but inactive. Intransigent on paper, in "real life" we conform; yet we do not feel ourselves to be dishonest, for to us the real life is rustling paper and the mental life is flesh. And even in our mental life we are critical and rather unproductive; we leave it to the "others," the best-sellers, to create.

The fluctuating character of American life must, in part, have been responsible for this dissociated condition. Many an immigrant arrived in this country with the most materialistic expectations, hoping, not to escape from a world in which a man was the sum of his circumstances, but to become a new sum of circumstances himself. But this hope was self-defeating; the very ease with which new circumstances were acquired left insufficient time for a man to live into them: all along a great avenue in Minneapolis the huge chateaux were dark at night, save for a single light in each kitchen, where the family still sat, Swedish-style, about the stove. The pressure of democratic thought, moreover, forced a rising man often, unexpectedly, to recognize that he was *not* his position: a speeding ticket from a village constable could lay him low. Like the agitated United Nations delegates who got summonses on the Merritt Parkway, he might find the shock traumatic: a belief had been destroyed. The effect of these combined difficulties turned the new American into a nomad, who camped out in his circumstances, as it were, and was never assimilated to them. And, for the native American, the great waves of internal migration had the same result. The homelessness of the American, migrant in geography and on the map of finance, is the whole subject of the American realists of our period. European readers see in these writers only violence and brutality. They miss not only the pathos but the nomadic virtues associated with it, generosity, hospitality, equity, directness, politeness, simplicity of relations—traits which, together with a certain gentle timidity (as of *unpracticed* nomads), comprise the American character. Unobserved also is a peculiar nakedness, a look of being shorn of everything, that is very curiously American, corresponding to the spare wooden desolation of a frontier town and the bright thinness of the American light. The American character looks always as if it had just had a rather bad hair-cut, which gives it, in our eyes at any rate, a greater humanity than the European, which even among its beggars has an all too professional air.

The openness of the American situation creates the pity and the terror; status is no protection; life for the European is a career; for the American, it is a hazard. Slaves and woman, said Aristotle, are not fit subjects for tragedy, but kings, rather, and noble men, men, that is, not defined by circumstance but outside it and seemingly impervious. In America we have, subjectively speaking, no slaves and no women; the efforts of PM and the Stalinized playwrights to introduce, like the first step to servitude, a national psychology of the "little man" have been, so far, unrewarding. The little man is one who is embedded in status; things can be done for and to him generically by a central directive; his happiness flows from statistics. This conception mistakes the national passivity for abjection. Americans will not eat this humble pie; we are still nature's noblemen. Yet no tragedy results, though the protagonist is everywhere; dissociation takes the place of conflict, and the drama is mute.

31

This humanity, this plain and heroic accessibility, was what we would have liked to point out to the visiting Existentialist as our national glory. Modesty perhaps forbade and a lack of concrete examples—how could we point to ourselves? Had we done so, she would not have been interested. To a European, the humanity of an intellectual is of no particular moment; it is the barber pole that announces his profession and the hair oil dispensed inside. Europeans, moreover, have no curiosity about American intellectuals; we are insufficiently representative of the brute. Yet this anticipated and felt disparagement was not the whole cause of our reticence. We were silent for another reason: we were waiting to be discovered. Columbus, however, passed on, and this, very likely, was the true source of our humiliation. But this experience also was peculiarly American. We all expect to be found in the murk of otherness; it looks to us very easy since *we* know we are there. Time after time, the explorers have failed to see us. We have been patient, for the happy ending is our national belief. Now, however, that the future has been shut off from us, it is necessary for us to declare ourselves, at least for the record.

What it amounts to, in verity, is that we are the poor. This humanity we would claim for ourselves is the legacy, not only of the Enlightenment, but of the thousands and thousands of European peasants and poor townspeople who came here bringing their humanity and their sufferings with them. It is the absence of a stable upper class that is responsible for much of the vulgarity of the American scene. Should we blush before the visitor for this deficiency? The ugliness of American decoration, American entertainment, American literature—is not this the visible expression of the improverishment of the European masses, a manifestation of all the backwardness, deprivation, and want that arrived here in boatloads from Europe? The immense popularity of American movies abroad demonstrates that Europe is the unfinished negative of which America is the proof. The European traveler, viewing with distaste a movie palace or a motorola, is only looking into the terrible concavity of his continent of hunger inverted startlingly into the convex. Our civilization, deformed as it is outwardly, is still an accomplishment; all this had to come to light.

America is indeed a revelation, though not quite the one that was planned. Given a clean slate, man, it was hoped, would write the future. Instead, he has written his past. This past, inscribed on billboards, ball parks, dance halls, is not seemly, yet its objectification is a kind of disburdenment. The past is at length outside. It does not disturb us as it does Europeans for our relation with it is both more distant and more familiar. We cannot hate it, for to hate it would be to hate poverty, our eager ancestors, and ourselves.

If there were time, American civilization could be seen as a beginning, even a favorable one, for we have only to look around us to see what a lot of sensibility a little ease will accrue. The children surpass the fathers and Louis B. Mayer cannot be preserved intact in his descendants. . . . Unfortunately, as things seem now, posterity is not around the corner.

(This essay first appeared in the magazine "Commentary.")

HOLLYWOOD IS A TERM
OF DISPARAGEMENT

Evelyn Waugh

It may seem both presumptuous and unkind to return from six weeks' generous entertainment abroad and at once to sit down and criticise one's hosts. In the case of Hollywood it is neither.

Not presumptuous: first, because a fortnight is ample time in which to appreciate the character of that remote community; there are no secrets under those unflickering floodlights; no undertones to which the stranger must attune his ear. All is loud, obvious and prosaic.

Secondly, because Hollywood has made its business the business of half the world. Morally, intellectually, aesthetically, financially, Hollywood's entries are written huge in the household books of every nation outside the U.S.S.R.; largest of all in those of America but, because of our common language, second only to them in our own.

Nor is it unkind, for one may say what one likes in perfect confidence that one is powerless to wound. No game licenses are issued in the Reserve where the great pachyderms of the film trade bask and browse complacently. They have no suspicion that in most of America and in the whole of Europe the word "Hollywood" is pejorative.

Even in Southern California the film community are a people apart. They are like monks in a desert oasis, their lives revolving about a few shrines—half a dozen immense studios, two hotels, one restaurant; their sacred texts are their own publicity and the local gossip columns.

The only strangers they ever meet have come to seek their fortunes; refugees from Central Europe for whom the ease and plenty and affability of the place, seen against the background of the concentration camp, appear as supreme goods, and astute renegades from the civilisations of the East who knows that flattery is the first step to preferment.

None of these will hold a mirror up to Caliban; all feel their own security threatened by a whisper of criticism. Artists and public men elsewhere live under a fusillade of detraction and derision; they accept it as a condition of their calling. Not so in Hollywood, where all is a continuous psalm of self-praise.

Place and people have the aspect of Philo's Alexandria; such, one thinks in one's first few days, must have been the life there in the great days of the Mouseion; some such withdrawal of the arts is necessary everywhere if culture is to survive the present century.

But this is a whimsy. Things are not really like that. The seclusion of these hermits is purely one-sided. They live for and by the outer world of which they know nothing at first hand and whose needs they judge by gross quantitative standards.

"No film of ours is ever a failure," an executive said to me. "Some are greater successes than others, but we reckon to get our money back on everything we produce."

There is the impasse, the insurmountable barrier of financial prosperity. Behold the endless succession of Hollywood films, the slick second-rateness of the best of them, the blank fatuity of the worst—and none of them failures! What goes on there?

Three groups are responsible for making a film, the technicians, the players and the writers. (Producers-directors bear the guilt of all three.)

Of these the least culpable are the technicians. It is they who make the studio the vast, enchanted toyshop which delights the visitors.

In only two respects are the technicians guilty. It is their fault that the studios are there, 3,000 miles from the world's theatrical centre in New York, 6,000 miles from the intellectual centres of London and Paris

They came there because in the early days they needed the sun. Now almost all photography is done by artificial light. The sun serves only to enervate and stultify. But by now the thing has become too heavy to move.

And the technicians are too enterprising. Their itch for invention keeps them always a move ahead of the producers.

Twenty years ago the silent film was just beginning to develop into a fine art; then talking apparatus set it back to its infancy. Technicolor is the present retarding revolution. Soon no doubt we shall have some trick of third-dimensional projection.

Mr. Charles Chaplin, abused everywhere as a "progressive," is the one genuine conservative artistically, in Hollywood. The others allow themselves no time to get at ease with their materials.

The technicians are almost anonymous. All the devices of publicity are employed to give exclusive prominence to a few leading players. They possess the popular imagination and excite the visitor's curiosity.

What of them? Dramatic critics often ask why the cinema has produced no actors comparable with the great figures of the stage, and point to the fact that in many "documentaries" and Continental films the best performances are given by unknown and untrained players. Even in Hollywood this year the highest Academy honours have gone to a man who was chosen simply because he had been maimed in the war.

The wonder should be that so many stars are able to give as much as they do, for the conditions of their work are hostile to dramatic tradition. Certain disabilities seem to be inherent in the film; others are peculiar to Hollywood; all are exaggerated there.

There is an essential inhumanity about a film star's life. Compare it with that of a leading actress of 50 years ago. The latter worked in the capitals of the world; once her play was running smoothly her days were her own; she lived a life of leisure and fashion in an infinitely various society of her own choosing.

The company formed a corporate unit with its own intimacies, scandals and jokes; each performance was a separate artistic achievement; the play was conceived as an artistic whole which was nightly brought into existence in a sustained and cumulative emotional mood which is the essence of acting.

The players were in direct contact with their audience. Each audience was different; the manager would nightly visit the dressing-rooms with news of who was "in front."

Above all, acting was recognized as an art which it took a lifetime to learn. Almost all great plays were written for mature players; the "juvenile lead" and the "ingenue" were for youngsters learning their trade.

The Hollywood star lives in a remote suburb. She sees no one from one year's end to another except a handful of people all in the same trade as herself. She remains in purdah in the studio, inhabiting a tiny bathing-machine, surrounded by satellites who groom her and feed her until the technicians have finished with the "stand-in" and require her presence on the set.

When her work begins it consists of isolated fragments, chosen at the convenience of the technicians. It is rehearsal, hour after hour, for a few minutes of finished acting.

At last in a Trilby-like trance she achieves the expression the director requires. She is "shot," and they proceed to another, often unrelated fragment.

And finally she has produced only the raw material for the "cutter," who may nonchalantly discard the work of weeks or dovetail it into an entirely different situation.

And she must be young. Her life is as brief as a prize fighter's. By the time that she has become a finished actress she is relegated to "supporting" rôles.

The work is physically exhausting and intellectually stultifying and there are no very great material rewards. A myth survives from past years that film stars live in Petronian luxury. The salary figures seem dazzling, and, indeed, she does live in a degree of comfort very enviable by contemporary European measure.

But it is no more than that. In fact her standard of life is precisely that of a moderately successful professional Englishman of 50 years ago. That is to say, she lives in a neat little villa with half an acre of garden; she has three servants, seldom more, very often fewer. Her antique furniture, collected at vast expense, would be commonplace in an English rectory.

Her main time of entertainment is Sunday luncheon when she asks half a dozen professional friends to share her joint of beef. She has more clothes than her counterpart, but her menfolk are infinitely worse dressed.

In only one substantial particular does she differ. She has a swimming pool which can be lit up at night. That is the mark of respectability, like the aspidistra in the cottage parlour.

And unlike her counterpart it is almost impossible for her to save money. If she attempted to live in simpler style she would lose "face" and be rebuked by her studio. She cannot live more elaborately, for taxation intervenes. She can make this maximum in one film. After that for the rest of the time she is working for nothing.

Consequently it is becoming increasingly hard to persuade her to do any work. Vanity is the sole inducement. She will therefore take no part in which she, and her male colleague, are anything less than the whole film.

She must be on the stage all the time in a continuously alluring fashion. A play which depends on a team of various characters has no interest for her. A film must be her personal romantic adventures and nothing else.

It is a short-sighted preference, for it means that when she is 50 there will be no adequate parts for her. But no one in Hollywood considers the possibility of growing up.

The infinite pains taken in Hollywood over all technical matters renders all the more remarkable their nonchalance when it is a question of ideas.

Go to the Art Research Department and they will tell you in a twinkling the kind of inkpot Dante used or the orders worn by the Duke of Wellington at Queen Victoria's Coronation.

Go on the set and hear the dozen or more experts wrangling round the "stand-in" about light and sound; wait until the star appears and see how men with combs and clothes-brushes, women with elaborate catalogues, cluster round and perfect her.

You will believe yourself present at one of the great achievements of human ingenuity and devotion. Then go to a "story conference" and you find yourself in a world that is at once haphazard and banal.

It is not that they are wrong-headed, that in the interests of entertainment they deliberately choose to disregard certain human values and to distort others.

It is not that, as is often suggested, they serve sinister interests aiming to preserve or destroy (according to choice) capitalist society and bourgeois morality, to advance American imperialism, Jewish internationlism, Catholicism, agnosticism or what you will.

It is simply that they are empty-headed and quite without any purpose at all. Thus anyone interested in ideas is inevitably shocked by Hollywood according to his prejudices.

The novelist is shocked by their complete inability to follow a plain story. For in the cinema, he would think, is the perfect medium for presenting a straight plot. The effects at which he labours so painfully may here be achieved with ease. All descriptions are superfluous. Here you have narrative reduced to its essentials—dialogue and action.

A great, simple art should have come into existence. But nothing of the kind has in fact occurred.

Literary considerations are as despised in the film studios as in those of modern painters. The producers, generally speaking, read nothing. They employ instead a staff of highly accomplished women who recite aloud, and with dramatic effects, the stories which filter down to them from a staff of readers.

The producers sit round like children while the pseudo-nannie spins a tale, two or three in an afternoon—classical novels, Broadway comedies, the Book of the Month, popular biographies, anything.

"Bags I," says the producer, when something takes his fancy. "Daddy buy that." Agents negotiate, a price is fixed. And from that moment the story belongs to the studio to deal with as they please.

Each of the books purchased has had some individual quality, good or bad, that has made it remarkable. It is the work of a staff of "writers" to distinguish this quality, separate it and obliterate it.

We all know frightful examples of favourite books we have seen thus sterilized. Perhaps of recent years the most notorious is Mr. Somerset Maugham's "Christmas Holiday," a brilliantly original story of an English schoolboy's awakening in Paris to some of the realities of life, eminently suitable for retelling in a film, which emerged from the mill as the adventure of an American airman with an escaped gangster.

Why, one wonders, do they trouble to purchase rights? I cannot believe that any action for plagiarism would lie if they had produced that film without reference to Mr. Maugham. It is simply, I think, that they like to have something to work on, and that the large sum paid to the author is an inconsiderable part of the total cost of production.

A film costs about $2,000,000. It must please 20,000,000 people. The film industry has accepted the great fallacy of the Century of the Common Man—epitomised recently in England by Dr. Summerskill's condemnation of good cheese—that a thing can have no value for anyone which is not valued by all.

In the old days a play which ran 100 nights was a success, a book which sold 5,000 copies might influence a generation. Even now a writer who sells more than 20,000 copies, instead of being elated, begins to wonder what has gone wrong with his work. But a film must please everyone.

The economics of this desperate situation illustrate the steps by which the Common Man is consolidating his victory.

It is not the large sums paid to the stars and producers and authors (the greater part of which, incidentally, goes straight to the Common Man in taxes), but the overhead expenses of the studio which overweight the costs, and these are imposed by the trade unions and their system of redundant labour.

It would not be impossible to get together a team of first-class players and producers and writers who would work for a fraction of their present salaries if they could take genuine pride in their art and make a film which appealed only to a limited audience, but this would barely affect the cost of the film.

Situations which seem fantastic elsewhere are commonplace in Hollywood. I know a "writer" who wished to put up a map on the wall of his room and asked for a hammer and four nails. He was told that all the carpenters would strike if he did the work himself.

A trade unionist arrived with his tools and found that a small bookcase had to be moved to another wall. The writer took one side and invited the carpenter to take the other. But that was a breach of rules. Two furniture movers had to be called in.

A special "florist" has to be summoned if, in rearranging a "set," the director wishes to move a vase of flowers from one table to another.

The unions determine the numbers to be employed in any film. If a band of six instruments is required, a dozen men will arrive and half of them sit idle on full pay.

Impositions of this kind, repeated hourly in a large studio, fix the exorbitant cost of a film. The capitalist at the head of the company is concerned solely with profits; the proletariat allow profits only to those who directly work for their pleasure; in this miniature class-war the artist vanishes.

The reductio ad absurdum of the principle of universal appeal is not in the intellectual or aesthetic sphere, but in the moral.

The American censors observe no such fruitful distinction as exists in England between films suitable for children and for adults. Nor do most American parents enjoy the authority common in Europe over their children. They cannot prevent them going to the cinema; all they can hope to do is prevent the cinema showing films likely to corrupt them. In fact, no one really knows what will corrupt anyone else.

There has been intense investigation of the question lately. It must be remembered that children seldom tell the truth to investigators, and that magistrates are usually sympathetic to the plea of the juvenile delinquent: "I saw it done in the pictures."

Moreover, it is the spectacle rather than the theme which impresses a child. That is to say, a boy is excited by the use of firearms whether in the hands of a gangster or a soldier; an embrace is equally inflammatory whether between licit or illicit lovers. Americans are devoted to a conception of innocence which has little relation to life.

But when all this is said it remains broadly true that some films may be harmless to adults and harmful to children. This, within all the essential finer distinction, the Americans ignore, and the function of the Hays Office is to enforce a Code which forbids the production of any film which can be harmful to anyone, or offend any racial or religious susceptibility.

No such code is feasible in a heterogeneous society. Logically applied it would condemn, for instance, almost the whole of Shakespeare.

The unhappy compromise is evident in all Hollywood films except those of Mr. Walt Disney. Every attempt is made by innuendo to pack as much lubricious material as possible into every story, while mature dramatic works intended for a morally stable, civilised audience have their essential structure hopelessly impaired.

The vagaries of the Hays Office may be quoted at indefinite length. One example must suffice here.

A script was recently condemned as likely to undermine the conception of Christian marriage. The story was of an unhappy married man and woman who wished to divorce their respective partners and remarry one another. They institute proceedings, but in the end refrain from remarriage precisely because they come to realise that this would not constitute Christian marriage.

At the same time the excellent film "The Best Years of Our Lives" was being acclaimed as the embodiment of healthy American domesticity. That story depends for its happy end on the hero being deserted by his Bohemian wife and thus being free to marry the banker's innocent daughter. This was passed because it was never specifically stated that a divorce would have to intervene.

I have attempted to show some of the disabilities under which Hollywood works. Are they insuperable? I sincerely believe that they are. As far as the home of a living art is concerned, Hollywood has no importance. It may be a useful laboratory for technical experiment.

The great danger is that the European climate is becoming inclement for artists; they are notoriously comfort-loving people. The allurements of the modest luxury of Hollywood are strong. Will they be seduced there to their own extinction?

TWO POEMS

Richard Eberhart

SESTINA

I die, no matter what I do I die.
Is this the sum of what man has to do?
There is no use to fly to be at ease.
Man flies, but knows not what he does.
It is in war you want to be in peace.
In Heaven, in Heaven I want to be in Hell.

The mortal span to find out Heaven and Hell!
No matter what I have to do I die,
The gods comply to cancel you to peace.
Before this then what is it man should do?
And after, does it matter what he does?
Will Christ-like Christ then put him at his ease?

Will will will him his own, a fabled ease?
Will, some say, is the whole road to Hell.
But man is bound to Hell whatever he does.
No matter what he does he has to die.
It is the dying that you have to do
Defies the hyaline luster of the peace.

Despair has not the end in view of peace
Nor has desire the purposes of ease,
But action, while you live, is what's to do.
Thought is three crossed roads that lead to Hell,
Your thought is fatal and will make you die,
For thinking kills as much as action does.

It is not what he thinks, nor what he does
Nor what cold mystery of the Prince of Peace
Avails—no matter what I do I die,
May nothing, nothing put me at my ease
Except the reality of Heaven and Hell.
No one told me what I ought to do.

The scriptures told you what you ought to do.
They are unreasonable truth, and what man does
Believe when most he believes in Heaven and Hell.
That passes understanding, that is peace.
But sky-fallen man will not be put at ease.
I die, no matter what I do I die.

No matter what I do I have no peace.
No matter what man does he has no ease.
Heaven and Hell are changeless when I die.

THE HELLDIVER GUNNER

This is the story of Johnny Dare,
O where did he go?
The dive bombing gunner of the upper air,
O where did he go, did he go?

He was a good mechanic, he was steady,
His was hard working, and thrifty,
His squadron mates said he was deadly
Behind his well boresighted twin fifties.

He would look through the Mark 9 Sight,
He would give short bursts with his tracers,
By instinct he knew how to fight,
He knew how to sight, and how to place.

He had been in combat, had Johnny Dare,
Far, far from the Iowa farm.
He had been in the melee out there,
Back he had come without harm.

Others had been shot out of the air,
Hit the sea with a mighty kiss;
And he knew, after the run, high, there,
What was known as a near miss.

Back from the wars came Johnny Dare
For a rest and a time of ease
With his aviation free gunnery mates,
Reading the comics and eating ice cream.

He put in for leave to get him home
To girls and rest instead of guns,
But there was no time to go home,
And he was assigned a new squadron.

They had new 2-Cs, he had a new pilot,
O where did he go?
Johnny Dare kept to his squadron duties,
They kept him on the go.

One day the squadron was revved up
And Johnny got in the rear seat,
He was in the last plane to take off,
It would be the same old beat.

He had on his flight jacket, and gloves,
His goggles and his parachute,
And just before they taxied out
He threw the mechs a salute.

The pilot had to taxi far
Way down to the end of the field
Before turning into the gray wind
And pausing to test his engine's feel.

There were a few trees and bushes there,
All was well and down the runway
Grew the Helldiver to the holding air,
Almost motionless upon the day.

Out of sight was out of mind
To all but those in the Operations tower,
They kept the news of weather and wind,
They had the bomber in their radio power.

In due time the squadron circled in
Came settling slow, one after other
Each pilot and each plane came in
All in the usual order.

The pilot of the last plane got out,
Out of the plane got he,
Back he looked, but Johnny Dare
He did not see, not see.

Only one glove on his bucket seat
Left Johnny Dare
When he went off that day
Into the upper air.

And his parachute harness was
Thrown back as over a chair,
Casually, rather gallantly,
Deliberate and debonaire.

ALPHA AND OMEGA

Isaac Rosenfeld

If my virtue be a dancer's virtue . . .
verily, that is my Alpha and Omega.
—Nietzsche.

1. *Introduction. The Postman, his story.*

THEY CALL me Little Giant. In the morning, when my work begins, the bag is heavy. I pull it onto my shoulder with a groan. All day it grows lighter and lighter; my head rises of its own accord, I take longer, quicker steps, my strength, courage and good humor return to me. Late in the afternoon, when the burden is gone, I am a new man. But it is late in the afternoon, the day's work is done, and tomorrow begins a new day.

This has been going on for years. Mind you, I do not complain. I am glad to hold my position in the service, the more so as I am now an old man and can soon expect a pension. There was a time, not so long ago, when many envied me. Those were the days when nearly everyone on my route was starving; the days when, in addition to letters, I used to load my bag with scraps of bread, meat, cheese, lettuce, the head of a chicken or a fish, lumps of sugar or candy, anything cheap and edible, and not always fresh, that I could lay my hands upon. I distributed food with the mail—first, out of pity, and then out of self-regard, by way of gaining the good will of the people, for the letters I brought them were, more often than not, notices of dispossessment and eviction and suspension of relief, news of the death of a relative, nearby or in a distant city. I will not soon forget those days.

But now only one thing concerns me: what effect has this work had on my character? Is it only because of my short stature and broad shoulders, my baggy pants and the rather, on the whole, ape-like swing of my arms and stoop of my body that I

46

am called Little Giant? The men in the post office have an instinct for choosing names: they appear to go only by externals, but in reality they work much deeper. Thus, lanky Garrity, our thin man, is called not, as you might expect, Slim, Beanpole, Reach or Noodle, but Cough Drop, and strangely enough, he really is very much like a cough drop. There must have been something of the same order that made them call me as they do. At least, I like to think so.

My work is somehow similar to that of both angels and hangmen. These creatures, blessed or damned, have surrendered their wills—they are in *service*. But why, since neither has a will of his own, should an angel be held blessed and a hangman damned? So with myself. What am I then, I who do not even read the letters I deliver? True, I know, in a manner of speaking, what they contain. I have developed a sense of content, I can judge by the size, shape, weight, color and feel of the envelope. But this merely reminds me that I am an outsider in the very thing I am most concerned with. For a time I considered steaming open the letters; I could have arranged to do it without danger of being found out. But I decided against it—rather, I resigned myself not to do so. After all, I am in service, too.

Then how shall I ever know the truth about myself? If there were a mystic society of postmen, such as, granted the proper conditions, might have existed in Roman days, we would have taken the matter up and evolved a rite for ourselves. The mystery would have its initiates. But now the mystery, poor thing, exists by itself and no one is instructed in it.

Concretely, this is how it goes:
One of my houses is a four-story tenement. On the first floor lives a large family. I cannot say how many children—it seems to me that each day I see new faces. The children, ragged and dirty—dressed in burlap and flour sacks, old tennis shoes, galoshes, and so dirty they might just have been plucked up out of the ground—rush out to greet me, gather about, cling to my arms and legs, climb onto my back and cry, "Mail, mail, mail, the mailman's here!" There is never any mail for them, and there hasn't been any for years—not since I brought the family its last relief check. Times have changed and things are looking up.

On the floor above lives the prostitute. There is never any mail for her either. Once there was a court order for eviction, but somehow she got around it. She comes to the window and looks out, sees the children swarming at my feet. Occasionally she clears her throat and spits; the gob of spit spatters on the sidewalk. More often, she gives me a forlorn look. I have no comment to make, neither of judgment nor condemnation, and with the direct, unblinking glance that I give her in return, I try to tell her so.

There are two other tenants. A dancer on the third floor, and on the fourth floor, a man with watery eyes who, from the way he drags himself to the window, appears to be a paralytic. There is always mail for the dancer—spicy, fragrant envelopes in many colors, addressed in back-handed, quaint, irregular, square, delicate or spidery scripts. Letters often from foreign countries, from France and Italy, Finland, Canada and Spain, and from remote corners of our own country such as Curtain Falls, Onion Terrace and Mahogany Creek. Fluffy letters written on tissue, bulky letters, clippings—all of them, I am sure, in praise of the dancer.

The man on the fourth floor also gets mail. Large envelopes, magazines, pamphlets, books, all very scholarly and serious, to be sure, but never a personal letter. It is strange that the people to whom I bring the most mail are the ones I know least. The large family of children and the prostitute I see every day, and though it is always the same, yet something new always passes between us. The dancer I also see daily—sometimes, barefooted and wearing her thin dancing costume, she takes the mail directly from my hand—but she is always preoccupied and remote and never looks at me, so that I do not really know her at all. I very rarely see the paralytic. He must have a hard time dragging himself up and down the stairs.

Such equations, I have noticed, are by no means uncommon: large families—no mail; steady customers (so to speak)—unknown to the postman; occasional customers—his best friends. The supreme touch, I should add, is that I myself seldom get mail. Precisely what this means I have not been able to find out. But I imagine it has some meaning, and is of interest, not only to postmen, but to the world at large.

2. *The Pleasures of Family Life. Antontonio Jeveves.*

Marthafoglia hung the last stocking on the line. "Zing-zing! Ding-a-ling! Chuka-chuka-chuka-chuka!" Lugubugu came tearing round the bend, steam up, throttle open, and collided with the post. The line snapped. All the freshly washed clothes fell to the ground.

"You watch where you go," said Marthafoglia, mother of

how many? and picked up the clothes and carried them into the house to do her washing all over again.

The child screamed several hours. There was a lump as hard as a stone on his forehead. He kicked out his legs, stiffened, collapsed, lay like a dead chicken on the ground, groaned and contorted himself and struck one pose after another, screaming. His brothers and sisters did not know what to do with him to make him keep still. They carried him down into the basement and laid him on the carpenter's bench, his head on the grindstone.

"I know what. Let's play hospital. Lugubugu must be sick. You must be the nurse. You must be sick too. Lie down in the wash tub. You must be another nurse. I must be the doctor."

"What can I be?"

"What can I be?"

"You two must take turns being dead and being the undertaker."

Lugubugu screams, and Ellabella, the eldest, never at a loss, builds a play about his screaming. Stuck away in her pocket book is a packet of picture cards—movie actors and actresses with their favorite smiles: Lola Cowley, Mark Thorp, Bucky Anderson, Charmaine Charmante. These must wait for another occasion to call them forth, when the child's desire distributes its other roles: I must be beautiful (Who do I look like?), brave (Stand back! Stickemup!), tender (I know, yes, I know, darling, but we still have each other), wanton (I'd let you kiss me good night, but I'm wearing pants). And the accessories of desire lie in a heap in the treasure chest, a cheese-box, behind a loose plank in the wall: a used-up lipstick, discarded high-heel shoes, cappistols, a doll's head, severed from the trunk.

Lugubugu falls asleep and they perform an operation on him with a rusty shears, snipping the air at his throat, the fuzz of his ears, and, very delicately, his eyelashes.

Antontonio Jeveves is a janitor with many houses to take care of and a family of his own in each. He has, all in all, in one place or another, some sixty children, not counting dead or jailed. He has three wives, two of them legal: Marthafoglia (see above) and La Paloma Pigeon; his common law wife is Clarissa Melissa, now big with child, who still has hopes of marrying him. His other women are Stella, who lives on Orchard Place in Cleveland, Sarah, who lives in Boston, street address unknown, Mary, Helen, Jewel, Rachel, Pearl, Gertrude, Pima, Pia, Ria, Mia, Nina, Parthenia, Virginia, Becky, Bessie, Anna, Suzy, Aida, Paula,

Polly, Cookie and Gertrude (known as "the other Gertrude"), most of whom give their last names as Smith. Antontonio Jeves has had children by nearly all of them.

Social workers, who have at one time or another been on his trail and have learned a little about him (though not, for instance, that he has more than one wife), have invariably given him up as an incorrigible idiot and stricken his name off their lists. Antontonio holds them in contempt. He made advances to one of them, a fairly young and, in a bloodless way, pretty woman, and nearly had himself turned in to the police. He attributed his failure, the first in many years, to the fact that he had been neglecting his nails, and for several days, waiting for the social worker to return, he kept after his nails, digging the dirt out with the blade of a screw driver. He would very much like to meet this woman again.

Antontonio knows that there are all kinds of women in this world (what doesn't he know?), and that some of them might, conceivably, have some reason to refuse him. But to tell the truth, he is eager to encounter one of these women, and for many years has been in search of her. (The social worker does not count, because, thinks Antontonio, he met her only in her professional capacity, and besides, she was not his type, her hips were too narrow. Here he performs a little trick, for whenever he does meet a woman who refuses him, he immediately concludes that she was not his type and therefore doesn't count; just as another man whose concern, the very opposite, is to find a woman who will love him, will also say that his failures do not count. But in spite of his little tricks, Antontonio's reckoning is substantially accurate in these matters.) He curses the luck which keeps him a poor man and cuts him off from access to the upper classes where, he feels sure, he would have no difficulty in finding a woman to refuse him. But on the other hand, he reasons, if he had money and could open doors that are now closed to him, he would again meet his old failure-in-the-form-of-success, and there he would be, right back at his starting point. Even so, poor as he is, and dirty, ugly (except for his beautiful, long, straight nose with the delicate nostrils), scarred and tattered—even so, he has met and enjoyed more than what one would grant him as his natural share of these women. There is no accounting for the upper classes, thinks Antontonio. What do they see in him? It all comes from being a janitor, from having worked round their homes. "Oh please, sir, won't you please fix my faucet?" And Antontonio, a complaisant man, fixes her faucet, and her daughter's, too. But what's the use of kidding yourself? Antontonio knows all about such romances, and he resents being included in the same category of afternoon- or odd-moment lover with the milkman, the iceman, the vacuum-cleaner- and brush-salesman. He feels that if he had a somewhat wider space for his explorations, if he could only move about a bit more freely in these circles, he would soon find what he is looking for.

Well, true now, there have been women who've said no. But Antontonio knows these nos, and is thoroughly weary of them. In each there is a sprout of possibility, just under the surface, thrusting its way up into the light. It is not a no, dead at the roots, an outright, absolute blank of a no, the no of a stone, past, present and future the same. It is the no of an onion (Antontonio eats onions raw); peel off the outer layers of negation, the middle layers of possibility and probability, and you come to the green core of willingness. Enough of such nos. Antontonio wants the absolute thing.

Why does he want it? He is as eager for it as another man would be for the very opposite, for yes—and for the same reason. He wants the truth. He feels that if he could but find a woman who was thoroughly dead to him, then perhaps he would begin to understand. He would study her as he studies a bit of machinery that needs fixing, examine the matter from all sides, probe into it, this way and that, and cast as much light as he could on the subject. He would study such a woman until he found, so to speak, the part that was missing; he would know in what respect she differs from the other women, and then, precisely because he knew why she does not want him, he would know why the others do. Then perhaps he would learn why he runs to them, adding woman to woman and piling up heaps of children, each with a straight, long nose like his own. Is it because he wants them or they want him? Or neither; or both? If both, in what proportion, and if neither, what then? He would very much like to be able to answer these questions. Now, while his sixty-first child (so far as he knows) is waiting to be born. He feels it is time.

One night he hit the pregnant Clarissa Melissa over the head with a beer bottle. (He was feeling rather depressed at the time, and some half dozen or so of his children were crying in concert. Antontonio thought it was because they were hungry, and Clarissa, because they were wet. In either case, they had neither food nor clean diapers to give them, so let them cry.) He hit her, but not hard enough to break the bottle, (on the return of which a five-cent deposit could be collected) or to break Clarissa's head. She did not fall unconscious, so, to occupy his time, he felt he should hold a conversation with her. He asked her immediately, without beating about the bush—such directness is one of Antontonio's greatest charms—he asked her why. Why did she think he came to her in the first place, why did they go about it the way they did, and why did they have so many children? Clarissa Melissa thought it was because they were poor. That, thought Antontonio, was a good answer, and it increased his respect for the intelligence of his common-law wife. But on second thought he saw that it was no answer at all. For if he was what he was because he was poor, what good did it do him to be told that he was poor? If he had money, he would no doubt have been able to answer many questions—but then what need would there be to ask any? Likewise, now, as a poor man, he asked many questions—but how can a poor man answer them? Clarissa Melissa hadn't much use for such subtleties and told him so, adding that in her opinion it was high time they were married. Antontonio hit her over the head again, not very hard—he was sensible of her condition—and taking the bottle with him to collect the deposit, he went off to see another one of his women.

In all probability, if Antontonio were ever to find the woman he is looking for, the woman who could give him the answer to his questions, he would kill her. Not that he would not be grateful for the enlightenment of a refusal; but enlightenment is one thing and a refusal is another—and besides, what could he do with such a woman after the enlightenment? He has not yet killed any one, and he has no particular desire to do so. But he is aware of his own strength and vitality that give him no rest and enable him to stay alive and well on a diet of onions and matchsticks, so to speak. So it is entirely possible that he would be capable of murder. He feels he has already committed deeds of great violence and daring, so why not another? Murder does not attract him, but all the same he is sure that he could commit murder very much in the same way that he now loves women —with disastrous consequences, which never catch up with him. But if he committed murder in the same manner, he would merely be adding a further fuddle to his present bewilderment, and would have to go about killing and racking his brains for the answer to the question—why do I kill? Whatever Antontonio does not know, intrigues him; whatever he has not had in his life, is an ever-present possibility, requiring study. But Antontonio knows that he is an insatiable man, and he is careful not to over-stimulate his appetite.

Unlike other men, he takes greatest pleasure in his children not when he comes home to them, but when he leaves. No sight is as rewarding to him as the sight of his many children, playing in the alley or the yard—at a distance of a block or more, when the dreadful noise they make grows dim and pleasant to the ear. He walks away with his head turned back and his heart filling with love. Just before turning the corner, he takes a last look, and there they are, blocks away in the empty lot, the whole family of them rolled together into one mass, impossible to tell one from the other. He blows them a kiss and goes proudly on his way.

Perhaps he does it all for the sake of the children. He loves children, of course—and who knows, maybe even more than other men do? Ever so much more, to such an extent that it is something morbid? He can't be sure, for he has so many children, that even his thick emotions must be stretched thin to cover them all. If he had only one child, or two at the most, then he would know for sure. But then, again, the question wouldn't even come up. There was a time, after all, when he was a father of only one by his own first, proper, legal wife, Marthafoglia, and then he never even thought to ask.

But perhaps that's it, who knows? Perhaps it is all for the sake of filling the world with his stock, neighborhood after neighborhood and city after city, and he still a comparatively young man with, God willing, many long fertile years before him. Who knows? Meanwhile, he goes about his work, a regular and decent man with no bad habits—rises early, starts the fire, carries out the ashes, carries down the garbage, leaves some food outside the door of the man on the fourth floor, mops the hall and the stairs and goes on to the next house and the next house, pausing, mid-day, for beer and a sandwich if he has money, and scratching his head and his neck if he has not. And when evening comes depending on where he is, he goes in to one of his women, and if there happens to be supper, has a bite to eat with her; then takes her to bed and snorts like a bull and a little while later snores like a sawmill. And while he sleeps, who can tell? perhaps a seed has begun to sprout into a child with a long, straight, delicate nose.

3. *The Prostitute, her story.*

Allow me my dignity. When I was a child, my mother, also a whore, said to me, "Never listen to what others say." I have followed her advice.

Most things bore me. I no longer derive pleasure from the so-called pleasant things of life. My plum must be all lined and wrinkled like a miser's purse, though—if I may be cute for a moment—I have never been miserly with it.

A word on language. By "plum" I mean vulva. Early in life I formed a strong dislike for the terms of my trade: *sexual intercourse, penis, vagina, prostitution,* the various diseases, etc., etc. There is something terribly vulgar, pedantic, self-conscious and condescending in these words, and I stammer and feel I am going to blush when I use them, as from time to time, say in conversation with a doctor, I find it necessary to do. The synonyms, which are called four-letter words, though many of the most essential contain five letters—and I can think of one of eleven—the synonyms would serve the purpose very well, but their use by a person of sensibility is full of danger. Above all one must be natural —especially in performing what self-conscious or inhibited folk call the natural functions. The difficulty in the thing is reflected in the word. A brutish person, a simpleton or a foreigner who is just learning the language can use "dirty words" (as they are called) with a clear conscience. But the rest of mankind is compromised. And who is not compromised? How well I could explode the myth of "the healthy truck driver!" But some other time.

To avoid compromising myself (and as it is, I sometimes think I am the most compromised of all) I have coined my own language. Plum is vulva or vagina (also flap and gobbet); penis is whacker, thrucker, dishik; sexual intercourse I call jim-jam, etc. I do not object to being called a whore, (especially with the middle-western pronounciation, *hoor*) but "prostitute" I dislike and prefer badger. As for the word "prostitution," which I abhor, or the trade itself (as my mother used to say, *"das Gescheft selbst"*), I say woodpile.

I've been on the woodpile all my life, ever since I began to assist my mother. (Her gentlemen called me "Mother's little helper." Thus it was that I came to regard my work as a kind of help, given in free will to mankind. It was also from this innocent phrase that I learned to appreciate the beauty of *double-entendre,* and not only double, but threefold, fourfold, and so on, until the whole world blossoms into a garden of hidden meanings.) I regret nothing. I've certainly had my time, and what with one thing or another, fizz, flapdoodle, stug and caracoca from here to Borneo and back, I can truly call myself a woman who left no lesson of life unlearned. God bless it, even now, an

54

old woman in a creaky bed, bitten by bugs, I can feel it descend
on me with a bang and a wallop, the life I've led! What a clear,
clean conscience—and what I value most, a sense of peace.

Soak me in salt water and you won't purify me. Preach at
me, pray, rave, threaten me, pour lye on my flesh—but me you
cannot touch, nor can you undo one single thing that I have done.
My life that has put me within reach of all, has also placed me
out of reach, out of reach of the hatred which burns in the gut
of the whole envious pack of you that would raise me from my
fallen estate, as you call it. It gives you no rest; but me it gives
great rest and a deep sleep—it is a pillow under my back. I have
plucked many a soft feather, my hearties, to comfort my deserving backside. What wouldn't you give for one of my secrets?
But the truth is, I have no secrets. I have had nothing that I
have not shared. Ponder that.

All the same, it is wise to have the good will of the public.
So my mother taught me, and so I have learned from my own
experience. There was my colleague, Rosalie, who was stoned,
just as it happened in the Bible. But one moment, please. My
impressions and memories rush at me, and I am entangled in
them, but they shall have to wait. Why do I call Rosalie *colleague*? Am I being cute again? The worst thing about whores is
their cuteness. The hats some of us wear, the cunning little
smiles and dresses, the little-girlishness! The angel of death in a
bridal gown—we are incurable romantics. One hag I know, a
real bag of a badger, went to the trouble of painting on her nose
life-like and life-size—freckles! Would you believe it? Another
wore a braided pigtail with a ribbon in it all her life. And when
her hair fell out as the result of one of the many occupational
hazards and diseases to which we are subject (see, more of my
cuteness), she got herself a wig which also had a braided pigtail.
Pouts, sniffles, giggles, even pimples—the little girl pursues them.
They think to regain what they have lost. . . . Thank God, I've
had none of that nonsense. But my own affliction, perhaps even
worse, is the cuteness of acuteness—my abnormal sensitivity to
words. I've just said that I have a clear conscience, which is
true. I don't consider myself a sinner—but I have all the symptoms of one, chief of which, in my own case, is a troubled speech.

But the public, its good will . . . Rosalie was stoned one
morning on the way home from the grocery. One stone bruised
her ankle, another cut her cheek, a third hit the bottle of milk
she was carrying and her coat and dress and shoes and stockings
were drenched in milk. She was also cut up by the broken glass,

but she didn't mind that half so much as the shame of having
to walk down the street in broad daylight, all covered with milk.
Everyone who met her on the way laughed out loud—and even
perfect strangers who couldn't have known who she was, it
seemed to her that they, too, knew and were laughing. It was the
grocer's son who did it, a lad of seventeen named Timmie, may
the crut give him no rest. Several days before, he had accused
Rosalie, falsely, to his mother, of having offered to cancel her
debt at the store in trade. Because of this accusation, the grocer's
wife drove the weeping Rosalie out of the store with a broom.
But the grocer, a wise father who knew his own son, saw no
reason to believe the charge without also believing that the kid
had accepted the generous offer. And so he beat him with the
same broom—in the course of which beating, the son confessed
his lie, and Rosalie's custom, but not her good name, was re-
stored. . . . I can't help remarking on the utter ignorance of our
psychology that this episode reveals. The grocer's brat, having
no experience of the world, was in a perfect position to indicate
the depth of the misunderstanding that so-called good and indus-
trious folk have of us. It is never a whore's malice, her venom,
contempt or desire to degrade her alleged betters that would lead
her to make such an offer. The offer itself is rare—and if it is
made at all, it is a sign of the whore's own degradation, the
misery and poverty and last extreme to which she has come. But
these good people imagine that we have nothing more to do than
go about plotting and planning to ensnare them—sure, run up a
debt and then wipe it out with one job, an easy life. As if they
would ever extend us credit beyond thirty cents—and when they
do it's a sure sign that they want to ensnare *us*. Which, in fact,
this whole incident proves. They think they have it coming to
them, they want it, the stinking hypocrites, they want it their
own way, which is a whoredom dirtier than our own, and whose
false motive is the cause of the bad name we must bear. We bear
it for the sake of their uncleanness. May the crab sadden their
days and nights.

Another unpleasant run-in with the people—this time, my
friend Phyllis taking the rap. She was living decently and quietly in a semi-retired way in a good neighborhood and paying an
exorbitant rent for her flat. (Landlords, like bugs, can smell your
blood.) One morning she awoke to find her door decorated with
two huge symbols, male and female, joined—a competent drawing of considerable detail, in red paint. The poor girl worked at
it desperately, for the house was up, but it would not wash away.

By the time she had run to the hardware store and come back with turpentine, the landlord and the neighbors had gathered at her door. The ladies, who had been enjoying themselves tremendously, retreated when Phyllis appeared, slamming their doors in her face; then opened them a crack and looked on. The men giggled and passed obscene remarks. The landlord made her scrub off the offensive drawing with the whole house looking on, then kicked her down the stairs and would not let her come back for her belongings. No one said a word in her behalf.

What redress do these poor girls have? None whatsoever.

Some of the girls say, jim-jam the public! This is not my attitude. Ours is a public calling, and it is useless to pretend that we can go our own way, taking no heed of the world. True, the profession amounts to a guild, of sorts, but it does not protect us or represent us in any way. Our only protection, and it's little enough, is the fact that we are necessary and ineradicable. I know, in some countries they register us and inspect us like so many cattle, and a certain percentage of our earnings goes to the state. I don't see much hope in that. It is based on a falsehood, which the whole scheme perpetuates: that we are wild, unprincipled and dangerous, and must be controlled at all costs. It's not only that this is slavery—it's an outright lie. Even if you were to put us on civil service with competitive examinations, sick-leave, paid vacations and old age retirement funds—so long as the lie remained that we are outcastes, occupying a special, degraded position, it would not help one bit. The falsehood would remain, the people would suffer from it, and we would suffer in turn. It is our lot to suffer from the evil in other's hearts.

What falseness and evil I have seen! It is evident in men from the very first moment of their approach. The way they look at you or talk to you—the way even that some avoid talking to you, keeping their mouths shut and pointing or grunting to make themselves understood—but expecting you, of course, to sing them hymns! There are some, however, whose silence is a blessing. They say nothing because they feel, as I do, that words are unclean—but in their actions, in their look, in the touch of their hands and in their very bones there is a sweetnes and a purity. It is these rare men who are our only hope, and the hope of the world. But the rest! I've seen strong and weak, crippled and sound, the long and the short, the black, the white and the in-between and in all of them a fury, a possession as by devils, of hatred, lust, uncharity, niggardliness, arrogance, stupidity, false pride and lies, lies, lies. A man's whole nature is expressed in the simplest act. There is a way of unbuttoning a button which is as cruel as cutting off a head. And to lie down in bed is to leave yourself open, wide open to judgment. It's a wonder how little they realize that we know them and can see deep into them, clear to the back. And not only we, but the whole sex, because a man lays himself bare in such an obvious, clumsy way, poor thing, and doesn't even know that he is known. But we especially have a power over them that is absolutely implacable. Perhaps that is why they hate us, or pretend, or feel that they have to hate us. It is only a strong man who has nothing to fear that can grant us, with his blessing, our right to exist.

I am reminded of money. Make no mistake, I love money. Gelt, mazuma, mahoola, kale—I can't get enough of the stuff. The things I have done for mere money I would have done for nothing else in the world—not for long life, good health, good looks. If the choice had ever been put to me: either do this, or remain as ill-favored as you are, I would certainly have refused. But the trouble is that such choices are never put to us, which is another reason the world misunderstands us. The choice always is: either do this, or you will not have this money. I for one always jumped at the money, promptly went down on my hands and knees, my knees and elbows, or stood on my head to get it. When it comes to money, there just is no choice.

And yet, believe me, though I say I love money, I also hate it, I really do, with all my heart. It embarrasses me, it disgusts me, it reminds me of the world's disesteem. But more important than that, it reminds me of the disesteem in which I hold myself. Money brings out the real whore in me. I am self-conscious in speech and obsessed with the avoidance of certain words; and uneasy before money. Quarters, pennies, dimes, dollars—they burn a hole in my hand. Words and money, money and words—you will find them at the bottom of the woodpile, in all its secret, dismal places. But all the same, when it comes to money I will instantly overcome my fastidiousness (and later hate myself for it) and there isn't a thing I still wouldn't gladly do for money, though the strength that some of these things require is now no longer mine.

Mr. Hubert Jackson is the ugliest man I know. He has been coming to me for years, and from the very first I wished I could drive him away. But he has the pertinacity of an old client and, apparently, a satisfied one. Hub follows me from place to place whenever I move or am forced to move; he has his distinct step on the stairs, his knock on the door, which I wouldn't mistake in a thousand. I hear it and immediately, as one would respond to a lover, something inside me says: It's he! My heart goes faster, though my hands turn cold and I shrink away in disgust.

Now, praise the Lord, he is too old for the woodpile. But this is not an unmixed blessing, and grateful though I am for it, I must say that it makes matters worse. For one, it prolongs his visits—and sometimes, when the caprice seizes him, I am at my wits end to chase him away. Then, when he sees me squirming in his presence, he loves to sit down and talk. "You know, we've both grown old together," he says, more often than not blowing his nose with a dirty handkerchief, as if to strike the note of confidence, or, without so much as a by-your-leave, taking a hairpin from my dresser and digging the wax out of his ear. He looks into his handkerchief after he has blown his nose, or if it's wax he's been after, he holds it up to the light on the hook of the pin and studies the quarry for a while. He knows how much these things disgust me. And then, because he knows how much I hate to recall his share of the past, he repeats, several times, "Grown old together . . . old together." There is engendered that false and clammy old-couple sentimentality which I would dislike with any man, and find absolutely intolerable with him.

But he does not keep on very long at this level. Before long he has switched onto a more familiar, and what is for me a more disgusting, plane, and he piles on the intimacy, as thick as slush. He begins by kidding me. Perhaps the religious pictures that I have hanging on the walls will catch his eye—say the picture of Him, enlarged, with the open streaming eyes, like a close-up in the movies, which hangs over the head of my bed. Hubert Jackson stops at nothing.

"What's He doing here?" asks Jackson. And when I don't answer him, he goes on, "Oh yes, I forgot, you told me. He dropped in one night and just stayed on." Or else he will say, "Very nice and cozy up here, just the two of you. But tell me, sometimes you must look at each other. Who blushes more, you or Him?"

I have stopped saying, aghast, "Hubert Jackson, don't you fear God?" It only encouraged his blasphemy. Now I keep still and hope he'll soon play himself out. But he goes on in this manner, offensive to man and God. Is there no way of getting rid of such a man?

I tell him he must leave—I am expecting someone. He offers to stay on—perhaps he can be of some assistance to me—I am, after all, not as limber as I used to be. Or I tell him I am unwell,

will he please go. He smiles very knowingly, congratulating me
on my prolonged youth. The vileness! What does he want with
me?

A rhetorical question. I know perfectly well what he wants.
He wants to make me play the whore for him, although he is too
decrepit to do it in the regular and proper way. The last time he
tried it proper, it was such a hideous scene that even Jackson has
not had the courage to try it again. Although he has an abomin-
able pride before God, like all such people, he hasn't even a spark
of dignity in himself—but the scene I am alluding to was too
ugly even for him to bear. He knows, however, that I have too
much decency to remind him of it, which is why he has the courage to face me. Now he is casting about for an opening, some new
trick to catch me on. I know what is coming and shrink back.
Jackson knows me too well.

He begins to speak in the vulgar language that he knows I
detest. The words the old letcher uses! I clap my hands over my
ears, but he goes on. I can see the movements of his lips, forming the obscene words. I shut my eyes, but I know Jackson is
still at it, confident that sooner or later I will look at him again.
I do what he expects me to do, look at him, take away my hands
and ask, "What do you want?"

"I want you to say '——.' "

"I won't!"

He takes out his wallet and places it on the table. "C'mon,
girlie, say '——.' "

"I absolutely refuse!"

He takes out a dollar bill and lays it before me. "Say '——.' "

"No!"

"——."

"No!"

"——. Come on, little girlie, say '——'!"

At last I give in. "——. Now get out of here!"

"Not so fast." He places his hand over the dollar bill. "Say
it again. And say '——' and '——'."

"——. ——."

"Again! . . . faster . . . say it again! Say it, girlie. Roll it on
your tongue!"

He excites himself inordinately. I'm afraid that one day
he'll pass out on me, die of a stroke. His face grows red, his
hands tremble, his eyes pop out of his head. When he finally
leaves, I feel dragged and spent and put to shame. My only de-

fense is to take the money, when he has at last had his fill of dirty words, and to take it with as great a contempt as I can call forth in myself, exerting every ounce of the whore in me. I make him feel my disgust, I make him see what he's like, how dirty, mean and vile, and give him a shot of my insight that penetrates his shrivelled old-man's loins and sticks like a barb in his spine. I don't even hide my self-disgust, the better to spew it out in his face. But he stares back at me in the same contempt, grinning in malice and triumph, feeling he has won his object, and we stare at each other in silence and hatred for several minutes before he leaves.

And he's right, too, the wretch! When he leaves, I feel so humiliated that I can think of only One to turn to. But I am too unclean, and I blush at the thought of His seeing me. I lie face down on the bed, not looking up, but it seems to me that He is looking down, and He, too, is blushing. . . .

So it goes, from one thing to another. Words, money, the public—all these simple things become complicated and unendurably ugly. Are they ugly in themselves or do I make them so? I began by suspecting the things, but now I suspect myself. Where does my clear conscience come in, the fact that I regret nothing, am glad of it all? But what shall I pin it to? I am reminded of the game children play and which we played at my birthday party when I was seven years old—and what trouble my dear mother went to, to get children to come to the party! Pin the tail to the donkey, it is called. There is the donkey on the wall, and here I stand, blindfolded, tail and pin in hand, dizzy, having been spun round and round. Go, grope, look for it, and see, while everyone laughs, how far you can come from the mark. Fantastic mistakes: the sofa, the clock, the umbrella stand. But now I know what the trick is. It is to pin the tail to yourself. One sharp jab and it's over—you're fixed up for life.

Hubert Jackson makes fun of me for keeping all these religious pictures. He thinks, Ah, so this is where you've stuck your tail! In a way, I don't blame him for laughing. It's so old hat among us to turn to religion in later life. It's just another one of the many clichés that rob our life of its freshness. The whore with a heart of gold, the whore with a daughter in a convent, with a sick mother, a mad father, a starving brother who is studying law, an ailing uncle, discharged from the police force on account of bursitis. The whore who goes to church ten times a day, and, in a single hour, crosses herself enough times to weave a rug. That's all stupid and trite, and so is the reformed whore, grown fat and rich, who supports all the local charities, is a pillar of the parent-teachers' association, keeps a clean house and is a mother to her girls. The poor things lack sophistication; they hang the tail in the most obvious place and go away feeling proud and justified, because they think they've hit the mark. Not one such whore has ever doubted that she'll go to heaven—and, I suppose, rightfully so. We all have, you see, a clear conscience— we just don't know what to do with it.

In my own case—well, I could just as easily have made the same mistakes, and at one time I did: the Last Supper, the Agony in the Garden, the Stations of the Cross, Christ Crucified among Robbers and the Descent from the Cross, all of which scenes hang from thumbtacks on my walls, are a testimonial to my errors, as are also the pictures of Mary and Joseph in Egypt, Pontius Pilate Washing his Hands (this over the sink; I said to myself when I hung it there, "Think well what you wash your hands of") and Lazarus Raised from the Dead. I have always had a religious streak a mile and a half wide, and lately you can tap gallons of tears from me just by saying the word 'suffer.' Of course, I control myself, I try to remember the difference between what's true and what's exaggerated. But after all, can you blame me, or any of us, if we take to it as ducks to the duckpond on a rainy day?

After all, think, it is natural for us. There's Mary Magdalen, and the woman who was taken in adultery, and Christ said, "He that is without sin among you, let him first cast a stone at her." Rosalie, who was stoned, wept bitter tears every time she read this passage, and covered it with kisses; the page on which this is written—she willed me her Bible before she died—is smeared with lipstick. And then when I think of my own life, the things I've done, the places I've been to, the men I've known, the lowest of the low, I think of Jesus, poor among the poor, and Christ in Hell. I don't mean to compare myself to Him, understand me, although some will even go so far as to do that. It's rather that when I begin to look around for something to cover myself with, any old rag to cover my shame, I hit upon *that*—and it's not a rag at all, but a piece of the finest silk, and on it is embroidered a message in red thread, and the message is meant particularly for me—and then I don't feel shame at all.

Didn't He say, take? Take insults, calumnies, misunderstandings, stones, bruises, wounds. Turn the other cheek. I have taken, and so have we all. I have turned both cheeks at once. And He said, give, give out. I have given. Give unto Caesar. I have given unto him. And to Peter and Paul and Tom, Dick and Harry, and Hubert Jackson. Take in, give out—it is the message, the rhythm of the woodpile and the rhythm of life.

And then as the preacher said who used to come among us, an old hand at converting the girls, "He was the greatest whoremaster of all. Didn't the Disciples procure for Him, Paul establish the syndicate, and Peter open the first house?" (He meant well, Christ forgive him these words, and me for remembering them.) "Bow down, you sinners, kneel, and then look up with shining faces to greet the Great Man who is come to call on you!" We kneel, we fling ourselves down, we sigh and cry out and gasp and clutch with our hands and dig with our nails, sink our teeth and call on His name. "Open the gates of righteousness, that I may enter and praise the Lord!" And then, with shining faces, cry "Sweet Jesus, I am coming! Hold me tight in Thy embrace!" But spent, let down, ashamed, we think, unworthy, of His Passion, and like wet, uncomfortable babies, having wet ourselves with tears, cranky and disconsolate, we whimper, "Jesus, Jesus, Jesus," His sweet name. In the asylum, in the hospital, in jail—nurse Christ, nurse us, doctor Christ, heal us, lawyer Christ, plead for us. Love us, sweetheart Christ, and father Christ, hear us, and do Thou weep for us. We have ourselves been dragged up the hill of skulls. Thy will be done, Jesus Christ, the same today, and tomorrow and forever. Forgive us, Christ, this humble flesh. The Father, the Son and the Holy Ghost. Amen.

But this overdoes it. I don't like blasphemy, I don't mean to be blasphemous (or blasphemious, as our preacher used to say) and I don't think I have been. But there's a limit, after all. To begin with, we are sinners, and though Christ said go and sin no more, we go and do sin more. Our sin is a mortal one, and we will burn for it, for sure. What's more, it is gall in His wounds, and lacerates His poor, hurt flesh. And yet I think He forgives us for it, for it is a humble sin, the very humblest sin there is, and done, the way we do it, not at all in pride. We are not like the rich man who has as much chance to enter heaven as a camel has to pass through the eye of a needle. We are not proud, not rich, nor do we take His name in vain, even when we call upon it in our beds. Nevertheless, we are sinners, and that leaves us out. His house is for whores who whore not, and we, for a fact, do whore. Now, if because I *am* a sinner I must be left out, all the more must I stand outside the gate because I do not even *consider* myself a sinner. I don't, and that's all. It's a matter of conscience, and my conscience, when all is said and done, will not support the claim. It is too clear—and though I am troubled with words and with money and with the complication of simple things, I seek not to be troubled, and see no reason to be so.

What then, is this not pride, to say I do not consider myself a sinner? A remarkable thing, take my word for it, it is not. That's the way it is, just so, simply so. I say it in simplicity and humility, humbler flesh has never been, and though I feel a tickling in my bones, I know it is not the smart of sin I feel, but a trickle of pleasure in the marrow, now almost dry, and I wish this trickle could flow and flood again, and it is not in pride that I wish it to be so, but in simple pleasure in the time I have had, and in regret that it shall not come again.

I think of my days and do not regret them. Rather, I am glad, and it does my heart good. I regard it as a plain and a pure thing, plain as rain and pure as snow. I know why the old Greeks, or was it the Egyptians or the Hindus? would keep the girls in their temples, for a pure thing it is. Mary, Mary, white as snow— but it seems to me that She is proud, not I, and I am pure, not She. (Forgive me, Mary.) Why is She now so still? I think of the girls in the temples and I think it would do Her good to have another Son.

A pure thing it is, pure in itself, unpurified. Just that, and nothing more. The act without consequence, the word without meaning, the ritual without belief. That alone. How often, therefore, is the bed without a sheet, the pillow without a case, the lamp without a shade. Even here in my room the bulb hangs, unshaded, from a chain over the bed, and you either turn it on or off, behold it or behold it not, and it can burn or just as well not burn. But when it burns, and seems to sway, and the bed moves, and seems to travel far into space, it is that alone, and we are all strangers.

It is neither a good thing nor evil, but pure, alone, by itself. And whether with the young man, his first time, and his pimples bright and round as cherries, or with the old man, dry and winded, or with that man, best of all, between age and youth, who knows how it is and how it should be—and then, sometimes, it is no longer sham, but true—even so, with one and all, we are all strangers. The impurity is in Jackson who would make it a familiar thing, to laugh at, not in myself, who would keep it strange and stern. It is the thing itself one has to have mind, heart and courage for, the jim-jam, nothing more. To that of the insects in the crack of wood, the mice in the pantry, the animals in the field, the beasts in the jungle and the birds in the air, we add our own, grounded, unable to fly, but our own, our human and inhuman thing, to crown them all, the greatest and the best.

Then the thing burns and is cold as ice, words fail and there is a stream of words in strange languages, one lives and dies and goes through the stages of life, crying baby, oh boy, daddy! We are all strangers, mother to son, you and I, and peace to us all. But suddenly we are strangers no more. Then bang, and the lights go out and the lights go on, it is all one, the darkness and the flashing lights, and in the act of devotion, the devotion itself, the Son of Man has come and redeems us one and all.

But Christ, I am mocked. My face mocks me, wrinkled and sagged like an overblown bladder emptied of air. My hair mocks me, tangled in the comb. My body mocks me, a tired, sticky, flabby thing, the widow of itself. My eyes mock me, dim, and not, after all they have seen, clear, the dimness burned out of them, but dimmer than the landlord's baleful look. And I must hustle for rent, drag myself up and down these stairs, beg, threaten, cheat, dissimulate, blow liar's dust and sneeze mercy on the saints; crouch, crawl, whimper, simper, fall, pick myself up, hobble, limp, skip, run, walk, creep, scratch, bleed, cry murder in broad daylight and Christ at night. Nothing touches me, grown old, grown cold. Nothing pleases me. I complain, grouch, grumble and scold—at the children below, the dancer above—they darken my days. Nothing pleases me, nothing touches me, nothing gives me a bang and a wallop, a thrill, a tickle, an itch any more. Last night I threw the clock at the door, and broke it, glass and all—I thought I saw an ugly thing there, painted in red paint. The day before a woman pulled my hair. Sew up the flap, I'm off the town. Off marbles, off robin's eggs, off bingo and cabbage and fantail for good. Lights out, roll up the flag. Empty the ash trays. Carry out the pails. Mop the floor one last time and lock up. Take off the sign. Closed for alterations, forced to close out, changed hands, under new management, under six feet, face to the wall.

But Christ, if the fat could still fry!

4. *The Dancer.*

Talia springs naked out of bed and puts on her leotard. This happens every morning. The time is eight thirty, neither one minute more nor less. She has time to brush her teeth—which she does standing on tip-toe, thereby enabling herself to see the full reflection of her face in the bathroom mirror, and to engage

in the day's first exercise, the strengthening of her leg muscles—
and to drink half a glass of tomato juice, which she has poured
out and set in the ice box the night before, before the arrival of
the morning mail. At the postman's ring, she leaps out the door,
another exercise, and goes bounding barefooted down the stairs,
taking them either two at a time, or jumping down three or four
at each landing, as a schoolboy does. Sometimes she gathers the
mail directly from the postman's hand, and, if she thinks of it,
collects the bulky packages and parcels of the paralytic who lives
on the floor above her. There are always many letters for Talia,
and, inwardly, she is delighted to receive them, although she does
not express her joy, for it is not in accord with her regime to release emotional energy so early in the morning, before the day's
work has begun. Talia runs up the stairs, gracefully, lightly, two
at a time, and arrives not winded at her door. Then she sits
cross-legged on the floor and opens her mail, pouting at the day's
first disappointment. Her big toes also pout, standing out from
the others, which are turned in toward the soles. There is an
expression something like disappointment on her big, bluish toe
nails. The letter she is waiting for has not yet come. She flings
them all away, frowns and sighs, and would certainly sulk—but
by now it is nine o'clock and time to begin the day's routine.

The first record she puts on the phonograph is the time-study
in metronome, which she had recorded, at considerable expense
and trouble, under her own supervision. The beat seems irregular—there are many different cadences, rests, irregular rhythms;
but the beats of the metronomes have a carefully measured relation, one to the other, and after one has heard the record several
times he perceives the over-all relationship which unites the
single time-patterns into a whole. Talia is convinced that this is
her own personal pulse and beat, the rhythm of her heart and
lungs, the cyclical rhythms, expansions and contractions, the
movement of her thoughts.

She begins to dance to it. Her motions, like the sounds that
accompany them, at first seem unjoined, sporadic, irregular. But
there is also a pattern in her dance, which soon becomes apparent. In the beginning, the movement is concentrated in the
lower part of her body and her legs, which are sturdy, with
square muscles. The toes grip the floor and release it, her feet
working like hands. The big toes no longer suggest disappointment; but as she has governed her body to make every part of
it expressive, her toes now have a look of something like disdain
about them.

Now it is her thighs and lower trunk that carry out the main movement of her body. Her feet move in smaller circles, their rhythm ebbing and coming to rest. Her arms and hands are not yet involved in motion. It is her thighs that carry the upward movement, suggesting the rising of water in the tree trunk.

The tree is now rooted, it can only sway, as in wind, which is brought to mind by the heaving of her belly. But this heaves like a sail in the wind, as one says, bellying. Then the tree is a tree no longer, but becomes a mast in full sail. But the mast is again a tree trunk, not yet cleared of its branches, which are her arms. The arms protest the transformation of the dance and refuse to bear sails. The fingers express ten alternatives, the wrists two, the arms and forearms supporting them. But even the protest and the alternatives are caught up in the transformation, and enter it, no longer distinct.

Now the movement changes and the image can no longer be tree or mast or sail. There is the movement only, withdrawn to itself at its fullest point, full of possibility which it does not discharge. Meanwhile, the rhythm of the record, nearing the end, goes:

```
tick-tock     tick-tick-tick          tock
tick-tick-tick-          tick     tick-tick     tick
tock   tick-tock-tock     tick-     tock-tick-tick-     tick
```

Now the dancer's head rocks from side to side, its motion at first jerky, then tapering off. Now the body is still and composed, and the head says in its wisdom, slowly nodding, that it is best to dance in one place. Then, as the record ends, it too comes to rest; as in the last moment of a spinning top, shudders and stands still, and what remains of motion, its departing soul, passes out of the top of her head in a moment of comprehension and silence.

Talia has her other exercises, other dances, other records. Some she performs, like the time-study, with her attention turned in to the essence of the dance; then she keeps the curtain drawn over the full-length mirror that covers one wall of her room. Other dances require her outward attention; then she draws the curtain aside and watches herself in the mirror, criticising her gestures and smiling at whatever is right, subtle or exact in them.

She pauses for lunch. Today, to suit the purpose of her dancing, and, as she thinks, the better to regulate her bodily economy, she is on a liquid diet. Talia drinks a glass and a half of pineapple juice and three quarters of a glass of milk. Then she rests on the couch in a position that she has herself discovered, after some research, to be the most restful and invigorating. Her limbs are neither relaxed nor tense, and her weight is so distributed that she both bears and yields it, sharing it with the couch. While she rests, she hears the stumbling, dragging noise the paralytic makes on the floor above, pulling himself about his apartment, and the noises of the many children in the courtyard. Their voices are shrill, frequently they quarrel and the younger ones wail and scream. There is a pattern in everything, the world is without chaos, and even chaos has an order—the order that it has. This Talia knows in her instinct for order. She has tried, with some success, to integrate the elements of a simple life—the things she sees daily, the daily events, sounds, rhythms, smells, feelings—into an over-all pattern of the most general proportions, which pattern she guards like a treasure and in guarding, seeks to perfect it. But the noises of the children do not fit the pattern —and this has for her a kind of horror, the kind that disorder calls forth in an orderly mind. Now she listens to the noises in the courtyard. There is a sound such as a tin tub would make, dragged over stones. A sound as of marbles rolling on the side walk, forever. The girls are jumping rope, and there is the noise of the rope striking the pavement, and the song the girls sing:

> *Buster Brown*
> *turn around*
> *Buster Brown*
> *touch the ground*

Talia listens in pain; a pain, as of the fear of death, which tells her she will never finish or perfect her work. . . .

It is time to return to the dance; time for three more dances until the arrival of the afternoon mail. She springs up, flexes her muscles and tenses and relaxes her toes, which are now all pink, devoid of expression and covered with the dust of the floor.

Again, records and phonograph, again dances, the mirror covered and uncovered.

The mailman's coming is made known to her by the shouts of the children in the yard. A glance out the window—she sees them climbing up his legs and back, hanging from his arms, from the bag, embracing his neck; and he plods on to the mailboxes, bearing their weight, neither laughing nor annoyed.

As before, she runs barefooted down the stairs, takes her

mail, runs up with it and sits cross-legged on the floor, hastily going through the letters. And as before, discards them in disappointment and gets up to dance again.

It grows dark, but she is still dancing. Certainly, by now, she is perspired and exhausted, and what sadness there must be for her in dancing alone, unseen and not leaving the house, must have made itself felt; but she has taught herself to incorporate even her exhaustion and sadness into the dance. So, too, the noises of this time—the whore who lives on the floor below has several times knocked on the ceiling with a broomstick in protest against the music and the thud of her feet, and the paralytic has dragged himself down the stairs to pick up the day's mail, which Talia has neglected to bring him.

Dinner, two glasses of milk and the remains of the tomato- and pineapple-juice, and again the dance. Her movements now are heavy, and severe with self-criticism. But there is no time to go back, to rehearse, repeat, refine. Each dance is new, and its execution and perfection must be spontaneous. There is no time to go back, for now is approaching the climax of the day's effort, which is the performance of an unrelated act, ungoverned in movement and uncontrolled.

Talia sees a hook in the woodwork, high up on the wall; climbs onto a chair to test it and finds it is strong. She puts a last record on the turn table, takes a rope out of the closet, makes a noose at one end and ties the other end to the hook; then places the noose over her head, and holding the slip-knot firmly that it may not constrict her throat, she kicks the chair away and dangles from the rope, kicking and squirming, gasping for breath, and slowly choking. She hangs for the duration of the record, which like the first consists of metronome beats. When the record ends and whirrs and scratches under the needle, she scrambles out of the noose, kicks herself free and falls, with a swollen face, heavily, not gracefully, to the floor, rolling over several times.

The panic movements of the hanging act have provided the topic, the theme for tomorrow's dance. Now it is bed time. She undresses, turns off the light and gets into bed, selecting a position which she thinks is best for her, considering the day, the time, the theme and the pattern. Talia holds this position all night, neither tense nor relaxed, in her sleep.

5. *The Paralytic.*

It was not always so. He had, at one time, the full use of his legs. As a child, he loved to ride his tricycle; as a boy in his teens, he went on many long hiking trips, and even as a young man, when he had already begun to limp, he loved to walk about the city, along the river, in the park and in the country. And he had full command of his other faculties as well; his health was always good and he was cheerful and optimistic. Even in those early days, he had a turn for books and speculation, and loved to seclude himself—but these attacks, which is what his family took them to be, were only sporadic, and even when he was seized with his scholarly fits, he remained the gay scholar, good-natured and bright, who lightened his serious work with walks and social affairs.

Winniker has suffered a general decline. He is lean, has a large, square head which no longer fits his neck or shoulders, a wrinkled, yellow face with watery eyes, and on his forehead and hands liverish spots have begun to appear, although he is just fifty. His legs are now almost of no use to him, though he can still walk with the aid of a stick. The stairs are an ordeal, but he is forced to live on the top floor (as if in illustration of one of the many paradoxes which he was all his life propounding), for he cannot get about well enough to find another place, and knows no one who would be kind enough to find better accommodations for him. Exchanging apartments with the tenants on one of the lower floors, supposing they would hear of it—the dancer, the prostitute or the janitor—is out of the question. He can't approach them normally, as another in his position might be able to do, and whenever he meets one of them on the stairs he is overcome with a shyness that forbids conversation. He stands stock-still, turns red, averts his eyes and waits until the stairs are clear, so that no one should see him struggling with his infirmity. There is besides some satisfaction for him in the fact that he lives above the dancer. It makes, as it were, for a well established point.

Winniker has lived what he considers a full life, and therefore does not very much regret that he must now live withdrawn and alone. His youth was not misspent, by which he means that the pleasures available to his earlier days did not entirely pass him by. In spite of his studious nature, he had many friends, among them several women, about whom he felt, as a young man does, that he knew all there was to know. He belonged, in college, to a rowing club—not, to be sure, the famous crew itself which competed with other colleges—but a society, which he had helped organize, in protest against the varsity team, and which ventured onto the river in flat-bottomed boats and tubs. This protest was directed against the abstraction of the athlete from man, and his development as a separate subspecies. Winniker believed, and still does, in the primacy of middle nature, the sound crafts- man, the good worker, and fought to have him recognized as the true hero and representative of mankind. Even when he dis- covered, shortly after the onset of his disease, that he had his own genius, and in this respect was, therefore, removed from the majority of the race, he continued to uphold the value of the re- presentative man, distinguished not by a highly developed single capacity, but by the presence in him of all capacities, all things human, all talents and skills. He had a number of followers in his youth, young men and women who valued his insight and pat- terned their own after it, though he discouraged their allegiance and was fond of saying, "He who follows me steps on my toes." In so many words—though with greater felicity and originality— had all leaders expressed themselves and admonished their fol- lowers: Zarathustra to his disciples, Buddha to his, and Christ had told Peter that before the cock had crowed, he would, three times, deny Him. A paradox, of course, for Winniker, in denying his followers, but further adopted the selfhood of the leader. But he was fond of paradoxes, and his desire to be let alone and re- sponsible only to himself was sincere, even if the attitude in which he expressed it was not original. Furthermore, he too much enjoyed what he called without meaning to be condescend- ing about it, his "lighter self," to care to remain in a public posi- tion, inconspicuous though it was. There were times when he devoted all his energy to improvisations of the moment, the more inconsistent the better. His happiest inspiration of this time was the wedding present he selected for a cousin of his, a very prim and prudent girl. Winniker sent her a barber chair.

Now the pleasures and diversions of social life are no longer available. Sickness and age have cut them off, but Winniker lives by the afterglow of his golden age, summoning it up, when he is gloomiest and most dismal, to reassure himself that he has lived well. But he manages to live pleasantly enough in remem- bered pleasure, and has even achieved a kind of serenity—though he has enjoyed this serenity only infrequently, and then it was more like a state of exaltation. He feels that the serenity which must be achieved, with a life devoted to it, as to an object, is not of the true kind which comes of itself. But even if his knowledge of the true serenity is for the most part theoretical, it has on several occasions come to him as the truth should come: pre- pared, but not contrived, uninvited, but not unexpected—a long-awaited surprise, a shock of peace. This true serenity is related to his major work and devotion, and whenever it has come it has been an expression of his joy in his work.

Winniker studies the dance. He has studied it in every phase and aspect, in its evolution and retrogression from place to place and period to period—studied its forms, motive, purpose, inspiration, its effect on the individual participant and spectator and on society at large. It is to him a concrete thing and a vast symbol, indefinitely abstract; he sees it everywhere in nature and in imagination, a thing prior to life and more primitive, life itself, and greater than life. And because it is so vast and great, the dance is to him the most representative activity, everything joining it in an ever-widening gyre.

Winniker's interest in the dance developed concurrently with his paralysis. At first he was unaware that the two existed side by side—there was his anxiety over his paralysis, but the dance was his refuge from anxiety and his forgetfulness. It was the dance itself that made him realize that there was a connection between the two states of terror and peace that alternated in his mind. . . . One night he attended the ballet (so long as he was able to walk without too great difficulty, he continued to go out, in fact, "ran about" wildly, from place to place). During the performance of "Aurora's Wedding" he felt so moved, and was transported so far out of his anxiety, that he unconsciously began to express his own joy, and the joy of the ballet, with the motion of his body. But his feet—at the very least, he had wanted to carry out the gliding rhythm—refused to respond—as if for the first time, so great was his surprise; and then he realized the intimate and terrible relationship between his joy in the dance and his incapacity for it. He left the theater at intermission; the shock had so unnerved him that he had temporarily lost even the degree of control he had hitherto been able to maintain over his legs, and had to be helped into a cab.

Then began the study that has occupied him ever since. The first question he asked himself was: Do I love the dance because I am paralyzed, or am I paralyzed because of my love for the dance? Winniker posed the question with wonderful subtlety, turning it this way and that, inverting it and restoring its original formulation, and arranging the probable and tentative answers in groups, series, pairs and classes of pairs. He recognized at once two poles, between which his thought was torn—the obvious and the recondite. Thus he saw that the hypothesis, the love of the dance is born of paralysis, was too obvious, and that the other hypothesis, that paralysis was born of the love, was too recondite. Was there not, he wondered, a third alternative, neither one nor the other, but nearer than both to the truth? An impossible necessity, an excluded ground between extremes? In which direction Winniker moved for a while, seeking the ultimate in the initial venture, the absolute answer at once. But he soon saw that his way was not prepared and that he must first study.

He began to study himself. No longer as the young student, grasping everything that came to hand—and all the more grasping in his belief in the value of representativeness—but now as the mature scholar, confident that his isolated interest is universal in scope. Thus the problem, What am I? became a world problem, as did also, and above all, the question, What is the dance? But this last question had first to be answered from within the questioner, so it became, What is the dance, that I am what I am?

Slowly, gradually, his work began. Winniker studied the dance and the history of the dance the whole world over. He published articles, essays, books and reviews and became known as an authority; books, periodicals, monographs, doctors' theses, magazines, reprints, lectures, addresses and miscellaneous papers were sent to him in the mails, as were also photographs and films, charts, diagrams, costumes and musical instruments. He amassed in a short time a valuable library and a veritable museum, all from the publications and artifacts which other authorities, admiring his work, begged him to accept with their compliments. He soon had the means to work uninterruptedly, the facilities for study and the double incentive of the desire for knowledge and greatness, which was renewed and given even greater force by his work.

But still Winniker was unsatisfied. He did not deprecate his great accumulation of knowledge, nor was he unaware of its orderly arrangement in his card files and his mind. It was a treasure which he would be proud to leave to the world. But as yet it represented only knowledge, which he considered to be but the first stage of work. After knowledge comes being, and this, he felt, he had not yet attained.

To be, as well as to know, what one knows! To be the war dance, the love dance, the rain dance, the bridal dance, the dance of fertility, of the benevolence and anger of the gods—and to have these dances issue from him, from his instinct, as they had issued from the instinct of the race. To be in himself that which makes one say, of one dance, that it is the assurance of immortality, and of another, that it teaches devastation, the subjection of the world to death. Then, only then, is the great representation, desired first in youth, achieved in maturity—Winniker, fully human, the man of all men.

But how does one achieve being? He encouraged all paradoxes, but had no patience with the scholastic paradox: the historian, lacking historical sense, the Story of Man's Courage, written by a coward. Winniker would have to be. He remembered that in his early adolescence he had come across a learned "Manual of Marriage"; reading it, though he had tried to preserve in himself the attitude of scientific detachment which the author had urged on the reader, he had nevertheless become aroused—and felt ashamed of himself for desecrating the proper spirit of the work. But now he felt, of course one should be aroused! A man responds with his whole being: the boy, in a furious study, to sex, and the astronomer to the stars, sucked up through his telescope to the sky, to become a constellation. And may the dance find the dancer, with eager feet.

But how? His own being gives no clue, his feet are still. And the world about him is not congenial—the noise, the cramped quarters, the long stairs to climb and the filth. Even his books and artifacts, once so highly treasured, have become a clutter of useless things.

Right now in the courtyard, interrupting his study, the janitor's children are playing a game, the rules of which demand that they beat the waterspout with a stick. Bang-bang-bang! Bang-bang-bang! Between blows of the stick he can hear the words of a conversation conducted by Mandalay and Panteley Jeveves. They are discussing the question, Are Pregnant Women Lucky? Mandalay says, Yes, they are, if you turn around three times when you see them coming. But Panteley maintains, No, you've got to touch it first.

Between Winniker and Talia there has for several years been an unacknowledged relationship. He met her on the stairs soon after she moved into the building, and at first had nothing but contempt for her: he mistook the sound of her metronome records for tap-dancing. Not that he held anything related to the dance alien to himself; but associating the young, rather muscular woman with a pinched face, whom he continued to meet, to his embarrassment, on the stairs, with the sound of tap-dancing, he concluded that her interest in the dance was not serious; and it was to protect himself from what he imagined would surely be her scorn of his work, that he scorned hers. Such defensiveness, unbecoming and inappropriate to an authority of Winniker's reputation, was, however, the direct result of that reputation. He wanted to avoid the disappointment of meeting her and finding that she did not know who he was. He was, moreover, by that time. very bitter—though unconscious of his bitterness—toward all healthy and, in particular, athletic people, and extremely suspicious of them.

But as time passed and he continued to hear without let-up the metronome beat in the morning and at night, the other records that accompanied Talia's dancing and the thud and shuffle of her bare feet, he acknowledged his mistake to himself. Evidently, she was no tap dancer; and since she worked indefatigably, with only the briefest pauses. and, far from dancing in night clubs and theaters, never seemed to leave the house, he felt obliged to admit that she was a serious student. But this, in turn, led him to the conclusion that she was a mediocrity, and he devoted a considerable sympathy to her under a general benevolence to honest, sturdy workers, all thighs and no talent, misled by unfounded ambitions. And then. her records disturbed him. All day long he cursed her music—though he had devoted a large part of his work to a study of the function of music in the dance. Music and bare feet, bare feet and music—and he, Winniker, must work with their noise always in his head. But in truth, it was the proximity of the dancer dancing that disturbed him most, the image of the unseen, active body. He found himself devoting more and more of his labors to human anatomy—a related topic, certainly, but altogether remote from the theme he was at that time working on. The longer he studied anatomy—in particular the bony structure and musculature of the legs and feet—the more closely he was drawn back to the preoccupation with his paralysis. which he had only lately managed to put down. Now it worked contrary to his instinct to consider the dance with reference to his incapacity; whether his objectivity, gained at such great cost, were truly objective, a desire to possess the object and nothing more, or whether he had thereby adopted merely a method in the most desperate subterfuge, hitting upon it precisely in the hope of a cure, he knew that self-concern, at the present stage of his work, was retrogressive and a danger. Nevertheless, the image of Talia gave him no rest, and whatever way he determined to regard her—as a serious student, a mediocrity, even as a fairly gifted dancer whose friendship might prove valuable to him—no sooner had he struck an attitude toward her than he found himself recoiling against the threat which she somehow exerted against him into a preoccupation with himself and his disease.

At last he resolved to put an end to his uneasiness by confronting the thing itself that unnerved him—he would have to see her dance. Then he would be on his guard, no longer vulnerable—and if she proved vulnerable, he would take advantage of her weakness to put her forever out of his mind; if she proved strong—and, it was to be hoped, truthful and representative in her dancing—then, perhaps, their association, placed on a level footing in the open, would be of advantage to them both. But he was incapable of directly presenting himself at her door and asking permission to watch her dance. It would most likely offend her. Furthermore, the necessity of descending the stairs and entering her room on his uncertain legs before her unsympathetic eyes—and all the worse if she chose to be sympathetic!—would certainly offend him. There was the possibility, of course, of inviting her to dance for him in his apartment; but extending the invitation involved the same difficulties as directly asking to be admitted to her room. There was no one to employ as an intermediary, except the Jeveves children or Jeveves himself, one of whom brought him food and a newspaper once a day; but the Jeveveses were not of reliable intelligence. And he could obtain no one else to act as intermediary without putting himself out beyond the limit of his patience, his endurance and his pride. He considered dangling a note from a string outside her window until it should come to her attention; but most likely the children in the courtyard would notice it first—and besides, the whole situation was ridiculous, as was also a variation of it, that he slip the note under her door. There was evidently no way of approaching Talia. And to rely on a chance meeting on the stairs was absolutely out of the question, as this method involved the embarrassment of all the others, to the highest degree.

Then it occurred to him that it would best suit his purpose to observe her, unseen. In this way he could take her true measure, and not have to reckon with her awareness of his judgment. He thought of peeking through her keyhole, of placing mirrors and reflectors outside her windows, of lowering himself on a scaffold to the edge of her window and peering in; none of these procedures was feasible. Fortunately he soon hit upon a simple expedient, the simplest and most direct. He asked Jeveves to bring him a drill, and set to work at once, boring holes in the floor; the holes, when completed, would look down through her ceiling. The work gave him the immediate satisfaction of know-ing that he had the solution of a problem in hand; at first it was not exhausting, and he could turn to it as a rest from his other activities, or a means of combatting the distraction of the records and the thudding feet from the apartment below.

But he soon found that it was more exhausting work than he had expected. He had to bore very carefully and quietly, not to call attention to himself. It went slowly, with little progress to show at the end of a week's labor. His arms and back tired easi-ly, and sometimes, when he had kept at it for an hour or more, he would find that from great exhaustion he had temporarily lost the use of his legs altogether. It was difficult enough to bore through the floor undetected; sinking the holes through the ceil-ing presented an even greater difficulty, for unless he proceeded with extreme care, the plaster would crack and chip, fall onto the dancer's floor and give him away. There were now well over two dozen holes in the floor, at various parts of the room, to af-ford a view of the dancer from all angles; before extending these holes further, he let water down through each hole, a drop at a time, to seep its way into Talia's ceiling. Then, working very cautiously, he enlarged the holes in the floor, and before lowering the drill bit to the ceiling he set his lips to the hole, prepared to suck up the wood shavings or loose plaster. Winniker was months at this part of the work, before he completed a few holes. Through them he could catch a glimpse, now and then, of an arm or a leg in motion, the gesture of a hand or the top of Talia's head, but never the whole figure or the whole dance, nor would his effort be rewarded until he had opened all the holes. Mean-while, his own floor was covered with plaster and wood shavings, and the holes that had been opened admitted even more of the disturbing music and thudding of the girl below.

Talia, all this time, had not been unaware of Winniker. Her encounters with him on the stairs had greatly excited her curi-osity, the more so as he would stand stock-still and refuse to move until she had gone into her apartment. Nor was he deceived by the mere closing of the door; guarding himself against a crack left open, he waited until he heard the lock catch before ventur-ing to move on. By his extreme embarrassment on the stairs, and the thumping, dragging noise he made above her, she guessed at his paralysis, and began to feel for him an impersonal pity, for the most part curiosity. As Talia thought, out of pity, but in real-ity, to obtain a better view of him than the brief glimpse in the hall gave her, she began to bring him his mail. But the stratagem failed. On several occasions he pretended not to be at home; and when she had at last made unmistakably clear to him the nature and purpose of her knock at the door, Winniker, in an unexpectedly gruff voice—it was the first time she had heard his voice, and for some reason had imagined that paralytics speak sweetly —ordered her to leave the mail outside his door. Thereafter she brought him his mail much less frequently, only when impelled by a very strong curiosity, as when the noise he made, dragging himself about, claimed more of her attention that she had assigned to it in her patterning of the surrounding world. But even so her curiosity was limited; she did not know or care to find out who he was or what he did. His whole existence was contained for her in the fact that he made a certain kind of noise, which she found it necessary to relate to other noises.

As soon as Talia began to come to his door, Winniker realized that his project was in danger. Though he kept his door locked, he feared that she might some day gain access to his apartment and discover the means he had devised for observing her. He therefore instructed Antontonio Jeveves to buy him a rug, and when the good janitor brought it to him, Winniker spent the day, in great difficulty, laying it over the holes. He made so much noise, struggling with the heavy brown paper in which the rug came rolled, that late that afternoon, when he had finally succeeded in unrolling it, and had placed books and dishes along the edge to keep it flat, Talia again brought him his mail. She knocked at the door.

"Leave it in the hall," said Winniker, in a gruff but weak voice. He was lying exhausted on the rug, where he had been trying to think of a simple way of rolling up the rug whenever he wanted to work on his peep-holes or look through the ones that were already finished.

But Talia's curiosity, though essentially as superficial as ever, was very strong that day. She knocked again. Winniker realized that he had neglected to lock the door after the rug had been delivered. He pulled himself up and began to shuffle to the lock, when the door opened. He stood stock-still.

Talia, her face pinched and her arms laden with parcels, barefooted and wearing her leotard, said, "I've brought you your mail, Mr. Winniker." Accustomed to the solitary life, each acquired character and social sense, as if from nowhere, when confronted with the other. The dancer turned sly, the dance authority, contemptuous. They stared at each other.

"Leave it, leave it! I said leave it!"

"May I come in for a moment?"

"You may not. Please go!"

"Where shall I leave these packages?"

"Anywhere. On the floor."

"I can't. My arms are full. You'll have to help me, or I'll drop everything."

"Then drop it, the devil take it! Drop it and get out of here."

"It'll break. This package, here, under my arm, sounds as if it has glass in it."

Winniker stamped on the floor with his stick. "Will you please go?"

"In a moment. Here—" She came into the room, moving toward him as if she were about to drop the packages; staggered, grasped the parcels, lost them and caught them again. "Help me!"

"The devil! Will you get out of here?" Winniker, forgetting his embarrassment and his rule never to be seen walking by a stranger, stumbled toward her, holding up his stick.

Suddenly Talia stood still, as if she were the paralyzed one. The spasmodic movements of her hands and shoulders stopped. She watched Winniker in great enthusiasm for the quality of his movements, observing his faltering legs, his head thrust forward and trembling on his thin neck, the crimp in his back, the twitching of his shoulders, the excited, spiderlike motion of his fingers, the stumbling, uncontrolled course of his feet. Her face lighted up in inspiration and she gave him a brief, satisfied smile; then flung the packages down on the bed, skipped out of the room and went bounding down the stairs.

Later that afternoon—exhausted though he was, he had completed several more peep-holes, working with extreme effort —he watched her do an imitation of his walk, executing a dance about it. She had gained her object, at once satisfying her curiosity, and extending the pattern, deriving a theme from his disease. And while he, too, had gained his object—that afternoon was the first time he had been able to catch more than a few disconnected glimpses of her dancing—it was in great disgust that he found that the object he had so long been pursuing, proved, on capture, to be nothing more than himself. Winniker was furious.

Whether from fury at the futile, senseless interruption of his work, the months lost in pursuit of a false object, or whether

from the mere passing of time, with no cause other than an inner
and inevitable one, Winniker's paralysis has grown worse. He
has thrown himself back into his work, hoping to regain wasted
time, but he must now work slowly. His arms and hands have
at last been affected, and he now has difficulty in turning pages
and taking notes. He still has voluntary motion in his hands, but
his coordination is poor and the time which elapses between the
conception and execution of a movement reminds him of the
passage of a sluggish nerve impulse in the brain and body of
extinct monsters. He now sits at the table all day, and no longer
drags himself about the room; he limits his movements to the
absolute minimum and has stopped going downstairs for his mail.
Now it is brought to him by the Jeveveses or Talia, when the
parcels and packages have cluttered up the vestibule. Talia no
longer attempts to come in to him, but from time to time she
leaves foolish notes with his mail, such as:

> These came for you.
> —Talia

or

> I brought these up.
> —T.

The notes are written in various inks on colored note paper,
gray, lavender, deep blue, and in white ink on black; the paper
is always scented. It is as if Talia had begun a flirtation with him,
or (he peeped down at her once again and found her dancing the
same paralyzed dance, now elaborated with all sorts of extreme,
disconnected gestures), or it may be that she feels grateful to
him and, too proud and selfish to thank him openly—too selfish,
perhaps, even to realize that it is gratitude she feels—she has
selected this means of thanking him.

After a week without notes, she left a particularly offensive
one at the door:

> Are you ill? Haven't heard you thumping about in
> some time.
> —T.

A few days later, another note:

> Worried.
> —T.

Then another note, which Winniker did not read. She came up

80

the next day and found that he had not taken in the mail and note from the day before, or the food and newspaper that Jeveves had left for him. Talia knocked on the door and got no answer; tried to open it and it was locked. She ran down the stairs, alarmed, but nevertheless leaping gracefully at each landing, with her spine straight, her chest thrown out and her arms outspread. The janitor, seeing her burst into his apartment, cleared the bed for her, knocking off several children who had been sleeping on it and shoving them into the kitchen. Marthafoglia was out shopping.

"Hot stuff, all right," said Jeveves, sitting down on the bed and reaching to pull off his shoes.

"The hot water has been fine all week," said Talia, misunderstanding him. "It's Winniker. He doesn't answer. We must get to him."

"Old man. No walk," mumbled Antontonio, hopefully wondering if he had the right to consider her words a refusal. He decided he had not. "No good. Old man."

"Quick, give me the key to his place. Key, key—a pass key. Do you have it?"

"Have got." He removed a huge ring from his pocket, the keys sticking out like the spines of a radial sea-animal. "Lots keys. More." He produced another key ring from under the pillow, reached for one under the bed, overturned a milk bottle and a stream of keys poured out. Antontonio swept them all into his pocket. "We open door."

He tried each key in Winniker's lock. None of them fit. "We break door," said the janitor, and did so.

Winniker was lying in bed, a sheet pulled up to his chin, staring dead ahead of him. "Mr. Winniker!" Talia did a split at the side of the bed. "Are you all right? What's the matter with you?" He did not answer. "Can you hear me? Do you know who I am?" Winniker lay still, alive but motionless. Only his watery eyes moved, glancing at the janitor and at Talia and quickly looking away. "Can you move?" She pulled his arm out from under the sheet, raised it and let it go. It fell lifeless to the bed, rolling a little, as if it were going to fall off.

"Knock out," said Antontonio.

Two days before, as he was working at his desk, he had felt himself growing heavy and cold, and had just managed to crawl into bed and pull the sheet over him, when he lost all power of motion. He had lain there ever since, hearing the children's noises, the mailman's ring, the janitor bringing food, Talia coming up with the mail and coming again the next day, her knocking and calling his name, the door broken in—but he had also lost the power of speech, and could make no sound in response. He could move only his eyes and his lips, soundlessly.

"Sick man," said Antontonio. "You stay with him?"

"I can't," said Talia, springing up. "It's late. I must get back to work."

"Me too. Go fix boiler. We get it old woman, who-ha, she live second floor, she stay." They went down the stairs together, Talia running ahead and leaping in very gracefully at her own door.

Jeveves knocked at the prostitute's door. He told her what had happened to Winniker and asked if she would sit with him, which she agreed to do. Watching her climb the stairs, he thought he might some day ask the question that he asked of all women but which, for obvious reasons, anticipating no refusal from this quarter, he had never asked of her.

The prostitute took one look at Winniker, screamed, blessed herself and ran down the stairs. She came back presently, her arms laden with religious pictures, and holding a bottle of hair oil that she had grabbed in her haste. She tacked all the pictures onto the wall above Winniker's bed, and then sat at his side, wondering what else she could do for him. She talked to him, but he did not answer, touched nim, and he felt dead—warm, but dead—and did not respond; she shook her fingers before his eyes, and they blinked. "Poor man, poor man," she muttered, and began to say a prayer over him; but she suspected, from the look in his eyes, that he did not want her to pray for him—or perhaps it was her conscience protesting against prayer. When I die, she thought, there will be no one to pray for me. But prayer was not necessary, the fact of dying was enough. What you wanted was something different from prayer, without words. But what was it; what could you do for another, not knowing what it was, what could you do, not having learned in your own life what it was? How will I die, who will do it for me? she thought. Still, she wanted to do something for him, and after a while she got up and began to straighten up the house. What a mess it was! All the books and daggers, knives, shields on the wall, the strange masks —it would have been a good idea to wear a mask on the woodpile—the dancing costumes, shoes, skirts, scarves. He had these things on his wall, and she had her pictures—it was all a matter of where you hung your tail. She arranged the books and papers in neat piles on his desk, aligned the books in the bookcase, dusted all the objects and swept the rug, laying on the strokes of the broom with considerable vigor and making the layers of puffy, dimpled fat dance at her elbows.

At the onset of the stroke, Winniker realized that he was going to die. Though he left his desk in haste, he left it reluctantly, and for an hour or so, as he lay awaiting death, he regretted that his work was unfinished, and that he had not stayed with it, to die at his desk. But when death was delayed in coming, and he saw that he should still have some time to live suspended over death, he gave his mind to his work again, thinking he might use up his remaining time in the best way that he knew, by following to its conclusion the particular problem he had been engaged on. But try as he would, he was unable to remember what he had been working on when the stroke came, and alarmed at the loss of his last power, he tried to get up and go to his desk, though he knew that he was unable to move, and tried to call out for help, though he knew that he had lost his voice. Winniker struggled with the paralysis, fighting it with greater will than he had ever done and all night long he lay afraid and struggling with it. But when morning came, he was more at peace with himself.

All that day, even when the door was broken in, he had been at peace. Now he considered it no loss that the work he had been doing remained unfinished. What was it, after all, but knowledge, further knowledge, a gap stopped here, a hole plugged there? The sieve would remain open, for all his effort. What mattered was that the stage beyond knowledge had not been attained—the being of the dance. There was this to regret, this to regret deeply, and nothing else. But as the day passed, he came to realize that he had reached the ultimate stage, had all along been on the edge of it, and had at last entered it wholly. The realization seized him in joy: it was his disease, growing in him since early in life and at last overtaking him, it was his paralysis, to which he had yielded step by step and day by day until it had achieved its final power—it was the paralysis that represented the ultimate being of the dance. By yielding all motion to paralysis, he had yielded to the dance and become part of its being, which was absolute motionlessness, forever at rest. So, in yielding completely to life, a man dies—and knowing this now, Winniker lay serene, at peace, and no longer afraid to die.

The prostitute had by now dusted and swept and cleaned

everywhere, and was taking up the rug to mop the floor, when she discovered Winniker's peep-holes. She dropped down on her hands and knees and peered into the apartment below, where Talia was dancing to the music of the phonograph. "Well, I'll be!" she exclaimed, but the dance seemed false to her, and did not please her. Winniker's holes, however, gave her great delight, and she felt a sudden love for him, as if they shared the secrets of a common self. She remembered, in tenderness, the days when she had worked in a peep-show, and it gave her a sense of triumph and achievement to find herself, at last, on the outside, looking in.

But one thing Winniker regretted. Now he felt the need again to have followers and disciples to whom he could impart what he had learned and have it live in them. To be vouchsafed being—but only for a moment, and not to grow great in it! Not to expand and explore its plentitude! To take up the dance again and go on—who knows?—perhaps even to a further stage, still higher. To have but one man to whom he could pass on the truth—with his eyes, since words now failed him; perhaps even to a number of men, perhaps to a generation, perhaps, if it were not too great a hope, perhaps, eventually, to all mankind, that they might all know the sublimity of the dance!

IN MEMORIAM FOR A WORLD

John Senior

I
The Problem

and what have we inherited?
They have known death before our age.
I think of Shelley lost among
the Euganean hills, half dead
with loneliness, and Arnold's rage
against the waves, weary of wrong.
The hope for death yet lingers
with the dead, we wait for dawn
clowns with tragic faces on.
I run the symbols thru my fingers
sand and straw, a clay for fools
fabric craft—the rhymes, rules;
but the body not the soul is there.
Yeats declared a blood stained stair
his symbol, and ancestral tower
a crumbled monument to save
against the hour when Christ would come.
He had the Will but not the power.
We hold this truth to be certain:
We have inherited a grave
twenty years after the second flood—
death masque of Byzantium,
descent of the final curtain
on god's great comedy of blood.

85

II
The Method

We observe this fact:
this man

this boy
this myriad of word and act
which follows without plan
or logical succession.
(There is joy
in remembered pain—
pain in passion.)
We must analyze them all again:
prepare the subject
dissect the heart
separate, inspect
each part
synthesize, ennumerate
list them
make them coordinate
within a system.
We must analyze them all again.
(There is pleaure in remembered pain.)

III
The Contradiction

We are gathered in this room to honor
a poet; surely there is good in this.
We sit at tables and drink wine together
wearing our love. O here no evil is
surely no sin is here. His eyes have seen
have known defeat to be a victory:
Poet! is it better to have been
in this world, lived out the irony—
ironic grin? better to acknowledge
Him and him, being both, not to judge?
or better beat heart's head, heart's blood
on stone?
    To be lost is not the worst thing
under this sun, for to be lost implies
having had a home; and he being
lost found loss less; comforted is wise,

wiser than we who had no need of comfort
but only of the loss. No, ours is not
the second lost generation; we fought
a war to find that death is no despot
but a distemper of the mind, a kind
of huge blood-clotted eye turned inward to sense
the huger Death inside—blind upon blind
to find the prayer become an insolence.
Let us wear love, then, here have drink and food
enough: a poet famed and honored
out of the logic, live, ununderstood—
this moment, then, we have inherited.

IV
The Consultation

If we could only call it madness
wrap the world up in a sheet
if he lapses into sadness
or attempts to masturbate
have him play a game of cards
with cooperative gorillas, have the guards
play doctor and the bars artistic
with coca-cola hypos, the latest comic
books to keep him occupied—
but for god's sake don't let him know he's dead.

        but who is mad
        is wrong is right
        and what is bad
        is good? we fight
        in symbol, go
        in sin
        not know
        which world what's in.

        or why.

V
The Debate of Body and Soul
The Body:
        I would like to speak for a moment about the atomic bomb.
In the newspapers I read that Laval has been shot, that a Titian
was discovered at a chattel auction. On the radio they say that

Venezuela is in revolt. In the lecture room I watch the blue bottle. On the streets they walk the way they walked yesterday, and I am struck with one unshakable conviction: men can never face the fact of their death.

I recall that discussion of criminal execution by Prince Muishkin. It is the certainty of the hour, of the moment, of death that drives the condemned man mad. But I doubt the thesis. The condemned deny death too. They go to the gallows with nothing more than a quickening bewilderment; there is as much wonder as fear—and that only in the last minutes.

I walk the streets. But with us it is easier not to wonder because the moment is uncertain, it is not precisely defined. We are more in the position of the old man, or the mortally diseased. Death is in fact always imminent, but we never believe in it. We have all always been about to die, but the fact is not kinetic. It is as if we were immortal because there is no other way to do business.

But there is much more than this. It is not only my death that impends, or yours. One does not have to believe in his own death. There is the curse of our age even in this: it is to be collective; a concerted signature. I always wished to pursue my own particular pathway to nothingness. There is something managerial about the word "disintegration." And then there has been the consolation of immortality for those of us who were never driven to the city of god—the immortality that fascinated the 18th century—the kind that Homer has enjoyed for three thousand years. Homer will be murdered too. That Second Death which Thomas Hardy talks about will be a part of the chain reaction.

Not that the human race does not deserve this death. I am not one of those who would defend. The fetish of our century has been its belief in the dignity of the people. If Christs have lived, it is small reason for pride. They spoke impossible riddles to a people without ears. The distinction between them and the Pilates is a microscopic dichotomy; good and evil being differences in quantity, not in kind.

This instant demands that we look into the mirror quickly before the image is blurred with our breathing. Look instantly at the glass and observe how mean and cruel and sick this specimen is. We have blamed it on poverty and conditioning and biology; but the simple secret remains—man is a putrefaction too loathesome to be petty, a cancer top-heavy hideous about to die without an ounce of dignity deserving neither gods nor tears.

And having seen us, go back to the fantasies of the newspaper columnists; it is too much truth to be remembered.

I find it difficult to think of Plato in connection with these things. For example, the Idea of the Good. And where is that ladder to perfection the Platonist climbs, searching out the singular in all the plural? We search out the Absolute with long range direction finders, the infinite extension of Self to be effected by nuclear brained sons of toothpaste manufacturers. This is to be a planned judgment day. John spoke of repentence when he was in this wilderness, and he composed us death-poetry. Now with the gods of utility and functional altars we have engineered our own Apocalypse consistent with filing systems and statistics.

And what have we to say? We have been for a few thousand years, ironic accidents with carbuncular spinal cords. We have created music and murdered gods, plotted things in our stars and charted a course of unspeakable misery and ridiculousness to our destruction. We deserve death. Let no man say he is innocent. I believe in guilt. Donne spoke about it in the figure of a continent. There is no justification for further interference—on with the execution.

Now let us return to our particular one of the ten delusions; or shatter it and run to the next and the next, considering each change a revelation. We will demand death for Ezra Pound. He will have his private kind of dying at least. And we will not understand that this justice is a farce. Who is guilty? We will not condemn the barbarism of the physicists, and if we do we will fabricate dignity out of the refusal of those who refused to work. We will not talk of crimes like the disintegration of an already beaten enemy, and if we do we will also talk about Karl Marx and psychoanalysis. Byrnes will prove that lives were saved at Hiroshima by a logic that jumps out of a hat. We will go to the lecture rooms and the prizefights. We will find comfort in theological absurdities convinced that minimum certainty is better than maximum intelligence. We will love, and in the teeth of disintegration speak our poems, discovering that even in the final hour is "time to murder and create."

There is something humorous about tragedy.

The Soul:

> Who mood the monad moon manmad
> (the moondog moandog madog moon)
> Who mode the moonman moanman mad
> (the manmoan manmode moon)

Hearo dog that bittiest me(a)n agen thanesalvesinwit and
seer the dark (hark) knightness hawrk
whowhen then fonders skip on skoal or bark to marck
o nightless) bright
on clift the leperds stalesong o
    o bran mantastic hightness thu o thu that mokest thrall are
gadness
goad sinlack the flailer on
on me
(perapathetic phalaxy imasculately contraskeptive
condoming distate of graste)
o why o why thou dog geared god hastow forstake in
me
    this aplombleastic paranoisium parapall
aboat the sadom
sumuprime fornor whose syn-
temest soles not in progency
but slife of lidiocrity
    waris this race rune rover yes
asouls not form egoneads crowed credooks are mode-
ornode pastheriority
butt s(h)ark
hark nonce agen the dinwit
bight the zoambat zombat moonen drawnce o witch
o wain wampiric sceanse wiltow ban seafurth agein?)
the dark the dark the dark shaff shoves of lightness
scend askend the lock outpeers'd
and moontranced weirs wear seedogsales
knot not infearm dimensity
faleaves but john o lanterns jack-
anights his hillish bonefire bearns to seewyrd
christfire calls the lea . . .
                   (Jappelauce!)[1]
    and the dog said:
I stond afart my mastefbatch and I, and indeffidately spear my
fingerbales.
    It is humorose henuf to be foney.
    Hearo dog the witlesses:
        for these are toments instant hours slantern
lanthorn sorrow teares like windshook rain moonmined blind
the souldrift sifts
soft silent treelass slow—
falls adoon alurk a pennyweys along the dark allone from

mountains wracks and rilling torns
boundborne to morrow rither
the faress treelight fathests of
          1(onely) dreams.

---

1. at this punkture the sole bows prefusely and pubicly abeises himselv three
times without stooping eviduncing mastegury of hind over hatter and the
supinority of the blody bole.

VI
The Witnesses

The Fisherman:

The other night when I returned from the sea
footsore, I found a woman kind enough
to wash my feet. What is it to me
if they always demand another proof?
It is a matter of indifference.
I busy myself with nets and tackle, fish
until evening, peddle my catch. The consequence
is neither my concern nor particular wish.

The Carpenter:

You call me here to find out what it is
I make. That's because of the story
they circulated about a pair of shoes
that cold night, my birthday. Well, for me
it's all a joke. I don't deny a word
of it and for the record I'll tell you
what it is if perhaps you haven't heard,
there's no secret to it, I make toys
in my shop for children—nothing new.
Some do important things, but I give boys
and girls toys. If you learned people call
that a crime it's not my fault because
I don't know anything about it at all
because my work has nothing to do with the laws.

The Sheepherder:

If the sheep get away? I don't know,
there are mountains beyond the upland pasture,
there are a thousand places for them to go;

and at night sometimes my dog, it's his nature
to keep warm too, he curls up by the fire
with me. When the snow flies again next year
the same thing will happen; it's not my desire,
I watch, but some are bound to disappear.

The Little Boy:
Gentlemen, it was the stoics who said
Jupiter is the light that men reflect
back to Him again, Him the greater gloried
for man the mirror. And again the intellect
the sceptics say, creates a Jupiter
and kneels before its own image humbly.
Religion is god and man, two mirrors,
looking at each other indefinitely.
This is the paradox I made apparent
that day in the temple when I played the cynic
for the crowd. It was part of the argument—
besides, I'm not responsible for logic.

VII
The Judgment

It is midnight
the revellers in the scarlet robes are gone
the final curfew struck, moonlight
hurries along the white edge of the sea alone
wrapping shadows about its thin shoulders
and then the rain

the roll of boulders
down the mountain-
side the sound of stone
rumbles
torrent of tone
the echo tumbles
down the rubble of flat lands
rivers of sound to the sea
and the fingers, the long white hands
grasp moonlight, grasp at the writhing river greedily.

It has been thus before
perhaps—but words are dubious stars
to hand our fortunes on—no more.

JOHN SENIOR

The after-image too recedes, the bars
are shut, the rains descend, choke
the gull's cry, the sea is quiet, the river silent
the moonlight safe beneath its cloak.

Night seeks its tent
and steals inside, makes fast
the flap and blows its lantern out, and in the deep
the universe content that it is time at last
curls into itself and falls asleep.

FLESH FAREWELL

Donald Windham

DISTANT strings of colored lights danced against the wind. Dusty Johnson walked along the highway not seeing them, not hearing the scratch of dry leaves along the concrete. The night was cold, and he felt the cold against his face and hands, penetrating his skin, muscles and tissue which covered his bones. He put his hands into his trouser pockets and walked faster down the highway toward the colored lights.

His walk was deliberate and angry, controlled by his cold, hurt pride. At an opening in the wire fence beside the highway, he cut off and followed automobile tracks through the pine-needled woods to the entrance of the fairgrounds. He came out of the trees by the ticket booth. A lighted empty streetcar stood at the end of the trolley line which half circled the fairgrounds and ended at the back entrance. Beneath the low outthrust trolley of the car he stopped and counted the change in his pocket; there was more than a dollar so he bought a ticket and went inside.

The end of the midway where he entered was deserted, tangled with ropes and rubber cables, but straight ahead a steady stream of people flowed between the two banks of sideshow posters. He walked proudly and angrily into the crowd. His heels were stepped on from behind, and he kicked the shoes of the people in front of him as he walked looking straight ahead. At the sideshow facing the rollercoaster, he stopped and looked about. He smelled the sweet odor of cotton candy in the stand which people were pushing past him to reach, heard the barkers' voices and the roar of the crowd, saw the posters picturing the alligator girl, the two-headed baby and the tattooed man, and watched the boy across from him tossing baseballs at wooden milk bottles to win for the girl beside him a mica-splattered pink plaster Christ. But he did not see anyone he knew and he walked on.

The midway thinned uphill into cane and weight-guessing stands, and at the top of the hill a few people stood around the dancing pavillion which was open to the night. The girls danced with their coats on. Dusty crossed to the rail which separated the pavillion from the midway and leaned on it watching for a particular face which he did not see. After five or ten minutes, he still had not seen anyone he knew and he dropped his eyes down from the dancers' faces to their feet as though no question of identity existed there. Without looking up, he reached into his pocket for a cigarette, lit it, and stood smoking. Someone behind him laid a hand on his shoulder and said his name. He turned and faced a boy named Robinson.

—By yourself? Robinson asked smiling.

Dusty nodded and turned back to the pavillion. The two of them leaned on the rail and watched the dancers. Dusty was silent, and Robinson talked about the girls he recognized, telling unbelievable stories of what he had done with them, speaking slowly and steadily, more interested in the effect of his story than in its contents, and watching Dusty's face as though he would completely change the gist of what he was saying if he saw that something else would interest Dusty more. His eyes shifted between the dancers and the boy beside him. Dusty listened partially, but the drama inside his brain was more real; and Robinson knew that his attention was divided.

—Do you want a drink?

—Do you have a drink?

Robinson smiled. He took his time in finding a cigarette and sticking it between his lips. He spoke without lighting it, with it wavering up and down in the corner of his mouth.

—Look at this.

The right pocket of his windbreaker was fastened with a safety-pin which he unfastened and took out a flat pint bottle of rum. He patted his other pocket and smiled.

—And there's another one in here!

When the bottle was back in his pocket, he lit the cigarette and, indicating for Dusty to follow him, walked away from the pavillion down the steep back of the hill. The incline was so sharp that to keep from running he walked with his weight thrown forward on the balls of his feet. Where the ground leveled, he stopped and waited for Dusty. The midway was above, the white-fenced racetrack circled the artificial lake beyond. He took the bottle out of his pocket, unscrewed the top, and held it out as Dusty reached him. Dusty took the bottle and drank.

—We can go back and pick up something when it's late, Robinson said.

—Not me, Dusty answered. I'm through with girls.

—Sure, Robinson agreed. Find them, feel them, fool them, fuck them, and forget them.

—You can say that again, Dusty said.

—Sure, Robinson answered. But I'm leaving this town next week. Really. I've got a job with the F.B.I. The girls may as well have something to remember.

Dusty did not answer. They walked on to a lunchstand which was isolated now that the racetrack was closed and they had another drink with a Coca Cola. They asked for a paper cup, but the counter-man said that cups went only with orders of food and refused to give them one. Robinson wanted to argue, but Dusty walked away.

He was thinking that he would never trust any girl again, and he did not realize that he had the rum bottle in his hand until Robinson joined him. With a gesture of independence, self-sufficiency and defiance, he threw back his head and drank. The warm sugar flavor of rum filled his mouth, and was followed by the metallic aftertaste of air. He exhaled through his lips, frosting the atmosphere. The warm sweet rum flowed with satisfaction through his stomach and limbs and encouraged him to think that he would never see the girl again.

He gave Robinson the bottle and looked at him for the first time. He did not know Robinson well and did not like him much. But Robinson looked like a friend now.

—Do you want to see a picture of a real bitch? he asked.

He took out his wallet and showed a photograph in it to the other boy.

—She said just wait until tonight. And when I went by, the place was dark and nobody home. She thinks I'll believe a note saying she's in town to spend the night with her aunt. But maybe I'll surprise her. Maybe I'll go back and wait till she gets in and tell her that I'm through.

Robinson smiled.

—She'd like that. She'd know she had you then.

—I'm through, Dusty said as though he were defying Robinson.

—Then you'd better find somebody else to give that proposition to.

96

—Not me, I'm through, Dusty said.

The rum filled him with action, and he climbed to the top of a bank and stood there rubbing his groins till Robinson caught up with him. They were behind the midway. In front of them was the back of an amusement where spectators threw baseballs at a target, and if the balls hit the center, a Negro man who sat shivering on a suspended board was dumped into a trough of icy water below. He fell as they were standing behind him, and they saw him climb back up, dripping and shivering, and sit on the board again.

—Want to see me get him? Dusty asked. Let's find the front of this damned place.

They were forced to walk to the end of the midway and go through the exhibition building. By the time they reached the building they had forgotten about the Negro. They walked the length of the exhibits between aisles of apples, corn, peaches and jars of brown preserves. The building was closing for the night and only the overhead lights remained lit. At the far end, in a dark corner by the chicken coops, they decided to have another drink.

—It smells in here, Dusty said.

Laughing, they went out into the high enclosed arch of the entrance. The first bottle was empty. They threw it into the corner and drank out of the second. Dusty watched people passing through the dark shadow of the building toward the ferris wheel at the beginning of the midway. Music tinkled. Robinson was talking again, this time about a special commission in the army; he drew a letter out of his pocket, unfolded it, and with all but the signature covered by his hand, held it out for Dusty to see.

—Dwight D. Eisenhower.

But Dusty was no longer standing beside him. He had followed a small girl into the midway. The girl stopped in front of the freak show and listened to the barker. Dusty saw that she wore no coat, only a cotton dress, and he opened his jacket as he walked toward her. The colored air of the midway smelled warm. When he put his hand on the girl's arm, she looked at him and said something about the fortune teller sitting beside a stuffed raven on the platform above them. Dusty talked to her, not caring what he said, and put his arm around her waist, caressing her. She did not stop him or seem to mind, and when he suggested that they go for a ride she agreed. They pushed out into the midway but were pushed back along the side of the platform into the corner at the end. Dusty took the girl's face into his hands, feeling the delicate bone of her jaw beneath his fingers, tilted back her head as unresisting as the hinged lid of a box, and kissed her long and hard. She did not resist, but when he stopped she said:

—I thought we were going for a ride.

—Right, he answered.

He kissed her again, then pushed a path through the crowd in the midway. The rollercoaster was directly in front of them. He stopped and stood in line for tickets, and the girl stood beside him holding his arm. He looked into her face. Her eyes were childish with the lashes distinct about the edges, her straight short blond hair faded into her cheeks, and she looked to him as though she might never have known a boy. He bought the tickets and put his arm around the girl again as they stood in line for seats in a car. He could feel the rum inside his body and the girl against it.

He was smiling down at her when he suddenly heard his name called from the midway. In the crowd he saw a girl, a friend of the girl who had tricked him, waving and shouting. All the warmth drained out of his body, and he became uncomfortably aware of his arm around the waist of the girl at his side. He was doublecrossed. All evening he had been alone and not seen anyone he knew, and now that bitch would accuse him of being out with another girl and he would be the one who had done wrong. It was not fair. He could say that it was a lie; he could deny that he had been at the fair at all; but other people might have seen him. He hated the girl beside him. He dropped his arm, but she held on to him. He did not move but he ached for action. He wanted the last half-hour never to have been, the girl to be annihilated, and himself to be alone. In his hate, he closed his eyes.

The train rolled onto the platform creaking and sighing metallicly. The girl pulled him forward. He wanted to run away toward the entrance, but he followed her, and they sat in one of the last cars. The attendant came and clamped the iron bar across them. He was locked in with her, and her loathed flesh which he renounced was pressed against him. People who were lined up waiting for seats enviously watched him.

The cars started the ascent slowly, pulled up the incline by a chain which seemed unequal to the weight it moved. Dusty felt as though he remained stationary with the earth grinding and sinking beneath him till he saw all of Lakewood Park spread out, and beyond it the green and brown trees, Capital Avenue with lights and houses along it. He was as high as a skyrocket which bursts over the lake, and he watched the balls of flame fall beneath him slower than seemed possible. Then the car was almost to the top where the track humped in a narrow peak.

—I don't want to see, the girl squealed in an ecstasy of fear.

She grasped Dusty's arm. He had almost forgotten her, but she came back into his consciousness now as the cause of all his misery. Only one car leveled at the summit of the track before it plunged, and though their car was still in ascent Dusty was jerked violently forward as he turned toward the girl. His face was close to hers, and he saw her eyes wide and helpless. He saw her close them as the car plunged downward dropping almost beneath itself. Every person in the rollercoaster screamed simultaneously. The girl clutched him, wanting him to hold her, and his stomach revolved as he was pulled up from the seat and thrown down against it.

—I can't look, the girl screamed happily.

—Open your eyes, he shouted at her.

The rollercoaster sank in the quick swing of the second dip. He was pulled away from the girl as he let go of the iron bar and caught her face in his hands. The car careened in the opposite direction, and he was thrown against her; but he held onto her face, determined that she should open her eyes and suffer. He shouted again:

—Open your eyes!

The cars had gone into a long climb, ascending on the momentum of their last downward drive, moving slower the nearer they came to the top. Still the girl did not open her eyes, and Dusty struck her in the face as they dropped out of the sky a second time. She moaned. His body was thrown almost out of the car, ripped upward like a flag in the wind, but he held onto the girl's head and kept his eyes intent on the girl's clenched eyelids. Sliding toward her, he pulled back his fist and drove it at her face. She moaned but did not resist. He felt his strength, saw that the girl's lip was cut and that there was blood on his hand.

—Open your eyes!

The train was tearing downward through a tunnel made by the supports of a higher track, then racing upward as though toward certain doom. The speed made him insane. He pounded at the girl's face hardly aware of her, cursing her and commanding her to open her eyes, pounding her as though he were part of the force hurling them through space.

Then the rollercoaster gaily sailed up and down the several hills which marked the end of the ride and coasted in toward the platform. Dusty stopped. The train stopped, and everything sprang into motion. The crowd in the midway was swarming and shouting, the music of the carousel was piping and wheedling, and the people in the rollercoaster were bounding out with valedictory cries of relief. Dusty felt the girl huddled in the corner of the car away from him. Without looking toward her, he leapt free and ran down the wooden ramp to the midway. If anyone noticed her, he was gone before it happened.

In the crowd he allowed himself to be carried along, passive and nescient; he was breathless but he tried not to look intent on losing himself. He let himself drift. At the freak show he was pushed across to the entrance so he bought a ticket and went inside, passing as he entered the tent of the gypsy in the fortunetelling booth about whom he had spoken to the girl.

—Hey. Boy. Cigarette! she called to him.

Self-consciously, without stopping, hoping that she had not recognized him, and thinking for a moment that he might have killed the girl on the rollercoaster, he threw the gypsy a cigarette. He walked slowly so no one would think he was running away. The inside of the tent was circled with platforms, and the show took place on one platform at a time. The crowd was at the far end of the tent now. He was alone, and no one was following him. Kicking the sawdust, he walked to the outside rim of the crowd and leaned back against a railing. On the first platform a girl was being suspended in air by a magician. Dusty tried to look everywhere at once and he saw nothing. He was dilated, spread out, exhausted but not satisfied. He needed a sharp sensation to focus himself upon, to make him separate and contained, and his name began to run through his mind as though he were repeating it under his breath, as though someone were about to call it aloud.

He spun around. A voice had snarled at him from behind. Leering down at him from the platform, blowing whiskey breath in his face, was the tattooed man. He stared at Dusty, sneered, and pointing to a sign, read it aloud.

—Do not lean on this platform!

He stared at Dusty as though he could read his thoughts, and Dusty stared back without dropping his eyes.

—Well, the tattooed man snarled.

Dusty asked the price of a design. Instead of answering, the man beckoned for him to come up on the platform. He climbed the stairs, rising above the earth as he had in the rollercoaster, and emerged in full sight above the crowd. The tattooed man gave him a cardboard covered with designs and said that he could not tell him how much a design costs until he knew which design he wanted. The girl who had been suspended in air on the first platform now appeared on the second as the three-legged lady and wiggled each of her three legs alternately. Dusty chose a single rose with a scroll around the stem. The tattooed man spat out the price and told him to pay in advance. He counted his change and placed it on the table. The tattooed man put the money away in a box on the floor and, while he was leaning over, produced a bottle from among a heap of dirty rags and drank. When he straightened up, he pushed a blank piece of paper across to Dusty and began to arrange his inks and needles.

Dusty sat staring at the khaki wall of the tent, thinking of his name, visualizing himself on the platform above the crowd as clearly as if he were looking into a mirror. He was so intently aware of this image of his identity that he was unaware of his actual self and his surroundings.

—Name, the tattooed man was repeating to him.

He focused on the man with sudden fear. He was double-crossed. The man had read his mind and knew what he had done. He was trapped.

—Name, the man repeated. I can't put a name on the scroll unless you write it down.

He pushed the paper toward Dusty and pointed at it angrily. Dusty looked down and comprehended. He took the pencil that lay on the table and wrote down the name of the bitch who had tricked him, though he no longer thought of her as a bitch. Sometimes people were better than they seemed, and when she saw her name on his chest everything would be all right.

The tattooed man told him to take off his jacket and shirt. He obeyed. The chair was cold against his naked back, and the sharp pencil tracing the design across the hard skin of his chest tickled him. He was again proud and strong. He looked down into the crowd that was gathering about the platform to watch and he saw Robinson among them. Robinson smiled and waved. Dusty smiled back; he was no longer angry. To appear natural, he leaned over and spoke to the tattooed man.

—At first I thought you meant *my* name, he said.

The cold needle pricked the skin of his chest until the pain became a hot steady cut. He clenched his jaw and smiled to prove that it did not hurt. Gradually he lost sensation. The girl who had been the three-legged lady appeared on the next platform and advanced to be sawn in half. The paper on which the girl's name was written blew off the table. The tattooed man kept on tattooing the indelible design across the boy's chest.

HEAVENLY CITY, EARTHLY CITY

Robert Duncan

Overture

Beauty is a bright and terrible disk.
It is the light of our inward heaven
and the light of the heaven in which we walk.
We talk together. Let our love leaven
and enlighten our talk! O we are dim.
We are dim shadows before our fiery selves.
We are mere moments before our eternities.

The youth of the man I am now has gone.
I have passed from its bright glare into its shadow.
Twenty-seven years have wrought their careful pattern,
worn in my flesh their inarticulate burden,
worn in my animal the mark and strain
of an inward heaven. Some bright and terrible disk
that lighted once this city of my passion
has dimmd and gone. Beauty
is a bright and terrible disk.
It is the light of our inward fire
and the light of the fire in which we walk.
When I see the figure of my lover,
—this is the eternal answer that the eye of love
sees in each being—then
from the years that have tried my flesh,
in the stain and age that trace in my figure
failure and betrayal of that golden vision,
man's possible beauty, th'eternal fire
in the guise of my manhood burns, burns bright
from the dim of my youth and consumes my youth
in its fiery self.

103

In the dark of my manhood the flamy self
leaps like the sun's hairy image
caught in the black of an obscure mirror.
This is the apish chiaroscuro of our source, the sun.
This is my age, my inward heaven.
The city of my passion is reveald in its beauty.

I

Earthly city in which I walk, the light, your sun,
is the golden heart of that deep body,
the darkened city that gleams in the tide
of an inward sea. Dumbly, I hear its voices,
voices that merge in a chaos of other voices,
murmur and surge of a bright confusion.
The song, your voice that in my throat
rises in praise of some pure spirit, lonely
and yet lovely human aspiration, breaks
in the chaos of a massd impurity.
So a single bird flying up from its field
claims above the clamor of a dismal century,
asserts, asserts, in its perishable body
the lone clear cry of its perishable beauty.
In the moment of song—earthly radiant
city of poetry—that golden light
consumes in its focus a world I have suffered,
the darkend city of my perishable age.

Yet never, never, can the heart meet the gaze
of that earthly paradise in which I walk.
It seems to accuse my heart; its quiet
and its song, the dappled mien of light and shade,
are like a beloved face that searches its reflection
and is torn in the rage of an inward flood.

The heart in the darkness of the city sings.
It answers the song of its source, the sun.
The darkness of the city protests, protests;
there is a throng of angry voices.
The heart in the darkness of the city sings:

I have seen the face of my Redeemer.
—this is th'eternal figure that appears and disappears
in the human flood. Momentary answer!
Never, never, can I meet the gaze
of that inward angel articulate of love;
and yet He touches me in passing.
His touch seems to penetrate and awaken
some answer, pure in its sleep, and is gone.
And now awakend I lie, dumbly changed,
too late, too late, inarticulate of love.
Could I but dream and dreaming gaze
upon the paradise of his eyes, but they are gone.
He, he is gone; he is gone; and knowing this
I know the heavy change upon the world.
I fear. I fear.
Tell me that my Redeemer will answer.
Tell me that my Redeemer lives.
For there's a kind of world remaining still
tho' he who did make animate and fill that world
be gone.

The voices of the night protest:

O lonely heart, too late, too late.
You cry out as if you were
some innocent, foundling of the angelic orders,
awakened by the passing of your Redeemer
to face the last long night alone.
Betrayer of man's possible beauty,
Thou art awakend to gaze upon thy dead
and speechless self, touchd by that angel
awakener of the dead.
Thou hast no Redeemer.
The ghost that walks in its reflected glimmer
is but the wraith that you call splendor.
O but you are dim before the fiery self
that is gone from your world.
Wrath is the ghost that walks in its glimmer
and pities, pities the lonely dead,
touches them in passing and awakens the heart
to face its death. Too late, too late.
There is no Redeemer.

The heart in the darkness of the city sings.
It answers the song of its source, the sun:

    I cry out as a child in the dark.
    I know that my Redeemer lives.
    The rage of my lover meets my cry;
    feasts upon my inward hell and shakes,
    shakes my spirit in his fury; tears
    from me the strain of life,
    inviolate song, and mocks my dim
    inarticulate heaven. Now in my wilderness
    where I have been driven by that blind
    Avenger, awakener of the damnd,
    betrayed by my Demon shall I in turn
    betray my Redeemer? I walk alone
    in that inward hell, shaken and riven
    from my Beloved, the lover of my inward heaven.
    Like Satan fallen in the weight of his pride,
    speechless I face that punishing spirit
    articulate of my own damnation.
    This was the lover who answered my cry
    as a wrathful father might answer a child
    who, dumb in the strain of the wrath inside,
    cried out in fear for the comfort of love.

    I know that my Redeemer lives
    who loves, who loves my lonely spirit
    and seeks in the darkness of my night
    to absolve my torture in his passion.

O my Beloved, in the night of my soul
I have thirsted for some passionate wrong.
I have lain in the arms of the destroying angel.
I have heard in hatred's sea the Siren's song and cast
my self upon that strand; held in love's cruel counterpart,
known the warm embrace and the inward cold.

Dumbly, I listen to the Siren's insistent sound,
that brazen counterfeit of song that charms
and fixes the soul upon its destruction:
this is the magnet of a massd impurity.
I walk in the eclipse of my Beloved.

But O the Earthly city remains.
In my dismal century the Earth replenishes,
replenishes her beauty.
Against the Siren's monotone, the fixed accusing glare,
your voice, Beloved, rises in praise
of that fair spirit, my inward heaven.
I know that my Redeemer lives.
The light, His sun, is the radiant song
that consumes in its focus a world I have suffered,
asserts, asserts, against the Siren counterfeit,
the Earthly paradise in which I walk.
This is the measure of my dismay:
to know its beauty like the face of my Beloved
that is torn in the rage of an inward flood.

II

Pity is the wrath in which we walk.
My heart like a burdend Icarus having struck terror
falls from its universe into the dark.
Then gaze deep upon my lover's gleam, feed my soul
upon the damnd perdition of his eyes.
The inward spark, the flamy self
dies, and its shadow leaps forward.
See, it is a demon lover to fill the abyss
as he falls.
Pity is the wrath in which we walk.
Then gaze deep, deep upon the gleam.
This is the true mirror of my face.
"No," I say. "No." In the shadowy room
I seek to disentangle myself from his arms.
Dumbly, unmoving he lies, having laid bare
his wrath, betrayed, he clings to me.
Pity is the gleam of the wrath inside,
a demon light to illuminate the face
and betray the heart. Like burdend Icarus
I would fall in the weight of my body
and damaged wings, in my knowledge,
into some dark and forgiving sea.
Pity is the unforgiving sea.

107

Traveler who would bring love's light into hell,
when that shadowy beloved turns from his hell
a face to gaze upon your face; this is a damnd
Eurydice, that catches in her mirroring quest
the gleam of love as a new perdition.
Sweep, then, Orpheus, the wild music from your lyre
as if you sang lost love, but remember
the beauty and charm are hate's machineries,
demonic art that catches the damnation into its disk
and lends to hell its immortal strain.
Sweep, then, Orpheus, the wild love from your lips
and when from the far room your forgiven lover
cries out from the rejection that forgiving is:
remember Eurydice's face because you turnd
is turnd toward her death; remember her cry
cries with love's final breath and is gone;
remember his face as your Eurydice
that was the woman's face in the lunar gleam of sleep.
The damnd in the fires of love wrap round themselves
and shriek. AI AI Orpheus, the brutal lyre,
beauty and charm to turn her face
toward its perdition.

Where is that dark and forgiving sea, flood
of rage or sorrow to sweep thru my body,
vast poem, ocean of the soul's resounding deep,
where falling Icarus falls to his rest?
In the blaze of his blinded eyes
the disk shows black, burnd in his mind
a charcoal sun.
Torn from his flight among the Bacchae of the sun,
those burning women of exaltation's fury,
he is hurld in the weight of wings and knowledge
into the forgiving depths of sleep.

J'ai dû tomber de très haut, de très haut,
très haut sur la tête?
Où est mon coeur? Où est ma tête?
Eurydice, Eurydice.
Que j'ai peur.
How heavy my heart falls with its burden.
There is no world than the world of my dreams
where the weight of my knowledge falls so far.

108

Orpheus of the bleeding wings among the beasts
in the shadowy meadows that extend in sleep
sings his sweet strain. Eurydice, Eurydice.
He closes his eyelids and in that inward light
Eurydice's dark face returns and is banished by his gaze
into eternity. Nightmare minister to pain!
Pity is the wrath in which he walks.

The Bacchae, furious women, drunk with lust,
close their eyes like their clenched fists
and see in the glare of their blinded eyes
a myriad burning destruction of the body.
AI AI these are sorrow's witch-like sisters
with their hair in rays like an angry sun; they cry
against earth's shady consolation, inviolate song.
How in our misery the calm of the grove,
and the calm of the evening's air, earth's
loving breath, commiserates and increases our fury.

We shall be redeemd and forgiven in passion,
washd thru by the fires of passion's sun,
and find in our bodies an immaculate quiet.
Pity is the wrath in which we burn.
The Bacchae in pure passion's roar
raise their clenched and violent hands
against the lonely and still singer,
Orpheus, who would sing love's praise.
He I am who torn in my flesh
return at last to my lost Eurydice,
the inward sea, terror's sister-face,
to receive my Icarus.

The Bacchae tear in my fleshly sleep
fleshly ribbons that gleam like gold.
I lie under the weight of the black water.
Eurydice toward whom I dare not look
—she is the bright spirit that sleeps in my heart—
returns to meet my inward gaze.

III

The praise of the sun is a didactic poem.
The ape in his raiment of gold or cloth of fire

apes the categories of the spiritual man
and, in the teachings, learns from his raiments
the torturous lesson of his apish form.
What man knows more in his cloth of gold
who fixes his eye upon his source? I know no more
than the fleshly life that clothes in its ardor
the bony rigor of my inward form.
The lineaments of my body are
a didactic poem,
the apish chiaroscuro of my source, the sun.

The praise of the sun is a solitary poem.
The lonely man can turn his skull sunwards
until that glory penetrates
and sears the confines of the bone;
can howl, can whirl his reluctant arms,
and measure his pride against the sun;
can moan in his incompleted image;
can howl for the bliss of his final mate.
He catches the sun in the mirroring heart
and praises that blazing solitude.
Then in the avenues of his earthly city
unearthly presences wink,
unfathomable eyes of an inward vision.

O with what pain I watch in my vision
my proud and reluctant animal self
where he sings in his lonely monotone;
he turns his beseeching enraptured eyes
and glares upon the heavenly scene,
cries, cries as if hurt by the surrounding beauty,
and apes the sound of a vaster heart.

He mimics the opulence of the sun,
and in that bright confusion, love,
he burns in exaltation's fires,
clutches, clutches at his animal mate
and whimpers against the pit of dark.

I watch with pain my hairy self
crouched in his abject sexual kingdom
writhe in that brief ecstatic span
as if he took the sun within himself

and became a creature of the sun,
became an illumined body of voices;
as if in the pit of his animal dumb
he heard the counterpoint,
the mimic tum-tum-tum of a vaster heart.

The praise of the sun is a nostalgic poem.
The tum-tum-tum in memory
is like the pounding surf in dreams.
The man in the solitude of his poetic form
finds his self-consciousness defined
by the boundaries of a non-committal sea
that washes, washes the reluctant mind
and carves from its shores its secret coves.

Sometimes our feelings are so mild
they are like a day when rocks
seem mere extensions of the sea
washd in a world of oceanic blue
and continents seem dreams of a watry deep.

Turbulent Pacific! the sea-lions bark
in ghostly conversations and sun themselves
upon the sea-conditiond rocks.
Insistent questioner of our shores!
Somnambulist, old comforter!
You right in passion's storm and passionate calm
your reasonless change and seek to restore
the aspiring man to your green remote.

The individual ape in the human sea
is worn, is worn by a non-committal tide
and shows in his unnecessary watching face
the necessary convolutions of that sea,
the memories of forsaken lands.

The praise of the sun is a nostalgic poem.
Sometimes the sea seems mild and light
as a luminous harp upon which the sun plays
threaded with indolent wires of gold
across the ruddy music of its waves
and its voices merge in a pulsing counterpoint
to sing the wonders of the sun,
the beasts of the sun and the watry beasts.

111

Sea leopards cough in the halls of our sleep,
swim in the wastes of salt and wrack of ships,
and sun themselves upon the resounding rocks,
or lie in the thoughtless shallows of the sun.
These are the tides of a poetic sea.
I drift. I drift. The praise of the sun
is purposeless. I dream of those forsaken shores
wrappd in the mind's redeeming haze.
Sea-leopards cough in the halls of our sleep;
disturb the course of the nostalgic sea,
casual hints where harmlessly they swim
of some brooding fear in the fiery deep.

The earth has tides of desolation and of bliss,
of shadows and of amber marbled surfaces,
laments and cries, vague intimations of the sun,
terrors, brightnesses of noon, and groves
of memory: in these her beauty is renewd.
The wandering man returns to his city
as if he might return to earth a light, a joy;
and find his rest in earthly company.

The praise of the sun is a renewing poem.
The earth replenishes, replenishes her beauty
and sings a green praise of her terrible source.
The sea reflects in her evening tides
upon a lavender recall of some past glory,
some dazzle of a noon magnificence.
The evening hour is eloquent of the sun.
This is no dominion of the pure terror
but soothes, soothes. We walk in the light
of beauty's calm; our city lies about us
murmuring, drifts in an evening humanity.
There is a wisdom of night and day,
older than that proud blaze of sun,
in which we rest, a passion, primitive to love,
of perishing, a praise and recreation of the sun.
My earthly city is seen in its beauty.

THE HOSPITAL

Seymour M. Krim

IT IS Sunday, and I am to ride on the bus. In the terminal a queue has already formed. I have purchased my round-trip ticket from the sweating Jewess imprisoned in the shrill cage, and now I assume a position at the end of the line.

Poverty informs our little group. Cloaked in shawls, twisting uncomfortably in shiny suits, my fellow-passengers stand guard over their bursting bundles. These contain rich foods—jars of sweet and sour pickles, smoked salmon, spiced meats—the robust delicacies of a poor man's table. They have been carefully husbanded for this Sunday voyage, and now they are being protected with vigilance. As we move forward the bundles are drawn painfully along; my associates are often allowed only one arm for this strenuous labor, for the other is laden with magazines and newspapers tied together in a fury of wild cord-ends. (I carry only four sliced-chicken sandwiches and a New York *Times*.)

Our 'warders' patrol the queue. "Only a single line," they bellow. "No pushing—*we've* got all day, and *no* one will get on the bus if there's pushing." We are not patient with this indignity.

Perhaps, in our eagerness to secure a seat (for the journey is long), we have jostled one another, breathed hot upon the neck of a fellow. Perhaps there has even been wrangling in our midst —a muttered word, an accusing eye. But surely this is excusable. We are agitated with waiting—ambivalent in heart—and the oppressive terminal air has contributed in no small measure to our discontent.

What right do they have to inflict gratuitous cruelties upon us? Those gross voices, for example. And the disdain in those insolent eyes. No—we stiffen suddenly—no, we will not suffer it! Our ranks close and we say: "Do you think we are children? Stop shouting at us!"

113

Our protest echoes petulantly. How naive we are—they are not disturbed in the least. In fact, they are rather amused. After a short pause, one of them booms impersonally: "Any monkey-business and nobody gets on the bus. That's final."

Ah, their curt brutishness is superb. Surely they are Spengler's *Naturmensch*—and we, bleating Ishmaels, hounded by pique and perspiration. Yet what can we do? Take another bus? An automobile, a train? Out of the question. There is absolutely no other means of transportation. This company, among many vast holdings, has an exclusive grasp on all roads and byways leading to and from our destination. We must ride upon the bus of pain, and we must abide.

At precisely high noon, the first of our party boards the bus through an aperture in the enclosed terminal. "Poppa! Come quick!" shrieks the tiny woman in front of me. With savage emphasis she has taken hold of her ancient father's left arm, and is hurrying him forward, filthy finger-nails threshing against his worn Sabbath cloth. The sullen silence which had pervaded our group has been ruptured; all are now seized with animation.

We have been stationed against the southwestern wall of the terminal. Our habitat, shadow, our symbols, cloaca and womb, but now—pace quickened—we are thrust into the raging neon that heralds interior commerce: drug store, luncheonette, bootblack cubicle. Suddenly, from one of these retail phantoms, comes a crusty jukebox lament which thumps through the terminal. At the ticket-window, a sailor boy, strutting and blond, begins to tease at a dance step by himself. Passengers waiting for other, more prosaic buses, are caught by the infectious rhythm: they beat their feet and chant, almost wantonly.

Our moving line stares numbly. These grave faces are unyielding in their censure. As the Harlem trumpet flails fortissimo my companions await their turn to escape this sportive display and mount the bus. The vehicle has been moored in the runway outside, adjacent to this obscure exit, and presently those of us remaining on line shall step out into the afternoon.

I follow close upon the heels of the daughter and patriarch. I hear him moan softly with the effort as he places his withered right leg upon the threshold of the bus. He holds grimly with both hands to the miniature bannisters and, with a supreme effort, hoists the remainder of his shrunken body onto the bus. I am prepared to follow when the bus's doors swing shut without warning. My entrance has been halted while the driver checks some rudimentary mathematical error—I see him fumble irritably through his till. Behind me a muted cry arises from those left on the line. You can't turn us away!

"Calm down. Everybody will get a seat."

At once, we are docile as lambs. How acutely our warders have sensed our insecurity—and how shamelessly we show our gratitude for what, in actuality, is hardly kindness on their part.

The doors open, and this time I am not to be thwarted. I hand my ticket to the driver who punches what appears to be an adding machine, then gives me a blue receipt bearing rather cryptic numerals. As I make my way back into the bus, I am again struck by the curious darkness of the interior. It is difficult to determine the precise origin of this phenomenon: perhaps there is a vast ceiling arched across the runway which obliterates all light; but if this is so, it has escaped my notice. Possibly the city's skyscrapers have conspired to seal this tiny avenue from the sun. But, assuming either of these instances, why then should the bus dispatchers wear white sun helmets with green visors?

I am cautious as I grope for a seat. I have never really adjusted myself to the conditions of our journey: despite more than a year's experience my attitude, it would seem, is resolutely Victorian. I finally slip into a seat and struggle with the window. "Weak, hah?" gleefully asks an old man standing in the center of the aisle.

Before I can answer, he brushes me aside and triumphantly raises the window. Before I can thank him, the old man disappears in the gloom. My eyes slowly accustom themselves to the strange light. I see that, as usual, it is mostly older men and women who sit silently by, waiting for our bus to start. They are flanked by a scattering of younger women, a brace of lone men and, finally, the children.

Our departure seems imminent when emerging from darkness limb-by-mountainous-limb, a vast Brunhilde comes marching down the aisle. She grows in immensity with each fearsome step, and slung about her girth are proliferous parcels of sour-smelling foods. I contemplate her coming with hostility—for the seat tangent to mine is among the few remaining vacant ones on the bus.

I had reserved it, in indulgent fantasy, for one young and comely—there is perhaps no greater anodyne for this trip than the sensual divertissement. And yet, as this unwashed, unblessed colossus advances toward me, I am deeply ashamed of my erotic reverie.

"That seat taken?" she asks bitterly, I having made no gesture to arise and let her in. I smile, "No," to assuage my guilt; she makes no answer, merely squashes heavily into the seat with her soiled treasures.

There is now barely room for me to sit on the pinpoint of my spine. If I were to turn my head a fraction of an inch, it would nuzzle a right breast three times its size. The woman suddenly belches, and a foul miasma engulfs me. I should like to change seats: but can I, justly? Are we not bound by a common knowledge not accorded most? And are we not, therefore, committed to a new tenderness toward each other? For what *is* man without pity?

Her eyes are dumb, her great arms weary with embracing burdens: I can not move . . . and then dart to a seat in the dismal rear. The poor woman stares blindly ahead: there are no ultimate humiliations for passengers on our bus.

The doors have closed, we are about to depart. An unseen hand pummels our flank—we can hear the sharp tattoo plainly—and at the signal, our driver puts the bus in motion. We creep slowly behind another bus nosing out of the runway and on to the teeming street. Done! In less than an hour we shall arrive at the hospital.

My comrades glisten painfully as we glide into a flood of fresh air and sunshine. I see them in what is perhaps a revelatory light. It is significant, for example, that they are mostly southern peoples: Italians, Jews, Spaniards, Negroes. Their Sunday clothes are worn with ritual deliberation; the more southern the heritage, the more lavish, and obviously Sunday, the clothes. My fellow-passengers are archtypal Latins, all animal and white teeth; Negresses, competent and grim, next large-boned husbands; an ambiguous blend of Mediterranean brunettes; and old Jews, disdaining the eliptical Americanese of wives and children, speaking a fierce Yiddish.

What unites us all is the wound, of course. After the first trip it is unmistakable: it would be no more apparent if it bled. Yet it is peculiar, most peculiar, that we are rarely menaced with memory and remorse during the week.

I speak from my own experience, but from what I have learned in conversation with other passengers, it would seem to be borne out generally. We traverse the normal week blithely or soberly, according to our tastes. I will grant that often before retiring, or when listening to certain types of music (notably Stravinsky and Bloch) we are subject to glimpses, fleeting re-

minders of the inevitable Sunday. But for the most part, even
the most sensitively wrought among us is much too absorbed in
gratifying the appetites to be but faintly disturbed. And is this
entirely fortuitous? We are described as warm-blooded peoples;
however inexact the generalization, I have little doubt concerning our voluptuous inclination. And, in one sense, isn't that why
we are destined (because of our coat of flesh) to know only the
sensation of pain and not its significance?

Even the children on our bus, naturally ebullient, are subdued. When they accidentally jest, or become too animated, they
start up guiltily, then bow their tiny heads. The children—how
touching, how ingenuous!—often forget their special fate even
while on the bus. We adults are, of course, not spared the duties
of full consciousness.

Our bus rides west toward the river and then turns north
up a great avenue. We pass dilapidated tenements, sprawling
ruins washed by the river's fever. From uncertain windows fly
"victory pennants," a florid display of multi-colored flags cele-
brating the end of the war. From what seems to be the last row
in the bus I hear a dry female voice exclaim: "Look! Real Americans!" The woman's comment is a pistol shot in our flowing
womb of gentle bus murmurs. "Will you look at Old Glory,"
she continues, with harsh pride. The passengers are coldly silent:
there seems to be little doubt that this foolish, rather arid voice
belongs to a newcomer.

The bus streaks northward from the vegetative slum. We
now enter an immaculate neighborhood dominated by stately,
phallic apartment houses. Uniformed doormen can be seen loung-
ing in baroque vestibules.

"Ah," cackles the neophyte, "no flags. They should be ashamed of themselves!"

My fellow-passengers can't help but show their scorn. It is
inconceivable to them that anyone who rides our bus should still
be enthralled by such secular devices.

In fact, the little man sitting next to me snorts derisively,
then looks up eagerly for confirmation. He twitches once, like a
coy bird, unable to contain a shrill, effeminate giggle. Then he
bends toward me.

"Have you been making this trip for long?" His voice is con-
spiratorial and knowing.

"For about a year," I say.

He makes the traditional empathetic response with tongue
and teeth. I smile impersonally, then gaze out of the window at

the portentous thunder-clouds gathering overhead. From the
corner of my eye I see him furtively peeking at me. When our
glances meet he turns away, the abashed schoolboy, his right leg
jerking involuntarily against mine.

It is fitting, I think, that my neighbor should be a homosexual: the guilt that infuses his every gesture, that provides the
intangible scenery for his fitful, tormented skirmishes, is locked
in struggle with a carnivorous passion. And so with the rest of
us, only less concentrated, less intense.

I too am lusting, only more quietly. Directly ahead of me,
sitting next to the window, is a handsome dark-skinned girl,
perhaps a mulatto—it is difficult to be sure. Her beauty, however,
is unequivocal. Every now and then she will incline her head
slightly and consent (how lovely!) to a shy, vague smile, almost
as though she is being enchanted by some bit of countryside we
are passing. (The city is far behind us now.) I completely accept
the conditions of our coquetry: her very obliqueness seems highly proper for the occasion, dainty and melancholy.

There is no opportunity for me to fathom this lovely girl,
however. My ardent companion has spotted a quarry, and he
brandishes his light artillery.

"The new buses are wonderful," he says, smiling up hopefully. "Yes indeed, I was on one last week that had marvelous
leather seats and chromium racks for baggage and things."

The dubious virtues of new buses are profaned at this moment; the heavens have burst, and our bus is transformed into a
tiny craft shuddering in a great sea. A tumultuous wind sucks
us this way and that, while thunder and lightning beat down
from their writhing crucible. The country road we are traversing
is cleft with the discharge: deep incisions are cut into the earth,
and all our driver's skill is called upon to maneuver us through
this battlefield.

My neighbor titters and places his hand upon my arm: "I
used to be terrified of thunder and lightning," he confides, then,
gaining confidence, he takes a further, more daring step. "When I
was a youngster I used to crawl in bed with my brother during
thunder-storms. He was frightened like me."

Our bus is plunged in darkness. We hurtle along in a Stygian
deep pierced only by flashes of lightning which illumine the
immobile faces of my fellow-passengers. The fury of the storm
is surely unprecedented: yet even the children maintain a unique
poise during its climax—but then, they know only too well that

118

nature doesn't descend to *grand guignol* for its most significant judgements.

As the storm subsides, the man at my side reluctantly loosens his grasp on my arm: under cover of darkness it was a secret thing, an indulgence we both accepted, but now, as a finger of light probes this vice, he looks away sadly, and his fingers fall from my arm one by one, like dead antennae.

Did I get wet? he inquires with tremulous concern. No. Did I mind that, because of some curious identification, he clutched my arm in the dark? Of course not. He raises his eyebrows in arch burlesque and licks his lips. I have a sudden impulse to shake him until his teeth rattle, to pinion those tailored shoulders and speak this dogma:

Mr. friend, pain is a priori. For special reasons, we have been selected to know it in this form. It is not pleasant, surely. But one must go on from there. If your strategy, as it appears, is gratification at any price, then you have not escaped; for with every coital spasm, as it were, you are again impaled. Understand: pain is the ring-master, and pleasure the tiger, but when the whip cracks, they are one and the same. Contain yourself— for God's and your sake!

But if he were to speak truly, and took delight in style, he would say:

Surely you are not naive—or are you?—but honestly, where would be the relish, let alone salvation, without my compulsive hunt? The Poet says life is a hospital and we are patients who think the next bed better than this one. I know the value of my unique bed. In the next lies heart-break and bewilderment.

As it is, I say nothing and he says nothing.

We have reached our destination. The sun shines merrily on vast grounds that seem to have been untouched by the storm. As our bus sweeps down the main thoroughfare I am impressed again by the architectonics of the place. White, sceptic buildings rise cleanly from the verdant green. On the periphery of the main grounds is that cluster of neat cottages which always remind one of some suburban culture—precise and secure. And in the face of the majestic anonymity which egulfs them—those glacial steel and concrete walls, that complex of stunning cubes and squares—the cottages seem warm and individual, one can visualize a dog smelling good things within. They are occupied, I believe, by the doctors and nurses.

At the first stop—which the driver announces as the "ad-

ministration building"—several of the passengers step slowly
from the bus under the weight of their huge bundles. Included
in this group are the dark-skinned girl (who faces me once, can-
did and serene) and my homosexual neighbor. He doffs his hat in
an ironic flourish, then waves good-bye with his left pinkie. The
driver collects the tiny blue receipts from those who leave.

The bus turns down a slight hill and stops a second time
beside a squat, oblong building. In front of this structure, upon
the freshly-mowed lawn, a group of Negroes are having what
seems to be a picnic. I see them quite clearly through the window.
There is great laughter in their midst, and two grey-haired men
are casually throwing a tennis ball to each other. The Negro
farthest from me is laughing softly with enjoyment of the game,
and as he laughs, a five-and-dime necklace quivers about his
throat.

I get off the bus at the final stop and enter the canteen. This
is a vast, low-roofed hall jammed with bare wooden tables and
hundreds of men, women and children. I have to fight my way
through this teeming mass in order to get within sight of the
counter. And even here people are ranged in great density, bar-
gaining with the men behind the counter for soft drinks and ice-
cream. These men, patients who have been selected for the task,
are unusually dextrous. They are neither polite nor are they
rude; they are rather as efficient and impersonal as machines.
With a bold thrust, I manage to reach the counter itself: at once
I smell the odor, sour and pungent. It is indigenous to all the patients; its ingredients are filth, sperm and perspiration. I buy two
bottles of Spur and make my way back through the howling
crowd.

Now for the overland foot journey. The building I seek is in-
accessible even to the bus. As I walk diagonally across a great
expanse of cropped grass I pass small parties sprawled on the
turf. One extremely tall boy, perhaps sixteen or seventeen, is
dancing about a middle-aged nurse lying on the grass. As he
swoops past her, the boy touches her head quite delicately with a
leaf; and each time he places the leaf upon her head, the woman
purses her lips and makes the sound of a wind instrument, much
to the boy's delight.

After a five-minute walk I arrive at the building. It is similar to the others except, if possible, more bleak, more implacable.
It has two entrances, I have been told, but in all my trips to the
hospital I have only been able to uncover one. Bearing my miniature bundle, I knock at what is presumably the back door and

wait for an answer. After a short pause, an attendant unlocks the door from within and holds it open for me to enter. When I am safely inside, he relocks the door with one of the innumerable keys that dangle from a chain fastened to his belt. The attendant wears the outfit common to all males who work at the hospital: a white shirt, with rolled sleeves, a tiny black bow-tie, and dark blue trousers. I am escorted into a small room—bare and functional—where a young woman sits at a table littered with charts.

"Ward?" she asks mechanically, without looking up from her papers.

"Forty-nine."

"Pass?"

I hand her my visitor's pass which she compares with one of the charts on her desk. On the wall behind her are two signs, placed about five feet apart. One says, in striking black characters: VISITORS MUST NOT GIVE MATCHES TO PATIENTS. The other: TO ENTICE AWAY OR ASSIST A PATIENT TO ESCAPE FROM THE HOSPITAL IS A MISDEMEANOR PUNISHABLE BY LAW. This latter caution is, I gather, required by the state. It is, however, the merest formality and has little to do with reality. In fact, I have often noticed the attendants joking about the incongruity of the sign.

The young woman stamps my pass and says: "You can go up now." I pass through a narrow exit and begin to mount the winding metal staircase. At the first landing I turn to the right and face the prohibitive door which I knock on with my fist. No answer. I beat it with my foot. I can hear nothing. Finally, I hear the inevitable rattle of keys and the door opens. A Negro attendant wearing rimless glasses asks me to wait on one of the benches.

I am in a huge waiting room. Unpainted tables and benches are arranged in arithmetic fashion the length of the room. At both ends of the room opened doors extend into similar rooms. Yet there is no *one* room—there are rather a series of doors within doors and chambers that have no tangible perimeter.

It is into this labyrinthine network that male patients of all ages are lead on Sunday afternoons. (Female patients are naturally quartered by themselves; and, of course, they may only receive female visitors.) The male patients' dress depends on what is available on any specific Sunday—usually a bizarre mismating of blue denim shirts, white duck trousers and thick, coarse shoes. During the week, in the confines of their cells, the patients usually go about bare-footed. And even now they do not

121

pretend to civilized graces: a patient next to me, with quiet non-chalance, blows his nose in the sleeve of his shirt.

Wherever I look, patients are eating and smoking. There is an incessant crinkle of wax-paper being removed, the grating sound of many jars being unscrewed. These, of course, are the foods that were transported aboard the bus; they supplement six days of the most frugal and tasteless fare. And on the tables, in heaping towers, are the plethora of magazines and newspapers that were brought for the patients' diversion.

Conversation between the patients and their visitors is spasmodic, unpredictable. The visitors sit solemnly beside the patients; they seem embarrassed, shy, and when they smile, it is to palliate an unknown quantity. The patients are at once oblivious, cunning and greedy.

Despite the contrast in clothing and expression, it is difficult for me to distinguish the visitors from the patients. This is especially true of the children (and, of course, the Negroes). One of the younger children, a boy of seven or eight with a bright, scrubbed face, is earnestly talking to his patient not five feet from where I sit. The patient is uncomprehending—he plays idly with a top that was brought for him—and the young visitor raises his eyes, perplexed and grave, to mine. There is no advice that I can give him.

At this moment I am signalled from the door by an attendant. The patient I have come to see has been brought up from below. I go forward and take his arm, careful to keep my head averted. We do not look at each other, for it is less painful that way.

"How's the boy," I ask, guiding him to a bench.

"How do you think? Join our little country club for three hundred years and find out."

I unwrap the chicken sandwiches—meager offerings compared to the swollen delights bared on other tables—and give him a bottle of soda.

"You've got to get me out of here," he says furiously. "I'm annihilated. Don't let them annihilate me!"

I light a cigarette and he rips the pack from my hand. I light a cigarette for him and he takes three breathless puffs, then lights another on the bright ash of the first. "Get out your pencil," he says, "I have two new inventions this week. Patent number one: an air-conditioned camel made of plastic, for desert travel. Patent number two: radar, the golden light!"

"That's already been patented," I say.

"No, not radar the golden light!" He puts his mouth to my

ear and whispers: "My radar will make six highways twinkle, water-power, motive-power, the banal eye-magic—" He breaks off and becomes silent, for standing in front of our bench is a young patient who has been listening intently to our conversation.

Suddenly, in one fierce motion, the young patient undoes his trousers and begins to urinate on my shoe. Two white-shirted attendants rush over and carry him off. They apologize for the incident and give me several paper towels to dry my foot. I take out my pencil and resume the role of amanuensis.

"Go ahead," I say.

"An impetuous monster," he grins, "we'll let him shower the naked city." I have learned of course to accept these startling changes in his conversation. When he was "admitted" to the hospital—or, rather, when I was informed that he had arrived there—a year ago, last July, the physician for Ward 49 frankly told me to expect just this conduct from him for the next five years. After that, I was told, his condition would depend entirely on myself.

"There's Uncle Harry," he says, pointing to a middle-aged patient sitting across the room.

"You're imagining it," I say firmly. "Uncle Harry's in Boston."

He looks at me shrewdly. "Don't contradict me. I know Uncle Harry when I see him. Hey," he shouts loudly, "Uncle Harry! Uncle Harry!" The man pays no attention to him.

"You see," I say softly, "you were imagining it."

He has just about finished the last sandwich when the voice is heard through the loudspeaker: "Time's up. Time's up."

All about me visitors stand up slowly; they tenderly, yet with fear and solemnity, embrace their patients. We too arise, holding hands. He awkwardly lays his head upon my shoulder and begins to cry.

"No," I whisper, soothing his head with my hand as one might a child. "Please, my dear."

And now, as always at this time, we may look at each other. I must not yield (surely this is a mirror, surely a dream). For, you see, it is myself. The eyes of tears, the lips I now kiss (as with Narcissus, out of humility) are mine. Each visitor is, of course, a patient; and in the great rooms, as far as my eyes can see, young and old men are kissing goodbye to their lost images. One child, obviously a newcomer, is terribly embarrassed, and all he can bear to do is hold his surrogate's hand at arm's length.

"You've really got to go now," the Negro attendant says to me. He takes "him" by the upper arm and they walk briskly away.

Our bus waits for us in the square. We walk down the green pathways toward it silent, bent. Many of the women and children are crying. Yet by this evening we shall all have forgotten.

ABC

Leslie A. Fiedler

"The slow torture of being a child. . ."

Art
 Will inherit
Play's etiquette, the use
Of the lie: the child's truce
With use and despair,
But more dear.

Beast
 Is the fist's
Ancestor. Be wary, Child; madrigal,
Fast nor prayer can let at all
Your hairless wrath, past innocence,
The dog's inheritance.

Circumcision:
 On this derision
Turns, the wolves' clamor, the sneer.
O Child, do not distrust the rite: Here
Your unfocussed anguish, the imageless dead come,
Are at home.

Dandelions,
 Rank, define
The child's disaster, to piss in bed;
Or ruined, will prophesy, broadcast by breath;
Betray, beneath their fringe, the threat of tense,
Their naked glans.

East
 Is the dream's crust,
Seaward the hardening rind. Waked
Out of the dance—doll, tower or toy shake
The motiveless morning city, dying
To things.

Fool!
 In school
Our first rebel: your dull hoof,
More imperative than order or love,
Stirs our titter. We see the teacher's afraid:
Are betrayed.

Ghosts
 Are lusts'
Eternity: the soul's antipodes. In what
We hunted, as in a mirror, caught
Forever. The child's not pure, but ghostless at least
Nearer peace.

Haircut:
 Swathed, caught
In the cage of his face, child into boy
Screams. Bloodless circumcision of the *goy*.
The innocent barber chastens our fur,
Perfumes the scar.

Islands
 Are the damned's
Arena. Men beached on the dream of boy or dunce
Survive, possess themselves not peace. But were one once
Immune to childhood, home more fabulous than laughter,
He'd walk the water.

Jew,
 Child, is you:
The eye's indelible ghetto: sober,
Whom once God beat like a lover,
Comic, genteel; now pray only for death—
Or less.

Kiss
 Is the price
Of the toy, the aunt's revenge; more
Red than cokes, the dream of girls, but more—
A strategy, a prayer to come where Moses stood,
Tongued by his Lord.

Lost—
 Our latest
News always. Around the child's corners
The enormous umbrage of adult mourners,
Who, knowing their names, the names of their street,
Yet also weep.

Medicine,
 Now begin
When the kiss fails, to scourge the desire of boys:
The vulgar color of measles, the cough's obvious noise;
Or later, the ulcer's dull bourgeois rancor,
The adult treason of cancer.

Negroes
 As nose,
Blue gum or raddled eye,
Betray the face the child's disguise denies:
History-less, unequal to its defeats,
Or bruised by sleep.

Ogre,
 Beggar
I am but let me please choose
For this boy rather to lose
Joy than you. Let his sisters
Fear monsters!

Pride,
 With its snide
Ambiguous notions of terror,
Is the child's mirror.
He remarks he is rather
Like his father.

Quest
   Is chaste
For Boy or Greek: Grail or Hesperides
Innocent for all their angelic police.
But if Jew or Man be not infirm
Let him burn!

Return
   Will turn
In the end hell's paradox like the rest;
The arch-immaculate garden blur to the breast,
The child's most pious explorer discover
Some lies of his mother.

School
   Is not cruel,
Though law for sullied love retrace
The mother in the teacher's face.
Starve! Starve! Eve chose gross bread; my son
Eats stone.

Time
   Will define
Our burden of terror. See, the ill-photographed
Father yellows to ancestor. Laugh,
But do not deny whatever dies is killed:
This is your guilt.

Unicorn,
   Do not scorn
The obsequious dog, the greasy rabbit
(To fawn for the caress, or between heat and habit
Bear—are innocent), tho sleep betray the boy to choose
Your delicate, unfertile hooves.

Virgin,
   Chuck, begin
To fret the sheets, be what, before
You were, you were: goat, goat or whore.
Yet some they say have died, before they died,
White as a Bride.

West
  Is our itch, lust
For loneliness, hunger for beasts; or your dream,
Boy, the meaningless dead: death between
Men a caress, hero and horse sharing one smell:
The innocence of hell.

X Is the text's
Inconsequent silence. We
Stutter and doubt—and suddenly
The child's anguish, the noise of the poem
Are one.

Youth
  Will lose
The child's earnest, be bored, grow hair,
Fear innocence. Beyond this frontier
Estranged, what children come,
Gawk—dumb.

Zion:
  The last sign
Of estrangement. The child inhabits
Our alien margins. His Sabbaths
Harden underground, crouch like coal—
Or the soul.

Christmas 1944.

AND WE'LL ALL FEEL GAY

Leslie A. Fiedler

MILLER had despite it all remembered through the morning, crouched on the rusting top of the truck's cab between the sun and the shouts of his children, his hands torn a little by the sappy branches and a disproportionate naif joy in him, the words. That he had the night before with difficulty and an intermittent sense of the dark's gravity gone to sleep, the words with him, in winter; and had waked to another season, to the accomplished spring, did not matter. He had not been able, it is true, to pick up his yesterday's work between the washed curtains whose wrinkles bellied out and were lost in the bland wind, and he had gone out to where his kids cried back and forth in the hoarse assumed voices of workers. "Jim" they called each other and "Jimmy" and he was "Joe" when he appeared to drag the branches newly sawed from the tree in the backyard around the difficult corner between the garage wall and the angle of the house; to stack them, their obscure buds black still as the bark, in the truck body to dry for the eventual fire.

Irwin worked with him, the neighbor's boy with his incomprehensible moron's stutter, the comparative peace of his unredeemable adolescence; and to his own children he payed the forfeit of attention—a mannered, absent acknowledgment of their soft gray paws thrusting up scraps and twigs; bending from the satisfaction of the larger bough caught at the precise point of balance and arched up and over the already difficult mat of branches. To the movement of muscle under his recent envelope of fat he responded with a child's pleasure, and he added it for good measure and congruously enough to the lyrical and dangerous pretense of sharing a child's game.

130

"Heave her up here, Jim," he would yell to Karl—or "Steady as she goes, Jimmy," to Ellery; and he would watch in their disproportionate eyes the great laughter of habitual and multiform paranoia mock his own careful indulgence. His clumsy regard for children was conditioned by the guilt he always felt before the shameful discrepancy, his own awful advantage, the gimick of adulthood.

"Okay, get a move on, Joe," they hollered back and their eyes were aware of the perils of insolence: dancing, dancing, the adult and parent in the sunlit moment merely Joe: "Come on, Joe," they shouted, "come on!"

That morning Miller, past the mirror that showed between bed and closet the fading soft belly of peace, the articulation of back and hip, already in these few months obscured, had carried his single first gray hair and laid it with precise sentimentality on the blackest object of the clutter on the dresser's top, an ebony brush, the gift of his ugliest uncle. The careful piety of the act was lost a little in memories of the uncle's nose, his narrow-lipped teasing and the last minute gift of a penny by which he assured himself that the solemn moment of torture had all been—a joke.

But Miller had said over then as if the discovery of some appropriate apparatus had made at last possible the completion of a begrudged ritual, the words: "The touchstone of our age is lost. . . ." It had sounded, however, even with the obvious slight monument of decay in his hand and only the two mirrors of closet door and dressing table to postulate an audience, as he had feared, dull in the delicate morning. "The touchstone of our age is lost. . . ."

It had seemed the night before apt and melancholy, with all the fragile sense of a sentence in a dream—of being a clue. Miller had been quite drunk and his friends with him, the stubborn objects of acquaintance with whom each year the nexus of shared experience became slighter, leaving at last only the residuum of a common past (the poor memories of adolescence: a first drunk, the puking together under the quiet shadowy trees in the park, the seedy ruses of revolt, the shabby meeting hall, the book under the desk), an increasingly minor aspect of their being alive—and a concomitant tenderness disproportionate to its causes; what, he supposed, surprised at its undramatic tone and texture, must be thought of as love.

They had all got drunk together after these longest unwilled absences—laughing, as they had reduced the remembered intolerable anguish of being young to its just comic dimensions, outrageously. And they had passed beyond that laughter for the first time; not only past the initial reassurance of common memories evoked with the air, tedious and tender, of a ritual; but even past the second stage, attained rarely enough when their moods improbably jibed and the liquor was good, the conspiracy by which, without losing the bond it slimly guaranteed, they were revenged jointly on their adolescence. They had not lapsed into the hostility that any commitment of opinion about a play or book inadvertently serious, could raise like terror, presenting a paradigm of their divergence and leaving them atomized, each convinced that some deliberate treachery of another had produced the monstrous disaccord none really willed at all.

Their disparate skills and vocabularies, the degrees of failure or adjustment were lost under their boy's names, their election of hilarity. All the dangers of recollection, even the customarily bad-tempered joke to which none was wholly immune, the implied rebuke of any old catchword of contempt that a heedless nostalgia evoked—"He has a small circle of friends and drives around in a Buick"—no longer mattered. Each was fixed as his own most delicate, lost symbol; Larry persisted under the now habitual mustiness, the uncertainty of regard no longer redeemed by the old air of the tentative, sat still in the innocent tableau under a running shower, fully clothed, his hand outstretched in the sensitive gesture of exploration. "Rain," he said with the old grace, "rain." No later commitments counted; the others each wore properly, as in some gentle charade or modest allegory, the unsuspected metaphor that fixed him most tenderly for that community, held for a small blurred while in the symbolic act no one could quite remember, the essential act of revelation perhaps never even quite committed.

It was the war, Miller permitted himself to reflect in what stress of thought was compatible with the deliberate measuring of drinks, and the war's ending which surrounded them like the guarantee of a common history, an undistorting medium; they could see each other through it with an odd, uncompromised clarity, and Miller frozen in his role of the ambiguous volunteer (uncertain still whether his motivation had been an inordinate respect for choice or a kind of quiet treason to his family, a pious flirtation with irresponsibility) looked through it and the bottom of his glass at Sid's drying hysteria of evasion, the leg broken like a transparent plot; at Dave's drying hysteria of allegiance, his

fine ridiculous hate and loyalty dessicating into the alcoholic joke
—drying.

Guilty, guilty, guilty: he cried his difficult secret inside his
head, with a precise and passionate emphasis as if it were a declaration of love. Marred, all the happy passionate faces drowned
in the hesitant light, by the undeclared implications under whatever surface avowal or denial; guilty in the end of being alive to
be sure, but linked too in a more obvious murderous complicity,
a shared and ponderable guilt that fit into his head even drunk,
did not evade him like the plausible, difficult abstractions of the
Fall.

"To hell with that," he escaped saying aloud; "that's for the
sober."

Guilty of not being dead; that was there, too and the concomitant joy of being alive that was so inexplicably easy to miss.
They all knew at once, and they toasted it unconfessed, that they
could afford against this the sentimental pleasure of being for a
while a little maudlin about their age; it was all a gag really, the
surface sorrow offered at a level that never tempted to despair,
to placate the immaculate and alien dead.

"The touchstone of our age is lost. . ." Larry had quoted.
"That's what Harry said to me: 'The touchstone of our age is
lost. . .' " He reached for it with an air of immense effort and
looked across to his wife to see if he had quoted right. Right, she
nodded, right, and the motion continued to certify the discussion
absently: Right, right—.

"My hair, too!" Lou cried and at the cue they laid their
skulls together with comic accord, exposing the ragged or naked
crown, aware of the quiet decay of teeth in them, postulating the
long implications of line and sag.

"He was so fat, too—around the middle," Larry explained,
hunting with them the context.

"Harry was always fat."

"Harry was always fat," he agreed, "but this was different,
a special sogginess around the middle, symbolic—not just fat, a
symbol of age."

"And Metzger," Dave cried more drunk than any with his
never quite dissipated, his cumulative, aftermath of alcohol—his
essential accomplishment; and everyone in their frantic round of
remembering now the obscure periphery of their time together,
calling them up like myths: "And Harnsberger"; "And Barnett";
"And Hannah."

But Dave cried above them all. "And Metzger," he said. "He believes in Relaxation, now. Do you remember his tic?" aping it of course over the dark remembering anguish of his face; "Now—no tic. He relaxes!" And they all roared with him; unaccountably it seemed to Miller now, but they had known then; *he* had known.

"He used to piss in bed," Phil bellowed when the conversation had grown for the first time loud enough for his comfort. His army-thinned body looked like a disguise; only the deaf voice without nuance, a sort of tonal innocence, confessed him. "His sheets were always hanging on the line. Now he relaxes?"

"No tic," Dave went on, assured at their center, "but no face. He asked me if I'd noticed a change and told me no tic; he held his face up; like wood, like water. How do you do it, I said. Relaxation. He relaxes. Relaxes." The simple-minded repetition had taken on all the aspect of some immense unconscionable gag, lashing them to laughter, almost to tears. Words were of small account by then, but with the merest half-phrase, the gesture that had gone with and had come to stand for the phrase, the picture with all its consequence was there: He relaxes: Metzger, not wholly alien to them but always disliked, with their special sensitivities, their tokens of marginality raised always to a power of the ridiculous.

Miller remembered an encounter with him at seventeen; "You have a face like a donkey's ass," he had told him trying to provoke a fight at a bar, and now he inherited for all his laughter the memory of that violence with the swish and thud of the shuffle board that had been behind them; he resented the unwilled persistence of the sound that ruined the integrity of the recollection. "A face like a donkey's ass," he had repeated, the thin soapy taste of anger in his mouth, senseless, fostered against a kid's ennui over his beer. He remembered anger easily as a taste and its failure; in the end Metzger, blinking a scared counterpoint to his grey twitch, had raised his comic face as explanation and excuse and had refused to fight.

"He lies on the floor," Dave had concluded, "relaxes one limb at a time. It's very difficult," he said. "I tried it!" The wry and sudden confession capped the joke; none of them any longer could laugh as hard as he wanted to; and all of them, weak in their chairs, knew that no organized mockery now could achieve the child's total act of exclusion, make the Fool completely and without peril the other. They fondled their laughter, its commitment to self-reproach.

134

Miller had watched over the heads of his guests, his own ambiguous drawing of Jesus, hung on an obscure bend of the wall, trying to temper the delight of his drunkeness in the ridiculous solution, maturity not less absurd than adolescence, salvation as comic as disease "This redeems us for despair," he told himself and started out of his chair, searching the sensitive face of his wife to see if he had said it aloud; such surrenders to rhetoric he was shamelessly prepared to indulge in silence, but shied at exposing himself, his need for the platitude of statement, except furtively, obliquely.

When he stood at the door, moving his head, flushed and slow almost to the point of sleep, under the last recollections, he felt oppressed by the gravity of even so trivial a parting. Larry had been the last to leave, repeating once more, "The touchstone of our age is lost. . ." and he had answered, "The touchstone of our age is lost. . ."

The words had lain over the whole party's-end business of collecting glasses and ash-trays and had ended by marrying the intimacy, that always in however brief a phrase, sometimes in a mere caress, was his special bed-time pleasure, of recapitulating with his wife the day.

"Silly, wasn't it" she had said not untenderly, and yet he had felt himself in his sudden weight of grief, a little her enemy; but falling away to sleep beside her warmth he had told himself that perhaps after all there might be something specious. . .

He had despite it all remembered through the morning, crouched on the rusting top of the truck's cab between the sun and the shouts of his children, his hands a little torn by the sappy branches and a disproportionate naif joy in him, the words. But the sun, simple flowers and his own sweat and motion had in the end defeated him.

The morning's work had been vain; the tree pruned nearly to nakedness, the shadow persisted still on the worthless grey soil of the yard in which his children searched hopefully for worms. The garage defined its shape now neatly in shadow, inhibiting the sun that lay casually on all the neighboring gardens. He laughed at his own dismay until the children joined him in a wild chorus and when they caught their breaths, asked him why, he teased them on with their own word, "Ish kabbible. Ish kabibble," until his wife came inquiring to the window.

He waved his stained hand at the waste of work and called: "Silly night last night," and she smiled at their predicament a

while and said, "Lunch is ready," closing the window and turning to the cool, dark inwardness of the house.

Miller awoke as he had for these three months with difficulty
and ashamed from the shallow indulgence of his after-luncheon
nap. There was no excuse now, out of the heat and the endless
insult of animal smells, for so much sleep; but the habit had
persisted and he rose shy and startled once more to the intimacy
of his own odors; to make the indifferent attempt at remembering his cagey dreams, or to watch the ceiling ruined by damp,
knowing that he no longer permitted himself the promise of a
drink to cut the muzzy aftermath of this daily surrender. That
decision, renewed each day, carried, he was not quite sure why,
a faint assertion of pride, made some amends for the nap.

His weariness was real enough, the unexpected legacy of
weariness, as real as the compulsive hunger that fed his new, uncomfortable fat; not merely the obvious device of evasion it
seemed but, vulnerable to exaggerated responses and eccentric
abdications, a continual latent tremor of tiredness.

The grey hair was gone from the dresser top; "I thought it
was *mine*," his wife said from the kitchen in a rustle of packages
to his shouted question; he no longer believed that he had meant
to save it.

It was almost time to set out after his older boy who had
been going to school afternoons for several weeks. "I'll call for
Karl," he said, hesitating between the red sweater and the green
field jacket, choosing at last, an election of anonymity, the latter.
It seemed important to delay a little the full sense of himself, and
so he continued to wear a shabby assortment of combat clothes
and bright salvaged ties to savor fully the interim, to achieve an
easy aspect of belonging, and to forestall for a while the entire
obligation of redefinition. That was a way, at any rate, of saying
it. He moved from masquerade to masquerade with a tired irony
at the expected focus of conviction, and no disguise could be
cruder than his exigencies.

"Don't rush me," he protested, "those *women* will be there."
He realized then for the first time that he was a little embarrassed
at the prospect of being, under the sombre harried regard of the
assembled mothers, the only male without function at mid-day,
rudely displaying his alien freedom. The old reflex that had sent
him for his own mother's sake, those summers when only idle-
ness had been adequate to his adolescence, through the shameful
pretense of job-hunting, kept him now in his symbolic green

jacket, an explanation, an excuse: "Pardon me, Madame, but you
see I've only just—"I haven't yet had time to—."

He walked slowly up the lucid dirty streets of the city where
he had not lived for so long, where he would never, after a few
months, live again, and he was glad no one knew him, did not in
the long windows of the stores watch himself.

The kids that had moved at noon slowly in space, holding
carefully a few daffodils, a balloon or book, towards school, were
exploding now in time from the school buildings, flushing the
sidewalks with noise—and Miller was all at once in that other
country he had begun to think the mere fantasy of his exile. The
red faces near tears arose like miracles from death and fell again
under the finger's bullets and rose; the cries of revenge and delight, the marbles, the shrill futile monsters, the short noises of
despair seemed the mere outward conventions of his own nostalgia, the landscape of his most familiar dream.

And when his own son in a haze of laughter broke at last
from the door, dragging a yellow-haired little girl with him toward the improbable kindly cop on the corner and left him to
pick up a loose shoe abandoned in the rush, Miller was oddly and
at last at home.

"Hey, Karl," he yelled "let's go"; and he was scarcely annoyed when swinging about together in a shared quick impulse of
joy, he and the boy had crashed into a large, blonde woman, who
had, in the most extraordinary tone of refinement, snorted at
them: "Bastards!" He was used by now to the extravagant violence of the civilian world; fresh from the orderly male anger of
war, he had found it at first intolerable, had been unable to
escape a continual sense of oppression under the monstrous rancor, incongruous with its apparent causes, that could make the
subway guard, the streetcar conductor, the clerk, a woman beside
a child—suddenly the howling enemy; the seed of wrath in every
passer, the underground, uncriminal terror no apparatus could
track. That he had foolishly hoped of the war in this respect a
wholesale catharsis—

"Dad— Daddy. Hey, Dad! *Listen* to me!"

"Yes, Karl," he said.

"Is 'bastard' a bad word, Dad?"

"There are no bad words," he began once more the unsatis-
factory explanation, not even completely convinced of its truth,
but sensing somehow that to be futile in this regard was important, patiently, hopelessly to explain.

"Is it a man's word, Daddy. A grown-up's word?"

"It is."

"Let's make an agreement. Let's not say it, Dad." They didn't but went on, hands clasped, into the slightly blemished afternoon. The children were, after all, still at it: secure in the blithe evasion of games or high on the jungle bars they committed their offenseless acts of pride. A small girl hung by her knees from a high place, her skirt down over her head and they watched her, through the wire grating of the fence, below them in the sunken schoolyard.

"I can see her pants, pants, *pants!* I can see her *pants.* I can see her pants, pants, *pants!* I can see her *pants.*" Karl howled and danced the rhythm with his legs flashing thin in the late sunlight.

"For Christ's sake," Miller cried, "haven't you ever seen pants before. Please tell me, what's so unusual about pants." But the boy continued to dance silently now, only the rhythm and his face persisting in the offense, the face dark and lost with a sour precocity of knowledge. Dee-dee-dee-dee-duh-duh-*duh!* Dee-dee-dee-dee-*duh!*

"Let's get on; it's late—" Miller made a show of consulting his new wrist watch, a futile decoy for the boy's attention; the afternoon wore badly and the kids grew merely shrill; there was, perhaps, only one country.

Karl began to move cautiously along the fence, edging sidewise in the direction his father was walking, but without permitting any space to show between his body and the wire grating; only his head and feet were free. It was a feat and he performed with quiet intensity; at the very end of the fence another boy, belly out, was fixed in the same sort of pose, but motionless, a half-eaten ice-cream cone in his hand, watching the ball players below.

Karl stood beside him for a moment their shoulders barely touching, watching him with a careful and pointless malice, and suddenly in complete silence knocked the cone to the ground and kicked it. For a moment his face wore a little absurdly, like his father's coat, the whole flush of rage and then it all trembled as he saw the answering anger above him, dissolved.

Against this only love, Miller thought in a kind of thin desperation; against this only love, and the word drowned in his hopelessness, his unfaith. He began to pull the boy roughly, jerking his arm upward, his own stride getting longer and faster. In a moment the child would be in tears; later there would be at home the solemn game they played at, the casting out of devils. Karl would lie limp on his bed and he would stroke him gently, calling out all the evil; "I'm sorry, Dad," the child would say at last as if he had invented the fault—but that would be afterward. Meanwhile he moved forward faster, faster, jerking the thin stubborn arm. In another minute the boy would be in tears.

NEW POEMS FROM PERU
(*A Little Anthology*)

translated by Ruth Stephan

AN INTRODUCTION TO MODERN PERUVIAN POETRY

WHEN JOSE Maria Eguren published his book *Simbolicas* in 1911 he became the unwitting parent of modern Peruvian poetry. He was the first to turn aside from the formal styles, the oratorical elegance and the pseudo-Indian prosody in vogue at the turn of the century to the intrinsic estheticism of an image. There was not only the difference between the outer and inner world of the imagination. There was the difference between seeing a man in court dress at a ball with glitter and crowds and music and hearing him whisper in the dark in a rose garden with fountains playing. Eguren dropped the obvious trappings of glamor for a more subtle natural enchantment. Quietly and independently he adopted the precepts of the French Symbolists and wrote a pure poetry. His form was lenient, his meanings delicately complicated, his symbols unornamented. Among his contemporaries he alone had genius comparable to the great European poets.

Although Eguren was seriously inspired by French Symbolism, it was not the single cause for his new direction. Symbolism was the bicycle and he was the rider. The Peruvian literati have kept closely in touch with French and Spanish writing, and every movement of consequence has had its local disciples. Eguren's friends were influenced by the Parnassians, later poets by the Naturalists, the Surrealists or by individuals such as Federico Garcia Lorca and Rafael Alberti. The European ties were bound more closely by the expatriation of César Vallejo who left Peru in 1923, embittered by the injustices of his native provincial town, to live the rest of his life in Madrid and Paris. Vallejo, the real

140

giant of Peruvian poetry, was a passionate humanist, affected first
by his own troubles in Peru and later by the Spanish Civil War,
who combined a singular mysticism with his deep sensitivity to
mortal problems. His vital individuality could not be contained
by any literary movement, least of all by Symbolism. Images
leapt up to propagate his ideas.

Today the poets who use the word "modern" as their particular epithet are a distinct and a comparatively small group. As
if to compensate for their paucity, they maintain a quickened
esthetic life among themselves and their fellow artists, giving
Lima the air of a slightly Indianized little Paris. At a staccato
rate they write poetry, art criticsm, dramas, and essays about
foreign writers and each other. They have only those within
their group as critics for there are no commercial magazine editors or book publishers to live up to or down to. Poets either
publish their own books or have them published by a friend or as
a supplement to a presently existing magazine or do not publish
their poems at all and let them make the rounds of the literary
underground in manuscript. So divorced is esthetics from com-
mercialism that it is unthinkable for a poet to place his book in
a bookstore. His standing, thus, does not depend on a public taste
but on a private taste.

In such a sympathetic atmosphere a poet is apt to mature
early and to become a national classic by the time he is in his
thirties. The three living leading poets, Martin Adán, Xavier
Abril, and Emilio Adolfo Westphalen, are all under forty-five
years old. Martin Adán (a pseudonym for Rafael de la Fuente
Benavides), a phenomenon in his work and in his own character,
is a removed member of the literary circle. He lives in an asylum,
insisting it is the only normal place to live in our time, from
which he occasionally "escapes" to see his friends or visit a tavern.
Although he established his reputation almost twenty years ago
with a novel in verse, *La casa de carton,* which immediately influenced contemporary literature, and although his poetry has
continued to be an excitement to all who read it, he has published
no other book. Some of his poetry has appeared spasmodically
in magazines but more has been irretrievably lost. One of his
most important pieces, a long poem *Aloysius Acker,* Adán destroyed in a fit of temper so all that remains are the fragments
which had been copied by friends. This year, in another reversal,
this esoteric idol who has lodged on the sky side of a cloud, made
a sudden descent into communal affairs. He submitted his poems
for a government competition which he promptly won.

141

Adán is such a master of technique he has a contempt for it.
He calls his sonnets "anti-sonnets" as he modulates their traditional tone to suit his own tenor. His struggle has been to describe adequately the arctic metaphyscial area where he wanders.
His poems are like letters from an unfamiliar pole where word
meanings and notes of music have the same vibration. He speaks
in eternal companionship to great abstractions. He, too, is a great
abstraction. He holds the philosopher's stone in his palm and
fears to look at it.

Xavier Abril is essentially a romantic who has passed through
several poetic phases. In contrast to Adán, he has traveled widely. He mixed with both Surrealist and non-Surrealist groups in
Paris and eventually was influenced by both. He was a close
friend of César Vallejo and was the one to bring back and edit
Vallejo's poems for a South American edition. Oddly, his poems
have little in common with Vallejo's apart from the spirited use
of images and the complete esthetic sincerity of each. Where
Vallejo saw man as a social being in conflict with mystical tides,
Abril drifts in a sensual dream. Vallejo saw love as the great
arm of humanity, "Love against space and time," he said. Abril
is aware of love as the figure of a woman, saying, "A woman or
her shadow of ivy fills this solitude with empty lamps."

Abril at the wellspring of Surrealism in Paris was not as
affected by it as Emilio Adolfo Westphalen, who never left the
borders of Peru, or the short lived Carlos Oquendo de Amat, a
poet of grace and humor, who ended his career as a political exile.
Westphalen became engrossed in watching the parade of images
in his subconscious. He stood at the crossroads of reality and the
imagination, fascinated with the ambivalence of life to death.
There is a slow moving rhythmical unity to his poems as if he
were swinging along on a never-ending walk. The tokens he
gives are frequently brilliant in their simplicity. Death is abolished, he says, for "I have forsaken my body like a glove to leave
the hand free." Westphalen's seriousness was like a foil to Oquendo de Amat who told his friends to "Take me like open violets
in bloom," no more. There was a careless charm in Oquendo de
Amat's attitude that permeated all his writing. He cared little
what happened to his poems, publishing only a few of them in a
book he called 5 *metros de poemas* which pulled out accordion-
fashion to measure just the five meters.

Among the younger poets there is one who is outstanding,
Jorge Eduardo Eielson. Without any apparent apprenticeship he
appeared in 1944 with a long romantic poem, *Cancion y muerte*

de Rolando, which indicated the sweep of his talent. The imaginative co-ordination of his succeeding poems is faintly reminiscent of Jean Cocteau. His vision is a park where he is a surveyor, a king or a weeping man sensible of seasonal movements and music, counting the fantasies of definite objects, seeming, without turning his head, to look at the same time over the stars, under the ground and at the hills of the surface horizon.

Javier Sologuren, the most disciplined of the new poets, was influenced primarily by Martin Adán, then by Westphalen. He is still uses their forms and rhythms as a trellis for his private images. Sebastián Salazar Bondy has experimented in verse, drama and criticism but his puckish humor is most at home in his surrealistic prose poems.

In a complete anthology many other poets should be included. Ricardo and Enrique Peña, César Moro who is now in Mexico, Rafael Mendez Dorich, José Alfredo Hernandez, Luis Fabio Xammar, Manuel Moreno Jimeno, Carlos Rios, Juan Rios Rey and Vincent Azar are all interesting poets. More should be included, too, of the *indigenista* poetry which has been inspired by the Indian life in the Sierras. This poetry of the land, as it is sometimes called, was initiated in 1926 by an educated Indian poet of Arequipa, Alejandro Peralta, who put the expressions and soundings of the people into a bold free verse. This strong new trend has become popular as being particularly representative of Peru. José Varallanos with his *chola* songs, Emilio Vasquez, Luis Niete, Luis de Rodrigo and Mario Florian are its finest exponents. Florian, a prolific young poet with an unusual melodious and sentient quality, has followed closely the beautiful Quechua songs sung in the Andes.

To translate the words or attempt to convey the spirit of these poets is not sufficient for their intelligibility, for their poems are like cosmic puzzles where the last jig-saw piece is an intuition of the country itself. It is inevitable that common symbols arise in a country like Peru surrounded by vast margins of desert, sea and mountainous jungle. Foreign ideas, like travelers, fly in and out. They may clarify and enrich but they do not change the basic symbols. To Peruvians, staring year after year at the pale sand stretching over the horizon, sand and eternity gradually merge in the mind. As distinctive from the distances of time, a metaphysical permanence is the flower at hand, a rose. Snow, found only on inland peaks where it is difficult to reach, has an exotic meaning. And among the Andean Indians the dove is the person loved or the song of love.

Even the poet who would escape these and other common symbols cannot do so for they are flags waving continually before his eyes. If he rejects them or turns purposefully to inner abstractions, they reappear in unsuspected speculums. The stream of consciousness has not been dammed nor diverted from its ancient course by industrialism. There is no super-realization of science advancing and mechanical change. Peru, in spite of its new oil cities, still is a hand-made country. The transitions of love, the apparitions of death, the peregrinations of the spirit are the great themes of the poets.

Ruth Stephan

fragment from ALOYSIUS ACKER

Martin Adan

Death! . . .
Inasmuch as I look upon, I see nothing
Except your ice nose.

What a perfect state!
As if God really would have created! . . .
The not born, death! . . .

Flowers, tears, candles,
Thoughts,
All useless, all useless;
Like the wish. . .

In my fiery shadow within,
Royal as God, in a manner infinite
And sensible, you lie down, dead:
I lie down, dead.

And for you the dog does not cry;
And for you the mother does not howl;
And for you the gravedigger keeps silent and does not wipe off
    sweat.
And no one is deafer,
And no one is blinder,
And no one is more no one, more I myself without any you,
You, the found, the refound,
The lost, I or you, if not the time,
And ever, and ever, and never
The you that I am and that is destiny,
The older brother, the little brother. . .

And I must be the life,
the Death.
How shall I be life,
You death! . . .

145

He who buys the house,
She who sells her body,
He, she, is the other,
No one but me, the one remaining
Or the gone on the round mat of the blind. . .

But I will dig—for what? . . . the grave in the deepest
Of me, in the most tender,
In the blindest,
Where my breath may not go,
Where my voice may not echo,
Where I alone
May go down, dead.

God will follow the winning of me, from afar,
With artifice and human
Frown, like he is; and the event
Will follow with pain; and in mystery;
And the son will be born:
And the grandson will be born;
And the fly will buzz in the summer;
And the rain will drench in the winter.
I will be startled on my couch.
I will correct and publish my verse.
I will wash my body.
I will go Sundays to the sea beach,
To watch the wave and the blowing.
I will write on State paper
Lustrums: "It is evident by the present document. . ."
The rose will open. They will kill the Christ.
More in the house of the dead,
Ay! in the house of the dead,
There where the dead live,
There where no one is and I am the dead
And the one alive is and the one alone and the one sad and the
    one eternal,
There only they meet
The penumbra and the event
Of God and his day,
Without night and without object.

fr.m SONNETS TO THE ROSE

Thou art not the theory, thy thorn
thrust very deep; nor art thou the teaching
of the rose the rose, since thy spear
opened a road to the moving rose.

Thou art the rose itself, sibylline
master who impedes the prospect
of the perfect rose that does not reach
to learn from the deluding rose.

Rose of rose, identic and sensitive;
to thy example, profound and changeable,
the poet makes the terrible rose.

Indeed thou art the rose eternal whose bough
steals the one who, foreseen, prisoner,
nibbles the rose of the love he loves. . .

ELEGY TO A ROSE *from* The Written Rose

Xavier Abril

Look thee at the pure rose,
Look thee at its death ghost.
How it once was without form,
without a hue, the opened rose!

Look thee, now no whiteness,
Look thee, now it is not real.
How the rose turns in the future
that once was motionless!

Love the rose secure
in the illusion held
or lost within the mind.

Hate the flower that endures
in the temple evanesced
of a rose perhaps repined.

from *ABOLITION OF DEATH*

Emilio Adolfo Westphalen

I have abandoned my head to rest sadly
In this shadow that falls from the noise of your footsteps
It turns to the other margin
Grandiose as the night to deny you
I have abandoned my dawns and the trees rooted in my throat
I have abandoned the star that ran between my bones
I have forsaken my body
Like the shipwreck forsakes the boats
Or like memory at the lessening tide
Some eyes strange on the beaches
I have forsaken my body
Like a glove to leave the hand free
If the merry pulp of a star must contract
You do not hear me lighter than leaves
Because I have freed myself of all the boughs
And the air does not chain me
Nor can the waters against my fate
You do not hear me coming stronger than night
And doors that do not resist my blow
And cities that keep silent so you may not warn them
And the forest that is opened like a morning
Wishing to press the world within its arms
Beautiful bird that must fall in paradise
Now curtains have fallen on your flight
Now my arms have closed the walls
And the branches bent to hinder your passage
Fragile deer dreads the earth
Dreads the noise of your steps on my chest
Now the fences are connected
Now your forehead must fall beneath the step of my eagerness
Now your eyes must be closed over mine
And your sweetness put forth shoots like new horns
And your kindness be outstretched like the ghost encircling me
I have let my head revolve
I have let my heart fall
Now nothing remains so that I am more sure of overtaking you
Because you induce haste and you tremble like the night

Perhaps I do not have to overtake the other margin
Now that I do not have hands that are caught
By the one resolved for the loss
Nor feet that weigh over so much forgetfulness
Of dead bones and dead flowers
Perhaps I do not have to overtake the other margin
If now we have read the last leaf
And I have begun music to plait the light in which you must fall
And rivers close the road to you
And flowers call you in my voice
Great rose now is the hour to detain you
Summer sounds like a thaw in hearts
And dawns tremble like trees on awakening
The exits are guarded
Great rose, must you not fall?

SIX POEMS

Jorge Eduardo Eielson

ODE TO WINTER

Winter is all fruits and lanterns
forgotten, and sacred skeletons of doves
in the wood. Winter kisses, enamored,
the glorious lips of the grape with his lips
of hail, and falls asleep over her.
Winter can come, one day, gently,
through the valley and, as a match in the hand,
carry a life to his city, like a thief.
Winter enjewels a man with sadness,
winter washes tombs of monarchs
and beggars, and crowns the gilt and aged autumn
with a ray of ashes on the head. Respect
winter, the antiquity of his soles,
his sceptre of dew on the brush; respect
the eternal features of the trees and the wind
of his dominion, when everything around him ceases and he
leans, wormeaten and sonorous, like a piano
in a pond or a death in a tomb.

THE TOMB OF RAVEL

Phantom, you who are in the harp and the ivy,
in bas-reliefs of music or tower, sleeping,
you have made your tomb in a piano, phantom.
Among golden chords, the sonorous faun
Blows your earth eyes to the moon,
and on stairsteps which go down abysmally burdened
to the bottom of the piano, by august moth
encircled, your cymbal head is heard.
No one knows who the horse is that daily
sobs on your obscure gravestone or half opens
the marble fingers of the niche in the shade.
My phantom, on your back has fallen
the funeral fly with wings of glass;

151

subterraneous pastor of the sun, now whistling,
or seated in veins of ivy, bronze and wood,
you have made your tomb in a piano, phantom.

TO A DEER WOUNDED ANOTHER TIME

Misfortune belongs to the nimble deer, the sky
confined to its glorious antlers,
that air that in fruition, far from the ground,
is like fruits the flight has devoured.

Impetuous descent with blue caution
in such affable winter, bland wound,
crowned with blood and grass and dust,
the buzzing is his palpitating neck.

Who may know the honey of your eyelids,
deer, over your troubled eyes, thus wounded
in the middle of the wood, how it may be

another obscure deer, dispossessed of himself?
Oh snowy tendril, oh life, oh beauty,
now all a deer that dies of whiteness!

PIANO OF ANOTHER WORLD
(*In memory of my dead brother*)

You open, youth, crypts of summer, solitary,
pantheon wings posed here; vulture eye,
Norman eye that looks at me, sadly,
wind that is loving me, eye, eye, eye,
forest eye, what do you search for in my eyes
—I should say to you—solitary youth, permanent and pure?
(Steady lantern the wall dividing and serpents
from the sky enclosed there, and teeth grindings
of misty flora opening your helmet or sinking
your skull into me, by sad, hard blows).
Is not this pure, sinister fern, golden ogre?
Is not this clear, black marsh, serene sky?
There is no one alive nor do I breathe—I should say to you—
only my hands, they search a face, a happiness.

INTERRED BOOKSTORE

What books are these, Lord, in our abyss, whose starred leaves
Pass through the sky and illuminate us?

152

Green, immemorial, they are opened in the humus, perhaps
They are drawing a prayer to our lips
Or are hushed lonely in their shadows, like unknowns,
Nature who prays even in them, at their iron signs
Kneels, with flowers on her belly,
For the human who on passing did not see them in the dust,
Did not see them in the sky, in the dampness of her grottos.
And they came down like an enormous block of the gods.
Since then only a green veil stays on them
from armours of bejeweled arms and chargers that returned
To their skeleton nobility between its leaves.
And dejected elm trees, pear cacti of the war, glory and rose,
Sleep too in them, covered with winter rust
And only to its old letters, very quietly,
Comes the subtle remata or the lily of the urine,
And a blue hand that turns its sodium pages
Among the rocks and fans its fish scales to the Death.
Wilt Thou allow me, Lord, to die among these books, from whose
    chest,
covered with fragance, flows out the black oil of wisdom?

PARK FOR A SLEEPING MAN

Brain of the night, golden eye,
jingle-bell, which trembles in the pine, listen:
I am he who weeps and writes in the winter,

Doves and snowsteps sink in my memory
and, before my head of thinking blood,
stone dwellings open their feathers, quivering.
Although fallen, among drowsy ice begonias,
I move the hatchet of the rain and bland fruits
and wakeful leaves are iced at my stroke;
I love my skull thus like a balcony
bent over a black precipice of the Lord.

I work stars at my side, oh ice!
and on the table of the lands, the poem
wheels among the deaths and, enflamed, crowns them,
then my shadow goes through all such glory
of bone, wax and humus that I kneel, majestical,
over the beautiful turf, on the burned gods.
I love, thus, this skull of mine, in its ashes, like the world
in whose cold parks eternity is the same
marble man who watches in a statue
or who stretches out, obscure and without love, upon the grass.

153

THE INHABITANT

Javier Sologuren

Resplendent umbel the dream spreads
between pearls which the mud stops:
on slight raising of the face is diffused
the duskiness of fishes' silk.

From the source that silences the steady
weight of the tide: fall, fall,
slowly fall, little cells, deserted
ruddy beings among tenuous green.

See perfect sands the reflections
of ivy in the silence; sediments
of transparent bones in the stone.

See the entire fern on the walls
of bats outstretched, and see
how in that fish time is leveled.

TO DIE

To die like a flower on the breast of two instantaneous waves
    before the indecisive splendor of an unexpected and near
        good fortune.
To die like a bird that falls among clouds of rose-colored hoops,
    among stalks of verbratile eyelashes and goblets of impal-
        pable light.
To die in a mercury castle at the radiance of an affectionate
    glance.
To die seeing the sun through gaseous hillsides.
To die like a rose cut by the night fire.
To die beneath a rain of silken fish-scales.
To die on the fragrant waves of some sensitive temples.
To die on this citadel sculptured on a deserted morning.
To die carried by the sea that breathes against the walls of my
    house.
To die on a sudden bubble of love on the point of being not more
    than vacuous.

154

To die like a small snail that the sea leaves oozing on the white
sands level as a blushing ear covered with summer rays.

To die to find the underground sculpture of an old human dream.

To die where the birds take unknown courses between waves and
the night, between a sumptuous rainbow and the dazzling
maze of a faun in ambush.

To die on the range of your nude body like a shred of inflexible
mother-of-pearl, of lacteous clusters and of sharp passion-
ately gay flowers.

To die alone on the ground at the lukewarm lash of air fallen
with pleasing weight and at the dread contact of a smooth
and recently filled skin.

To die in a fastidious duet of narrow gold flutes at half-water of
your eyes beneath the incandescent earth,

To die fastened to a strong throat on the noiseless froth of the
foliage.

To die joined to a head of hair that sweeps the bottom of mines
of precious flames that must be brilliant gas in the hidden
nocturne of my love.

To die at the level of a delicate smile.

To die in a lake of cold silk where the fiery stones of midday
seethe, in your eyes of little solitary fruits where the afternoon is a leaf of untrampled honey.

To die on a body embellished by the most remote snow.

To die feeling that on earth blood, disorder and the dream still
are beautiful.

THE KANGAROO SAVES WORDS

Sebastian Salazar Bondy

For the villain of tomorrow I write my koran of filth, my biscuit of orthopedic arms I prepare slowly. I know that the metropolis will die in gelatin, in a deluge of dwarfs, with all the sister cousins biting each other and full of muscial injuries, of words without owners, dry trees and burnt suspensories. Let them now read my book who may have closed forever the revolving doors, those who await the cruel Sunday without giraffes.

I do not write for anyone especially but listen to what a water-carrier directs here and there, with his imperishable angelical, tired of sitting on the stones the river disarranges. And I speak to him of clay and other rutted songs. I speak of geography, of eight watchmen and eight ruins. I speak to him of my country of cubes and tin, of conger eels and black soldiers. I speak to him about everything. Do you understand me, etymological sailors, fish of the red-stocking water? Ah, you understand me, obstetricians, Mexicans!

Few words, my friends. To tell lies, few words. The latest is privy, is rag, ghost, plough, vomiting necktie. He leaves me alone, half relative of sweet bran, high and sonorous as metal. The pus, the celestial pus of the priests, the brown pus of the lover, the ancient pus of the occult goddess.

THE HARD WAY UP

Mario Florian

The hard way up on the road.
To climb it
the strength of the legs
breaks;
froth of weariness
in the throat.

It must be afflicted blood
the dull sweat that drops from us.
By this heroic way
by this pure hard way up
how many times—whip, destiny!—
my father must have walked, must have walked
my grandfather, the father of my grandfather
—all the river of my race—
hurting themselves, falling down, complaining. .
The trees along the edge heard them,
the trees along the edge tell everyone.

—Hit strong, fell, burn,
my axe,
destroy bark;
eat trees,
triumph. . .
So, tomorrow,
there will be no tongue
that speaks to my sons, to what men,
if I have slumped, if I have cried,
if I have abolished God,
on this hard way up.

Bent with burdens, with poor home-made sandals,
how many eternally,
will pass by here!

from INDIAN DOVE

Grieve, spring, that saw so much of her
drinking at your edge and combing her wings.
My little dove has died!
She has died!

Grieve, burning stones of the earth
that, hard, bit her pink feet.
My little dove has died!
She has died!

And you flowers of the evergreens
that left the forests for her love.
My little dove has died!
She has died!

And you full tassels of wheat
that never gave her the sweet rusk of grains.
My little dove has died!
She has died!

And you files of little doves that
encircled her like a thrashing plot.
My little dove has died!
She has died!

And, finally, you wild cooings
that made love to her from winter to summer.
My little dove has died!
She has died!

TWO STORIES

John H. Porter

ROBINSON

HE WORE a well-tailored civilian suit, but the monocle and the ramrod back were a dead give-away. Robinson watched him out of the corner of an eye. He didn't look at Robinson. When the waiter came lurching down the aisle of the club-car, he said: "Waiter! Brandy!" Then he went back to reading his paper with strict attention and a faint disdain.

Robinson looked out of the window at the fleeing landscape. He tried desperately not to think, to remember, to go over his plans. It had all been arranged. There was nothing to do. Telephone poles and trees flashed by the window, houses appeared in a smudge and were gone, the distant mountains loped like blue leopards at the end of the plain.

The man in the grey suit turned a page of his paper.

. . . the red earth, thought Robinson, with cotton, with trees and with rocks. The farmer's house. The farmer's wife with thick brown hair and nipples the size of my thumb. They scratch the back of the earth; the earth in gratitude gives forth. When they die, the priest's robes flap in the wind and the priest says *Oremus Domine.* In the early light, they come out to see the express train whistling along the rails.

Robinson looked around in the club-car; a girl with red hair smiled at him warmly and the scent of her perfume came to his nostrils. But the tall man in grey was talking at last.

The reports, he said to the woman who sat beside him. The reports? Are they in order? The woman was small, and looked lovely and kind. She handed a sheaf of papers to the man in grey. Ah, he said, ah yes, the reports. All in good order: Peterson, Smith, Robert St. Clair. He thumbed through them carefully.

159

Robinson's eyes closed tight and the darkness washed in. The skin on his face began to shrink like the skin on a mummy. He thought of various poses, cacti, statues, an aluminum chair. Peterson had been shot nine days before; no one knew where. Smith, hanged in the prison. St. Clair, clubbed in an alley. A spike, thought Robinson, a spike between the rails—that's what I should have been. Still, the voices continued.

This Robinson, said the man in grey. Very interesting. It is all here, in the files.

Robinson? asked the woman. She was a little astonished, a little shocked. I hadn't known about Robinson. Why Robinson? Why Robinson? echoed the man with a shrug in his voice. Why anything?

Robinson, said the woman. He may be difficult. Perhaps we should wait. No, purred the man in grey. No. We are—shall I say ready?—for Robinson.

Doubt—in the woman's voice. He has friends, she suggested. The man laughed for a long moment, enjoying the laughter. Delicately he said: he has not quite as many friends as he had.

But he has been so resourceful, the woman said. And he knows the passes. Ah, the passes, said the man with a note of respect. The mountain passes. Yes. I wonder which pass he will try—if he gets to the passes. It will be quite amusing to see. The passes. I may profit by the occasion to fish for some mountain trout.

Tentatively, the woman said: Of course we are always right. We have never been wrong. Ice tinkled in her glass as she lifted her glass from the table. I should not like to be wrong.

The man laughed indulgently. Really, Alma, he said, you're delicious. So sympathetic! It's a pleasure to work with you. You needn't be sorry for this boy, this Robinson. It's all in the files.

There was a rustle of paper. They are reading together, thought Robinson.

Yes, said the woman, yes, yes, I see. But it is not just the same as the others. You see, here he was only five. Five, five, said the man, what does five matter? There are always excuses. So here he was twelve? The woman murmured. But in Buenos Aires: twenty, the man continued. Twenty, in Buenos Aires! No longer a child! But why should we bother? We had the same story with Peterson.

Robinson opened his eyes.

The man was leaning back in his chair, relaxed and comfortable, caressing the woman with a smile. We have often had this story. It is part of your charm. And we have never been wrong. He touched her hand lightly. The woman looked up at him, melted and pleading. You're not angry? she asked. Not in the least, not in the least. How could I be angry with something so special?

But nothing is changed, thought Robinson. The trees flash by, the moutains lope like leopards. And in the early morning the peasants watch the train. He looked around the car. He thought that the look in his eyes was as brittle as the muddler in a whisky glass, but the concept didn't amuse him. The girl with the red hair smiled at him, fragrantly. He went over and sat by her.

You *have* been a long time, she said, rubbing her back in the chair like a kitten. You're getting off near the mountain? Near the mountain, said Robinson. It was part of the plan. The girl smiled, lifting her short upper lip and revealing her even white teeth and pink tongue. But how wonderful!—she said delightedly. She stretched and put her arms back of her neck. We can have the last night together.

The last, Robinson started to say, not the last, but his voice rattled and was still, like a twig in dry grass. With the woman on his arm, the man in the grey suit was strolling up the aisle.

He was very tall and elegant and cool. The light from the afternoon sun broke on his monocle in a thousand splinters. He walked up the aisle as steadily, as casually as if he were crossing a lawn at a party, drawing a cigarette from a cigarette case. As he came up to Robinson, he glanced at a waiter. Brandy?—he asked of no one in particular. Brandy soda? Then, preparing to sit down, he smiled at Robinson. His smile was courteous and he tapped his cigarette on his thumb-nail and bowed faintly from the waist.

Ah, Robinson, he said, Mister Robinson. His smile was broad and his eyes, amused. We've just been discussing you, he said.

THE INDIANAPOLIS STORY

ONCE I was in jail in Indianapolis, on account of a watch I really hadn't stolen at all, and one of my fellow-inmates said: "Christ, what a town! It's the asshole of the nation!"

That was the first time I'd heard the expression and it had, then, a fruitiness it's lost a bit since. But except for a certain lack of anatomical exactness, it's a splendid description of that city. I couldn't do better myself. Oh, I should feel differently, I know, after all these years; I should be able to accept Indianapolis as a *fait-accompli*. But if it's necessary that Indianapolis should exist, perhaps it's equally necessary that I should exist to despise it.

For Indianapolis had a truly overwhelming power to ignore me. In that, it surpassed all the other cities of the world. Chicago? I laugh at Chicago! Indianapolis could have given it spades. In Chicago, I would have been able to hole in with some little coterie and there, among the beaded cushions, the tea in glasses, the reproductions of Matisse, I would have found the bearable wretchedness I later found in Greenwich Village. I could have made my misery articulate. But not in Indianapolis. No one would listen. "Shad-ahp!" said Indianapolis.

Up to this point, I have been deceiving you, somewhat. You think this a story about Indianapolis, but it's really an essay on fiction. The question is, how does one write about old experiences in the light of a new attitude toward life, a new clutch on things? It's a problem to be solved.

And so I have told this story a dozen ways, like a schoolboy caught in a lie. I have made phrases to delight you, *mon hypocrite lecteur, mon semblable, mon frère.* (I have been highly cultured in my time.)

"There was once," I wrote, "a young man who hated Indianapolis because it was hot and flat and far from the sea, because each spike of grass and clump of bush seemed shrivelled by the smell of gasoline; because the young man saw so many people with dull, baked faces walk into the marble monuments through the shimmering air."

But these *made* phrases, well. . . . They are tacked together, like some montage of tin and felt, and carried about to elicit admiration from people with a taste for oddity. They do not grow! And you have heard about the writer being a catalyst.

But perhaps the trouble is that I am not a writer after all; perhaps I have become blunted from too much hackwork; and yet, are writers happy?

To leave the marble monuments alone, Indianapolis is the asshole of the nation. And so I'll tell you what I did in Indianapolis in the effort to escape it altogether.

Of course, you realize one must escape from Indianapolis. There's no doubt about that. The town did stink of gasoline when I was there and things looked shrivelled. The air went quivering. And I swear to God, the faces of the people had a dull, baked look, a look of frustration, boredom and perhaps brutality. It was the sort of clenched expression I have seen on the faces of alcoholic veterans of the First World War. And then, there were some vast public buildings I especially loathed. Such enormous nothings! There were tiny people crawling up the stairs. But this is not an accurate description and has nothing to do with my reasons for hating Indianapolis, which I hated because I was desperately alone, like a man on a raft far out at sea.

You know what they promised me before I went to Indianapolis? A job on a paper! And that meant: reporting. He who did not accept such a definition deceived me and was the son of whores. And reporting, well, it's hard to remember just what I saw in that. Wearing my hat on the side of my head, for one thing; letting a cigarette droop from a corner of my mouth; knowing it all; and hanging around with all sorts of sporty girls. That, and the idea of being on the fringes of literature. Perhaps I am making this up, but perhaps I am the only man in the world whose very ambition it was to become a frustrated novelist. Then the pleasure of scribbling, itself! "A red wheelbarrow stands in the rain." "Hope for settlement of the week-old truck strike increased last night. . . ." You see, you bang out the words, things happen on the sheets of paper, and there's a life—of sorts.

Jackson, of the Indianapolis *Globe!*

When I got to Indianapolis, I went to the *Globe* and found out that I was to work in the morgue. That's where the newspaper kept its pictures and mats for me to file and to pass around. I was bored as the devil, and hot as grease because we worked under a flat tin roof. Now and then I went out into the press-room and into the glaring, blue-lit inferno of the engraving room, where it was cooler, and agreeably weird, and then I hurried right back, for, in the presence of other people, I tended to blush and to fall all over my feet.

The hell of it was, I was such a superior young man; I'd read Mallarmé; I'd travelled; I counted on starting some novels which, no doubt, I wouldn't finish. And there I was, trotting about with mats and pictures instead of being a reporter. I envied the reporters, of course, but mostly because of the happy love affairs I was sure they had. In the office, however, they seemed to be dolts, though I found myself in the contradictory position of wanting the dolts to admire me.

The greatest ninny of all was a fellow-alumnus from a prep-school in Switzerland. This fellow, the financial reporter, was a bit older than I and he had all the easiness of manner I loathed so much in the seniors at school. Good God, if I had to feel such a worm, why did the others make it worse with their strutting around? To be sure, the financial reporter didn't strut in the office; he just sat behind his typewriter and smirked urbanely, but that was presumption enough. I tried to talk with him; nothing came of it. The fact is, I'd been reading John Maynard Keynes and his seemed a fine book to discuss with a finanical reporter, to make him sit up and take notice. But all he said was:

"I haven't read it!"

And though he appeared willing, in a faint-hearted way, to introduce me to some of the better families in town and to take me out drinking with "the boys," we had had our say.

So, mostly, I stayed in my lair. I chaffed a good bit, about dates and parties, with a buck-toothed young woman who worked alongside of me; and sometimes I even thought of accepting her invitation to come home to dinner. I pictured a sort of Booth Tarkington routine, if you know what I'm talking about—lawns, and waltzes, and young girls in muslin, and a creaking swing on a porch. But, I felt, something was expected of me that I didn't choose to give. And then those teeth!

My other companion was an old artist who had the adjoining cubicle and with whom I attempted a few conversations. Only, my interest was in Art, and his, in pictures—and never the twain could meet.

Eh, ah! I was a mouse in an empty milk-can, thrashing about! And so the days went by in a scratchy silence, in the heat and fear, and I waited for the night.

Often, after work, I'd go to the public library and get a book and read it while I had my dinner in a dog wagon. I'd read anything. I guess I felt that if I knew all there was to know I'd be fine and dandy. I'd see in effect how the oak came from the acorn and dissolved into dust, and how the generations rose and fell, what all connections were, and how all things were really something else. I even read *The Philosophy of Law.* But it was solitary sledding. I had that trouble in concentrating which the popular magazines deplore.

No matter how much I prolonged my dinner, there always came the hour of going home, the dreaded hour. For I was so *one*, do you see? I had the most romantic notions about the night and I phrased them in the most romantic way, with "The leafy dark," "The yellow light on the turning leaves," so that phrases and experience alike could only raise the curtain on an empty stage.

And for all that I expected so much to come out of this dark, and despaired so greatly of finding it, I had to go back to my rooming house after the fruit and the cheese.

Horrible as this rooming house was, it couldn't hold a patch to the one I'd been in before. The first one was full of a lot of young garter-snappers just out of college who drank a great deal of "brew" and called the landlady "Ma." My own roommate was musically-inclined but he had the brain of a metronome. And then the college boys used to lock themselves in their suite once a week with the most bestial intentions. I was curious, of course. But it was really too much. (Such a way of expressing hostility!) So I had to depart.

I departed not knowing why, though I know it now, and there's the problem of fiction I have mentioned before. I departed full of joy and hope because I was moving to a rooming house near the University where lived three girls who were studying art.

Art!

"It seems to me one should paint the soul of things!"

"Yes, Jackson," she says, looking softly into my eyes and in spite of herself sliding a hand into my trousers, "that's what we ought to paint!" And I'm in.

Belle, maternelle, gaie, a real Roxanne. What tender, lubricious, wonderfully responsive little artists lived in the Indianapolis of my dreams.

The second roominghouse, in which I expected to find these nymphs was an imitation Swiss châlet, bulging with paranoia, dizzy with its load of gables, cupolas, dormer windows, bulls' eyes, turrets—and everything else a hypo-manic designer could load on before his pen ran dry. A porch went teetering along its front, crowded with chairs that sagged from the weight of long-gone, fat-assed landladies. Inside, the parlor, a dark cave, was jammed with furniture and more dead birds under glass than you'd think it possible for a few old women to collect in a single place.

I made my arrangements with the landlady, a red-faced, eccentric old bitch who told one and all that her husband had been done in by the city administration, which was why she had to take in boarders; I settled the questions of soap, sheets, rent, no loud noises, et cetera; I moved into a room on the second floor. Soon after, I was introduced to the girls, which is to say we asked each other how we did, and went our ways. (It may have been that they had engagements.) I hoped we'd really get to know each other later on, but the thing that amazed me for years and years was that we didn't!

Not that I didn't make what I thought were attempts. I knocked on one of their doors, turned red as a fez, choked, said: "Uhm!" and stared, as if to announce that here I was and why didn't they do something about it. The girl dropped her hair-brush, giggled and called to her room-mate. There was enough giggling right then and there to last me the rest of my stay in Indianapolis, and out I slinked, completely crushed. Such idiots! Artists, eh! They were little fatheads getting ready to teach the scale in rural schools.

Nevertheless, I tried again a few days later, this time by way of getting to know the two young men who lived in the house. This, too, must be counted among my less successful social engagements. We chatted a bit about jobs, prospects, good places to eat, like a trio of drunk printers mixing up pages from a "Come to Indianapolis" pamphlet. I thought the young men rather vicious, simply because they were practical. And gone was the notion that somehow they might, well, pimp for me in a nice way, take me out with the girls, get me going on Art, Rimbaud, Valéry. . . .

"Je ne puis plus aimer seulement qu'en dormant. . . ."

And so I was left to face alone these girls who wouldn't even let me stick a foot in the door. I used to hear them running up and down the stairs, chattering, cheeping, twittering in their nasal, flat, but soft girl-voices. I seem to remember a flutter of white dresses whisking through the hall, pink young faces and thick dark hair, and a perfume that was sweet and young and of women. But no *rapport!* So I moved to the attic.

166

One of my notions was that to live in an attic in Indianapolis would somehow be like living in an attic in Paris; and in an attic it is so much easier, without thinking or writing, to fancy oneself a student and artist. And then I was removed from the sound of the girls and the scent and the doors always opening.

I used to go up to that attic in the early evening and shut the door and for a moment look out of the tiny window. Almost anything at all, the faint light on the leaves, the cough of a starting motor, made me lonely and sorry for myself because I couldn't say: "See!" or "Listen!" And then I read or wrote in my journal until it was time to go to bed, a time I approached with fear and longing and put off for hours by every invention known to man.

Of course, I considered alternatives, such as the whorehouse section of the town, of which I'd heard but had never visited. I was too afraid. Afraid of the night, of thugs, of dirty streets. Afraid of my lack of luck, so that I couldn't expect a tender young tart but a shark-hided old hag and a dose to boot. And how far could I go on my fifteen dollars a week? Nevertheless, I used to look out of my window at the dark streets and wonder what sort of joyous thumping was going on where I couldn't see it and how the whores were making out on their backs, and then I'd read a few poems and hit the hay coked to the gills on pure ideas. But not for long.

Man and boy, I'd probably taken enough solo flights with my look-lively, my hey-you-rascal, my one-eyed-winker to satisfy King Solomon's harem. I used to pretend the bed was a woman, and after being seduced long enough, I'd let her have it. I had them all, art students, models, strip-teasers, whores, the jail-bait I'd seen on the streets, actresses, "Girl with a Parrot," The Duchess of Alba. (Thank you, ladies!) And then I felt weak, despised and cast out. "This is the last," I would say to myself. I had to stop! My God, I thought, if I could only stop I'd be powerful, aggressive, scholarly—the darling of women. Somehow, I figured, the pressure would be reduced if I felt more effective with people. But how be effective in Indianapolis? I wound up with the idea that I'd be more effective among people if I didn't need them so much and that's why I took such a shine to John Cowper Powys' *The Philosophy of Solitude.*

Essentially, the idea is: there is a common bond between all animate and inanimate objects, since they're all made of atoms. Furthermore, there is a "universe," far beyond Indianapolis, out of which we have come, into which we can return. The trick is, to establish such a feeling of closeness with this inanimate world that it can stand in the place of all other connections. If you think that's a whacky idea, let me tell you it's a pisser to put into practice. I agreed that a madman staring at a dry leaf on the window ledge of his cell had the means to be at one with the world, and that I myself needed to look at, fondle, and identify myself with inanimate objects, to get the hang of the thing. I, too, used to stare at leaves and trees and bits of rock in the effort to get in touch with something warm and gentle and understanding, outside myself, but I couldn't make it work.

Night after night, I came home, read, scribbled, peered at a twig; and I went to bed feeling as split off from rock and root as I did from the girls in the roominghouse, the girls I gave up so that, in the long run, they'd have me. That total independence I could never quite reach; the stones in Indianapolis had hearts like women. If I had really studied metaphysics, I'd have perished of brain-fag because I was in a philosophical rat-race anyway, thank you.

All the same, I decided that the idea was all right; the trouble was I couldn't put it into practice in the roominghouse that was so loud with distractions. When I read an advertisement for an apartment to rent at a price I could pay, you couldn't have excited me more had you announced the second coming of Christ.

The apartment was described as having a bedroom, living room, bathroom, all furnished, with a piano, for $20 a month! Already, in my imagination, I played the piano in the twilight. (I had taken to the piano the way a nightingale takes to song.) I strolled about in my bathrobe and slippers, book in hand; the cosmos and I were like two bugs in a rug. The picture was tinged with sadness, too; I was quite alone. So, lovely young women would hear about me and come to call, those poetic young women who fall on their backs if you give them the time of day. All I needed was the apartment, for the Lord would provide the rest.

And then, the roominghouse people wouldn't be about me all the time, the men, the girls, the landlady. Roominghouses, I had always loathed. There were so many possibilities! So many fears! And in that setting, one's melancholy is played upon so small a stage. I went to look at my apartment.

It lay an ungodly distance from the center of town, a matter of one street-car ride, two bus-rides and a ten-minute walk. The region was desolate, neither residential nor slum nor suburb, but I didn't care. I was nearing home! I passed one rickety building

on a corner, somewhat afraid it might be mine, then I hesitated
and turned up an alley, to the right, which meandered towards a
stream between two high, moss-covered walls.

Behind those walls, I thought, there were two charming
girls, young and gay and profoundly read. Their father was a
professor, with flexible ideas. A little man with a beard. He
played the piano while his daughters sang. In the evening, one
of the girls and I would walk in the garden, hand in hand, talking about things . . . ideas . . . man's loneliness upon the earth.
And then we would embrace in the shadow of the trees whose
thin branches touched the top of the wall.

Thinking this, I came to the stream which, broad and slow,
was moving its phlegmatic, oily, blue-green waters along a bank
that was paved with cobblestones, as I remember. It was as if I
had come out of the nightmare of Indianapolis into a quiet corner
that was Paris by the Seine. And me with my own apartment,
and people I could love! I sat there dreaming for three-quarters
of an hour, closer to the world than I had been in months, tossing
crumbs of cement, or pebbles, into the water, just to hear them
go ker-splash.

Then I roused myself to go back and look at the house on the
corner. The lean-to roof extending over the porch rested its
weight on two sagging pillars, like a drunkard sprawling with
his elbows on a bar. In the doorway stood a pregnant young
woman who stared at me sullenly.

I compared the house number with the address in the advertisement, and asked to see the apartment.

"Ma!" bawled the young woman in a resentful tone of voice.
She was so unprepossessing I imagined her seducer must be a
long way out of town by now. And yet as I looked at her dark
face again, I thought if worse came to worse. . . . .

In a moment, a whiskery old crone in a black dress came out
on the porch and blinked at me.

"It's a kinda ole house un the rooms ain't clean yet but you
kun look," she said, whining, and led the way upstairs to the
apartment.

It was appalling. The bed lay dying in the middle of the
floor, its wirey guts springing out at all angles, as if it had been
gored by a bull, a tattered coverlet over its face. There was a
broken chair, a chest of drawers on three legs, and the piano.
That, I saved for the last. I went to look at the other room, a
large, bare closet; and the bathroom, deep in thick, grey dust,
whose plumbing might have been picked up in a junk-yard. All

the while, the old lady kept up her keening, in a high, flat voice. The apartment was really O.K. just needed a little teching up un I could buy a few things if I wanted um then there was this pianner un all.

I walked back to the front room and tried the piano, which grinned at the ceiling with its dingy, carious teeth.

"Plunk! Plank! Plink!" the piano said.

I went to the window and looked out at the broad highway that ran past the house, now loud with the humming of trucks and passenger cars, and stinking of gasoline. It ran on and on, until the sidewalks seemed to meet in the distance, past shops and filling stations and houses as wretched as the one in which I stood. A hundred yards down the highway, on the opposite side, a vast storage tank ballooned against its network of cables and runways, and for a moment I stared at that and at the endless parade of cars.

A tugging at my elbow broke into the hypnotic trance. "It's real nice out there," said the old woman, desperately eager to rent the apartment. She pointed to the window with her other hand. "You can always find someth'n to see. Why, I could spend hours just watching them automobiles, because it's like they was keeping me company. You'd never be lonely if you was to live here!"

As God is my judge, I could feel the blood ebbing in from my hands and my feet, leaving them cold with fear and paralysis. Never be lonely! The traffic roared on in a kind of silence, as if the cars rushed by on a muted screen and the roaring was in my ears; and the silence was not the expectation of sound but the silence in which no human voice is ever heard. I jerked my elbow free from the bony old gravedigger's grip and threw one horrified glance around the apartment. There was dust, there was dust, there was dust! And I fled, without saying a word.

It is not true that I tore out onto the sidewalk, and ran along, and, seeing a dull, baked face reflected in the dust-smeared window of a grocery store, hurled a brick at it to discover that the face was my own. And it would be a pack of lies to say that I returned to my roominghouse and there collapsed in echolalia, or burned my bridges, and my book, or studied taxidermy by mail and became a great success. I merely went back to my room and hoped that one of the art students on the floor below would think of me sitting there.

Ah, Indianapolis, asshole of the nation! Sometimes I wonder what else went on in the town that day. If life was not bearable for the others, then when, then where? Did they have any fun? Did they say hello? Did anyone ever come to help the swollen girl whose bastard was being born in hatred at the burnt-out end of the world so few escape?

YEATS IN DUBLIN

In memory of W. B. Yeats

Vernon Watkins

A rich lupin-garden,
A long, amber room,
A bronze head, bookshelves
Glittering in that gloom;
And threads, threads, threads of the sea,
Threads of the birds of doom.

Impression of rain-wet, moving leaves.
A dog upon the drive
Casts a questioning shadow
Where secret flowers connive.
A terrible seabird. Folded wings.
Then the gannet's dive.

'From such a treadle of the sea
Your foot may never come,
Never without breaking
The pattern of the loom:
All the ages go to make
The thread around your thumb.'

'O come back', the seabirds cry,
'To the raindrops' hammerings,
Down to the ignorant Irish sea
Crossed by encircling wings;
Under the sea dumb grains, great rocks:
Think of these old things.'

But Yeats, Yeats the poet
Under Dublin skies,
After the ten years' journey
On which no seagull flies,
After the waves of silence
I look him in the eyes.

Fresh from the shining sunlight
We came on his dark seat,
Shook hands, paused, were dumb there
Fearing to tire him out,
Though his raised head was noble,
His voice firm and sweet.

'Tell me about that young group
Of Welsh writers', he said,
'Whose poems in that paper you sent me
The other day I read.'
An image stands on carmarthen sands
With the black birds overhead.

'The young poets', he murmured,
'Toil too much. They lay
Something on their table,
And dissect, and wear it away
Till nothing but the grits is left;
But all song is gay.

There must always be a quality
Of nonchalance in the work.
The intellect is impotent
Labouring in the dark,
For a poem is always
A piece of luck.

Who can foretell the run of luck
Or where the luck may fall?
Watching the roulette-wheel
We see the spinning ball,
But where it stops and comes to rest
The place is magical.

The Psychical Research Society
Lately has found
It can experimentally
Foresee that resting-ground
A second before the fall of space
And the death of sound.

Much the treasure-hoarding mind
Values its sum,
But to a breath's vibration
All is held there dumb;
All is reduced to nothing;
Then the luck will come.

Against blinding darkness
A man's blood is thrown,
Striving for that intensity
Which danced before time ran;
That thing, for lack of a better name,
I call 'Eternal Man'.

A poet seeks his deepest thought,
Then finds, when it is made,
A loyalty has held it,
Not by time betrayed,
The very distance measured
By the blood's shade.

In an early poem I set myself
The task to unite
The myths of all ages
In a single night,
To draw their tale, not on the wall
But in the tip of the light.

I might have made it with the myths
Of Ireland alone,
But somewhere in my mind's eye
I saw Priam's throne.
Usna I wanted, and Troy too,
So I put Troy down.'

174

'Did the idea come slowly,'
I questioned, 'did it unfold
At once, or from the leaves themselves
As from a sculptor's mould?
Was it your mind that saw the words,
Or was your mind told?'

'I made it,' with a slow smile
Said that Irishman,
'Looking at a lady's photograph
Where all those myths began;
So naturally it came slowly.'
And he went on:

'A critic who has pleased me
(Though the best attack)
Says that the style is public
In my latest work;
That near to my youth, with a difference,
Song is going back.

That difference is important
In poem or in play.
Hard as thoughts in the bone to find
Are naked words to say;
Write, get rid of rhetoric;
Cut the dead wood away.

To-day I summon boyhood's reed
But bid that same reed break,
For broken things are powerful
Being bruised and trampled. Blake
And Burns had a public style;
But others found a fake,

The trick and slang of a slippery speech
Trite and second-hand;
Pandering to the popular ear
They did not understand
That truth must cut harder
Than the diamond.'

175

I asked, had he stirred enmity.
'Yes, my work was banned.
It was the laymen squeaked and squealed
And would not let it stand,
Never the hand of blessing,
Always the felon's hand.

But before my book 'A Vision' appeared
The Bishops began to urge
A ban on its publication
Fearing its views at large;
Then they heard it was a guinea,
And they dropped the charge.

'The Resurrection' would not have been played
But for a general strike.
Men who insist on vessels
Dare not see them break,
Terrified should the dead walk
Or the sleeper wake.

I met, in America,
A holy man who said:
'There will always be miracle—
(He raised his old, white head)
There will always be revelation,'
That old saint said.

A saint. I met his follower then.
He professed belief in all
The tenets of the Church's creed,
Mass and ritual,
Except the immortality
Of the human soul.

Another priest I asked which road
To salvation lay.
'Go to Mass, go to Mass,'
Was all that priest would say.
'It will take just twenty minutes.
Go, and you need not pray.'

Then, when I put a question
In salvation's track,
'Read what you like,' the priest replied,
'A great or a holy book.
I take when I go praying
A Dante bound in black.'

Yeats justified the parish priest,
One that could curse and bless,
Especially curse, and blame bad crops
On the peasants' wickedness.
'They must have their magician:
He is neither more nor less.'

We from two countries coming
Took tea, and talked of things,
Behind us threads of sunlight
And the path of wings,
Before us thought and images
Beaten into rings.

Thought, grief-impassioned, drifted
To Coole, and Lady Gregory:
'Have the trees grown a little
Around Thoor Ballylee?'
One by one he raised those names
Between the waves of the sea.

Lionel Johnson, Dowson,
And political men betrayed,
Murdered by their excess of love
Or by a dream they made;
Synge's mighty statements;
The brightness of the shade.

'We have the folk in Ireland;
The English make it up.
How can a country's language thrive
If an abstract shape
Battening on the vigorous man
Sucks the blood-drop?

When I first went to London
I was looking for a technique.
I had the folk behind me,
My food was there to seek,
But without the subtlety London taught
I could not learn to speak.

I got technique from a man who was
A very bad poet indeed.
He taught me to appreciate
The small stops of the reed;
The Minutiae of a poem
He first made me heed.

What if the labour all seem vain,
What if years are spent
Chiselling and chiselling
The stubborn element?
All is rewarded on a breath
By an accident.

My quarrel with those Londoners
Is that they try
To substitute psychology
For the naked sky
Of metaphysical movement,
And drain the blood dry.

All is materialism, all
The catchwords they strew,
Alien to the blood of man.—'
One ranting slogan drew
That 'Poetry must have news in it':
'The reverse is true.'

I questioned him: 'How can there be
A national poetry?
What can we make or what resist
When all is like the sea?'
He said: 'You must resist the stream
Of mechanical apathy.'

Speaking of leaders, he affirmed,
'The best is he who knows
The fancy-dress of politics
From his garden-clothes,
Who understands the popular mask,
Those deceiving shows.'

He spoke of de Valera,
A charming, cultured man
Who found upon the platform
True culture under ban,
Then uttered out of vehemence
Words he would say to none.

We talked of national movements.
He pondered the chance
Of Welshmen reviving
The fire of song and dance,
Driving a lifeless hymnal
From that inheritance.

I thought of rough mountains,
The poverty of the heath.
'Though leaders sway the crowd,' I said,
'Power is underneath.
The sword of Taliesin
Would never fit a sheath.'

'The leaders and the poets
Are not in unison.
When Hitler struck a medal
He knew that George won,
But he had not served his movement,
So slept in Avalon.'

He questioned my French friend,
And his words remain
Shining like pebbles
Under the flow of the Seine,
Where Synge had walked with him,
Where he had met Verlaine.

Spirits whirling about us
Were laid by a look,
Ghosts turned in delicate light
To gold on the edge of a book,
Wound in the shroud of a still page
Which no man took.

Light in the drawing-room,
Daylight on the lawn,
Book-shadows in the corners
Seemed to have drawn
Spirits from the back of the mind,
From conception's dawn.

Yeats and his wife once more
Asked of the Tower
Where I had stood last year
A dumb, low-breathed hour,
Watching the blade of the grass
And the grass-flower.

Then, as the heron
Raises from the stream,
He raised from the haunted chair
His tall, proud frame
In that dazzling background
Of heroic dream.

Now, as a child sees
Daybreak on a wall,
His image showed me in a flash
Birth and burial,
The trouble of the lovely song,
Parnell's Funeral.

'I must work' and 'I must rest'
In one breath he said,
Unconsciously, a blind man
By a blind hand led,
All creation hanging
On that double thread.

My friend and I were silent
Witnessing that thing
Which of the sacred rivers
Had touched the secret spring
Making, in the youth of age,
The dumb stone sing.

With visionary footsteps
Slow, he crossed the room,
He who had made the dead lips sing
And celebrate love in doom,
About him the sages
Of Byzantium.

To that broken vision
What could we bring,
Blinded by the shadow
Of the mounting wing?
Had he not loosed the tongue of dust
And made the dead lips sing?

The river that fed his fingers
A pagan sun would parch
Did not the soul throw writing there
On the vaulted arch,
Clash and flash of irrational love:
A Full Moon in March.

Silence falling from the moon
Beating to brass
The towering labours of the sun
Bids Herodias'
Daughter dance more madly
Till all but love must pass.

Words and the flight of images,
That unerring dance,
Passionate love of wisdom,
Hatred of ignorance.
Words laid on silence.
The tragic utterance.

'I am sorry you have come so far
For so little,' he said.
The music of the mounting wave
Crashed into my head
In which the spray confuses
The living and the dead.

I have seen kindness
In true, loyal eyes.
Who prophesies from the lip of a shell?
What raging water cries?
The blue wave moves beneath me:
Above, the white bird flies.

THE PROJECT

Brom Weber

I USUALLY reach the Library between ten and eleven o'clock each morning. But before entering, I walk along Fifth Avenue. I let myself be caught up in the crowd that moves up and down the street. Everyone seems so sure and certain about his direction, his glances, his smiles.

Some people look into fancy shop windows at imported jewelry or at the latest books. Others stare upwards through telescopes at the Empire State and Chrysler Buildings. I do likewise, though there is no real need for me to consider things to buy or buildings in which to rent an office. Nevertheless, so strong is my desire to be one of them, that I merge with them. There walks a girl in bright ballet slippers. She walks confidently, because under her arm is a cover design done for BEWITCH-MENT. Here is a man with bright eyes and well-cut moustache. He has just finished a series of sparkling ads for a liquor concern. Now he marches along with pay check tucked in his wallet. With these evaluations, I become a part of the city's life. I am not outside. I move with it and feel with it.

On this morning, like other mornings, I tore myself regretfully out of the promenade and ascended the sprawling marble steps of the Library building. I never enter the Library on the Forty-Second Street side. It is so commonplace there. On Fifth Avenue, the structure is imposing, and resembles one of the solid banks to be found on Wall Street. And it ties in nicely with my banker's hours to be entering a building designed to resemble an intellectual depository. For, after all, my daily visits to the Library are not just sojourns without meaning. I have a project to complete, and it requires hours and hours of the most patient research to gather the necessary facts.

As I climbed the steps to the great bronze doorway, I felt more and more like a business man calling at his office to a job.

183

My portfolio with its paper and pads was tucked securely under my arm. My hat, while not a Homburg, sat jauntily on top of my hair. I climbed slowly, so as to enjoy my pleasure to its fullest extent. There is also my health to consider, for I am delicate.

I scanned the bronze bas-reliefs on either side of the doorway while passing through. Just as they were yesterday. That's good. It gives me a feeling of stability to know that things haven't changed overnight. The guard stood in his usual spot, near the turnstile.

"Hello, Joe," I said quietly.

He turned to me, almost as if he didn't recognize me. Then his lips stretched into a welcoming smile:

"Good morning."

Joe doesn't like to talk much. I've tried more than once to draw him into conversations. But he persists in keeping quiet, I concluded some time ago that he's probably ashamed of his Italian accent.

Without haste, I walked across the marble floor. The room is made entirely of marble, and I am respectful. I make a special effort to walk quietly here, since I don't think it's dignified to draw attention by walking noisily.

Two men were in line ahead of me at the coat checkroom. I couldn't avoid feeling contemptuous of them. Slightly of course, because I'm not a snob, but contemptuous. It wasn't that their coats were shabby, or because one of the men was unshaven, or that neither of the two had a briefcase or notebook. It was just that their entire appearance indicated their lack of appreciation in making use of the Library. These are the people who come to the Library aimlessly, because they have nowhere else to go. Here it's warm . . . they doze in large armchairs and dream of hot lands and busy offices. Despite the fact that I have a job to do, I waited patiently behind them.

Suddenly, just as the attendant was ready to take my overcoat and hat, a shrill female voice shattered the peaceful silence. Startled, I turned around. A small thin-faced woman, clad in a tight-fitting jersey dress, came running down the steps leading from the upper floors. Following close behind, seemingly trying to pacify her, was Joe, puzzled and irritated.

"I'll report him, that's what! I'll report him!" I heard her say as she ran across the floor. Meanwhile, Joe had taken up his stand near the doorway.

The coatroom attendant had been smirking bitterly throughout the episode, shaking her head from side to side and holding
her hands behind her back. Finally, she lifted up my hat, but
made no effort to take my coat. With what was meant to be a
sympathetic smile, she leaned forward in Joe's direction. As
though in response to her plea, Joe walked over to us. His face
bore a mocking expression.

"They are in love," he announced in his soft voice, "two love-
birds. . . ."

Who are they? I wondered. But Joe didn't enlighten me:

"*She* claims *he* spit on her first. *He* claims *she* spit on him
first. I always get mixed up in these love-affairs."

Leaning his body over the counter, Joe whispered in the
attendant's ear. I couldn't make out the words. No doubt he was
telling her something about the incident. I was more absorbed,
however, in the fact that Joe actually said more to this woman
in a few minutes than he had ever said to me in all the time I
knew him. This puzzled me. Yet, I reflected, the vagaries of
friendship have no equivalent relationship with true values.
Friendship is, after all, only an emotional link in which feeling
plays a more important part than reason. I really couldn't condemn Joe too harshly for his attitudes. These two lonely people
needed each other.

After Joe went back to his doorway post, the attendant
picked up my coat and said wryly:

"You get some nuts in this here place."

I made an effort to smile, although I had caught her glance
at my overcoat.

My overcoat is like any other coat. But there is something
about it, something I consider unimportant. In its way, it looks
exactly like the coats of the two men who stood before me in
line, frayed, worn. But it's not torn! I'm proud of that, and
proud of my combed hair and clean shirt! It's not wealth that
marks a man, but the manner in which he keeps those possessions entrusted to him by life.

Poor woman, I thought, she is tired from standing on her
feet all day long. Life must get very tiresome for her. Indeed,
her face did look exhausted, and her fingers gnarled from fastening and unfastening themselves endlessly on overcoats and hats.

I climbed the steps to the upper floors. At the turn of the
staircase, I saw the male "lover" crouching on his knees. Gesticu-
lating with his hands, his flabby lips quivering with words, he

appeared to be making an unintelligible effort to persuade me that it was "she" who had spit on him first: "She . . . she first . . . she." And he spat before him to make himself clear. But I didn't care. He or she!

I looked down at him from the second floor landing. Bundled up in his clothes, as though hiding from someone who stood directly over him, he no longer mumbled. But his yellowed fingers crawled fantastically in the air as though exercising for a pianistic exhibition. I burst out laughing as I thought of this preposterous "love-affair." Joe's satirical use of the expression amused me as much as the thought of the lovers themselves.

"Such nuts," I exclaimed.

In the Catalog Room, I rested my arms on a table in order to catch my breath. My eyes closed for a moment. Such relaxation fortifies my strength. And I needed energy for the day of work that lay ahead of me.

Turning to the card catalog set in the wall, I picked out a tray of cards. As I set it firmly on the table, I noticed a girl standing alongside. Her back was towards me, and she was shifting her weight from one foot to the other and back again. I sensed immediately that she was attempting to attract my eyes. With each movement, her body changed its shape. These flowing lines were meant to entice me. But how pathetic were her efforts to be alluring! Even if I were not busy with a project, it would be impossible for a blatant type like this to attract me. It amazes me that wherever I go, there is always some girl ogling, twisting, hopeful in the delusion that such is the way to interest me. They can't seem to understand that their pitiful posturings have absolutely no effect on me. As though to demonstrate her power, the girl beside me defiantly tossed her head in the air.

Angrily I averted my gaze and began hastily writing the titles and authors of the books I needed on the library call slips. But my fingers kept slipping on the pencil's smooth and shiny sides, and I erased more than I wrote. The flames of humiliation began to burn in my cheeks as I realized that she had upset me. I looked at her again. She had moved closer, still with her back towards me. What does she look like? I wondered. Are her eyes green and her nose small? Is her mouth open slightly, so that her teeth bite into her lower lip as if in passion?

I drew my breath in with dismay as I understood the meaning of my thoughts. Momentarily, I had a vision of the girl whom I had seen yesterday in the Periodical Room. Her sweet refined beauty and manner constituted my secret ideal. Had I in any way proved myself unworthy by this weakness? I questioned myself harshly.

Suddenly my hand was jarred and the pencil it held slipped to the floor. She had deliberately fallen against me. Involuntarily, I reached out to prevent her from striking the floor. Her face was a startled mask as she faced me. In a voice honeyed with innocence, she said:

"Oh, I'm sorry. I didn't know you were behind me."

Angered at this deception, I derided her silly excuses:

"Didn't know you were behind me, did you?"

She pulled herself out of my grasp with surprise.

"I said I was sorry," she gasped.

I fled into the Reading Room, after hurriedly sweeping together my belongings. My sense of decorum, my reserve, are attributes on which I pride myself. Furthermore, I had a job to do and must get on with it. So I resolutely determined that this synthetic Eve would not be allowed to upset me one bit!

I sat down heavily on a chair in the rear of the Reading Room. The further back you sit, the better off you are, because thus you can avoid the draft that slices through the front of the room. I dried my perspired forehead with a handkerchief. Then I was appalled to see the call slips clutched in my hand. I had forgotten to hand them in at the call desk in the Catalog Room. Now there would be no books delivered to me. Nor was my pencil in my coat-pocket. It must have been lying on the floor in the other room. But I didn't want to go back there, either to hand in the slips or to reclaim my pencil. I didn't want to see that girl again, nor did I want her to see me. Bitterly I felt around in my vest pockets and found a pencil stub. It would have to serve me for the rest of the day.

In order to occupy my time fruitfully, I picked up several of the books scattered on the table. One had an interesting title, and I opened it. The book was worn, and its pages dirty with fingerprints and age. The type was small. How do they expect anyone to read in the Library? The lamps burn ten-watt bulbs; books are encrusted with dirt; chairs are hard; no matter how you squirm, aches gather. Behind your back, the attendants walk catfootedly in their gray coats . . . peering over your shoulder and breathing on your head. As a good citizen, however, I stopped myself from grouching.

At first glance, the book seemed interesting. Someone called Bardunius had the brilliant idea of writing on the use of reason. It's an important subject. If more people were able to use their heads, the world would definitely not be the depressing place it now is. I myself make a point of treating every problem reasonably. I try to understand the good and bad sides of everything, so that I'll make no mistakes.

But instead of telling you how to use your mind to best advantage, Bardunius kept on bleating in high-toned language about "moral responsibility" and "ethical consciousness." All proper in its place. But is there a practical good to be derived from such talk? Would it help me, for example, to develop my brain so that I could forge ahead and complete my project in the best possible way? Absolutely not! This book had as much real value as a philosopher in a courtroom!

I don't make a practice of writing in books. However, I've never thought it fair for an author to be able to provoke his readers, and yet be so far removed that he remains unaffected by their complaints. So I sympathize with those impassioned souls who make a writer prove every implication, every contention, and who emblazon their approvals and disapprovals on the very pages of his book. . . .

Someone brushed by my chair and I looked up. The bronze hands of the big wall clock stood at 2:30. A whole morning and part of the afternoon was gone, with nothing accomplished. I strode from the Reading Room, and hurried through the Catalog Room. In the corridor, I stopped for a moment near the phone booths. I had no one to call. It was probably time to eat lunch. I felt for the coins in my pocket. In company with my keys and pocket-knife, they had sung a comforting, jingling music. Handled now as coins by my fingers, they were pitiably few in number . . . tokens which would serve me better as carfare during the next few days.

Eating now was time-consuming anyway, as well as being costly. One has to stand for hours in the sandwich shops waiting for service. Far better, I thought, to read some magazines and make the day count for something after all.

Magazines are very important in my work. At one time, I used to read only the few specializing in the subject with which my project is concerned. But I grew uneasy. I worried about missing articles of importance in neglected magazines. I reflected that some of this material, all of it unknown to me, might even be so significant that it could probably cut the time required for my project by a third . . . by a half! In this state of agitation, each magazine transformed itself into a staring reproach that I was not reading ten others. Finally, I'm proud to say, I read almost every current magazine on the shelves.

The Periodical Room was almost empty. I selected several magazines and looked around for a seat. Not far from the magazine shelves, I caught sight of the girl whom I had seen yesterday. I sat down at her table. She was still as sweet and demure as the girl upstairs had been evil. Today she must talk to me.

Yesterday, I had been sitting dejectedly before a heap of magazines. My mind was reeling from articles on everything, ranging from sewage disposal equipment to seal-meat vitamins. And the stories! Even the accountants' quarterly review carried a strange tale about the romance of figures. I seemed to be getting exactly nowhere with my work. My eyelids were dry. My head ached.

Then this girl had walked gracefully over to my table, her short round body swaying. She had smiled shyly as she noticed my interest, and moistening her lips delicately had begun to read. I knew instantly that this girl would mean a great deal to me.

So I wrote a note to her without delay. Motioning to the high school boy who replaces discarded magazines on the shelves, I had folded the note. He had come over unwillingly.

"Yeah?" he had asked.

"Sh. . . ." I replied, pulling him closer so that I could whisper in his ear. "Give this to the girl sitting across the way." I pressed the note into his hand.

"Whyn't you give it to her yourself?" he had asked.

"I don't want her to know right away that it's from me," I told him in a whisper.

He appeared convinced, because he walked off. But he was back in a few minutes. Flushing, he had thrown the note onto the table, and said:

"I ain't carrying love letters for anybody!"

Love letters! I didn't even have the temerity to believe that this girl could possibly love me. I simply wanted her to realize how much I admired her. But this brat had opened the note and misinterpreted it. There wasn't an ounce of decency in his body!

Well, I'd see to it myself that she talked to me today. I wrote a note again, and placed it in the center of one of the magazines before me. Then I put the magazine directly on top of her purse. The girl was so interested in her reading that she didn't look up. Soon she would probably be reaching for a pencil or a handkerchief, I thought. She would lift up the magazine, and my note would fall out onto the table. I expected to hear her voice shortly thereafter, and I allowed myself to revel in the ecstasy which her tones would bring me.

I occupied myself meanwhile by opening another magazine. I wanted her to observe that I was a man who had a job to do here in the Library. If she asked me later, I would tell her everything about my project. And I felt that I could trust her implicitly to keep the details confidential.

The first page of the magazine had an advertisement with a humorous cartoon. I chuckled, and then I noticed the coupon at the bottom. It offered a free booklet on molded plastics, no strings attached. Plastics is an up-and-coming field. Why, they're even making houses from plastics these days. Despite that, I made no effort to cut out the coupon. I believe there's always a good possibility that later readers may be interested in something on the other side of the coupon. And if that's gone, they can't read the full page.

I was growing impatient. Still no word from the girl. I'd wait a little longer, though. She was shy, I knew, and how can you speak to a stranger just off-hand? Give her some time also to let the note make an effect upon her, I cautioned myself. Its words will encourage her. For there could be no misunderstanding their tenderness and devotion.

In this state of excitement, I wanted nothing to distract me. The atmosphere must be absolutely tranquil. I must hear her first words as soon as they were spoken. It was almost as if the pages of my magazine made too much noise in turning, so I closed it. My body was trembling, and I closed my eyes.

I raised my eyes after what seemed an eternity. Suddenly, behind the girl's back, appeared the high school boy. His ugly face, spotted with pimples and covered with down, smirked at me as he tapped her shoulder. I leaned forward slightly, horrified yet gladdened. Was he going to tell her how much I wanted her to speak to me? Yet it seemed so crude. Nevertheless, I warmed to his haggard face, weary from working long hours after a hard day at school. How can one hate a child for long?

As the girl looked up at him in response to his touch, the boy placed his hand on the magazine containing my note and asked:

"Have you finished with this magazine, lady?"

He knew! He had spied on me from some corner, watched me place my note in the pages of the magazine. Now he was determined to thwart me, to take away the magazine, before she had a chance to read my note. How rudely he had interrupted her reading, banging her on the shoulder with his grimy paw.

Before she could reply to him, I stood up, feverish and distraught. I gripped my portfolio so violently between my hands that I felt it give way and tear.

"Let her alone!" I screamed at him.

He retreated, but not before he had grabbed the magazine. The girl looked up with alarm, her eyes widening.

"People can't read here with the way you bother them," I shouted. "All you do is crack your heels on the floor, push against chairs, make off with magazines before people have finished reading. What are you being paid for? What do you mean by smashing people when you ask them a question? Answer me, you scrawny runt! You rotten pup!"

I could see the boy edging away more quickly as I continued to shout, but I couldn't stop.

"Haven't you any manners? Can't you see that people are trying to read, trying to work? Keep quiet, for God's sake!"

Breathlessly I fell back into my chair. The reverberations of my words in the high-ceilinged room pounded against my ears. The others stared at me. Let them stare with their worried squirming eyes! It was high time they heard someone with the courage and intelligence to express himself when the need arose. If you stepped on *their* toes, they groaned and apologized. But not I. Resolutely I put my belongings in order, straightened my tie, and buttoned my vest.

Through the open door, Joe walked in. Dancing behind him in excitement was the boy. The gray guard's uniform dried the exultant saliva in my mouth, and I lowered my head on my chest. When the footsteps reached my chair, I looked up at him. His olive-skinned face was sallow and cold.

"We've had enough complaints about you to fill a book," he said, and stopped. Someone laughed appreciatively at his little joke.

"We've seen you tearing pages out of books . . . cutting coupons out of magazines. You've scribbled filthy words on the lavatory walls, and scratched tables with your pen knife. You think you're pretty smart. But we've been on to you all along. Now you've gone the limit . . . insulting girls and fighting with the Library staff. You're nothing but a bum! Get me?"

"I—I—I. . . ." I stammered. I wanted to say it was all a lie, but the words wouldn't form themselves in my throat. He continued as though I hadn't said anything:

"I'll tell you this much. Get out of here, or I'll throw you out. Don't come sneaking back, or we'll put you where you really belong. . . ."

I pressed myself down in my chair, overpowered by this naked revelation of myself. Where would I go tomorrow, and the day after, when I left the Library never to return? What would I do? The girl glanced at me with contempt, and turned away. Tears melted my eyes.

192

THE RUINS OF MUNICH

PHOTOGRAPHS BY HERBERT LIST

THREE POEMS

Peter Viereck

FOR TWO GIRLS
SETTING OUT IN LIFE

(*A morality-play*)

"The two young ladies separated. Juliette, who wanted to become a grand lady, how could she consent to be accompanied by a girl whose virtuous and plebian inclinations might dishonor her social prestige? And Justine, for her part, how could she expose her good name to the companionship of a perverse creature who was looking forward to a life of vile lewdness and public debauchery? They bade each other an eternal adieu, and next morning they both left the convent."—Marquis de Sade, *Justine or The Misfortunes of Virtue,* 1791.

I

The sick man, though, had wit who thought you up.
Who can not picture you that fatal morning?
Homeless, not even knowing where you'll sup,
You sigh, "Adieu!" and ask yourselves, "What next?"
I sound like old Polonius—don't be vexed
If I give too avuncular a warning;
But having scanned your futures in a text,
I gasp at all the ways you'll be misled
(Your nuns behind you and your males ahead)
And want to save you from your author's plot.
When he says, "Follow me," you'd better not!

193

II

Justine, by all means do be virtuous
But not in so provocative a fashion.
I'm being frank; please listen: solely thus
Can you elude that lamentable passion
For which your author lends his name to us.
The night he ties you down in Bondy Wood,
You'll learn what happens to the gauchely good.

III

Yet you'll endure, Justine. Most stubbornly!
To love mankind, to preach tranquility
To Etna or reverse a spinning planet
By bleating trustfully your Pauline tracts—
Such supernatural smugness is sheer granite:
No, not eroded by whole cataracts
Of fondlers groping through—beyond—your body
To sate in flesh the spirit's old distress
And plunge their seekings in some final sea.
Meanwhile, far off, a certain chic Grand Lady
Half-hears a voice each night (too kind for spleen)
That weeps for all her daytime wilfulness:
"Juliette! Juliette! What have you done to me?
It's I—your other self—your poor Justine."

IV

And you, Juliette: have fun while doing ill.
Be un-immaculate *while yet you may*
(I drop this hint to give the plot away).
But when you dance with sweating stable-lads
Or tired Dukes who giggle at your skill,
Don't think it's you who dance; the ghosts of gods
Who died before our oldest gods were young,
Twirl savagely in your polite salon:
That sofa, where reclining comes so easy,
Is far more haunted than you'll ever guess.
Your lips raise shrines as mystic as Assisi
From whiteness they so piously caress.
O you are very wise (your playful nights,
That seem so casual, are primordial rites)
And very silly (promise me you'll stay
A pretty little girl who'll never spell

194

"Chthonic" nor learn her Freud too sadly well).
Last week I think I met you on Broadway.

V

Two truths, two sisters. An obsessive pair:
Serene in their unalterable roles
Whether their frantic author flog or kiss them.
And either truth rebukes our limbo where
Girls are not Bad but merely Indiscreet,
Girls are not Good but merely Very Sweet,
And men are filed in their own filing-system
With frayed manila-folders for their souls—
Once labeled GOD'S OWN IMAGE: USE WITH CARE
But now reclassified as OBSOLETE.

VI

Justine! Juliette! We need you, both of you,
'Girls of mild silver or of furious gold'.
Revoke your spat; it is our own feud, too.
You smile? Yet you can bless us if you will.
And then—and then—identities unveiled,
Tall tales rehearsed and poutings reconciled—
    Two opposites will find each other
    And sob for half a day together;
For heaven and hell are childhood playmates still.

STIFLING OF HEARTS
A HUNDRED TIMES A DAY

'God is dead'—Zarathustra

Sometimes a waitress laughing from a window,
To plates a truant and with comet's hair,
Enchants his snakes of longing like a Hindu
Till they sway anciently and learn *la chair
Est triste.*
A tryst?
        But plates need slaves: *la chère
Est triste,* and now from window back to table
All hips strut out of sight and into fable
With Helen's scorn—and Cindarella's prayer.

195

YOU ALL ARE STATIC; I ALONE AM MOVING

(a young tree addresses humanity)

You all are static; I alone am moving.
Racing beyond each planted Pullman wheel,
    I pity you and long to reel
You through my thousand outstretched ways of loving.
Are you alive at all? Can non-trees *feel*?

Run while I may, for at my pith gnaws Night.
The winds—these are great stacks of anchored air;
    I thresh them with my hard-pronged hair;
I jump right through them, roaring my delight.
Live while I may—run, run, no matter where.

How marvelous—if you but knew—is speed!
You all must wait; I am your overtaker.
    Striding to green from yellow acre,
I toss you Spring. Each dawn, my tendrils knead
Stars into pancake-suns like a tall baker.

Trudging toward snowtime, I could weep for hours
To think of birds, the birds I leave behind.
    Why did the God who keeps you blind,
Instead give sight and sentience to my flowers?
Black questions in my sap outwear my rind.

Humans (I almost envy you your peace)
Are free of this gnarled urge for Absolutes
    Which sweetens and saddens all my fruits,
Dragging my twigs down when I'd fly towards bliss—
While bugs and diamonds agonize my roots.

WHO KILLED THE UNIVERSE?

(A who-dunnit-thriller of that arbitrary
universe of the Existentialist prophets)

Peter Viereck

"Search! and tell me if thou seest a certain shape or shadow,
making way with wings or chariot fierce to repossess a heaven he lost
erewhile. Yes, there must be a golden victory; there must be gods
thrown down and trumpets blown . . . beautiful things made new, for
the surprise of the sky-children."

—Keats, Hyperion

"LISTEN, Mr. Jones, it's not that I mind his staring at my wife.
Staring is no crime. But why did he knock the safety valves off
the boilers this morning?"

Gaylord Jones held the combined job of roving superintendent and Public Good Will expert for an apartment house syndicate in up-state New York, autumn of 1949. His flabby plump-
ness was noticeable only at second glance; at first glance it was
neutralized by his imposing tallness. This afternoon he had
been urgently summoned to the advertising man's apartment; he
had just arrived but had already stopped listening as his sum-
moner continued,

"Why does he talk so full of 'haths' and 'damnations' like the
Bible? If I were his boss, I'd force him to talk janitor talk. Where
will it end if janitors start talking long-haired? But above all,
I called you here because of those radiators. Why doesn't he send
us tenants some heat up, like you promised he would?"

Mr. Jones answered as affably as ever, Yes I guess you admitted it in your own words: staring is no crime. So now we
can say goodbye in a spirit of friendly agreement. I'd better get
back to my own little nest, that oil-heated little mansion the
syndicate gave me when I won the Economy Prize for cutting

heating costs in their other buildings." The portly superintendent began edging towards the door of the advertising man's
apartment, while continuing to talk rapidly. "All day I'm slugging away for the rights of the tenants; so I just don't have the
resistance left to stand the cold here. Can't expect me to turn
into an icicle just to listen to a lot of undermining remarks about
my janitors and radiators."

"Who said that anybody minded his damn maddening staring," resumed the advertising man, "or his mumbling either?
The cold radiators, that's what I minded when today I caught
him telling his parrot, *Death by freezing for the pagan ad man,
but one more chance for his betrayed wife. Oh, why do they all
laugh together behind my back?* 'At it again!' I shouted from
behind, real loud to scare him; 'You're always mumbling against
the tenants in secret, but now I've caught you *at* it red-handed;
you're always *at* it.' He didn't even try to weasel out of it, just
answered with a funny word I don't understand: '*Armageddon
tonight.*' Well, I don't mind all that so much as I do when the
two of you—not to mention that Great Dane of his, that dog's up
to no good either—and the parrot, he's also to blame, distracts
him from the radiators—all my sinus and all your promises, and
also when—."

Gaylord Jones had disappeared.

There was a reason why the mumbler in the basement, the
little janitor of the big cold house, could spare no time for the
steam heat. He was busy writing page after page in a cardboard-
covered book labeled *Dear Diary*. For example, last summer:
"Proclamation: NO MORE MOSQUITOES; all top-ranking
archangels please note." Or this autumn: "The real trouble is
finding a cobra with guts enough to crawl up the radiator pipes."
Or still more recently: "Dear Diary, when I think what's going
to happen this week to Tempter Jones, sometimes I almost feel
sorry."

Gray. The janitor exuded grayness: the nice old guy,
loyally incompetent, with eyes harassed but acquiescent, the
eternal conscientious bore to whom people ought to say, "Little
man, what now?"

What now? Can a blank cartridge blow up or a mouse roar?
Can grayness redden into a will-to-power? Mr. Jones never
glimpsed the spark nor heard the sputtering fuse of one ex-
plosive forgotten little brain-cell just below the janitor's con-

sciousness. This made the misunderstanding mutual, for in turn the janitor never glimpsed the grayness of the scarlet villain of his diary.

Superintendent Jones symbolized in *Dear Diary* all the thwarting Powers Of This World. In contrast with the janitor, he was everywhere treated as an official and a gent. "J. Gaylord Jones" he signed his checks. Always tipped a nickel more than ten per cent. Had a wife who respected him. Made his barber, whom he called by his first name, cut rather than shave the hair just behind his ears so that it wouldn't look fresh from the hairdresser. Supervised at serenely unhurried intervals the whole chain of apartment houses owned by the corporation syndicate. Soothed in a friendly infuriating manner the ruffled clients, such as the advertising man, who now brought to a final crisis the mystery of the mumbling janitor.

Like a turtle's cozy shell gone soft in one spot, so did the invulnerable normalcy of Mr. Jones contain one lone and fatal eccentricity: vain about his qualities of tolerance and understanding, he dabbled in collecting amiable fuddy-duddies and harmless old crackpots as his janitors. "My characters," he would call them patronizingly. "Say, you should get a look at my mumbling janitor."

In order that Gaylord Jones might wake up each morning with such a smile of well-being on his face, it was necessary, thousands of years ago, that a famine took place east of the Ural mountains. Necessary that a geological accident hung peculiar peninsulas on the northern shore of the Mediterranean. And necessary that apartment syndicates paid good salaries in a New World city which would not have been built if nomads in Asia on shaggy ponies had not shifted some trade routes.

The final product of all these varied centuries and aspirations was J. Gaylord Jones, strolling home to his wife from a celebration of "Be Kind To Trees Week," with a slightly audacious feather in his quiet dark hat. To him the cosmos, with all the known and unknown results of its particular diffusion of atoms, was a family restaurant, the sort of restaurant where beer was preferred jovially to coffee and prudently to whiskey, where reliable investment councilors argued tolerantly with suburban commuters and remarked in well-modulated voices:

"Very worthwhile."

Yet in this man's own solar system and own city and in his very own apartment house, a small gray janitor was tinkering with the boiler in order to murder him.

199

The lingo of the janitor's will-to-power derived from two books. He knew every sentence of both by heart. The first was the Apocalypse, the Revelation of St. John the Divine. The second was an English translation of Fourier's long forgotten prophecies. These had prophesied the transformation of the salty ocean into free lemonade and of ferocious lions into kindly "anti-lions," who would purr and carry children on their backs. As prerequisite to such civic-spirited transformations, Fourier had demanded that the earth stop exuding what he called the Stench of Immorality, which was poisoning the perfumed harmony of all the other planets.

Continuing logically where Fourier had timidly left off, the janitor reasoned in his nightly jottings:

"Whatever lives, misbehaves. Only one cure for the Stench of Immorality: to abolish all living things. Memo: the ribbon on my little finger is to remind me about the new T.N.T."

Some years ago, with clerkish efficiency, he had circled a specific date on his calendar and labeled it "Doomsday and Armageddon". The years passed, and this week the date was due. "Dear Diary: Doomsday very, very soon; and I'm as nervous as the day I addressed my high-school forum on *Saintly Meekness*. Just like then, I keep asking myself: will I bungle the job, will I forget any little detail, will the angels Michael and Gabriel say I was a FLOP? Memo: to try to remember what I meant with that ribbon on my finger."

During this ultimate week, the janitor was revising his last will and testament. His will was quite a separate document from his diary. Imaginary slights provoked ceaseless new wills. Each will changed the proportions in which he allotted his non-existent millions to his nephew named Boone, to a manicure girl named Mimi, to his parrot who had no name, and to his dog, a Great Dane named Sitting Bull. The parrot was green and talkative. Nobody knows what color Sitting Bull was originally; his habit of napping in the basement coal-bin gave him a hue which made the children of the tenants whimper in their sleep.

The large kindly animal was smudged coal-black from snout to tip of tail except for his eyes. Friendly and sad and just a little reproachful, the eyes of the Great Dane became flamingly blood-shot from the irritating coal dust, so that to the non-veterinary they appeared red with rage. Every Sunday evening the advertising man from upstairs would tell his wife, who did not know the janitor was always out Sunday evenings, that he must go to the basement to complain about the cold radiators.

One day Anna-Maria, the young Sicilian masseuse who used to meet the ad man in the coal bin, failed to show up for their usual Sunday tryst there, although up to now her enthusiasm had even exceeded his own. Ever after, she spent her Sunday evenings in church and became the apartment house's most lavish contributor to the League of Decency fund. Pressed for an explanation by her disappointed Sunday friend, Anna-Maria would only shake her pretty head at him, crossing herself and sobbing hysterically:

"*Malocchio* . . . red in the dark, red and black . . . *Dio mio* sends *diavolo* with the Evil Eye to punish me . . . red in the coal bin . . . oh *malocchio, malocchio* . . . "

Quite a different young lady was Mimi, the peroxide blonde manicurist. Reserved, business-like, and not over-rouged, she worked in the hairdresser shop on the next block and once had been listed in the janitor's will. Her unevenly dyed hair lacked that skill and good taste which adorn an unsoundly spent life. Stars of red ink in the margin of the janitor's diary marked the day when she suddenly ceased to be named "Mimi," being rechristened "the Great Whore of Babylon" — happy phrase coined by Saint John.

The janitor had never met Mimi, had seen her only at a distance. Nor was she ever to have any inkling of his existence. Once on a windy morning he had peeked upward at her from his basement window as she was skipping wholesomely along the street, humming:

"Mama don't want no rice, no peas, no cocoanut oil."

Of course, she did not notice him next day when they accidentally entered the same streetcar.

Not notice him? After yesterday's intimacy, not to recognize him today? Betrayal! Mistakenly he assumed she was only pretending not to know him.

A whole month he devoted to brooding over the Mimi incident. This was the historic month when he proclaimed a new fast for ascetics: "O noble Great Dane, give me the strength never to touch breakfast foods that crackle." Month of neglected furnaces during his spiritual trial. Month of lonely experiments with black and white magic, of bitter renunciation, and of final hard-won rebirth. Month of self-purification when he wove his omnipresent hair-shirt out of the small strings he salvaged from trash-baskets.

Truth at last! Suddenly Mimi's identity was revealed to him in a vision sent from a more sweet-smelling planet. "O

Fourier, truth is bought with suffering; how Lonely but how Great we are!" The very flames she thwarted on the streetcar were, it now appeared, flames she had fanned in him on purpose: by wildly disporting herself above his basement window. Why? To distract him from his mission! "Listen, parrot who hath no name: this — this — this *body* of hers — ah, how blind I have been!" He had never known what the word "fleshpot" meant, so recurrent in his readings, and had never dared look it up in the dictionary. But obviously this body of hers—"Dear Diary, how clearly I see life now!"—was one of those vast, gaping fleshpots of the Wild Parties of Egypt about which the Good Book had so many things to say.

His hands trembling with moral zeal, the janitor recorded his new discovery. At Armageddon his diary would unveil exactly who it was who lurked behind her camouflage. How the world would gasp if only it knew! Each night he jotted down some new strategem for warning a complacent solar-system against her plots of interplanetary pollution.

"Hell's proud empress of beauty and damnation," he lyrically raged against her, more attracted to her than he had ever been during her more demure role as Mimi the manicurist.

"O Sitting Bull," he intoned in that inconsistent hybrid diction of his, one-third Apocalyse, one-third Fourier's romantic 19th-century diction, and one-third janitor-argot. "O Bullsie-pupsie, you big innocent beast of woodsy Nature, lend me the simple wisdom of your brooks and trees against my passion. And say, don't let no more devils of Babylonian temptation go hanging around my bed tonight while I sleep. You just bark at them, see, bark and nip them; there's a good pup."

All that night the loyal coal-black animal whined in sympathy beneath his master's cot, hearing him groan again and again into his pillow:

"Mimi, you ratted on me."

2

The beneficiaries of Mimi's unmasking were the nephew named Boone, the Great Dane named Sitting Bull, and the parrot who had no name. To them the janitor transferred in his will, in ever fluctuating proportions, her former share of his imaginary estate.

The nephew, an orphan since boyhood, was being sent to the local college by the generosity of his bachelor uncle, who was poor but nepotist-minded. The boy's first name had been given

him by his parents in honor of Daniel Boone. The great back-
woodsman had been their favorite American hero in their Good
Citizenship class in highschool. This common historical interest
was what first brought them together. Later as scholarly zeal
ripened into a more tender sentiment, they exchanged their
first kiss behind their secret rendez-vous, a brass statue of the
pioneer erected by the Junior Chamber of Commerce and labeled: "In reverent memory of our Danny Boone, blazer of new
trails for the Youth of America."

At the christening of the first fruit of their married love,
Boone's parents insisted that every one, including the congregationalist pastor, wear a Daniel Boone masquerade costume.
After weakly protesting, the pastor declared, "The way I figure
it, fellows, the eleventh and chief Commandment is to be a Good
Sport." With these words he donned his big furry Boone cap
with the rest of the revelers and ever afterwards referred to the
occasion as "the most glamorous night of my life."

Boone's mother was promoted to assistant secretary of the
local Y.W.C.A. the same year that his father rose to the rank of
calisthenics instructor at the Y.M.C.A. Taking these new honors
not as selfish privileges but as a spur to new duties, the happy
pair organized a community rally which successfully raised funds
for a new gymnasium, called *The Daniel Boone Fireproof Gym.*
Soon came the gala inauguration of the new structure; their
loftiest dream was about to be fulfilled. Out of sheer excitement
over the great day, Boone's father lit the first and last cigarette
of his life, exclaiming "Whee!" There ensued the first and last
quarrel ever to trouble their affectionate comradeship when
Boone's mother knocked the offending commodity from her husband's lips. It fell amid the open gasoline cans left by the
chauffeurs.

As the Congregationalist pastor put it in his simple and
dignified funeral sermon, their ever cheerful service to the youth
movement had accomplished so much good in so short a time
that their lives were full and rich even though their passing was
tragically young.

"And at least," he concluded, "they passed away on the
same night, always together up to the end; and I, as their
spiritual adviser at the christening of their first-born, can assure
you that this is how they would have wished to go: together."

When the orphan reached his sixteenth birthday, he was
solemnly invited to his uncle's apartment-house basement.
There, with one hand reposing on the head of the Great Dane

named Sitting Bull and the other hand on his nephew's shoulder, the janitor looked Boone straight in the eye and said:

"Boone, you're going to be a man now. That means you'll meet girls; and especially when you go to college with all those cocktail parties after football games, you'll have to face strange and new temptations, just as the earlier folks did at Babylon. Since your Dad and Mom are no longer with us, it's my job to warn about that side of life. Read the books of Fourier and the Apocalypse. I kind of can't put into words what I mean by temptation and by being — well, clean-limbed; there's things we know and never talk about; but when you're older you'll catch on to what I mean, get me?

"Well, every time you meet temptation and you feel as how you can't control yourself one minute more, that's the time to ask yourself just one simple question, which'll never fail you, and that question is: *Would Daniel Boone have done it?* If you'll never forget that question, you'll always be a young gent, like your Dad would've been proud of if he was here today and if only he hadn't touched tobacco during that awful Babylonian party at the opening of the Boone Gym."

In the autumn in which the janitor was to proclaim Armageddon, Boone was beginning his Freshman year. He despised his uncle for being what Boone's room-mate called "bourgeois." The janitor was always too conscientiously busy (as Boone complained to his room-mate) at some homely domestic task, such as tinkering—with a grim smile—at the safety valves of the boiler system or jotting things in that prosaic-looking diary into which no one ever bothered to glance.

"I'm not like my uncle," Boone would boast in front of his mirror; "I'm a Free Spirit; I defy all sorts of conventions."

In contrast, the janitor regarded Boone, the last of his clan, with hero-worship. Doubtless there were gloomy moments when the uncle considered the nephew too recklessly advanced in his mildly agnostic views on religion. But the janitor, too, as he mellowly remembered, he, too, had doubted the Apocalypse in his youth. What of it? In the end at Armageddon, such a rosy-cheeked Prodigal Son would undoubtedly see the light and join the shock-troops of the angels. So the uncle, with the tolerant smile of Us Who Know, refused to worry even when he received the following letter from Boone:

"Uncle, I want you to know I have become an ICONO-CLAST. I feel completely emancipated from medieval superstitions. Progress is all that matters, and we American youth should wake up and race in its front ranks."

Soon thereafter, as the uncle had hoped, Boone wrote a hasty correction to this letter:

Dear Uncle,

In my last letter I was an intellectual. But anything becomes extreme if it goes too far. So my philosophy now is: sound mind in sound body. On account of this philosophy about being sound in body as well as intellectual, I'm going to take up football.

I don't mean I'll really play it, but I'll watch it from our new stadium. For this a fellow needs a pennant. Too bad I don't have enough money to buy one. Also a fellow needs a coat. It sure would be nice to have one.

Your loving nephew,
Boone.

P.S.1. I looked at the works of that foreign writer whom you told me to read: Fourier. Deep stuff; makes a fellow think. Just like Kipling's poem about "If."

P.S.2 Thanks for all those pages you sent me from the Apocalypse about "the Beast that was, and is not, and yet is." I've put both Fourier and the Apocalypse at the top of my "must" list, the way I would any book you so kindly suggest. I am looking forward awfully to reading both of them just as soon as I get free time again: say, after I graduate. College keeps me too busy to read books.

And still more recently:

"Dear uncle, I am taking a course in government. I am getting ever more Liberal, and it feels wonderful. It all ties up with what is called the Industrial Revolution, which alone caused free government by the man in the street without losing sight of the fact that commerce is the lifeblood of trade. Naturally by 'liberty' I mean true liberty, not the kind which is always debunking but the kind which is sound."

As a postscript to this last letter:

"I'm so emancipated I don't mind at all that my own uncle is only a janitor. Naturally I won't go too far out of my way to mention it at my frat house. But don't think for a moment I'm ashamed of it. I believe in equality and in ignoring class lines."

The small gray janitor replied to this postscript with the

most magnificent gesture of his life. He sent his nephew a check
to buy a racoon coat.

The uncle's profound understanding of the academic world
derived from the movies. Over twenty years ago this source had
informed him that all unperverted young gentlefolk are panting
to become "collegiate" by wearing a "coonskin coat." Hollywood
found in these oversized coats the same magic that totemistic
savages find in the beast-skins used during puberty rites. The
coats conveyed a borrowed virility to the young campus war-
riors who could afford to pay for them. The janitor's mysticism
responded joyously to this shaggy pageantry of football rallies.
In his basement he prayed for the day when his nephew, attaining manhood, might join in the great furry ritual, preferably
accompanied by a torchlight parade under a full moon. Meanwhile, America's coonskin folklore died out even in Hollywood
with the death of the 1920s—but not in the mind of the gray
janitor, for he saw no new movies after that era.

His last movie, a romance about higher education in a speak-
easy, widened his esthetic horizon by introducing him to a dare-
devil musical discovery called "syncopation." This sang out at
him through a tireless young lady in short skirts with a boyish-
bob hair-do and a hat shaped like a flower pot. Snuggling with
hip flasks and fellow scholars in the rumble seat of a fast car,
defying the gods at a speed of 40 miles an hour, she was raced
from saxophone serenades to dance marathons—and spent her
spare time sitting on flagpoles or swallowing goldfish. Blushing
prettily, the janitor recalled for the rest of his life every word
of one of her songs in America's new music:

> If it's naughty to rouge your lips,
> Twist your shoulders and shake your hips;
> Let a lady confess, "I wanna be ba-a-a-ad!"

"Dear Diary, never again a movie," he had written after
staggering home from this; "they'll get theirs all right at Armageddon. Tobaccogindamnation."

3

The check for Boone's raccoon coat (plus certain more furtive expenditures for nitroglycerin) used up the janitor's modest
bank account. Liberated from these material bonds of the universe, he decided to bring about its spiritual climax at once:
doomsday. If only somebody would first make a martyr of him
by doing him some monstrous or even petty injustice! For martyrdom was the surest and most traditional route to sainthood.

In the past he had tried to provoke martyrdom by muttering insults to his superintendent. Each time, the only reaction of the latter, who never listened carefully to such blurred mumblings, was to force a cigar upon the mumbler and call him "my pet character." Mr. Jones was proud of "my tolerant understanding temperament."

How the pious gray janitor prayed and prayed for persecution at the hands of Gaylord Jones! Always had prayed for it but today more than ever because this evening Mr. Jones was scheduled to inspect the basement. "Dear Diary: here I sit, waiting for Goliath to storm my basement and thinking maybe it's been plain petty of me to bear grudges. I'll forgive him, that's what I'll do, and save his life and call off The Explosion at the last minute if only he'll do me that one little favor of martyrizing me. But if he still refuses to persecute me. . ."

The little janitor was not an authority on blowing up buildings. He had never blown up any buildings before. So he played safe or, rather, unsafe by using all possible methods at the same time.

First and simplest, he began feeding the boilers to the bursting point this evening, removing all safety valves. But this would not have done enough damage alone. For more than twenty years, with the money he saved by giving up movies, he had found subtle ways of buying and hiding explosives. He included dynamite because the dramatic connotations of its name appealed to him. He included other varieties with more prosaic chemical names but even more deadly. Each seedling of doomsday he nursed with the same impartial gentleness. "My roses of wrath," he called them in his diary. At other times, more often of late, he called them "God's roses of wrath."

While waiting for Mr. Jones this evening (an event heralded in *Dear Diary* with initial captials as "the Descent to the Basement"), the janitor killed time by piling angry roses into an unflaming corner of the furnace. There the fire would not reach the explosives until after a time-span, a span long enough to coincide neatly with the time needed for the steam to blow up the boiler system. He calculated that this assault on two fronts would storm even so Satan-protected an apartment house.

At this moment, as the janitor stood at the furnace calculating, J. Gaylord Jones made his long awaited Descent. He was pondering the advertising man's demand for hot radiators and was thinking to himself something like this:

"Oh these tenants! You'll never know what they'll quibble about next; when it isn't the cold, it's the cockroaches. Want to live like sultans; think they're too fancy for ceilings that leak even a tiny bit and wiring that gives them even the tiniest electric shocks and good old pipes that flood their kitchens not even an inch deep. But I show 'em; the landlord still has a few democratic rights left; I let 'em wait a full month each time before I phone any plumber or electrician. Ha! might as well enjoy this housing shortage while it lasts."

To his surprise Mr. Jones found the boilers already glowing with heat. Tonight was the night: ecstatically the janitor was heaping ever more coals into the furnace as if officiating in some orgiastic ceremony, a fire-god frenzy. Perched on his left shoulder was the parrot who had no name, shrieking at the flames, while the Great Dane trotted back and forth at his master's side with ever more excited yelps.

Normally the superintendent was observant. But so amazed was he to discover heat in any of his agency's apartment houses, that he overlooked two related facts. First, all safety valves were missing. Second, none of this heat reached the complaining advertising man or any other apartments; for days the janitor had been sawing the connecting pipes in half and soldering them shut.

"That's the spirit we like to see, busy as a honey bee," rhymed the superintendent to break the conversational ice. "Just thought I'd drop by for a gab-fest. The corporation likes me to be kind of a big brother to its personnel. Any favor I can do for you?"

"So Lucifer has come to spy on God again," was the quick reply. "Martyrize me; that's the only favor I need. Persecute me right now; I stand ready. The oceans will taste like lemonade. Everywhere lots of anti-lions, all around."

The mumbling was so faint and slurred that, as usual, Mr. Jones could not understand it. But politely he pretended to:

"Certainly, certainly, whatever you say. And I suppose you'd like me to stroke Sitting Bull. Children and dogs always love me."

The Great Dane growled so malevolently and the parrot screamed so warningly that Mr. Jones hastily withdrew his hand. "I feel like browsing around a bit, instead. See you've painted two posters on the walls. I'm a great one for art myself, and inspiration, and all those things. If there's one thing I can't stand, it's a Babbitt; that's why I always lived in the State of

New York; you couldn't drag me with ten horses to the Middle West. The pen is mightier than the sword any day of the week."

Getting no response, he began assessing the janitor's two drawings esthetically, speaking half to himself:

"Now, I go for paintings I can feel. They've got to hit me where I LIVE. This first poster really hits the jackpot with those gold and white sketches of harps and wings. Mind if I read what it says underneath? Ha, it says: 'List of the Saved. First, Boone. Second, Sitting Bull. Third, the parrot who hath no name.' Very nice, very nice. But hmmm, under the flaming red poster on the other wall you've written: 'List of Those Who Die To-night. First and most of all, the superintendent. Second, Mimi, the Great Whore of Babylon. Third, myself in her repentent arms. Fourth, the advertising man because of all those giggles in my coal bin. Fifth, the universe.' Hmmm, wonder which superintendent you mean; must be that has-been whose job I got as reward for my secret report on how I caught him mollycoddling the tenants. Well, I'll always back a practical joke to razz some has-been; your second poster, the humorous one, suits me even better than the first."

"A Beast will rise up out of the sea," recited the janitor, "having seven heads and ten horns and the name of blasphemy. War in heaven. And a Sign, great and marvelous. Seven angels victorious over the Beast, singing the song of the Lamb."

Inside the janitor's skull, the overlooked little restless cell had now conquered all the other brain cells, which no longer dared hold back its will-to-power.

"The sea; sure, the lamb and the sea. Chin up, man; easy does it," oozed the superintendent, having no inkling of what was up but wanting to soothe the nice little fellow. "I must say I've never seen a boiler puff so with heat. More than they deserve upstairs. Better not give 'em too much service, or they might forget who's holding the whip-hand this year, we or they."

The soldering-shut of pipes and removal of safety valves and excess of fuel and steam were creating an eerie atmosphere of vast pressure, striving and pushing and ever hotter. Pressing and puffing.

"Since your bad nerves come from overworking for *them*," continued Gaylord Jones, "you'll always find me out there slugging for the rights of the basement against all the upper floors. I've my own ways of finding out the income of everybody upstairs, and beLIEVE me, they're all duds. I've also ways of rewarding your personal loyalty to me. I'll have your basement air-conditioned while you enjoy a paid vacation in a sunny cheerful nerve-clinic."

The superintendent beamed with relief. Surely his white-lie promises of air-conditioning and paid leave had now ended the crisis.

"Uh huh," replied the small gray janitor, reverting from his Apocalyptical tone to a tone of respectful meekness. "Uh huh. Pardon me, Sir, while I keep the fire from going down." Into an unflaming sector of the furnace he threw a thick wooden box. Unknown to his visitor, the box contained an additional batch of assorted explosives.

"Guess I'll be trudging along now." Nonchalantly the superintendent was strolling toward the cool safety of the basement door.

In an instant the janitor's small body was shielding the doorknob. Contemptuously the towering Mr. Jones shoved him aside. But at once the still more gigantic Great Dane bounded to his master's aid with a roar of rage. A pair of enormous jaws closed upon the visitor's right ankle. The fangs closed with coy self-restraint, not quite drawing blood but with just enough pressure to hint what they could do.

"Greatwhoreofbabylon," commented the shrieking parrot who had no name. "Doomdoomdoomsday. Iwantacracker."

During the rest of the conversation, Sitting Bull kept his strategic grip on the ankle. Every time the ankie's owner tried to escape, the jaws began tightening. Meanwhile, the practical-minded janitor bolted the thick basement door. Through it no shout for help could reach the apartments upstairs, where the freezing ad man was at this moment opening a new package of paper handkerchiefs.

Mr. Jones resorted to applied psychology, confident, patient, persuasive:

"Of course, you know you don't mean to harm anybody. Only a bit tired. The old nerves need a once-over; every new-model streamlined janitor knows it's smarter to see a saw-bones than to be pushing up the daisies. Here, smoke one of my Havanas, and let's talk it over man to man as two old colleagues of the little old housing game."

"Visions, visions, seven heads, the breaking of nations. Who dares to laugh at me now behind my back? Who'll try to boss me around in my basement? For tonight I officially predict the explosion of Satan Jones and myself and the whole universe— except for Boone and Sitting Bull and the parrot who hath no name. Everything is completely official. Whoever is not with me is against me."

4

Boone had missed the great game.

The unusual expense of the raccoon coat, so difficult to order, so utterly out of fashion, used up the check from his uncle. After the nephew had also bought the football pennant on which he set his heart, not a penny was left to buy a ticket to the football game itself. But he vowed to act afterwards as if he had attended. He planned to lose himself among the spectators after the game and to act as if he belonged among them and to wave his pennant with neither more nor less fervor than they. What if he ran into any girls he knew and they stared at him with scorn or half-suspicion? Well then, he would say, "Some game!" and stare right back, just as normally as ever you please, as if to say:

"You can plainly see MY conscience is clear. But what about YOURS?"

How proud the uncle would have been, had he seen the nephew today! How splendid was Boone's splendor as he waited, haughty and raccoon-decked, outside the barred ticket-gate, wistfully hearing the football cheers inside the stadium! Unbowed, there he stood in his outer darkness, not with gnashing of teeth but like an emperor lordly even in exile.

At last the game was over. Boone's college happened to be the winner. He waved his pennant, yelled, and infiltrated into the core of the crowd leaving the stadium. Sincerely he felt himself into the role of the well-seated patriot who has been watching every pigskin nuance and yelling all afternoon. Sounding convincingly hoarse kept him too busy to wonder why the crowd seemed interested in other questions than whether he had seen the game.

Back to the campus he marched with the victors. There he paced haughtily up and down the soggy lawns. For hours. Though cold, the day was not yet cold enough for such a weighty overcoat. But functionalism be damned! Half smothered, he had been wearing it until evening now, so furry and sleek and black and imperial, up and down the campus for all to behold.

"Cracker!" the parrot was shrieking at this very same moment. "Beastlambwhore. Bab-bab-babylon."

"I understand," the understanding superintendent was saying. "So we disagree. Let's be frank about it. But let's be reasonable about it also; let's agree to disagree, like in the British parliament. But say, it's getting late; must be time for me to hit the old feedbag again. You know how wives are, haha, about waiting late with hot grub; guess I'll head for home now and call it a day. OUCH, get that damn dog off my leg!"

By now, both men were talking past each other; but by talking alternately, they still kept up the convention of address and reply. It was the janitor's turn, and he "replied" to the superintendent:

"A new calendar! You are now listening to an official announcement. No more seven days in the week. No more seven anywhere. Because the Beast has seven heads. A new national holiday to celebrate my parrot's birthday. He who hath no name. No months allowed more than 29 days each unless they pay tribute to my nephew. Sitting Bull as Santa Claus, dressed in a red robe with sleigh bells that jingle. No anti-lions allowed to swim in the lemonade if they laugh at me openly or—in secret."

"Seven days; so that's it? Your health, your—hmmm— mental hygiene, can't stand working all seven days? Why didn't you tell me sooner? From now on I need your work only six days a week. In fact, you've my permission to go away right now. This very minute."

Back and forth paced the nephew, from lawn to lawn. The football game was long over. It was a nipping evening in late autumn, ever cooler. Perhaps cool enough, after all, to justify his coat.

"Big unclean Fleshpot of Babylon. Destroy, destroy. Manicurist across the street. Kill and kill. They're sending thoughtwaves against me from the fourth dimension. Whore, whore, whore of Babylon. Kill, kill, kill."

"Killkillkillacracker. Crackerofbabylon. Iwantawhorewhorewhore. Iwantacrackercrackercracker."

"How about Atlantic City? A really long rest. For as long as you feel like it. Now, hold on; don't worry about expenses. Old J.G.J. takes care of such details. The stork never blest my wife and me with little packages from heaven so I like to think of all my little janitors—and their Great Danes also—and their parrots, too; that is, if they have parrots—the way I would think of my own dear children. Now if you and that nice hard-working dog will only let me get out of this building quick, then I can get you all—that parrot, too—that parrot's playing on your team, too, isn't he?—can get you all a whore; no, I mean a cracker— no, I mean can buy you some presents, yes presents, wonderful presents; excuse my nervousness, slip of the foot—I mean, slip of tongue; losing my foot on things—I mean, losing my grip on things, but the pain in my foot, those sharp—HELP! those teeth again."

The flames were at last penetrating the wooden boxes in the far end of the furnace. The pressure in the basement grew ever intenser as the steam in the boilers seemed to be racing with the dynamite in the furnace as to which would explode first.

"Kill and kill. Armageddon. Mimi, my thoughts are with you in this hour. In a couple of minutes the building blows up."

Up and down strode the nephew. Lonely orphan of that famous fire in the Daniel Boone Gym. Waving his football pennant with corybantic abandon.

Why couldn't he run into any girls he knew? Why did nobody pay attention to his shaggy new coat? It felt so wonderful to be a Free Spirit, a Lone Wolf and young, instead of being a slave of Bourgeois Convention like his cautious gray uncle. To Boone, furrily triumphant, this was the greatest day in history.

"Doomsday right now. The greatest day in history. Will you still gyp me out of being a martyr? In one minute the steam in the boilers blows up. In one minute the dynamite in the furnace explodes; universe likewise. I'll explode also but not Boone. I also: *even God must end*"

"End," echoed the parrot who had no name. "Iwantadoomsdaycracker. End. End."

The Great Dane named Sitting Bull, so formidable a minute before, began whining and cringing like a scared puppy, as if his canine nervous system were feeling the sudden increase of pressure in the bursting boilers. Feeling the animal's grip relax, the superintendent regained his usual composure.

"Why, the way you're talking," he chided archly, "I'd almost think you're going to blow your top."

"Oh my God!" he added a second later, noting for the first time that the dial of the boiler system was really and truly at the explosion point. "Then you really mean what you're saying? And you'd rather be a martyr and pretend you're God or something than get dandy presents like an air-conditioned basement? Oh, I'll do anything you say if you can stop the explosion. I swear I'll make you a martyr. I'll be very tactful and understanding about it. Yes, yes, my friend, YOU'RE GOD—"

The minute ended. The boilers exploded. The furnace exploded. The explosives exploded. The apartment house came to an end. So, of course, did the universe (because in an arbitrary cosmos a little gray janitor did happen to turn out to be God).

The whole universe and all things in it. The end. No more stench of earth to excruciate the perfumed stars. No more stars either. End of all, with one inscrutable exception: up and down strode the unharmed nephew of God, heeled by an ethereal parrot and the wraith of a Great Dane. Triumphant in his raccoon-skin coat, round and round he strode on the empty air where once had been a campus. Round and round and up and down. Forever now, through an eternity of repetition,

In his sleek and glossy new coat.

SEVEN POEMS

William Jay Smith

ELEGY

For Bateman Edwards, died September 1, 1947

I stood between two mirrors when you died,
Two mirrors in a dimly lighted hall,
Identical in all respects.
Two mirrors face to face reflecting endlessly
Reflection's end.
The wind had blown a few faint notes upon a pipe,
And died away, or seemed to die.
I stood between two mirrors in the hall.
Outside, the wheels had cut the gravel, and the sun-
Flower nodded to the sun; the air was still.
The deer that browsed upon a distant hillside
Lifted his antlers like a coral tree
Forgotten in midsummer undersea.
And from the delicate dark bridges which the spider
Spun from branch to branch,
In desolation hung
One leaf, announcing autumn to the world.
The world that evening was a world of mirrors
Where two great dragons from opposing caves,
Mirror their eyes and mirror all the scales
Of their long bodies and their giant tails,
Emerged. And all that had seemed human was confined
In terror in the limits of the mind,
And coiled, uncoiled within my memory.
In your sudden dying you became the night
Which I must add to darkness now

215

To make the morning bright,
To have day break, and daybreak
Melt the mirrors. But I know
You cannot hear me, hear me,—O
Dear friend, good morning and good night.

CHRYSANTHEMUMS

I had, here in the room before you came,
A dark delight announcing as with drums,
Your coming, and the closing of the door,
Upon a table top, obese and tame,
These lion-headed flowers,
Four chrysanthemums.

A painter would have loved them, and been glad
To have them within reach: to see
Is mad, and madness teaches
Nothing if not love.
Great kings lay murdered in the flower beds:
I had, upon a table in this room,
Their four crowned heads.

In life we are often lonely, wanting death,
A kind of love, not quite
Like this, a somnolence of light,
A glory which is native to the sun,
A poem in the landscape brooded on.

Dark springs, how dark;
And from the world's four corners, flowers
Like the heads of shaven Danes,
Huge and listless lions' manes,
Look down upon us where we lie
In darkness now, and overpowered die
Of love, of love.

BALLAD FROM BEDLAM

'Let Huldah bless with the silkworm—the ornaments of the
Proud are from the bowells of their Betters.'
—Christopher Smart

The firefly corresponds in urgent letters;
He is repaid in the notes of the nightingale.
The gullet of the shark rides out the gale:
Our ornament derives from the bowels of our betters.
My grandfather, Billy Smith, had an Irish setter's
Piercing eye, and a temper quicker than quail.
Our ornament derives from the bowels of our betters.
Faith was the name of his wife; she was hard as a nail:
Undertakers are the real go-getters;
Give me the Glory Road, the Oregon Trail,
A worm to clothe the Proud, a peak to scale:
Our ornament derives from the bowels of our betters.
God bless the hermit crab, the Veteran
Of Foreign Wars, the intestine of the whale,
The old man's rattle, and the infant's wail:
Our ornament derives from the bowels of our betters.

WATER COLOR

The boy in swimming is out to prowl,
Break wind and water round the orange rind,
Naked trip and nip the homing owl,
Not unlike the hawk, unlike the hind.
In cobwebbed caves lie poisoned arrowheads;
The sunlight strikes the water like a gong.
Marigolds are reeling in their beds;
All the clocks in Switzerland are wrong.
Bobbypins for little Goldenlocks,
And for the happy fisherman a fly.
The coffee bubbles over on the rocks:
Draw the shade against the morning sky.

A FEW MINUTES BEFORE SUNSET

Heir apparent, prince of purest majesty,
His throat a fine and fluent question mark

Of eloquent and almost aquiline intensity,
The swan invades the pool, the polar dark,
And glides into a hall of mirrors, all
Reflecting him: the world is destitute.

Let every eye then follow him forever
Down marble passages, in golden rooms,
Until this work of reverence is done.
All one can remember is a river,
And a mother who must mourn a dear, dead son,
Summer and the swan, the cold, white plumes.

ON HER ARRIVAL

On ocean's peacock blue, on seas of flame,
Across the cold Atlantic, crowned, and foam-
Encircled, comes the girl who bears my name,
Now moves my love toward England, and toward home.

Halyards leap with signal, time, and tide,
Ships their courses keep in claret sounds,
While earthward moves my life, my wife, my bride,
Over the sea my huntress and her hounds.

Diana, darling, quickly, death must die,
And absence, meaning death, give life, give birth.
Then let me live forever in your eyes:
They are the darkest corners of the earth.

SEASCAPE

Each abandoned shell
A habitation and a cell,
Abode and refuge to a desert band,—
My eye moves with them, and the beach tonight
Goes forth to greet the solemn anchorite,
The hermit crab out walking on the sand,
Bonsoir, Bernard l' Ermite.

Tonight there are other lovers in our bed,
And those are skeletons upon the shelf.
I—I am a stranger here myself,
Ben Franklin in a cap of marten fur
Among Europe's powdered heads.

A wind from the sea; the crab darts
Back into his hole,—and home is where one starts,
The barbarous ocean breaking on the reef,
All that internal structure of belief,
The world that is outside that is the heart's.

THE AMATEURS

Howard Nemerov

"OF COURSE something must be done. That could have been said six months ago." Anna jingled her golden bracelet, pulling it by one of its bangles round and round her wrist. "You all sit here and say something must be done, somebody has to do something —no wonder his life's a mess, for he does get to hear about it, you know."

"Will you stop rattling that bracelet, please?"

"Does it make you nervous, Osmin? You've been very easily upset, since you started working for *Time*."

"Me—nervous? Ha. I've noticed that compulsive little gesture of yours with the bracelet, Anna, I've seen it for a long time now. You're sure you're all right? I mean, quite certain, are you?" Osmin, a lean young man, dark-complected and with silky black hair, settled back in the corner of the sofa. His insolent smile seemed to suggest that he had scored a hit, a very palpable hit with his remarks; but no, it was only the smile he automatically assumed after every sentence, and his friends had long since stopped looking for the profundity which, it was implied, lay hidden in every trivial observation.

"Why not beat me, dear," said Anna, twirling the bracelet. "I only do it to annoy."

"If you would only stop it," said Malibron, turning as he always did a silver ring on his fat little finger, "we could get back to the question of Allan. While it's certain that nothing will be done," he added, "I think our concern for our friend is kind and amusing, in a grubby sort of way."

"A wife, or a mistress—or even a job . . ." Nancy suggested vaguely. She frowned, then smiled and shrugged her shoulders.

"Oh yes, yes indeed—" Malibron picked up her words. "But that's typical, absolutely typ-ic-al. The wife, the mistress, the

220

job—or the needle, the bottle, the grand tour. And let me say
I've seen it happen before. You don't know, none of us know,
what would be good—really good for him. So like a grand shop
window, we offer the stock solutions, the ready-made things that
are valuable in case of troubles like his. And like the manager,
well-disposed on Christmas Eve, we come out, very grand, rubbing our hands together, and we say to this poor, poor urchin,
who is rubbing his nose on the glass, 'well, son, what do you
want? Just say the word, anything at all—for we are God, you
know, we are very grand and we want to treat you right'. And
the poor bloody little urchin—"

"I think, somehow, we've heard this before," Anna said, pretending to yawn.

"In somebody's book, wasn't it?" asked Osmin.

After a silence, Anna said, "We might give him Angel.
Would you like that, Angel? You've never met him, have you?"

"Never met Allan Hastings, Angel?" asked Osmin. "My God,
you've got a treat coming. Do you like simple people—I mean,
but really simple?"

Angel uncoiled herself slightly at the other end of the couch.
"I don't know," she said. "It's so long since I've met any." This
got a laugh, for Angel was still 'new' enough in this little circle
to be taken for a wit, a phase that would not last long, since she
was undeniably as serious as she was beautiful. Also she was
younger than the rest, and already their appreciation of her began to give way to their somewhat fussy pedantry, which they
called 'introducing her to things' and 'making arrangements'.

"Well, you'll meet one tonight," Osmin said. "Presently he'll
come in through that door—"

"Osmin will now favor us with a 'character'," muttered
Nancy, getting up. "I'll go in the kitchen, Anna, and fix drinks."
She turned to Angel. "When you've heard this as often as I
have, dear—"

"He'll come in through that door," said Osmin loudly. "Handsome as a somewhat decayed Greek god, neatly and not at all
originally dressed—you won't suspect in the least, until he slides
on the throw-rug in the entrance—" he pointed to the rug. "He
won't fall down, not quite, but as he recovers he will smile
apologetically, take off his hat and look at it as though it had
suddenly been invented in his hands. He will say nothing. He
will sit down, still with that smile on his face, and he will listen.
Like a spectator at a tennis match he will turn his face to the
person who has the ball at every instant. The quality of his

listening is respect, even devotion, coupled it seems with the most imbecile lack of understanding—"

"That's about enough, Osmin," said Anna.

"Oh, no. Enough? Never. He is simple—exquisitely— but *deep,* you know, profound. And when he does say something, everyone attends, deeply, profoundly. 'What about death?' he will say, possibly, 'what about that?' And this, in our complex little group, is a triumph, is a success. 'Ah,' someone will say, 'why didn't I think of that?' Oh, he has, Hastings has, the secret, the key, to all things. He calls Satan by his first name, whatever that may be, he appears the confidant of angels—no pun, darling, was intended— the familiar of principalities, thrones and dominations, the friend of seraphim, the toady and sycophant and courtier of God himself—all because he has said, 'what about death'."

"Aren't you getting somewhat bitter, Osmin?" asked Anna. It was true that Osmin had become very serious in delivering his 'character'—more, even, than serious. His breath came faster, his little smile broadened disclosing sharp, even radulate teeth— altogether his expression seemed fit as much for biting as for speech.

"And after all," said Nancy, who had come back from the kitchen in time to hear the last remarks, "he *is* so right. What about death, indeed?"

"But when Nancy says it," Osmin laughed, "it's not nearly so impressive, it hasn't got that je ne sais quoi—" he kissed his hand mockingly up at the ceiling, and said in a basso profundo: "What about death, what about that? That's the way it should be done."

"My God, Osmin," said Nancy quietly, "how I should enjoy watching your death agony." She set down a tray of drinks on the coffee table, conscious that everyone was staring at her. That sort of remark, everyone silently agreed, was carrying things just too far. After all, you had to know where the game leaves off and becomes something entirely different.

"Well, really," said Osmin at last, "that's a revelation, isn't it?" Osmin had always, if the truth be told, been frightened of Nancy. A year ago, he had been "very serious," as the phrase goes, about her. But something—no one of their friends knew just what—had happened to break that up decisively and in an instant. And what it was, actually, was that Nancy, who was taller and stronger than Osmin, had hit him one evening as the climax to a disagreeable interview which he had intended for a seduction. The blow had been more ways damaging than he cared to recall. Her ring had torn his cheek slightly—but worse, she had stood over him and dared him to strike back. A matter for quick decision, and he had decided for prudence and regretted it nightly ever since.

Now he stood up. "You have that quiet bestial charm," he said, and his smile stretched itself to its automatic suggestion of the greatest profundity—"the sort of thing that Orpheus was able to tame, O virgin and brute." And before any reply could be made Osmin bowed slightly and retired to the bathroom, where he noted without surprise that his hands were trembling terribly.

Of the friends, only Nancy fully appreciated Osmin's remark as referring not to the immediate scene but to an evening fully a year removed in time; thus through her local resentment she admitted a gratitude almost tender to him for this insight—deeper for being accidental—into the heart of another, into, as she put it, a 'foreign power'. She saw at this moment, she felt, deeply into Osmin.

"Like certain saints," she said with prim lightness, "who posthumously reveal the image of the Virgin imprinted on their livers, in color." This too, was very imperfectly understood by the company.

"You see," said Malibron to Angel, "this is entirely the result of talking about Hastings. We never behave this way when we talk about other people."

Angel, however, looked very serious and said, "Why did you say that, Nancy?"

"Oh, why does one say anything? I don't know."

"But it was unkind. He might just be very frightened of dying." Angel made this remark with the most unaffected simplicity of voice and manner.

"God," Anna said softly. "Another one."

"The perfect match for Hastings," said Malibron. Angel blushed. "How charming," Malibron said. "To blush, I mean. When was it, Anna—ten years ago at least—the last time some one blushed in this room?"

"Oh, please," Anna cried in a kind of disgusted supplication. "Please stop." And then, to Angel: "You don't understand, I know. But it's a fact that no one else understands either, and I think no one really wants to."

"About Hastings?" Angel asked.

"Yes, about Hastings," Nancy broke in. "And that's enough. Night after night, and week after week, for six months now. Soon he'll walk in. And then next week Angel will have something to say, she'll have her opinion of Hastings too. Then will you be happy?"

"You see," Anna said, still to Angel, "he was, well, a quite ordinary person until one night—"

"Oh nonsense," said Malibron. "He was never ordinary. He simply did the things you expected from—"

"How absurd. Are you going to pretend he was some kind of genius, then?"

"No, simply a person who—"

"Well, what's wrong with the word *ordinary* then?"

"Oh, never mind. Go right ahead."

"*Critic*," Anna threw him the word with fastidious loathing. "As I said," she went on, "a quite *ordinary* person. Then, one night. . . ." She paused and looked at Nancy and at Malibron, with a look that seemed to say: I hadn't really intended to go through all this again.

At this point Osmin came in again, apparently as perky as ever. He sat down next to Angel, took her hand and said in a conspirator's hoarse whisper: "Whatever they tell you will be a lie. You see, I really know him."

And now the doorbell rang.

While Anna went to answer the door, Nancy stepped back into the kitchen. They could hear, now, deliberate steps upon the stair, ascending. Malibron looked steadily at Angel, who had simply let her hand remain in Osmin's possession, but entirely as though unaware. She was, he considered, a remarkably beautiful girl, tall and very thin, with a serious face and golden hair. For a moment Malibron, who was not usually sensitive to such things, felt a tension in himself, an anxiety, a perturbation, a fear. It was indescribable. She is so . . . uncontaminated, he put it melodramatically to himself—so unknown. For what, after all, do we know about her?

She came—so much they knew—of a rich Boston family. She had run away to New York, and Angel was not her real name. She lived with another girl in what must have been the most unmitigated poverty, and gave lessons in needlework where and when she could get them. Nancy had met her through friends whose children took lessons of her, and under these auspices Angel had been introduced into the circle. But that was all. No one, except perhaps Nancy, knew where she lived, she never met any of them singly but only in the group, where she seemed invariably affable though slightly abstracted, as if thinking of something that had to be done later, when she left them.

Just now it seemed to Malibron oddly important that the scene should be as it was, with Osmin holding Angel's hand, with the heavy steps coming up the stairs, with Anna impatiently twisting the door knob, waiting. If I knew, now, he thought, I could say to them; This is the last time that—but though he felt this with almost obsessive intensity he could not make out what it was that seemed so ominous, what sort of "last time" he meant. With a sigh, between boredom and desperation, he threw the whole situation (whatever that meant to him) away. I don't want anything to change, he thought finally. I know we're trivial, and foolish, and even bored a good deal of the time with each other's company and talk: but I don't want anything to change. When people open doors, the world walks in. It tracks dirt on the carpets, doesn't remove its hat, sits heavily on pathetic little chairs, says the wrong thing at once. You feel you've been accustomed to insolence, but this is new. Compared to this, Osmin is a harmless child. Having said so much to himself, Malibron felt rather stupid. One knows so well, he added, that nothing will change.

Osmin meanwhile looked down at Angel's hand, that rested so limply in his. He noticed with revulsion that the nails were dirty—not much but a little, which to him was worse than if they had been coal black. He could not repress a shudder. Then he saw the red weal of a recent burn that went the length of the girl's thumb, and this seemed to him pathetic, beautiful, he wanted to weep over it. He really did, very much, want to weep. But as the scream of a man wounded and in agony may, out of control, issue in a sound like laughter, Osmin knew himself for one capable of producing, from the deepest and most genuine feelings, only some cheap travesty, a sneer perhaps, immediately to be misunderstood. Angel had made a lucky guess about his fear of death: it was true, and every slur, every embarrassment, the slightest sign of violence, at once related itself for him to his own death, which was a confused vision in his mind both of a time when he should not be, when his body should rot in the grave, and of the terrible last moments when he should feel the sheets grow cold around his legs, and be scarcely able to breathe: this last scene appeared to him with terrible intensity and frequency in dreams.

Our hands, he thought now, are like feeble monsters that we send into the world, to get, and be damaged. How they take the beatings that our greed deserves!

225

Anna pulled open the door, and Allan Hastings stood in the entrance, smiling uncertainly. Angel could not for the moment see what the fuss had been about. He was indeed fairly good-looking, quite tall but not slender—almost powerfully built in fact. And he did not, as he came in, trip or slide in the least, though he did hold his hat somewhat (she thought) apologetically for so large and masterful a person. In his left hand he held a brown paper bag, clutched it really as an object of the utmost fragility and importance. Finally, still smiling, he gave the hat to Anna—it was funny, actually, she curtsied mockingly as she took it, but he didn't notice—and said Hullo Richard, to Malibron, then Hullo Osmin, I hope you're well. And then his eyes, which seemed to Angel somehow vague and unfixed in their regard, took in and tried to focus on her hand in Osmin's. She felt, guiltily, at this moment, that meanings were being drawn, alliances and divisions made, all very falsely, but it would have been too much, now, to take her hand away. And it did not last long; in a moment Anna had come up and introduced them. If he was surprised at finding a stranger there, a new person, it did not show. Unless, she thought, he's just a shade *too* normal, *too* ordinary; and she called to mind some ridiculous bit from a farce, about a half-wit who was coached for the first minute of an interview—the hello, the how are you, the delighted I'm sure —and kept repeating these formulae while his vis-a-vis became more and more desperate.

"How are you," Hastings said to Nancy, who had just re-entered the room; and Angel, as soon as he had turned round, removed her hand abruptly from Osmin's, while he, also, moved decorously further away.

"You're quite late," said Anna.

"Yes. I've been walking." A slight emphasis on the last word made the reply seem to Angel the least bit pompous, as of a person who, without saying so much, wished you to understand that all his activity was significant and remarkable. Osmin possibly felt this too, for he could not resist saying: "from going to and fro in the earth, and walking up and down in it."

"Forgive our literary man," Malibron brought out after a space of silence. "What's in the paper bag?"

"Oh." Hastings seemed surprised and pleased that it should be noticed. "I'd forgot. A present for Anna." And he gave it to her. "It's best to bring presents," he said. "I know how it is. Times are hard."

"Thank you, darling," Anna said, opening the bag. She looked inside, then around at the company but especially at Osmin. Just one word, just one smile, her glance said to him. Then she took the bag into the kitchen. It contained a dozen eggs, six fresh sprats, and about a pound of chop-meat. She put it all back in the bag, which she stuffed into the refrigerator. Then, shrugging her shoulders helplessly, she returned to her friends. It was nothing, really, nothing. *Times are hard.* Well, what was wrong with that? Times were hard. But people didn't bring you eggs and fish and meat, here, to your house, did they? So plausibly, so naturally, with such an air of humble apology for the times, which were hard? They brought, others brought anyhow, cakes, pastry if they came to dinner, brought something excessive and luxurious which you wouldn't have bothered with; they didn't come with the basic elements, did they? picturing, perhaps, the eggs cooked morning after morning for the sullen, lonesome breakfast, the fish—she hated fish—staying till they stank and had to be thrown out?

"You forgot the bread," she couldn't help saying as she passed his chair. But he was listening to Nancy, and didn't hear. Osmin heard, though, and looked sharply at her.

Nancy had been talking quietly but intensely to Hastings. In general silence they heard her say decisively, "You've been wasting it, all of it, letting yourself go—it's like a living death. If you don't want it, if holy poverty is what you're after, give it to me, give it to us—do something with it."

"How nice!" said Osmin bitterly, "how lovely."

Nancy sat up straight and said: "He must realize the position. I don't care how you interpret it. What he's doing is a crime."

"And what is he doing?" This from Anna.

"His money. He gives it to people, strangers. He's just confessed as much."

"And whose business is that?"

"Nancy's, obviously," Osmin said.

"I think we'd better leave this subject," said Malibron. "Interesting as it might prove to be."

Nancy got up. "You don't any of you understand," she said. "Not just little money. Big money. Hundreds of dollars, thousands in a day—all to people in the streets, to anyone."

Everyone now turned to stare at Hastings.

"Obviously," said Malibron, "we must all try to run into you in the street as often as possible."

"And quite possibly," Osmin added, "one or two of the

people he meets in the course of a day belong to the deserving poor."

Then a strange thing happened. Hastings took out his wallet, opened it and handed Nancy a hundred dollar bill. He did this gravely, without the least irony or condescension.

"Oh Jesus," said Osmin. "This is too much. Nicely begged, Nancy, well whined for." He turned to Hastings. "Who are you, anyhow? God? St. Francis feeding the birds? You're mad, you know. I suppose you do know that? Do you think I'm going to ask you for a hundred dollars? Do you want me to ask you for a hundred dollars? That would suit you, wouldn't it?"

Quietly Hastings opened the wallet and extended a bill between his fingers. Osmin looked at it without moving. He laughed.

"The eccentric millionaire! Mass-produced loaves and mechanized fishes!" Then, more quietly, "What is it you're trying to buy, Allan? Give me that." He snatched the note from the extended fingers and, with the elaborate motions of the stage magician, bowing and smiling to the audience, he began tearing it up. Pieces fluttered to the floor, while all stared and were silent.

"Don't, please," whispered Nancy. Osmin laughed again, tore up the last of the note and ostentatiously washed his hands in the air. "I come," he said, "at a higher price."

Malibron stared at the floor. "It was a thousand dollars," he said quietly.

Osmin looked as if he had not understood, then turned very pale and began to shudder uncontrollably. Then, "It doesn't matter," he said. "Not in the least." And he spat on the floor where the torn note lay.

"Bravo, bravo," cried Angel.

"Oh shut up," said Anna. "I've had enough. These are my rooms, you are my guests—either behave or get out." She turned away and spoke more to herself than to them: "One of them spits and the other yells bravo," she said with vast resentment.

This summary made the whole episode modulate quickly into absurdity. Malibron laughed uncertainly, then Nancy, then even Osmin. Finally they all laughed except Hastings.

The laughter was succeeded, nevertheless, by a prolonged and uncomfortable silence. Then at last Malibron spoke, with effort and obviously painful sincerity:

"Maybe it would be a good thing, Allan, if you told us— tried to tell us——what all this is about. What it means to you. I was going to say that we're all your friends, but since a moment ago I've had some doubt of that. Still, if we could . . . *do any thing* . . . understand, even—if we could . . ." He left off helplessly, making odd gestures as if weighing things in his hands.

"It would be better if we forgot all this as quickly as possible," Anna said.

"No," Nancy said. "He owes us an explanation."

"He owes . . ." Osmin laughed once, in her face.

"Well, why not!" Nancy turned on him. If the hundred dollars is what's bothering you, remember that you tried to buy me for less. You think it's greed, I know, and to you that changes everything. Well, it's not greed, it's not. It's something . . . it's . . ." her tone of controlled fury gave way to vagueness. "It is greed," she said in a faint voice. "It is, oh it is."

"That's right, tell me your troubles." said Osmin. "Right this way, folks," he declaimed, "this way to the sin eater's where you will see wonders worked, miracles performed. Come, Allan— slip that camel through that needle's eye."

The sarcasm of the invitation seemed quite lost on Hastings. He sat with his head slightly bent forward, hands on his knees, and began to speak.

"It's hard to explain," he said. "You'll probably laugh. I don't mind that, and I can't argue with you." He took a deep, labored breath. "I'm quite well off, as you know—"

"You surprise me." Osmin sniggered.

"And that may have been a lucky thing," Hastings imperturbably continued, "because as you also may know, I'm not very quick or clever—I haven't anything like your mind, Osmin."

"A tribute! Thank ye kind sir."

"Because I'm so slow, then,—ah," he cried, "it's nothing to be explained. I just, one day, woke up. You people, you're clever enough—when someone says to you, "The World" in that awful and disapproving voice—you know?—why, you're able to surround it quickly with thoughts. Here's a dissatisfied creature, you say, or, Why does he tell this to me? why not to the priests, or the kings, or the senators? But I couldn't get all that on my tongue. And besides, really, no one said anything."

It was comprehensible. That, to them, was the worst. Despite his incoherence there could be no pretending that he did not make himself understood. And it grew worse. Hastings rocked gently back and forth in his chair, as though wrestling to bring up some poison that sickened him inwardly; but all that issued was the word, the jagged, uncut phrase which landed among them as though he spat rocks.

"I saw a blind man. My own blindness, I said to myself. Blind men are angelic, they have merciful faces. I always thought that. He tapped his stick in the gutter, and his face was malicious, was guileful. The evil—innocence of the face, like some awful child. Very fat. This was a rainy day, and I stood there. As if somebody had said The World, in that disgusted voice, and suddenly you felt it. You would never forget, never.

"I can't explain. It was an infection. Everything I ate tasted hot, wicked and dirty. For weeks I could only take water and a little bread. I went to doctors. But it always came to this: that they were puzzled, and I had to explain. Then I knew they were laughing. They sympathized, but they were laughing. And I too, I was laughing at them because they were so helpless. We never said anything, but they must have known."

Speech seemed to become more and more difficult; his breathing, even, was rapid and unnatural.

"I said, we must cut it out, cut it away, get rid of it all. Burn all the junk and go down in the waters, I said. Burn. I said—"

He stopped, seemed to search for a word. His mouth hung open helplessly.

"I don't know, I don't know . . . I don't know."

Although Hastings had been speaking quietly enough, what he said was evidently costing him much, in strength, even in humility, since as so often occurs, the belief that was held with such courage and modesty, such chastity in silence, became in speaking of it outrageous, vulgar and illogical, absurd.

"But you don't *stop*, do you?" cried Nancy. "You don't kill yourself?"

"It's difficult to explain," he muttered. "I said that before." He had been sitting with his head somewhat bowed. Now he raised his face to Angel, and it could be seen that he was passing into some phase of crisis. The muscles of his jaw were set as though in paralysis, there was sweat on his forehead. His eyes, Angel thought, might have been a blind man's eyes, unfocused as though in irrelevant and universal concern.

"You mustn't ask me questions." he said, "because I'm not good at explaining. I only know what is right . . . for me." The last words were spoken in a whisper.

"Into the fold," said Osmin with a triumphal sneer. "The bloody Catholics have got him."

"Now that's good," said Malibron heavily. He stared at the little crucifix on the wall, and stared at it until the others turned to look. Anna said nothing.

230

"Osmin, you're a cheap miserable little bitch." This from Nancy.

"But it's not enough!" Hastings suddenly said, and got to his feet. He stood there and repeatedly struck his fist into his other hand; yet it was not a gesture of anger or even of resentment, but rather somehow of the completest helplessness. "Something definite, final, conclusive . . . the end." He began to walk up and down among them, repeating "the end" at every step. He came to a halt finally before the crucifix—almost he clicked his heels together or made a slight bow, but this might have been unintentional. "Some *pain*, some *pain*" he said, with the utmost emphasis.

Malibron got up and stood behind him, expecting obviously that he would collapse in a moment and Hastings did in fact look like a person on the edge of some hysteria: he seemed to struggle for breath, and his whole body trembled slightly and incessantly.

"Some—conclusive—pain." He brought this out with difficulty. The others were frightened now, not knowing what to expect. Eccentricity had definitely gone over the edge, but into what land, what territory none of them wanted to say or know. It was very well to talk of madness—he's mad, absolutely mad, they said— when a person did something quaint and amusing; but this eccentricity and odd humor of the blood was a joke they had no taste for it. So that at first they were curiously grateful to Osmin for laughing.

"Pain—you talk about pain," Osmin cried. "That's a different thing, a pain, a real pain, you understand—not just the sharp sting in the pocketbook which is the morbid essence of your affair with Lady Poverty. But pain—" he stood up and pointed at the crucifix—"the spear in your side. Allan, the nails. Do you think you could stand up to the nails, Allan?"

"Yes, pain, what do you know of pain?" Angel cried, and Osmin glanced gratefully at her. "Or poverty either? Have you ever been poor? Answer me, have you ever been poor?" She too seemed struck by a curious enthusiasm, elation, difficult to understand or explain. There was such an excitement in her voice as she threw him her question.

"Believe me," Osmin went on. "Believe me—I know pain. I know how to bear it."

Nancy said something aside, obviously vulgar.

"It's not bearing it—that's not the thing," Hastings said in a low voice.

I could stand that pain, even that!" Osmin said. "Even His

231

pain." Obviously he meant it, theatrical as he was. "You could
—truly—drive a nail through this hand." He held up his right
hand, pointed to the palm with his cigarette; then, with no more
ado, drove the burning tip into the hand and ground it out
there.

"Schoolboy stuff," said Nancy distinctly. "We did it for
amusement, winter nights at Vassar."

And there the thing might have—should have—ended. Osmin
was so absurd, standing there with his burnt hand still raised,
but looking otherwise white and drawn and ready to faint.

But Angel said, almost in a whisper, her eyes burning, "That
was wonderful. How many of you could stand that?" Her voice
was intense with admiration, even with love.

"If you two damnable little perverts will stop—" said Anna,
just as Nancy struck Angel across the mouth.

"Look, please!" said Malibron. "That's about enough, isn't
it? Here, Osmin, I'll get some burn ointment. Where is the
burn ointment, Anna?" He hurried into the bathroom.

"Damn the burn ointment," Osmin said. "I meant every
word."

Hastings took a slow step towards him.

"You would?" he asked. "A nail?"

"I've said so," Osmin replied.

"Bluff," said Nancy. This word did it. Or would it perhaps
have gone on anyhow? At any rate, like a vault that opens to a
password in the owner's voice alone, Osmin swung to smoothly
and at once.

He knew (he said) what they thought of him; he knew
especially what Nancy thought of him. He was a buffoon, he
played the fool, he let her beat him—yes, all this came out,
greatly exaggerated—it was because they were unchristian, had
no charity in their hearts, they didn't realize how miserable
life was, how often he had thought of ending it, how he had
endured pain like Prometheus (yes, this famous comparison
also was used), how he studied, learned pain, was one of its
graduate students, its proficients, because in charity, in humility,
in self-loathing and abasement, turning the other cheek . . . and
so on. "You all measure your pride in pains inflicted," he said.
"You count it a good day when you come one over another
person; but I am proud of suffering pain. I *will* to suffer pain."

"Sexy little brute, isn't he?" said Nancy with critical admiration, as though she were, in some proprietary sense, exhibiting him.

"Do you mean it—the nail?" Hastings asked harshly.

"Yes, of course I mean it. Are you frightened? Look, people," Osmin said "I will take the pain, but he is the one who's frightened."

"You will teach this lesson?"

"No." Anna said decisively. "No."

"Oh, yes, yes," cried Angel almost gaily. "I know where there's a hammer and nails." She ran into the kitchen before anyone could stop her, if anyone had proposed to do so.

Anna shook Hastings by the arm. "You don't mean it, you don't mean to do it." He did not reply. "I won't let you do it."

"Do what?" Malibron had returned. "I couldn't find any ointment." Just then Angel came in with a small metal hammer and a nail. "Oh my God!" breathed Malibron. "Is this still going on?"

Hastings took the hammer and nail without looking at Angel. Indeed he and Osmin had all this time simply stared at one another across a space of perhaps five feet; and this silent regard began almost to hypnotize the others.

If it had been simply drunkenness, Anna thought, it would be easy. We'd take away the hammer, we'd have a little fight, but it could be done. Everyone would be relaxed. But no one is drunk, and there's nothing childish about it. They are going to do it.

The realization had by now struck them all and it seemed to produce a paralysis. Malibron said, plaintively, "What will it prove? What is it going to prove?" and sinking into a chair he continued to say just this, this formula, in a voice that was becoming no more than a moan. Angel was evidently and horribly ready to enjoy herself; she accompanied Osmin, holding his uninjured hand, as he backed to the wall. Anna looked away, looked at the crucifix. Only Nancy seemed either unaware or incapable of believing in what would happen.

"They won't do it, it's a joke," she assured everyone in confident tones; then she too began to repeat the phrase as if it were a prayer.

Allan Hastings towered over Osmin. His face was impassive, his eyes dull and without expression. He held the nail in one hand and, in the other, the ridiculously small, dainty-looking hammer.

Osmin put up his right hand to the wall. He was smiling, for this scene represented, perhaps, an ultimate ambition with him. The smile was strained, grimace-like, but the intention to smile was unmistakably there.

233

"For you, I do it for you," he whispered to Angel, and she whispered, "yes, I understand."

"Begin, then," Osmin cried with an awful insolence. "What are you waiting for? I forgive you, you know. I forgive you, I forgive all of you." More quietly, he said to Hastings: "You called it a lesson. That's right. My God, how you will learn from this. And me —" he brought back his hand and touched his breast dramatically — " a minute of pain, and then I'll spend my lifetime laughing while you learn about pain. I'll even let you give me the thousand dollars again—for the tuition."

"Stop." Hastings said. "We'll talk about that later."

"What is it, hate? Do you hate each other?" Malibron groaned. "What will it prove, even if he does stand up to it, what will it prove?"

Osmin threw his hand back against the wall, and Hastings set the nail against it.

He struck gently at first, and the nail went in easily enough. Then it hit a bone, and Hastings seemed to go completely to pieces. He smashed with increasing force, sometimes not touching the nail but letting the hammer thud directly on the flesh. Osmin's eyes were open and very bright.

But it did not take long. Soon, with three final blows, given with more strength and less accuracy than was needed, the nail was driven fully in.

"All right," Anna said, as firmly as she could. "That's enough. Now draw it out."

"No." Osmin said. "Let it stay a minute." He was evidently in terrible pain, perhaps only now (as his elation subsided) realizing the pain. "Let him look. Look, Allan. The nail. Look, damn you."

Hastings had turned away, shuddering terribly. The hammer fell to the floor.

"It's not a claw hammer," Malibron remarked. "It's not got anything to draw nails out."

"Oh Jesus." Nancy began to laugh. It didn't seem a hysterical laugh; but rather brilliant, bold and pertinent. Anna went to the kitchen to get — lord knows what, pliers perhaps. But before she got out of the room, the plaster about the nail gave way and Osmin simply fell in a bundle on the floor. The back of his hand was bloodied and raw. Angel went at once to her knees and began to fuss tenderly over him. Now that the crisis had passed, her fierce and perverse exaltation seemed to have gone too; she was almost matronly, there on the floor, and when she raised her face she was crying.

"I'll phone a doctor," Anna said. But Malibron looked intently at her and she stopped.

Hastings was standing in a far corner—a neutral corner, Anna said later—with his back to the room. His fists were clenched at his sides, his posture rigid and strained, his head thrown back.

"He's dead," Malibron said. "Anyone can see he's dead." He knelt by Osmin and took up the wrist, with the nail still in the hand. "He's dead." The wrist fell stupidly back to the floor. "Obviously dead."

They all looked at Hastings. He turned round to face them. He seemed gripped by some spasmodic internal constriction, his face was red, he struggled to breathe, to speak: "My God. Six Hours. Until the ninth hour. And this. Oh my God!"

And now, unbelieving, they saw what it was inside him that struggled, that had perhaps struggled all evening, or all his life, to come forth. Laughter. It came up chokingly at first, then in stronger surges it poured forth like blood from the mouth. Helplessly, holding his stomach as if in pain, he roared with deep, healthy laughter.

AN OLD SCHOOLBOOK

James Laughlin

Principles of Geometry
a long time and patiently
you have been waiting for me

to understand your lesson
are your margins still
nervous with my messy scrawl

yes there's the square
head of my roommate Henry
Barkhausen and that one must

be Dick Pinkham who payed
me eighty cents a week
to do his Cicero and there's

fat old Mr Kenington himself
scratching his stomach on
the corner of his desk

during his lectures to us
on the figures that we never
understood but learned

by rote to parrot back
to him in daily tests and if
we got them wrong we used

to run back to the classroom
during lunch & change the
papers in his desk be-

fore he marked them marks
marks I hungered and I
yearned and burned for marks

the way the other boys
craved girls or being on the
hockey team nothing could

stop me nothing did until
I was head boy in school and
now here is my book a-

gain here after twenty
years principles of geometry
turning these pages now I

think I understand the
figures look at these paral-
lelograms & squares these

hollow shapes aren't they
the spaces empty spaces that
spread out through all

the grown-up lives we waited
for with such desire &
see the lines that cut a-

cross the spaces are they
not the things the women and
the money the ambition

and the wars & all the false
ideas that destroy our
life & eat into our soul?

DESIRE AND THE BLACK MASSEUR

Tennessee Williams

FROM HIS very beginning this person, Anthony Burns, had betrayed an instinct for being included in things that swallowed him up. In his family there had been fifteen children and he the one given least notice, and when he went to work, after graduating from high school in the largest class on the records of that institution, he secured his job in the largest wholesale company of the city. Everything absorbed him and swallowed him up and still he did not feel secure. He felt more secure at the movies than anywhere else. He loved to sit in the back rows of the movies where the darkness absorbed him gently so that he was like a particle of food dissolving in a big hot mouth. The cinema licked at his mind with a tender, flickering tongue that all but lulled him to sleep. Yes, a big motherly Nannie of a dog could not have licked him better or given him sweeter repose than the cinema did when he went there after work. His mouth would fall open at the movies and saliva would accumulate in it and dribble out the sides of it and all his being would relax so utterly that all the prickles and tightening of a whole day's anxiety would be lifted away. He didn't follow the story on the screen but watched the figures. What they said or did was immaterial to him, he cared about only the figures who warmed him as if they were cuddled right next to him in the dark picture house and he loved every one of them but the ones with shrill voices.

The timidest kind of a person was Anthony Burns, always scuttling from one kind of protection to another but none of them ever being durable enough to suit him.

Now at the age of thirty, by virtue of so much protection, he still had in his face and body the unformed look of a child and he moved like a child in the presence of critical elders. In every move of his body and every inflection of speech and cast of ex-

239

pression there was a timid apology going out to the world for the little space that he had been somehow elected to occupy in it. His was not an enquiring type of mind. He only learned what he was required to learn and about himself he learned nothing. He had no idea of what his real desires were. Desire is something that is made to occupy a larger space than that which is afforded by the individual being, and this was especially true in the case of Anthony Burns. His desires, or rather his basic desire, was so much too big for him that it swallowed him up as a coat that should have been cut into ten smaller sizes, or rather there should have been that much more of Burns to make it fit him.

For the sins of the world are really only its partialities, its incompletions, and these are what sufferings must atone for, a wall that has been omitted from a house because the stones were exhausted, a room in a house left unfurnished because the house-holder's funds were not sufficient—these sorts of incompletions are usually covered up or glossed over by some kind of make-shift arrangement. The nature of man is full of such make-shift arrangements, devised by himself to cover his incompletion. He feels a part of himself to be like a missing wall or a room left un-furnished and he tries as well as he can to make up for it. The use of imagination, resorting to dreams or the loftier purpose of art, is a mask he devises to cover his incompletion. Or violence such as a war, between two men or among a number of nations, is also a blind and senseless compensation for that which is not yet formed in human nature. Then there is still another compensation. This one is found in the principle of atonement, the surrender of self to violent treatment by others with the idea of thereby clearing one's self of his guilt. This last way was the one that Anthony Burns unconsciously had elected.

Now at the age of thirty he was about to discover the instrument of his atonement. Like all other happenings in his life, it came about without intention or effort.

One afternoon, which was a Saturday afternoon in November, he went from his work in the huge wholesale corporation to a place with a red neon sign that said "Turkish Baths and Massage." He had been suffering lately from a vague sort of ache near the base of his spine and somebody else employed at the wholesale corporation had told him that he would be relieved by massage. You would suppose that the mere suggestion of such a thing would frighten him out of his wits, but when desire lives constantly with fear, and no partition between them, desire must become very tricky, it has to become as sly as the adversary, and this was one of those times when desire out-witted the enemy under the roof. At the very mention of the word massage, the desire woke up and exuded a sort of anesthetizing vapor all through Burns' nerves, catching fear off guard and allowing Burns to slip by it. Almost without knowing that he was really going, he went to the baths that Saturday afternoon.

The baths were situated in the basement of a hotel, right at the center of the keyed-up mercantile nerves of the downtown section, and yet the baths were a tiny world of their own. Secrecy was the atmosphere of the place and seemed to be its purpose. The entrance door had an oval of milky glass through which you could only detect a glimmer of light. And even when a patron had been admitted, he found himself standing in labyrinths of partitions, of corridors and cubicles curtained off from each other, of chambers with opaque doors and milky globes over lights and sheathings of vapor. Everywhere were agencies of concealment. The bodies of patrons, divested of their clothing, were swathed in billowing tent-like sheets of white fabric. They trailed barefooted along the moist white tiles, as white and noiseless as ghosts except for their breathing, and their faces all wore a nearly vacant expression. They drifted as if they had no thought to conduct them.

But now and again, across the central hallway, would step a masseur. The masseurs were negros. They seemed very dark and positive against the loose white hangings of the baths. They wore no sheets, they had no loose cotton drawers, and they moved about with force and resolution. They alone seemed to have an authority here Their voices rang out boldly, never whispering in the sort of apologetic way that the patrons had in asking directions of them. This was their own rightful province, and they swept the white hangings aside with great black palms that you felt might just as easily have seized bolts of lightning and thrown them back at the clouds.

Anthony Burns stood more uncertainly than most near the entrance of the bath-house. Once he had gotten through the milky-paned door his fate was decided and no more action or will on his part was called for. He had paid two-fifty, which was the price of a bath and massage, and from that moment forward had only to follow directions and submit to care. Within a few moments a negro masseur came to Burns and propelled him onward and then around a corner where he was led into one of the curtained compartments.

Take off your clothes, said the negro.

II

The negro had already sensed an unusual something about his latest patron and so he did not go out of the canvas-draped cubicle but remained leaning against a wall while Burns obeyed and undressed. The white man turned his face to the wall away from the negro and fumbled awkwardly with his dark winter clothes. It took him a long time to get the clothes off his body, not because he willfully lingered about it but because of a dream-like state in which he was deeply falling. A far-away feeling engulfed him and his hands and fingers did not seem to be his own, they were numb and hot as if they were caught in the clasp of someone standing behind him, manipulating their motions. But at last he stood naked, and when he turned slowly about to face the negro masseur, the black giant's eyes appeared not to see him at all and yet they had a glitter not present before, a liquid brightness suggesting bits of wet coal.

Put this on, he directed and held out to Burns a white sheet.

Gratefully the little man enveloped himself in the enormous coarse fabric and, holding it delicately up from his small-boned, womanish feet, he followed the negro masseur through another corridor of rustling white curtains to the entrance of an opaque glass enclosure which was the steam-room. There his conductor left him. The blank walls heaved and sighed as steam issued from them. It swirled about Burns naked figure, enveloping him in a heat and moisture such as the inside of a tremendous mouth, to be drugged and all but dissolved in this burning white vapor which hissed out of unseen walls.

After a time the black masseur returned. With a mumbled command, he led the trembling Burns back into the cubicle where he had left his clothes. A bare white table had been wheeled into the chamber during Burns' absence.

Lie on this, said the negro.

Burns obeyed. The black masseur poured alcohol on Burns' body, first on his chest and then on his belly and thighs. It ran all over him, biting at him like insects. He gasped a little and crossed his legs over the wild complaint of his groin. Then without any warning the negro raised up his black palm and brought it down with a terrific whack on the middle of Burns' soft belly. The little man's breath flew out of his mouth in a gasp and for two or three moments he couldn't inhale another.

Immediately after the passing of the first shock, a feeling of pleasure went through him. It swept as a liquid from either end of his body and into the tingling hollow of his groin. He dared

242

not look, but he knew what the negro must see.

The black giant was grinning.

I hope I didn't hit you too hard, he murmured.

No, said Burns.

Turn over, said the negro.

Burns tried vainly to move but luxurious tiredness made him unable to. The negro laughed and gripped the small of his waist and flopped him over as easily as he might have turned a pillow. Then he began to belabor his shoulders and buttocks with blows that increased in violence, and as the violence and the pain increased, the little man grew more and more fiercely hot with his first true satisfaction, until all at once a knot came loose in his loins and released a warm flow.

So by surprise is a man's desire discovered, and once discovered, the only need is surrender, to take what comes and ask no questions about it: and this was something that Burns was expressly made for.

III

Time and again the white-collar clerk went back to the negro masseur. The knowledge grew quickly between them of what Burns wanted, that he was in search of atonement, and the black masseur was the natural instrument of it. He hated white-skinned bodies because they abused his pride. He loved to have their white skin prone beneath him, to bring his fist or the palm of his hand down hard on its passive surface. He had barely been able to hold this love in restraint, to control the wish that he felt to pound more fiercely and use the full of his power. But now at long last the suitable person had entered his orbit of passion. In the white-collar clerk he had located all that he longed for.

Those times when the black giant relaxed, when he sat at the rear of the baths and smoked cigarettes or devoured a bar of candy, the image of Burns would loom before his mind, a nude white body with angry red marks on it. The bar of chocolate would stop just short of his lips and the lips would slacken into a dreamy smile. The giant loved Burns, and Burns adored the giant.

Burns had become absent-minded about his work. Right in the middle of typing a factory order, he would lean back at his desk and the giant would swim in the atmosphere before him. Then he would smile and his work-stiffened fingers would loosen and flop on the desk. Sometimes the boss would stop near him and call his name crossly. Burns! Burns! What are you dreaming about?

Throughout the winter the violence of the massage increased by fairly reasonable degrees, but when March came it was suddenly stepped up.

Burns left the baths one day with two broken ribs.

Every morning he hobbled to work more slowly and painfully but the state of his body could still be explained by saying he had rheumatism.

One day his boss asked him what he was doing for it. He told his boss that he was taking massage.

It don't seem to do you any good, said the boss.

Oh, yes, said Burns, I am showing lots of improvement!

That evening came his last visit to the baths.

His right leg was fractured. The blow which had broken the limb was so terrific that Burns had been unable to stifle an out-cry. The manager of the bath establishment heard it and came into the compartment.

Burns was vomiting over the edge of the table.

Christ, said the manager, What's been going on here?

The black giant shrugged.

He asked me to hit him harder.

The manager looked over Burns and discovered his many bruises.

What do you think this is? A jungle? he asked the masseur.

Again the black giant shrugged.

Get the hell out of my place! the manager shouted.

Take this perverted little monster with you, and neither of you had better show up here again!

The black giant tenderly lifted his drowsy partner and bore him away to a room in the town's negro section.

There for a week the passion between them continued.

This interval was toward the end of the Lenten season. Across from the room where Burns and the negro were staying there was a church whose open windows spilled out the mounting exhortations of a preacher. Each afternoon the fiery poem of death on the cross was repeated. The preacher was not fully conscious of what he wanted nor were the listeners groaning and writhing before him. All of them were involved in a massive atonement.

Now and again some manifestation occurred, a woman stood up to expose a wound in her breast. Another had slashed an artery at her wrist.

Suffer, suffer, suffer, the preacher shouted! Our Lord was nailed on a cross for the sins of the world! They led him above the town to the place of the skull, they moistened his lips with vinegar on a sponge, they drove five nails through his body, and he was The Rose of the World as He bled on the cross!

The congregation could not remain in the building but tumbled out on the street in a crazed procession with clothes torn open.

The sins of the world are all forgiven, they shouted!

IV

All during this celebration of human atonement, the negro masseur was completing his purpose with Burns.

All of the windows were open in the death-chamber.

The curtains blew out like thirstly little white tongues to lick at the street which seemed to reek with an overpowering honey. A house had caught fire on the block in back of the church. The walls collapsed and the cinders floated about in the gold atmosphere. The scarlet engines, the ladders and powerful hoses, were useless against the purity of the flame.

The negro masseur leaned over his still breathing victim.

Burns was whispering something.

The black giant nodded.

You know what you have to do now? the victim asked him.

The black giant nodded.

He picked up the body, which barely held together, and placed it gently on a clean-swept table.

The giant began to devour the body of Burns.

It took him twenty-four hours to eat the splintered bones clean.

When he had finished, the sky was serenly blue, the passionate services at the church were finished, the ashes had settled, the scarlet engines had gone and the reek of honey was blown from the atmosphere.

Quiet had returned and there was an air of completion.

Those bare white bones, left over from Burns' atonement, were placed in a sack and borne to the end of a car-line.

There the masseur walked out on a lonely pier and dropped his burden under the lake's quiet surface.

As the giant turned homeward, he mused on his satisfaction.

Yes, it is perfect, he thought, it is now completed.

Then in the sack, in which he had carried the bones, he dropped his belongings, a neat blue suit to conceal his dangerous body, some buttons of pearl, and a picture of Anthony Burns as a child of seven.

He moved to another city, obtained employment once more as an expert masseur. And there in a white-curtained place, serenely conscious of fate bringing toward him another, to suffer atonement as it had been suffered by Burns, he stood impassively waiting inside a milky white door for the next to arrive.

And meantime, slowly, with barely a thought of so doing, the earth's whole population twisted and writhed beneath the manipulation of night's black fingers and the white ones of day with skeletons splintered and flesh reduced to pulp, as out of this unlikely problem, the answer, perfection, was slowly evolved through torture.

April 1946.

SIX POEMS

Eleanor Ruth Hesthal

JOURNEY TOWARD TRANSFIGURATION

There are other signs tonight:
St. Elmo's light nibbling and flicking
Honey phosphor on the javelin mast
Which, for meaning, pierces the sky
As I with words inthorn my thought.

There are other signs.
The fish with their Byzantine scales
In the boat-side seas
Float in white lustre,
Belly-up, myriad, shining,
And dead.

Other signs. Falling barometer,
Roar-bodied storm, winds enwintering air,
Rail of lightning, anger sufficient for death.

But the ship accomplishes the night
To incite the cockle tide
One day more.

And on the ocean haven docks.
Signs also on the sun.

FRIDOLIN

Fridolin lives but his mouth hangs down at the corners;
The flood has passed over and gone, and his kin
Are as safe as were Noah's and even
The cat and the dog have dried out by the fire.
The storm has passed over and Fridolin lives,
And the live birds come back
To the marsh-footed trees.

And the house was loosened and floated down
The strange Ohio: a Charon's boat
On the mistful river, unhappy house
With watery windows, upon whose roof
The children and Mary and Fridolin
Crossed the Ohio and entered Hell.

It is strange that there was no weeping
And no Judge,
No thunder-brained limbo, no rejected,
Earth-spumed sorrows, no depleted,
Weather-withered human breast,
No undecipherable, cried-out words, no woe,
No twilight and no sun
Nor any night.

Only this: that time himself was there
With Hell and Heaven equal in his hands
Like North and South or any dual thing.
His substance was of lark-song, colored gray,
And all earth's meadowed hills piled to his feet.
And life and death here loved each other
And as one
Caressed the humming-bird and blessed the gull
And sea-wise cormorant, and over all
Was such a quietude as windless space
Conceals between the stars at early dawn.

But Fridolin and Mary did not see
But felt their seeing with immortal eyes.
And they came back alive with children safe
And warm by fires that burned out fear and night.

But Fridolin withdraws, and jaw in hand
Sits at the flood's white edge, seducing death,
Like Hamlet loosening time from Yorick's skull.

SESTINA

The sparrow splashes the pool; the ferns arrange
Their fronds upon day's going, going whole
And one into the west. The winds that come
Puffing upon the fingers of the sky,
Hurling aside the dusk's most passionate hand,
The winds blow draughts along the night.

And man holds marking scales to measure night.
He squares all runes, sees firmaments arrange
One little trillionth star. He feeds the whole
Appetite of law, sees soul-larks come.
God stares upon it all: reveals the sky
In comet-lustres flashing from his hand.

And knowledge spreads a many-fingered hand
As lawyer-prophets justify the night,
Dissecting circumstance. While men arrange
The stench and rite of war, seers harvest whole
Acres of reality, see the ripe fruits come
And coming lightnings frost upon the sky.

The sparrow fog pecks seedling stars from sky,
And wet, the darkness floods on every hand.
The black begins, begins now all the night,
Lonely, while the hawk-head men arrange
Carrion catastrophe, mankind whole
And healthy, cracks the sky for worlds to come.

Time winds man's waste away and griefs that come
Transfix in ice our tears. The wordless sky
Converses through man's throat only. Avid the hand
Stretched out for understanding in this night,
What scholarship shall chaos so arrange
That beauty springs to form and stands here whole?

The dark is going. Sparrow-dawn takes whole
Disasters on his wing and lifting come
The sucking sun-mists out of fen to sky.
And hope is of the spring. Man's unlocked hand
Lets go the wars. He brims the day and night
With solace while the continents peace arrange.

In dreams revival, loam and sky arrange,
Whole-orbited, the spring that sets the hand
Of peace upon night's sill when mornings come.

LITTLE JACK HORNER

Between the line of bone and sun,
Rock and cloud, tense and liquid—
What agitations! What syllables!
Stone aflood with tides of art!

Into that dough from which all hills
Are kneaded, spiced with bulbs,
With grass farinaed, with sugar winds
To delight the frosting with a cloud,
Time has put his finger and pulled out
The nodule of all wisdom—lucky plum!
What is such a taste to our flesh-wise appetite?
Let's stand back and listen with our harsh and thirsty ear,
And see, through tears, but faintly with our hungry, light-deaf
    eye

> —The juice upon the lip
> —The crunch of fruit
> —The sucked stone spit out
> —The finger licked

ON A NEW-FOUND TRUTH

Integrity, with no lines on which to write
The symbol of its image, strikes the air
With new wisdoms suffered out of May-wept tears
Cried under the willows of the never years
For never dreamed-out dreams and never grace.

Among the hedges wanders truth,
Looking into the marrow of the trees,
Inspecting the license of spring, weighting,
Weighting and lighting, the fleece of earth.

So to rear and float
With the air let in
And the light turned on.

NIGHT FEAR

The deadly carousel of shadows round a mountain
Riding in angles, in the shapes of beasts,
Terrifies the watchers who watch from the valley.
They rouse light to their windows,
Rush noise to pace silence,
Defend, defend with laughter,
—But the great shades march the hill.

Heart praise for heroes does not avail.
Pride is in flight. The hill-birds are asleep.
Forsaken by fame, without longing or trust,
The watchers are watching, in envy of day.

But the stars begin. But the moon springs up.
Leaves return to their night-lost branches.
The rocks are recognized. Elegies uttered
In terror are murmured now by birds.
Subdued is the pant and quiet the throat-pulse.
Day-rise, and fear goes home.

DEDICATION DAY

Rough Sketch for a Moving Picture

James Agee

On an afternoon in the early spring of 1946, in the noble space between the Washington Obelisk and the Lincoln Memorial, crowds, roped off from a great square, watched the statesmen, diplomats, military officials, scientists, clergymen, college presidents, newsreel cameramen and *Life* photographers who had assembled upon special platforms, under the unsteady sunlight, and under the uneasy motions of the flags of nearly all nations, to dedicate the heroic new Arch which was for all time to come to memorialize the greatest of human achievements.

The Arch, which had been designed by Frank Lloyd Wright, was the master-builder's sole concession to the Romanesque; at that, he had made it proof against frost, earthquakes, and the inscription and carving of initials. Glistering more subtly than most jewels—for it was made not of stone but of fused uranium—it stood behind the billowing, rainbow-shaded veil which as yet concealed its dedicatory legend, like some giant captive royal slave of antiquity, face masked, the body nude.

From loudspeakers fairly successfully concealed within the ⸱Arch, or sprouting tall above the wide, renewing lawns like rigid quartets of zinc morning-glories, poured a special performance of the choral movement of Beethoven's Ninth Symphony, in a new translation by Louis Aragon and Harry Brown, done under the supervision of Robert E. Sherwood, conducted by Arturo Toscanini in Studio 8-H in Rockefeller Centre, where an invited audience watched the dedication ceremony on the screen of television's first major hookup.

Even by still not wholly perfected television, it was a stirring sight. The many preliminary speeches, to be sure, had been rather more protracted and less satisfying than speeches on great occasions generally are; for it was not clear either to the speakers or to the listeners precisely why or to what purpose or idea the Arch had been raised, and was to be dedicated: they labored, rather, purely under an irresistible obligation both to indicate their recognition of a great event by erecting a permanent altar to it, and to sign their names to the moment in a few authorized words—as is still found necessary by many people, for instance, when a dead man is buried. The speeches, accordingly, were more notable for resonance, eloquence, and on every speaker's part a most scrupulous courtesy and optimism, than for understanding, far less communication of understanding. But once the speeches were over, the ceremony was a peculiarly simple one and achieved, as several Europeans and many of the more sophisticated natives were afterward to agree in semi-privacy, a level of good taste hardly to be expected of ordinary Americans.

All it amounted to, in the long run, was a moment of silence, during which only the restive flags and the sighing of the great veil especially distracted the eye. It involved, on the part of Maestro Toscanini (who was playing as even he had never played before), a Grand Pause, just before that majestic instant in Beethoven's Symphony in which the basses, endorsed by trombones and emulated by soprani, intones the lines

I embrace ye, O ye Millions!
Here's a kiss for all the World!

—lines upon which, after earnest discussion whether to substitute for the somewhat fulsome and perhaps over-Teutonic word *kiss* the sturdily alliterative, more Whitmanesque and manly, more comradely, altogether healthier word *wink,* the re-translators had agreed that it was impossible to impove. During this pause, also, it was possible to hear the subdued rattle of Latin as four ravenous Cardinals raced towards the Consecration in all but perfect unison, their voices blended with that of the Pontifical Benediction, relayed from Rome; a group of eminent Protestant clergymen, each, between his closed eyes, pinching the bridge of his nose between thumb and forefinger as if adjusting an invisible pair of pince-nez, knelt each on one knee at the spread center of a new lawn handkerchief; the most prominent and progressive of American Reformist Rabbis all but inaudibly intoned *Eli, Eli,* intimately, into a neat small microphone; the twenty best Allied marksmen of the Second World War presented their rifles; and many members of many national bands lipped their reeds and mouth-pieces or, heads bowed to deft fingertips, tested their drum-heads and ravanastrons.

253

The climax was simple indeed. Dressed in white organdie, an exquisite little girl, recently judged the healthiest three-year-old in the United States (for it had been quickly and courteously agreed, shortly after the termination of lend-lease and Mr. Herbert Lehman's three hundred and seventy-first appeal to Congress in regard to U. N. R. R. A.'s more urgent needs, that no other nation should enter competitors), upon receiving a soft shove from her mother, a former screen star, and a whispered "Now, Lidice", toddled alone into the open, along the sulphur-pale grass, towards the great Arch, bearing in her right hand a taper which had been lighted from a light which had been taken from the light which burns eternally in Paris, above the tomb of the Unknown Soldier. At the same moment, from a small hole at dead center of the pavement beneath the Arch, (an orifice bound by a platinum facsimile of Martha Washington's wedding ring), and from the center, as well, of an embossed lucite medallion which, within a zodiacal wreath, indicated the direction of, and the air mileage to, the capital city of every civilized nation, shyly, rather the way the early worm might try the air in an especially lyrical Disney cartoon, stood up a few inches of gleaming white cord. As the child approached, her bladder a trifle unstabilized by privilege, the Cardinals, and the Monsignori and Papal Knights who served as their acolytes, could not perfectly restrain the sideward sliding of their eyes; among the Protestant clergymen there were several who saw what happened through the rainbow swarming of their eyelashes; the Rabbi's vocal chords thickened, necessitating a slight clearing of the throat, during which he forgot to turn from his microphone; a few even of the superbly disciplined riflemen (and women) uncrossed their eyes from the muzzles of their weapons; one of the musicians permitted his instrument, a tuba, to emit a strangled expletive; a boy on the outskirts of the great crowd could be heard hawking Good Humors, which were not moving very satisfactorily, for the day was chilly; a woman, moaning, fainted, falling double over the rope; and an Eagle Scout, masterfully brocaded with Merit Badges fiercely repeating to himself his terrifying last-minute change of instructions (for it had been decided only in afterthought, in bitter and desperate haste), *No! No! Not Taps! Not Taps!*", raised his bugle to his beardless, though freshly, and electrically, shaven lips.

And now the child stooped, in one of the more rudimentary postures of ballet, and, extending her sanctified taper, touched the bright cord with the flame; and in the exquisite silence there

began, audible even to the distant boy who stopped saying Good
Humor in the middle of the first syllable, a faint, searching, rustling noise, not unlike that which a snake elicits as he retires
among dead leaves. And now, while the musicians poised their
instruments and the marksmen slanted their rifles upward; and
while the Cardinals slowed or accelerated a little as need be, in
order to reach their genuflections, and the threshing of the bells,
at the precisely proper moment; and while, in New York, the
Maestro held one hundred and seventeen instruments and nine
hundred and forty-three pairs of eyes suspended as by one
spider-thread from the tip of his baton; and while the woman
who had fainted was softly and quickly shunted toward the rear
of the crowd; and while the voice of America's Number One
Commentator continued its description, in such expert unobtrus-
iveness that although he was thrillingly audible to every one
among the millions in his unseen audience, not a single person
among the onlookers could hear a word he said, though nearly
all were straining with all their strength, in order that they might
know what was happening before they read it in the late editions,
which were even now being purchased along the periphery of
the crowd; while all these things were transpiring, or held themselves balanced intense in readiness, trembling, the chosen Scout,
who in innumerable rehearsals had perfected a rendition of Taps
so heartrending that, in recorded form, with hummed accompani-
ment by Bing Crosby, the Andrew Sisters, the Ink Spots, and the
Westminster Choir, it had already sold better than a million
disks, did as best he could, disconsolately, lacking reheasals, with
Reveille, which he had had no occasion to play since Camp broke
up the previous summer, and which many people agreed he managed really very prettily, considering the circumstances. As his
last note melted, the twenty marksmen fired the first of their
twenty-one salutes, flicking the silver-gilt padlocks from a long
rank of cages which exhaled a brilliant flock of homing doves,
somewhat frustrated in their breathing by wired-on imitation
olive-branches, and banded with appropriate messages with
which, after wheeling briefly, luminous against the clouds, they
set off in haste for the several and all-inclusive quarters of the
globe; the Cardinals genuflected; their bells threshed; the Rabbi
collapsed his microphone stand and smoothed his hair; the woman
who had fainted opened her eyes, gazed up the sharp chins of
sympathizers and, with a heartsick groan, miscarried; the clergymen rose from their knees and carefully folded and pocketed
their handkerchiefs; the Good Humor salesboy resumed busi-

ness; and in perfect synchronization the military bands of forty-six nations and the National Broadcasting Symphony Orchestra and the Westminster Choir attacked respectively their respective national anthems and their continuation of the Choral Symphony, all somewhat modified, in the interests of euphony, by Morton Gould, but virtually all still recognizable to the untrained ear; and the iridescent veil, its release cords pulled, on a signal from James Bryant Conant, by the President of the United States, Charles De Gaulle, a reluctant veteran of the Chinese Purchasing Commission, and undersecretaries from the Embassies of the other two of the Big Five, sank laboring on the March air from the crest of the Arch, revealing, in Basic English, the words:

THIS IS IT

,A soft cheer of awe moved upon the crowd; then a flowering of applause like the rumination of leaves before rain: for this secret had been successfully kept, and very few of those on the outskirts had managed to buy extras until the veil fell.

Below the legend, the Eternal Fuse continued to exude and to consume itself, one inch above the pavement at the rate of one inch per second. The fuse was chemically calculated continuously somewhat to intensify the noise of its consumption, enough to be distinguishable to anyone who kept attentive vigil for so much as twenty-four hours; at the end of precisely one hundred years, it was further calculated, this penetrating whisper, grown continuously more acute never dynamically more loud, would become audible at the point most distant from its origin, on the planet. Some stayed, now, and held vigil; others, many, listened a half hour, even an hour, then lost patience; slowly, towards the early neons, the crowd dissolved. Few were left, at dusk, to witness the lowering and folding of the flags.

During the earlier stages of planning the Memorial there had been considerable discussion whether the fuse should burn down at the rate of an inch per hour, or even per day; but an inch per second had ultimately been agreed on not only as peppier and somehow more in keeping, but also because this rate of consumption measureably helped solve, or at least proved awareness of, certain delicate social and economic problems. Some 7,200 feet of the fuse would be consumed each day; approximately 4,897.6 miles, which amounted to roughly 322.17 bales of cottor each year. The cotton would be the finest Egyptian long-staple, grown by members of a Sharecropper's Rehabilitation Project in one of the richest of the condemned areas of the Delta. Bales would be furnished, alternately by a white and a Negro family, and would be purchased at cost, the cash to be applied against the interest on Rehabilitation Loans. The purchase of the chemicals used in impregnating the fuse, a mere few tons of those substances so recently and abruptly rendered obsolete for military use, was to be sure a mere token, but as such it assured various embarrassed manufacturers of archaic munitions of the Government's enduring sympathy, and concern for their welfare. Moreover, the manufacture of the fuse itself made gainful and honorable employment available to a number of persons otherwise unemployable, and added no little not only to the symbolic dignity but also to the human warmth of the entire Project. For beneath the Arch, in a small, air-conditioned, irradiated workshop so ingeniously contrived by Norman Bel Geddes that it was possible for those who found it more efficient to do their share from hospital beds or even, a few of them, from streamlined baskets, the fuse was manufactured on the spot. Its creators, who were by unanimous agreement among those in charge of the Memorial called Keepers of the Flame, worked perpetually, wheeled in and out, as shifts changed, through silent tunnels of tile and plastic, by women physicians who had been rendered redundant by the termination of hostilities. They were at all times visible even while they slept, to tourists who used other tunnels, through thick walls of polarized glass. The tourists' admission fees, even though ex-servicemen and children in arms were to be passed at half price for the next two years, would clearly better than pay both the initial cost and the maintenance of the Project; the surplus monies were to be applied toward the relief of those who should have neglected to redeem their War and Victory Bonds by 1950.

One of these twelve-hour shifts (for the work was light) was composed of such disabled winners of the Distinguished Service Cross, the Congressional Medal of Honor, and the Navy Cross, as did not wish to be a burden on their communities or to languish in Veterans' Hospitals, and as were alert to the immense therapeutic value of honest work. It was required of them only that they wear their uniforms and decorations, during working hours, and, as a reminder and incentive to youth, show their wounds, scars, or stumps. They were paid whatever their rank and injury entitled them, in pension. The other shift was composed of depreciated but surviving collaborators in the experiments at Hiroshima and Nagasaki, who had been forgiven, and were, indeed, aside from a few unfortunate incidents which marred the course of their journey across the less progressive reaches of the nation, treated with marked civility, even being permitted to shake hands with Secretaries of State and of War, who laughingly apologized, through an interpreter, for wearing radiation-proof gloves and masks throughout the little ceremony. There had at first been some talk of accepting, for this work, only such Japanese as embraced Christianity, but it was generously decided, in the interests of religious toleration, that this should not be required; indeed, a number of the Nagasaki colleagues, formerly Christian, were known to have renounced Christianity; it was an open secret, even, that two of them were privately practicing the out-lawed Shintoism. This too (though care was taken that the fact should not become known among the general public) was smilingly disregarded, on the grounds that in their present occupation, and distance from the homeland, and fewness in number—not to mention the efficiency of the magnificently trained Project Guardians—no great harm was likely to come of these atavist diehards. It was required of the Japanese only that they keep on display, during working hours, those strange burns which have excited, in Americans, so much friendly curiosity—an exposure necessarily limited, of course, in a number of cases, in the interests of decency. These Japanese were paid the wages customary for prisoners of war (the funds were deposited in their names in a Subtreasury vault, their board and keep being deductible) and, in accordance with the rulings of the Geneva Convention, were required, in their eating, to fare neither better nor worse, nor other, than men in our own armed services, being forced, in fact, to ingest one can of K Rations, two four-pound porterhouse steaks, one carton of Camels, eight squares of Ex-Lax, two boxes of Puffed Rice, the juice of twelve oranges, a tin of Spam, a cup of Ovaltine, a prophylactic, a tube of nationally advertised toothpaste, and macerated or liquified overseas editions of *Time, Readers' Digest* and the New Testament, each, per day, plus roast beef, apple pie and store cheese on Sundays and proper supplements, including third helpings, spoonlickings and ejaculations of "Gosh, Mom," of the special dishes traditionally appropriate to the major Holidays; all to be administered orally, rectally or by intravenous injection, as best befitted the comfort of the individual patient—a task which many of the little fellows found so embarrassing, and which the tourists found so richly amusing to watch, that even after the first few days, feeding time created something of a traffic problem.

It was agreed that in due course these invalids would be supplanted at their jobs by their children if they should prove capable of breeding and bearing them, and that such children, if their behavior should prove unexceptionable up to the age of 21 years, would be granted the privileges of American citizenship and of absentee voting. The male children of those veterans capable of siring them would be offered their choice between the same lifetime guarantee of gainful employment, and a scholarship at Peddie. In that event—as to some people seemed quite conceivable—that this turnover plan too rapidly diminished the personnel, it had already been arranged that the Japanese and American ranks be filled out respectively by Mission converts to any one of the accredited Christian faiths, and by divinity students, who would receive fullcourse seminarial credits for their services per year, tuition halved.

Raw materials were conveyed to these workers each midnight, promptly, by armored truck. Before the day of the ceremony they had produced a spool of fuse so thick that it was decided to give them a holiday. In the morning, on the White House Back Lawn, there was a picnic, with a sack race, and a baseball game (won, amusingly enough, by the Japanese). In the afternoon they were all brought to reserved areas (segregating, however, the Japanese and Americans) at the very brink of the ropes, to witness the Dedication.

One pathetic incident marred this otherwise perfect day. One of the more elderly of these scientists who contributed their genius towards the perfecting of the bomb—he shall, in these columns at least, remain nameless—had begun, not long after the Japanese surrender, to strike his colleagues as a little queer in the head. He was known to have attended Mass, at first secretly, then quite openly; later, to have spent several evenings of silence among the Friends; later, to have sought out a poet of his acquaintance, of whom it had been learned, he asked Mahatma Gandhi's postal address, whether a letter might be kindly received, and answered, and approximately how far into the East it might be advisable to journey, insofar as possible on foot, or on his knees ("perhaps to Lhasa?" he asked), in what he called "atonement." The poet, according to his own account of this singular interview, merely laughed uproariously, murmuring some obscurantist figure of speech—which with great amusement he repeated, when questioned by friends of the scientist—about "locking the stable after the horse had been stolen". It was not long after this—early in October—that plans for the Arch began to develop. Once the scientist learned of the idea of the underground personnel he did not rest, or indeed let any of his associates or of their contacts among the officials rest, until he had gained permission to become one of the Keepers. This was granted him the more reluctantly because he insisted on working with the Japanese shift and, to the further embarrassment of everyone, gave warning that he would refuse to eat the carefully balanced diet offered the Japanese, preferring, rather, just so much boiled unpolished rice per day as he could hold in the palm of one hand. In view of his immense services to humanity, and out of a kind of pity, and a perhaps overconscientious sense that the community as a whole, having so greatly benefited through him, shared, in some measure no matter how small or indirect, a certain responsibility, or at least concern, for his broken mind, it was, after prolonged consultation with eminent psychologists, agreed that he should be humored. Unfortunately, the best will in the world, on the part of those officially and medically responsible, was not, as it turned out, enough.

In the course of those "Arch Prevues", so-called, which many readers will have glimpsed in the newsreels, it became painfully clear that it was entirely unfeasible to permit him to persist in his wish. It was not that the Japanese misbehaved; indeed, they left the old man severely alone. It was rather, the behavior of the physicist himself, and the disturbing effect of his behavior upon Prevue tourists. Although the thick glass rendered him inaudible, it was only too clear, to the more observant of these onlookers, that as he worked he spoke, and that his speech was evidently a terrible blended stream of self-vilification and of pr-y-r. And even to those insufficiently accustomed to these retrogressive attitudes to decipher them correctly (for many thought, as they put it, that he was "just cussing out the Japs"), it was nevertheless excruciatingly embarrassing to see a white man working among those of a different pigmentation, and to see how, so often as the limited gestures necessary to his work permitted him, he tore at his thin hair and beat his bruised face with clenched fists and tore at it with his nails, and to see how at all times his bitten lips bled copiously onto his starched laboratory jacket, immediately soiling it regardless of its ever more frequent change; and how his torn face was wet with continuous uncontrolled (and perhaps uncontrollable) tears. Some took to rapping on the glass with coins to draw his attention, then, according to their wont, either jeering at him by gestures of their hands and by contortions of their faces, or attempting to revive his courage and self-esteem by showing in their faces, or by making the sign of Victory and smiling their sympathy, or by clasping and shaking their hands and grinning, that however regrettable his present plight they continued to honor and to befriend and to congratulate him, in view of his past achievements. Such gestures, however, appeared to offend the Japanese, and were discouraged by the Guards. Others of the spectators passed on quickly in revulsion; and that too, in its own way, impaired the intended dignity, charm and decorum of the exhibit. Still others, however, and in considerable numbers, blocked the tourists' tunnel by following the example of one young soldier who, late in the afternoon before the Dedication, quite without warning fell to his knees and burst into tears. To be sure, few of his imitators wept; most of them, indeed, and this was especially true of those at the edge of the sudden crowd, did not know what was happening, and knelt only because they saw that those ahead of them were kneeling. Scrupulously conducted interviews immediately following the disturbance, in which prominent churchmen and psychiatrists were assisted by Gallup Poll experts, thoroughly established the fact that the soldier himself, despite his many campaign-stars and decorations for valor, was a psychoneurotic, that virtually nobody had understood the cause of his outburst, and that nothing whatever need be feared, notwithstanding the insistence of certain evangelistic types, in the way of a so-called "religious revival". Even so, the kneeling was of itself an irregular and far from convenient action; the more so because for every tourist who, out of a courteous desire to do what was expected of him, dropped to his knees, there were at least two others (2.29, by the Gallup count) who, mistaking this for some kind of vulgar sentimentality, in natural impatience and contempt, and no little anger, clambered among and through and over the close-packed kneelers, creating a severe jam and, ultimately, a mild panic; for an overwrought woman at the far edge of the commotion screamed that the Japanese had broken loose, others took up the cry, and those in front of the exhibit split and bruised the unbreakable glass in their effort to protect their women-folk. (The Japanese, it must be said, were entirely innocent in this affair.) From this confusion many of all types, kneelers, non-kneelers, defenders and defended alike, emerged with minor contusions, and instituted suits against the Arch Authority for damage to their nerves, clothing, and earning power. Such are the unfortunate effects of a single man's unbridled individualism.

It was at the end of this shift, accordingly, at midnight, that the physicist was told, in all possible kindliness, that his services, greatly as they were appreciated, would no longer be required, and that he had his choice of lifelong residence and treatment, gratis, in whatever sanitarium in the nation he might prefer. Instantly he stopped his crying and asked, in a manner which seemed entirely rational, whether he might not, before retiring, have at least the privilege of throwing that switch, in the underground workshop, which would start the fuse on its eternal journey. He did not like to think, he said, that any one of his fellow-workers would be deprived of his day off, or of witnessing the climactic moment from the best point of vantage possible. Such was the unworldliness of the man, that it had not occurred to him that this was, after all, a crucial part of the ceremony; in fact, a switch had been arranged on the Number One Platform (its knob set with the Hope Diamond, on loan, and heavily insured for the occasion); and it was to be thrown—since both Drs. Albert Einstein and Lise Meitner had declined the honor— by Major General Leslie Groves. It was decided not to embarrass the poor old man. Quickly, by telephone, the General's magnanimous withdrawal was secured; the scientist was then told that everyone would be delighted, and honored, if he would consent to "start the ball rolling", as they said, in a position of the greatest possible conspicuousness and eminence. Courteously, even gratefully, he replied that he really preferred to be underground. After careful consultation, it was deemed entirely harmless to grant his wish—a decision which, as nobody could have foreseen, was to prove tragically ill-advised.

Within a few minutes after the Dedication he was found next the great spool, dead by his own hand (by prussic acid); it was deduced that he must have swallowed the poison in the instant of throwing the switch. Pinned to his immaculate laboratory jacket was a note, written clearly and steadily in his own hand.

Out of deference to the deceased and to his surviving relatives, it was instantly and unanimously agreed not to publish this short, singular document (though qualified students will be granted access to it), whose contents could only puzzle and offend sane human beings, and establish beyond possible question the piteous derangement of a man of former genius. By rough paraphrase, however, it seems not dishonorable to say that in unimpeachable sincerity he regarded his suicide as obligatory—as, indeed, a kind of religious or ethical "sacrifice", through which he hoped to endow the triumphal monument with a new and special significance and, through the gradual spread and under-

standing of that significance, once more (as he thought) to assist
the human race.

Even in death, however, this unfortunate but brilliant man
again made history. Psychoanalysts are even now busy exploring the hidden depths of the already celebrated case; the nation's
leading philosophers are rushing a symposium to be entitled *The
New New Failure of Nerves;* and clergymen of all denominations,
united in agreement perhaps more firmly than ever before, are
determined to preach next Sunday (and, if need be, on the following Sunday as well), using this tragic incident by no means
unsympathetically yet sternly, and with controlled ridicule, as
an object-lesson, and grave admonition, to such in their spiritual
charge as find themselves for any reason of pride, or a thirst for
undue publicity, liable to the grievous error of exaggerated
scrupulousness. "Some things are best left to Jesus Christ",
will be the burden of their argument; the text will be, *Render
unto Caesar the things that are Caesar's, and unto God the things
that are God's*

The body will be interred, with military honors, at the centre
of that area in New Mexico in which this gifted scientist, and his
colleagues, first saw the light of the New Age. And it does not
seem too much to hope that perhaps he will be remembered,
not, surely, as he had intended, yet a little wistfully, in the sound
of The Fuse itself as it increases upon the world. For misguided
and altogether regrettable though his last days were—a sad warning indeed to those who turn aside from the dictates of reason,
and accept human progress reluctantly—he was nevertheless,
perhaps, our last link with a not-too-distant past in which such
conceptions as those of "atonement", and "guilt", and "individual
responsibility", still had significance. And, in a sense, his gift
to mankind was greater, perhaps, than that of his more stable
colleagues. For, though "sacrifice" is a word to be used only
with apologies, it would be hard to define what, if anything, they
"sacrificed" in the giving; but he gave up his sanity.

IN TIME OF ORDER

Alex Comfort

Night after night as they lay imprisoned, stars
moved in their faultless order overhead
speaking aloud their old threats and promises.
So moving as we fight, they still assert

to one God's finger assenting to the Right
but to us a cold wind from the edge of time
their hostile, bright neutrality of aim
saying that to the just and the unjust is one end

and seeing them set me thinking of the time
when Newton still looked out among green leaves
and saw the hand of something like his thought
in light or flowers or the plains of sea.

For us who fight now, there are no signatures.
No kings or godheads set their names on leaves.
Beauty like us has a more perilous life
and Freedom is not written on the stars—

the stars did nothing for Connolly or Sacco
nor for the endless million in the soil
who, since they died to give this thing a name
having no names are silent.

Yet we are not losers. What we make we have,
we have made Freedom in an empty place
we have brought light into a lightless cave
and in the end we are makers of new things.

And still we, the sentries, at the wood's edge stand
and see the people a cloud that moves and rises
that bears in itself a dark yeast
pillared and brooding, filled

with churnings of its own, smoking, headless, afloat
under whose sleep the swine root without fear
while that great anvil stands across the sky
and under the moving cliff the fields fall one by one silent

until amazing, a blue elbowed stream
suddenly flies like light tyrannicide
and through the forest of rain the long hills give back
echoing bank by bank the flat cheers of thunder. .

For Freedom and Beauty are not fixed stars
but cut by man only from his own flesh
but lit by man, only for his sojourn
because our shout into the cup of sky
brings back no echo, brings back no echo ever,
because man's mind lives at his stature's length

because the stars have for us no earnest of winning
because there is no resurrection
because all things are against us, we are ourselves

A DISTANT EPISODE

Paul Bowles

THE SEPTEMBER SUNSETS were at their reddest the week the Professor decided to visit Aïn Tadouirt, which is in the warm country. He came down out of the high, flat region in the evening by bus, with two small overnight bags full of maps, sun lotions, and medicines. Ten years ago he had been in the village for three days; long enough, however, to establish a fairly firm friendship with a cafékeeper, who had written him several times during the first year after his visit, if never since. "Hassan Ramani," the Professor said over and over, as the bus bumped downward through ever warmer layers of air. Now facing the flaming sky in the west, and now facing the sharp mountains, the car followed the dusty trail down the canyons into air which began to smell of other things besides the endless ozone of the heights: orange blossoms, pepper, sun-baked excrement, burning olive oil, rotten fruit. He closed his eyes happily and lived for an instant in a purely olfactory world. The distant past returned —what part of it, he could not decide.

The chauffeur, whose seat the Professor shared, spoke to him without taking his eyes from the road, "*Vous êtes géologue?*"

"A geologist? Ah, no! I'm a linguist."

"There are no languages here. Only dialects."

"Exactly. I'm making a survey of variations on Moghrebi."

The chauffeur was scornful. "Keep on going south," he said. "You'll find some languages you never heard of before."

As they drove through the town gate, the usual swarm of urchins rose up out of the dust and ran screaming beside the bus. The Professor folded his dark glasses, put them in his pocket; and as soon as the vehicle had come to a standstill he jumped out, pushing his way through the indignant boys who clutched at his luggage in vain, and walked quickly into the Grand Hotel Saharien. Out of its eight rooms there were two available—one facing the market and the other, a smaller and cheaper one, giving onto a tiny yard full of refuse and barrels, where two gazelles wandered about. He took the smaller room, and pouring the entire pitcher of water into the tin basin, began to wash the grit from his face and ears. The afterglow was nearly gone from the sky, and the pinkness in objects was disappearing, almost as he watched. He lit the carbide lamp and winced at its odor.

After dinner the Professor walked slowly through the streets to Hassan Ramani's café, whose back room hung hazardously out above the river. The entrance was very low, and he had to bend down slightly to get in. A man was tending the fire. There was one guest sipping tea. The caouadji tried to make him take a seat at the other table in the front room, but the Professor walked airily ahead into the back room and sat down. The moon was shining through the reed latticework and there was not a sound outside but the occasional distant bark of a dog. He changed tables so he could see the river. It was dry, but there was a pool here and there that reflected the bright night sky. The caouadji came in and wiped off the table.

"Does this café still belong to Hassan Ramani?" he asked him in the Moghrebi he had taken four years to learn.

The man replied in bad French: "He is deceased."

"Deceased?" repeated the Professor, without noticing the absurdity of the word. "Really? When?"

"I don't know," said the caouadji. "One tea?"

"Yes. But I don't understand . . . "

The man was already out of the room, fanning the fire. The Professor sat still, feeling lonely, and arguing with himself that to do so was ridiculous. Soon the caouadji returned with the tea. He paid him and gave him an enormous tip, for which he received a grave bow.

"Tell me," he said, as the other started away. "Can one still get those little boxes made from camel udders?"

The man looked angry. "Sometimes the Chaamba bring in those things. We do not buy them here." Then insolently, in Arabic: "And why a camel-udder box?"

"Because I like them," retorted the Professor. And then because he was feeling a little exalted, he added, "I like them so much I want to make a collection of them, and I will pay you ten francs for every one you can get me."

"Khamstache," said the caouadji, opening his left hand rapidly three times in succession.

"Never. Ten."

"Not possible. But wait until later and come with me. You can give me what you like. And you will get camel-udder boxes if there are any."

He went out into the front room, leaving the Professor to drink his tea and listen to the growing chorus of dogs that barked and howled as the moon rose higher into the sky. A group of customers came into the front room and sat talking for an hour or so. When they had left, the caouadji put out the fire and stood in the doorway putting on his burnous. "Come," he said.

Outside in the street there was very little movement. The booths were all closed and the only light came from the moon. An occasional pedestrian passed, and grunted a brief greeting to the caouadji.

"Everyone knows you," said the Professor, to cut the silence between them.

"Yes."

"I wish everyone knew me," said the Professor, before he realized how infantile such a remark must sound.

"*No* one knows you," said his companion gruffly.

They had come to the other side of the town, on the promontory above the desert, and through a great rift in the wall the Professor saw the white endlessness, broken in the foreground by dark spots of oasis. They walked through the opening and followed a winding road between rocks, downward toward the nearest small forest of palms. The Professor thought: "He may cut my throat. But his café—he would surely be found out."

"Is it far?" he asked casually.

"Are you tired?" countered the caouadji.

"They are expecting me back at the Hotel Saharien," he lied.

"You can't be there and here," said the caouadji.

The Professor laughed. He wondered if it sounded uneasy to the other.

"Have you owned Ramani's café long?"

"I work there for a friend." The reply made the Professor more unhappy than he had imagined it would.

"Oh. Will you work tomorrow?"

"That is impossible to say."

The Professor stumbled on a stone, and fell, scraping his hand. The caouadji said: "Be careful."

The sweet black odor of rotten meat hung in the air suddenly.

"Agh!" said the Professor, choking. "What is it?"

The caouadji had covered his face with his burnous and did not answer. Soon the stench had been left behind. They were on flat ground. Ahead the path was bordered on each side by a high mud wall. There was no breeze and the palms were quite still, but behind the walls was the sound of running water. Also, the odor of human excrement was almost constant as they walked between the walls.

The Professor waited until he thought it seemed logical for him to ask with a certain degree of annoyance: "But where are we going?"

"Soon," said the guide, pausing to gather some stones in the ditch.

"Pick up some stones," he advised. "Here are bad dogs."

"Where?" asked the Professor, but he stooped and got three large ones with pointed edges.

They continued very quietly. The walls came to an end and the bright desert lay ahead. Nearby was a ruined marabout, with its tiny dome only half standing, and the front wall entirely destroyed. Behind it were clumps of stunted, useless palms. A dog came running crazily toward them on three legs. Not until it got quite close did the Professor hear its steady low growl. The caouadji let fly a large stone at it, striking it square in the muzzle. There was a strange snapping of jaws and the dog ran sideways in another direction, falling blindly against rocks and scrambling haphazardly about like an injured insect.

Turning off the road, they walked across the earth strewn with sharp stones, past the little ruin, through the trees, until they came to a place where the ground dropped abruptly away in front of them.

"It looks like a quarry," said the Professor, resorting to French for the word "quarry," whose Arabic equivalent he could not call to mind at the moment. The caouadji did not answer. Instead he stood still and turned his head, as if listening. And indeed, from somewhere down below, but very far below, came the faint sound of a low flute. The caouadji nodded his head slowly several times. Then he said: "The path begins here. You can see it well all the way. The rock is white and the moon is strong. So you can see well. I am going back now and sleep. It is late. You can give me what you like."

Standing there at the edge of the abyss which at each moment looked deeper, with the dark face of the caouadji framed in its moonlit burnous close to his own face, the Professor asked himself exactly what he felt. Indignation, curiosity, fear, perhaps, but most of all relief and the hope that this was not a trick, the hope that the caouadji would really leave him alone and turn back without him.

He stepped back a little from the edge, and fumbled in his pocket for a loose note, because he did not want to show his wallet. Fortunately there was a fifty franc bill there, which he took out and handed to the man. He knew the caouadji was pleased, and so he paid no attention, when he heard him saying: "It is not enough. I have to walk a long way home and there are dogs. . . . "

"Thank you and good night," said the Professor, sitting down with his legs drawn up under him, and lighting a cigarette. He felt almost happy.

"Give me only one cigarette," pleaded the man.

"Of course," he said, a bit curtly, and he held up the pack.

The caouadji squatted close beside him. His face was not pleasant to see. "What is it?" thought the Professor, terrified again, as he held out his lighted cigarette toward him.

The man's eyes were almost closed. It was the most obvious registering of concentrated scheming the Professor had ever seen. When the second cigarette was burning, he ventured to say to the still squatting Arab: "What are you thinking about?"

The other drew on his cigarette deliberately, and seemed about to speak. Then his expression changed to one of satisfaction, but he did not speak. A cool wind had risen in the air, and the Professor shivered. The sound of the flute came up from the depths below at intervals, sometimes mingled with the scraping of nearby palmfronds one against the other. "These people are not primitives," the Professor found himself saying in his mind.

"Good," said the caouadji, rising slowly. "Keep your money. Fifty francs is enough. It is an honor." Then he went back into French: *"Ti n'as qu'à discendre, to' droit."* He spat, chuckled (or was the Professor hysterical?), and strode away quickly.

The Professor was in a state of nerves. He lit another cigarette, and found his lips moving automatically. They were saying: "Is this a situation or a predicament? This is ridiculous." He sat very still for several minutes, waiting for a sense of reality to come to him. He stretched out on the hard, cold ground and looked up at the moon. It was almost like looking straight at the sun. If he shifted his gaze a little at a time, he could make a string of weaker moons across the sky. "Incredible," he whispered. Then he sat up quickly and looked about. There was no guarantee that the caouadji really had gone back to town. He got to his feet and looked over the edge of the precipice. In the moonlight the bottom seemed miles away. And there was nothing to give it scale; not a tree, not a house, not a person. . . . He listened for the flute, and heard only the wind going by his ears. A sudden violent desire to run back to the road seized him, and he turned and looked in the direction the caouadji had taken. At the same time he felt softly at his wallet in his breast pocket. Then he spat over the edge of the cliff. Then he made water over it, and listened intently, like a child. This gave him the impetus to start down the path into the abyss. Curiously enough, he was not dizzy. But prudently he kept from peering to his right, over the edge. It was a steady and steep downward climb. The monotony of it put him into a frame of mind not unlike that which had been induced by the bus-ride. He was murmuring "Hassan Ramani" again, repeatedly and in rhythm. He stopped, furious with himself for the sinister overtones the name now suggested to him. He decided he was exhausted from the trip. "And the walk," he added.

He was now well down the gigantic cliff, but the moon, being directly overhead, gave as much light as ever. Only the wind was left behind, above, to wander along the trees, to blow through the dusky streets of Aïn Tadouirt, into the hall of the Grand Hotel Saharien, and under the door of his little room.

It occurred to him that he ought to ask himself why he was doing this irrational thing, but he was intelligent enough to know that since he was doing it, it was not so important to probe for explanations at that moment.

Suddenly the earth was flat beneath his feet. He had reached the bottom sooner than he had expected. He stepped ahead distrustfully still, as if he expected another treacherous drop. It was so hard to know in this uniform, dim brightness. Before he knew what had happened the dog was upon him, a heavy mass of fur trying to push him backwards, a sharp nail rubbing down his chest, a straining of muscles against him to get the teeth into his neck. The Professor thought: "I refuse to die this way." The dog fell back; it looked like an Eskimo dog. As it sprang again, he called out, very loud: "Ay!" It fell against him, there was a confusion of sensations and a pain somewhere. There was also the sound of voices very near to him, and he could not understand what they were saying. Something cold and metallic was pushed brutally against his spine as the dog still hung for a second by his teeth from a mass of clothing and perhaps flesh. The Professor knew it was a gun, and he raised his hands, shouting in Moghrebi: "Take away the dog!" But the gun merely pushed him forward, and since the dog, once it was back on the ground, did not leap again, he took a step ahead. The gun kept pushing; he kept taking steps. Again he heard voices, but the person directly behind him said nothing. People seemed to be running about; it sounded that way, at least. For his eyes, he discovered, were still shut tight against the dog's attack. He opened them. A group of men was advancing toward him. They were dressed in the black clothes of the Chaamba. "The Chaamba is a cloud across the face of the sun." "When the Chaamba appears the righteous man turns away." In how many shops and market places he had heard these maxims uttered banteringly among friends. Never to a Chaamba, to be sure, for these men do not frequent towns. They send a representative in disguise, to arrange with shady elements there for the disposal of captured goods. "An opportunity," he thought quickly, "of testing the accuracy of such statements." He did not doubt for a moment that the adventure would prove to be a kind of warning against such foolishness on his part—a warning which in retrospect would be half sinister, half farcical.

Two snarling dogs came running from behind the oncoming men and threw themselves at his legs. He was scandalized to note that no one paid any attention to this breach of etiquette. The gun pushed him harder as he tried to sidestep the animal's noisy assault. Again he cried: "The dogs! Take them away!" The gun shoved him forward with great force and he fell, almost at the feet of the crowd of men facing him. The dogs were wrenching at his hands and arms. A boot kicked them aside, yelping, and then with increased vigor it kicked the Professor in the hip. Then came a chorus of kicks from different sides, and he was rolled violently about on the earth for a while. During this time he was conscious of hands reaching into his pockets and removing everything from them. He tried to say: "You have all my money; stop kicking me!" But his bruised facial muscles would not work; he felt himself pouting, and that was all. Someone dealt him a terrific blow on the head, and he thought: "Now at least I shall lose consciousness, thank Heaven." Still he went on being aware of the gutteral voices he could not understand, and of being bound tightly about the ankles and chest. Then there was black silence that opened like a wound from time to time, to let in the soft, deep notes of the flute playing the same succession of notes again and again. Suddenly

272

he felt excruciating pain everywhere—pain and cold. "So I have been unconscious, after all," he thought. In spite of that, the present seemed only like a direct continuation of what had gone before.

It was growing faintly light. There were camels near where he was lying; he could hear their gurgling and their heavy breathing. He could not bring himself to attempt opening his eyes, just in case it should turn out to be impossible. However, when he heard someone approaching, he found that he had no difficulty in seeing.

The man looked at him dispassionately in the gray morning light. With one hand he pinched together the Professor's nostrils. When the Professor opened his mouth to breathe, the man swiftly seized his tongue and pulled on it with all his might. The Professor was gagging and catching his breath; he did not see what was happening. He could not distinguish the pain of the brutal yanking from that of the sharp knife. Then there was an endless choking and spitting that went on automatically, as though he were scarcely a part of it. The word "operation" kept going through his mind; it calmed his terror somewhat as he sank back into darkness.

The caravan left sometime toward midmorning. The Professor, not unconscious, but in a state of utter stupor, still gagging and drooling blood, was dumped doubled-up into a sack and tied at one side of a camel. The lower end of the enormous amphitheater contained a natural gate in the rocks. The meharis, lightly-laden beasts on this trip, passed through single-file, and slowly mounted the gentle slope that led up into the beginning of the desert. That night, at a stop behind some low hills, the men took him out, still in a state which permitted no thought, and over the dusty rags that remained of his clothing they fastened a series of curious belts made of the bottoms of tin cans strung together. One after another of these bright girdles was wired about his torso, his arms and legs, even across his face, until he was entirely within a suit of armor that covered him with its circular metal scales. There was a good deal of merriment during this decking-out of the Professor. One man brought out a flute and a younger one did a not ungraceful caricature of an Ouled Naïl executing a cane dance. The Professor was no longer conscious; to be exact, he existed in the middle of the movements made by these other men. When they had finished dressing him the way they wished him to look, they stuffed some food under the tin bangles hanging over his face. Even though he chewed mechanically, most of it eventually fell out onto the ground. They put him back into the sack and left him there.

Two days later they arrived at one of their own encampments. There were women and children here in the tents, and the men had to drive away the snarling dogs they had left there to guard them. When they emptied the Professor out of his sack, there were screams of fright, and it took several hours to convince the last woman that he was harmless, although there had been no doubt from the start that he was a valuable possession. After a few days they began to move on again, taking everything with them, and traveling only at night as the terrain grew warmer.

Even when all his wounds had healed and he felt no more pain, the Professor did not begin to think again; he ate and defecated, and he danced when he was bidden, a senseless hopping up and down that delighted the children, principally because of the wonderful jangling racket it made. And he generally slept through the heat of the day, in among the camels.

Wending its way southeast, the caravan avoided all stationary civilization. In a few weeks they reached a new plateau, wholly wild and with a sparse vegetation. Here they pitched camp and remained, while the meharis were turned loose to graze. Everyone was happy here; the weather was cooler and there was a well only a few hours away on a seldom-frequented trail. It was here they conceived the idea of taking the Professor to Fogara and selling him to the Touaregs.

It was a full year before they carried out this project. By this time the Professor was much better trained. He could do a handspring, make a series of fearful growling noises which had, nevertheless, a certain element of humor; and when the Chaamba removed the tin from his face they discovered he could grimace admirably while he danced. They also taught him a few basic obscene gestures which never failed to elicit delighted shrieks from the women. He was now brought forth only after especially abundant meals, when there was music and festivity. He easily fell in with their sense of ritual, and evolved an elementary sort of "program" to present when he was called forth: dancing, rolling on the ground, imitating certain animals, and finally rushing toward the group in feigned anger, to see the resultant confusion and hilarity.

When three of the men set out for Fogara with him, they took four meharis with them, and he rode astride his quite naturally. No precautions were taken to guard him, save he was kept among them, one man always staying at the rear of the party.

274

They came within sight of the walls at dawn, and they waited among the rocks all day. At dusk the youngest started out, and in three hours he returned with a friend who carried a stout cane. They tried to put the Professor through his routine then and there, but the man from Fogara was in a hurry to get back to town, so they all set out on the meharis.

In the town they went directly to the villager's home, where they had coffee in the courtyard sitting among the camels. Here the Professor went into his act again, and this time there was prolonged merriment and much rubbing together of hands. An agreement was reached, a sum of money paid, and the Chaamba withdrew, leaving the Professor in the house of the man with the cane, who did not delay in locking him into a tiny enclosure off the courtyard.

The next day was an important one in the Professor's life, for it was then that pain began to stir again in his being. A group of men came to the house, among whom was a venerable gentleman, better clothed than those others who spent their time flattering him, setting fervent kisses upon his hands and the edges of his garments. This person made a point of going into classical Arabic from time to time to impress the others, who had not learned a word of the Koran. Thus his conversation would run more or less as follows: "Perhaps at In Salah. The French there are stupid. Celestial vengeance is approaching. Let us not hasten it. Praise the highest and cast thine anathema against idols. With paint on his face. In case the police wish to look close." The others listened and agreed, nodding their heads slowly and solemnly. And the Professor in his stall beside them listened, too. That is, he was *conscious* of the sound of the old man's Arabic. The words penetrated for the first time in many months. Noises, then: "Celestial vengeance is approaching." Then: "It is an honor. Fifty francs is enough. Keep your money. Good." And the caouadji squatting near him at the edge of the precipice. Then "anathema against idols" and more gibberish. He turned over panting on the sand and forgot about it. But the pain had begun. It operated in a kind of delirium, because he had begun to enter into consciousness again. When the man opened the door and prodded him with his cane, he cried out in a rage, and everyone laughed.

They got him onto his feet, but he would not dance. He stood before them, staring at the ground, stubbornly refusing to move. The owner was furious, and so annoyed by the laughter of the others that he felt obliged to send them away, saying that

275

he would await a more propitious time for exhibiting his property, because he dared not show his anger before the elder. However, when they had left he dealt the Professor a violent blow on the shoulder with his cane, called him various obscene things, and went out into the street, slamming the gate behind him. He walked straight to the street of the Ouled Naïl, because he was sure of finding the Chaamba there among the girls spending the money. And there in a tent he found one of them still abed, while an Ouled Naïl washed the tea glasses. He walked in and almost decapitated the man before the latter had even attempted to sit up. Then he threw his razor on the bed and ran out.

The Ouled Naïl saw the blood, screamed, ran out of her tent into the next, and soon emerged from that with four girls who rushed together into the coffee house and told the caouadji who had killed the Chaamba. It was only a matter of an hour before the French military police had caught him at a friend's house and dragged him off to the barracks. That night the Professor had nothing to eat, and the next afternoon, in the slow sharpening of his consciousness caused by increasing hunger, he walked aimlessly about the courtyard and the rooms that gave onto it. There was no one. In one room a calendar hung on the wall. The Professor watched nervously, like a dog watching a fly in front of its nose. On the white paper were black objects that made sounds in his head. He heard them: *"Grand Epicerie du Sahel. Juin. Lundi, Mardi, Mercredi......."*

The tiny inkmarks of which a symphony consists may have been made long ago, but when they are fulfilled in sound they become imminent and mighty. So a kind of music of feeling began to play in the Professor's head, increasing in volume as he looked at the mud wall, and he had the feeling that he was performing what had been written for him long ago. He felt like weeping; he felt like roaring through the little house, upsetting and smashing the few breakable objects. His motion got no further than this one overwhelming desire. So, bellowing as loud as he could, he attacked the house and its belongings. Then he attacked the door into the street, which resisted for a while and finally broke. He climbed through the opening made by the boards he had ripped apart, and still bellowing and shaking his arms in the air to make as loud a jangling as possible, he began to gallop along the quiet street toward the gateway of the town. A few people looked at him with great curiosity. As he passed the garage, the last building before the high mud archway that framed the desert beyond, a French soldier saw him. *"Tiens,"* he said to himself, "a holy maniac."

Again it was sunset time. The Professor ran beneath the arched gate, turned his face toward the red sky, and began to trot along the Piste d'In Salah, straight into the setting sun. Behind him, from the garage, the soldier took a pot shot at him for good luck. The bullet whistled dangerously near the Professor's head, and his yelling rose into an indignant lament as he waved his arms more wildly, and hopped high into the air at every few steps, in an access of terror.

The soldier watched a while, smiling, as the cavorting figure grew smaller in the oncoming evening darkness, and the rattling of the tin became a part of the great silence out there beyond the gate. The wall of the garage as he leaned against it still gave forth heat, left there by the sun, but even then the lunar chill was growing in the air.

THIRTIETH CENTRIFUGE

Warren Wirtz

These poems were motivated by an approaching thirtieth birthday which seemed numerically neat enough to deserve a record.

Specific references to the occasion are to be found in The Morality of History and The Central Extreme. Otherwise it was intended to serve as a point of departure rather than a theme, and it will be seen that the various relationships existing among all the poems have more importance than any one theme. It may be well to indicate also that The Central Extreme is placed in the middle of the set, and that with the linking of the descent to history in the last poem to the invocation of history in the first, the circle of relationships is closed.

THE MORALITY OF HISTORY

Unkind history, be kind to him
    As communists will give brave men a red
    Revolver. That now, by Julian year and policy
    Alarm may quiet, enemy stumble, example
    Multiply before a second bracket.

If Each count ten, then thirty is a holy
    Number, and twelvemonth more is time for the festive
    Watermelon in a woman's furrow to split
    With ripeness; there may yet be time to postulate
    The proper passion, for the male muse planteth,
    Woman tendeth, and their oval seed is flat black.

And, history, be graciously old and strange
    Or sharp and new; prate not your spate of romantic
    Rückblicks, reasonable naïveté, late season
    Rotting, for the ectoplasmic Third has prospered
    More than helpless Christ or (even then!)
    His twilit super-daddy.

If I knew

A good address for answers, I should pose as prophet
And pray: Blank, for Lord, I have seen young men
Flourish in youth and die, ah soon, and fertility
Bless the aged. Untangling will from ambivalent
Ignorance, look into this man and follow
The strange arrow of subconscious probability.

CONCERTED PLAN

Internal success, requiring marvelous balance
Between the ego and the id, accepts
The ragged answers to the vehement questions
Children ask. So *logos* for you will grow lambent
With wonder: your electric adventure will glow with
    empirical
Delight.
           But an untoward crab nibbles each hero's
Privates. *Philosophia perennis,* canon
By crab—six centuries ago lascivious and stupid
Monks miscopied, and now he is a hundred
Years ahead. Take brilliant X, whose silver
Tongue is *à la page* and will not pun
Philosophy. His illuminated art
Fogs back to comfort.
            And you wishfully wonder,
Muttering your rosary of unite, unite!

Impoverish not nor overpeople this silly,
Hopeful world, nor walk the indifferent tight rope,
But suffer and reclassify. Believe,
In the cool dazzle of eternal light, believe
The magnificent, ridiculous moment, pronouncing chiefly
The starchy white collars strangling immoral scholars.

MURDER

Reduce absurdly, seduce the mask in the pane
Which names the murderous butcher who splintered the deer
And with three clean strokes of his hatchet killed your dear,
Your true love. The pillow's crusted stain,
The powder on the stair, your rifled drawers,
Crumpled cravats—they will not lead you to the man:
Only the actor outside your window, whose moan
Is low and who is trampling on your prize flowers.

279

Oh, that this should happen to you, whose blot
    Was a mere mildly necromaniac aunt
    And a crazy religious cousin! Why could you not
    Have heard the warning tom in the alley last night?

That most wonderful woman followed and remembered
    But never understood. What does she say,
    Lying deep in the earth dejected and dismembered?
    Is she praising love and singing to your baby?

Night follow black night, you draw the tight blind.
    If you heard his name whispered, you have forgot.
    Garotted in your study's wilderness, hear only the wind
    Repeating the to-him-who-hath it cannot forget.

DELUSION

By Lake of the Isles, where autumn's ordeal
By fire and the poplar's phallic death-yearning
Remind me of Y, I review his burning
To see what story the ashes will tell:
On dock, in boat, by gate, through wicket,
Practicing apostasy
They perpetrated ecstasy,
And love gushed from a wide-lipped spigot.

Too fast. Sun on the polished disc
Of the bronzed leg razed the hotel
Which took with it several innocent people,
And several people running the risk
Of ivy found only a girl and a man
Down by the water getting a tan.

By the water's edge, under the birch
On pneumatic moss in the humid thicket,
Young lover forever clutches the ticket
Padding and smoothing a substantial berth
To heaven, but the ninety days flame by
Effacing hotel and ancient ivy,
And the ticket will be for a color movie
With a cypress lake and a postcard sky.

           * * *

Let him bury only such pleasure
   Boys bury: razor blades, tinfoil
   Old knives, that x not telling a spoil
Uncover a quaint and fabulous treasure;
So that pleasure coiling with gratitude
Or couchant with pity may not seem
The pigment of the Indian traveler's dream,
But the amorous shade from the brittle hood.

And if the vain tiger poised in the liver
   Rehearse life, pant ecstasy,
   Conduct love, deny frenzy,
Drown him in that stream quasi-river
Between gift and giver and cortex and liver.

A CASE FOR DEFENDANT LOVE

If love be not exhausted,
   And so progressives think,
Such licence ought really be trusted,
   Pen ever craving drink;

Whose demented variables, or tame,
   Pedantically alter by phase,
Incurring mostly blame,
   But several deserving praise.

Praise speechless eye, praise lip,
   Color, suave demean,
And highly inflected hip
   For old, imperative routine.

Chant priceless babe, sweet thing;
   Speak roses to the one:
Lovers equally sing
   Infrequent solos of swan.

Curse pressure's bagatelle,
   The gadfly's intuited sign
Of easy direction to hell,
   But stop, for they malign

Young lover holding too tight
  Because he lacks technique
And the hapless, long-tailed kite
  Let out by possession gone weak.

                * * *

Whether love be get or talk
  Or do or sit or give;
To learn, to feel, to walk;
  Whether love be eat to live

Or live to grow, elicit
  Palpitate or mope;
Be visitation or visit,
  Be moan, be trust, be grope;

Be pure idea, sheer dove,
  Or action involving curtain;
Whatever totals love,
  This much is fairly certain:

That being essentially water,
  It hankers after vapor
And the suck of a greenhouse blotter;
  Love dries quickly on paper.

Though it needs a whore-heart bigness
  And a well-fed diaphragm laugh
To counter objection to harness
  And complete distaste for chaff,

The cycle itself holds interest
  And zigzags nice on a chart,
With up the heave of the chest
  And down the valves of the heart.

ILLUSION

Lacrymonious, my favorite Krenekism,
  Rolled like a legless drum to the Mississippi.
  And you, too, have probably after schism
  Crossed the logical street to avoid that unhappy

Encounter. Over the hazardous terrain between
    The mogul puffing limericks through a post-prandial cigar
    And the great, sober man, who shouted and was lean,
    Because it had no landing strip, you could hear

The sadistic tree like a slapstick on your back,
    Guess spoil-sport snipers in the bush. Unproved
    By the gigantic bee humming through cloud and flak,
    The fatal sting was pointless from that altitude.

Twice I wept real tears, not *lacrimae rerum,*
    And I must admit as well I heard a host
    Of angels making merry in a celestial room
    As big as this earth. They were laughing and leaping; they
      danced
    And sang, and the end of their pure white revel was a toast
    To heaven's and devilish laughter's plenum.

THE CENTRAL EXTREME

Kouskous from Syria, Mazaryk Czech,
    Furor biographicus;—
    Thirty is the time of year when thick
    And fast, the legal mind makes case

Of case, relies on distance, counts
    The clockwise day, and the wary mentor
    With blank for face and mood for tense
    Watches erg and atom fleeing center.

In short, it may not seem a waste
    To have gone all the way to Monte Carlo
    For a fling at a fortune and a lightning taste
    Of elegant fashion and such easy dough,

For Nicollet Avenue is not the Azure
    Coast, and travel broadens the mind;
    And you have a clear idea of adventure
    Which otherwise might have been hard to find.

Airing his fairly impractical statistic,
    The poet and possible intellectual
    May happen to whittle a walking stick
    For tapping his way into an effectual

283

And anonymous happiness. Or the pine,
Soft and yielding to luck, may shape
An opener for the cautious letter the ship
Carries. So let your light shine.

But if he trade interest for chance
Under a blanket decadent or mellow,
What will it profit if he dance
To the wentle-trap's sad *ritornello?*

Refusing to underline the shock
　　Prescribed for professional conversation,
　　He will choose the careful hero, then look
Away. And wound with jubilation,

Washed and combed, he will laugh from his belly
　　When the lily trumpets under the chin
　　How once he married a pleasantly silly
Old woman to a relatively dirty old man.

THE SOCIALIST'S PROGRESS

L'enfant prodigue, a prodigy
　　Like little Mozart at his clavier,
　　Had soft, industrial palms and a tear
To tug at the nourishing cord; tragedy
Loomed bigger than a broken heart
On Hollywood's broad and silky screen.
But birds sang, and fields were green,
Under the stinging, under the smart.

Music was sweeter far when, returned
　　And selfless, the man reached out his hand
　　To sweeten preposterous pay, and friend,
Years dead, forgot how once he mourned
The prodigy; mother's pride
With characteristic ease, devotion,
And skill dived into the churning ocean
And played his music on the tide.

My sister's heart is a hospital where clinical
    Calm questions to health and delegates
    No deed. Nor do poets or renegades
    From ease, beginning or ending financial,
    Though for them the absolute test
    Is the lights flashing in a million houses,
    Which tell what changes and what pleases,
    And flatter the diamond of each man's interest.

DILETTANTE

Having tickled thirteen humorless muses
    In thirteen distinct languages with tolerable success,
    Our butterfly will woo Cro-Magnon man
    For a capacious skull like Da Vinci's. Cultivated
    Ladies once played the harp, sang, danced
    The minuet and painted, but the sub's oil slick,
    Which is its very maximum of love,
    Though it cover Minnetonka, will never reach
    Pacific.
            For, oh, the world is full, too full
    For living if heart have wings to fly and eye
    A need to dance! And not before return
    From Mecca and the final revision, which ends as it
    Began at the starting place, can the truly voluptous
    Understand that we shall never rest
    Outside of death, if death itself be rest.
               *   *   *

The paramecium divides. In love
    Open to suggestion, the chartreuse negress
    With the fuschia gloves checks only her bird's pulse:
    So, one, Philemon, whose lactic luck ran over;
    So, two, the ant wrestling with his locomotive;
    So, three, the poet with a social worker's soul;
    And since every man is certain of his own identity,
    The moot fool must depend on the grasshopper's meager
        charity.

ALLEGORY OF THE THREE ENEMIES

"Because I would kill myself for love of me,
    Because I looked in the mirror and saw an ape,
    Because I daily sabotage my hope
    Which was blind hope you loved and meant to keep,
    I chose you for my perfect enemy."

"At first it was not clear. I was too young."

"You were young, and then I sought a stronger weapon
    To fight the growing harm which might one day happen
    To me, an innocent man. And if bitter tongue
    Grow sweet and hate grow weak, I die disgraced."

"Speech, yes, is strange. I would have killed you then
    When I was drunk with hate from hurt for man."

"I was strong, a careless victor; your chaste,
    Your splendid, your elaborate dying kept me pure.
    What do you ask to live now I have lost?"

"My pure revenge will please most exquisite taste:
    You will eat the fancy fungus of your fear
    And with this delectable mushroom take your life."

"You give too much for the honey and the small loaf
    I stole, and I have never died before."

"With such simple gesture I put down the pack
    Which bruised my back and leaves me bent and aged.
    How in little time is all changed!
    Because the vacuum cherished only pique,—"

"I die, and mine is a violent, unjust fate."

"Because this man surprised me into hate,
    Beat prisoner and sacked his land, I have sent
    Him to his death with hate that I may live,
    For he was much too helpless to repent,
    And I was far too weary to forgive."

CONTEMPORARY CRISIS

Some aesthetes and all reformers, when the sun goes down,
    Focus their five immaculate faculties
    On the century's mutations and find them not good.
    But the igloo's nights are long, and this will be
    The glass brick tower where the specialist may go
    To study the habits of deep sea fish or the Italian
    Primitives, where, *le frileux* would say, there are lampsful
    Of light but oh so little heat.   From here

    He will write an important letter explaining theory
    And discovery; it will be to his wife who will understand
    Because she loves him.   In Yellowstone, he left
    A pot boiling over with mud, and he will be sorry
    Once each night.   He will converse with the penguin Bach
    And the holy fathers who walk in a ring wearing seal.

Love is much bigger than one and warmer than seal.
    But what shall we do with the Prussian who fires the mud?
    What do with the moneys that daub the lurid poster
    And snag the frightened fish?   When engineers
    Design a cable from the silent circle of penguins
    To the greatest geyser, psychoanalysts, referring
    To pleasure's postponement, will prefer to speak of patience.

    But in fleet car, the solid act must splinter
    Steel, and the chiseled thought make dust of ivory,
    For a man's memory is both fortress and apology.

THE AESTHETE'S POSITIVE APOLOGIA

"The mental exercise, the pursuit of reason
    And the doctrine that plush and poison can kill a bull,
    Though none is so useful in winter as close-woven wool,
Have sent me packing to the Louvre in every season.

"Strange that the clerk's spine, which tingles to facts, should
        be mine
    And dictate the eccentric microcosm's unholiness,
    And that I should not feel a spastic loneliness,
When the atrophied will resigns, for whiskers and wine.

287

"St. Augustine was a vagrant aesthete and drunk
  Who apprehended the naughtiness in beauty.
  His metamathematical cinch was duty
And alum, but for me, faith is a rather large chunk.

"And the singular cult of conservative beauty, if you like,
  Plus the plural hopes which rest on the senses' proof
  Are my present ritual. *A leaky roof,*
You will say, *the picture is lacking, the bung of the dike,*

"But swimming forever through religion's and art's fluidity
  And holding too long to your rock, beware lest you sink
  To the floor, or making a crag of what you think,
You break your bill pecking at time's quiddity."

TIME'S RHETORIC

Tail in mouth, streamliners whoop
  From city to village along the moralizing
  Parallels of steel and of these lines;

  The gandy dancer's moment shines,
  But the sight from the jerky platform is paralyzing:
  So fades the rose; thus tulips droop.

  Who knows the flash of their pyrotechnics?—
  Playboys always jump at a chase,
  While oaks record with a fat or thin ring,

  Nonagenarians find them amazing,
  And astronomers, speaking in terms of space
  And years of light, explain light tricks.

That turtle we found today on the track,
  He had no schedule except the one
  That played accordion on his back,

  But then, *bon voyage!* May there be
  Calliopes and elephants and fun
  At your circuses, all free.

288

Go to the attic before you leave.
 Behind the form and in the trunk
 You will find a letter you must believe.

 It will tell you all you need to know
 About yourself. Study the junk
 There, close the heavy lid, then go:

Say fair weather time is the very best
 Time, spindling the early spring,
 Loitering in autumn, bringing rest

 To watches, giving wing to wing
 Before snow whitewash bud and nest,
 ¡And a measure of song for the goldfinch to sing.

But do not answer the night the stars
 Broadcast the catchy, fool-proof quiz
 Which puzzled Jurassic megalosaurs:

Look away far through the foam and fizz,
 Then tote this life in hermetic green jars
 To the mouldy cellar which history is.

EXISTENTIALISM: A NEW TREND IN PHILOSOPHY

Paul Kecskemeti

I. A New Language in Philosophy

MOST PHILOSOPHICAL SCHOOLS in the past, from antiquity to the nineteenth century, no matter how much they differed among themselves, agreed in one thing: they placed the abstract and universal above the concrete and particular. The older philosophies sought to formulate truths valid for all time and for every person. They encouraged the tendency to look at things as mere instances of the working of universal laws. Hence, when a burning practical question arose in the life of an individual, this philosophical tradition required him to trace it back to the pertinent general laws. Philosophy as such was concerned merely with great, all-embracing questions, such as the Meaning of Life, the Fundamental Laws of Nature, the Essence of Truth, and so on. In so far as there was any application of these abstract verities to practical problems, the individual was supposed to work it out for himself; the philosopher merely gave the general framework. He was convinced, of course, that the general framework was all that mattered; the application to individual cases followed all by itself. Thus, philosophy spoke a truly abstract language, every term of which impartially had the same meaning for every individual.

It was no less than a complete revolution in philosophy when an isolated thinker in small Denmark, Soeren Kierkegaard, in the '40s of the nineteenth century began to speak in a new language. Opening any of Kierkegaard's works at random, one may well doubt whether his subject is philosophy at all. There is no mention of the "great questions of life," or rather, we hear about "great questions of life" in an entirely different sense. For instance, Kierkegaard discusses the question whether a person should marry or not; this question is raised, not as the abstract problem of marriage which is the same for every person, but as a concrete problem facing one particular young man in connection with one particular young girl. Kierkegaard discovered that these were the really important problems, since they were the ones that made a difference to one's life. He called these problems the "existential" problems, and put them squarely before the philosopher.

"Abstraction," Kierkegaard said, "is without interest; to exist is the highest interest of the existing subject." Or again: "What is abstract thinking? It is a kind of thinking for which there is no person who thinks. It disregards everything except thought, and thought can exist within itself as its own medium. Existence, on the other hand, is not thoughtless, but in existence, thought is in a foreign medium."

The novelty of this language consists in the fact that "existence," "interest," and the like, are used as primitive terms. Older philosophies used as primitives such terms as "idea," "sensation," "emotion," etc. That is to say, the world as a reality was built up out of sense data, ideas, and emotions, or whatever the "x" was that "caused" sense data, ideas, and emotions. What these sense data, ideas, and emotions "meant" for the individual subject was entirely *his* affair. His "existence" and "interests" were whatever followed, in a particular case, from a constellation of the primitive data (the sensations, ideas, emotions); they were secondary and derivative. For Kierkegaard, however, existence as such, interest as such, belong to the primary stuff of reality.

Since the existence of the individual and his vital interests cannot be deduced from primitive terms, the philosopher must not be preoccupied with impersonal sense data and ideas but must become a "subjective thinker." As such, he is endowed with "imagination, feeling and dialectic in the immediacy of existence with passion." To the extent that the thinker exists in subjectivity, his thoughts have real pertinence.

The supreme interest of Kierkegaard's hero, the subjective thinker, was "becoming a Christian" as a condition for salvation. For him, it was necessary to abandon abstract living and thinking primarily because there was no other way to become a Christian. According to Kierkegaard, it is the isolated individual who has to work out his salvation by becoming a Christian; this is achieved in a supreme "moment" when one embraces "faith" in an experience incommensurable with the regular happenings of everyday life. The essence of the "moment" of achieving faith is a passionate risking of everything for the sake of something that is not accessible to reason. The content of faith is absurd and paradoxical; but then, nothing except the absurd and paradoxical can be existentially relevant; whatever is logical and reasonable is necessarily abstract and neutral with regard to existential questions.

Kierkegaard's writings remained virtually unknown for about fifty years after his death. Since the beginning of the century, however, his fame and influence have been spreading. It was by no means only theologians who were interested in him as the exponent of a paradoxical idea of Christianity; his "existential" approach, his stand against abstract thinking, deeply influenced philosophers who did not share his religious preoccupation. Among existentialist thinkers today, there are nihilists and atheists as well as Christian believers.

The basic idea of existentialism is that the individual human being always is in a situation; that his situation means something to him; and that this meaning cannot be derived from elements devoid of such existential meaning.

What, then, is the task the existential philosopher sets himself? Obviously, he cannot hope to solve all existential problems of every individual human being. Yet, he wants to give some guidance to individuals enmeshed in their respective situations. In order to do this, of course, he has to take up a position outside the various concrete situations. In this sense, he must remain abstract; no philosophy can be anything else. In another sense, existentialist philosophy contrasts with abstract philosophy in that the former deals with the concrete material which makes up situations, whereas the latter's material is situationally neutral. The existentialist teaches his pupil to derive meanings from primitive terms which are themselves meaningful, whereas the abstract philosopher gives directions for constructing meanings with situationally meaningless raw materials.

This cleavage is, it seems to me, an extremely radical and important one. Existentialism is (to use William James' phrase) tender-minded and pessimistic; abstract thinking is—in the form in which it is influential today—tough-minded and optimistic. I mean that the existentialist does not dare to break up the stuff of human experience too radically; he fears that if one lets go of meanings, they can not be recaptured again. The abstract thinker, that is to say, the pragmatist and scientist, on the other hand, feels confident that meaning will emerge all by itself if the analysis of experience is pushed far enough in the direction of unanalyzable and uninterpretable ultimates. It is important to bear this in mind, for it is easy to be misled by the often seemingly "tough," disillusioned and misanthropic language of many existentialists. Basically, as Jean-Paul Sartre, the leader of French existentialism, put it, existentialism is humanism. As such, it is opposed to anti-humanistic scientism and pragmatism.

Which type of thinking is appropriate to our age? This question cannot be answered impartially, because one of the main issues disputed by the two schools is precisely whether the one or the other is more appropriate to our time. The time has not yet, so to speak, made up its mind; the only thing we can be sure about is that it is about as easy to interpret our time in "existentialist" terms as in "abstract" ones. In the present situation, it is just as "natural" to hold that the understanding of the condition of man and communication between human beings alone can avert doom, as to hold that the resolute application of scientific method alone can save humanity. At the end of this paper, I shall indicate my own stand with regard to this alternative.

II. Existence and its Limits

Present-day existentialism can be traced back to two German philosophers who were deeply influenced by Kierkegaard, Martin Heidegger and Karl Jaspers.

Heidegger starts from what he calls the problem of "ontology," namely, the question what we mean when we say that something "is" or exists "in reality." Do we mean—or, rather, should we mean—that this really existing thing is something that can be sensed? or that it can be measured by scientific instruments? or that it can be thought of? or that its existence can be logically proved? Or, if none of these "definitions of being" is correct, which one is?

In Heidegger's opinion, all the definitions given above are inadequate. He feels that whatever presupposes another being that senses or measures or thinks it cannot be the example of "being" in that emphatic sense he has in mind. He finds only one type of "being" which is not derived from the being of something else but is self-contained, namely, the existence of the individual human being. The human individual, Heidegger says, not only *is*, but in so far as he is, his existence *matters* to him. This "being-that-matters-to-the-thing-that-is" he calls "existence," and he holds that all modes of being have to be defined in terms of their relation to "existence." All this is rather close to the Kierkegaardian conception of existence.

But older philosophies also come to mind at this point. We may think of the Greek Protagoras who said that "man is the measure of all things—of the existence of the real ones as well as of the non-existence of the unreal ones." We may also recall Descartes who found that there was just one proposition which withstood his persistent, systematic doubting, the proposition "I think, hence I am." In these older philosophies, however, the standards by which "being" is judged are situationally neutral; in Protagoras' case, if we accept Plato's interpretation in the "Theaetetus," they are sensations; in Descartes' case, they are thoughts. Heidegger's standard, on the other hand, is a sense of urgency, of anxiety, which belongs to a situational context. Heidegger's "existence" is not only recorded like a datum but "means" something to the being that exists and is anxious to exist.

This "existence," Heidegger holds, always projects a meaningful, functional world around itself. "Being-in-a-world" is one of its essential characteristics; this is how Heidegger disposes of the old philosophical teaser of the "existence of the outside world." Within the world which is thus an attribute of the existence of the individual, reality is encountered, first of all, in the shape of the functional roles or "handinesses" of things. A chair as "something-to-sit-upon" is more real than a "physical object" or a "sense datum."

Existence essentially "cares" about things; it can be interpreted as "care" and "anxiety." The latter is an especially fundamental aspect of the reality of existence: it is a "metaphysical" emotion in which existence senses the "possibility of non-being." In "anxiety," existence comes nearest to a complete and adequate understanding of itself, because anxiety contains in itself the most fundamental and radical piece of knowledge that is given to man, namely, the knowledge that his existence is finite. It is bounded by death which alone makes it whole. Even during life, existence is "conditioned by death,"—not in the sense that man knows it as a fact of experience that he will die, and not in the sense that he explicitly thinks of his own death all the time, but in the sense of his "anxiety" as a motor of existence gives urgency to all things that matter. There is "reality" because man dies, that is, because he has not infinite time on his hands. If one could wait indefinitely, nothing would "matter"; hence, nothing would be real.

Existence, however, is not only "conditioned by death"; it also *forgets* death and builds up a fictitious world of sham permanence and trivial understanding around itself. This is the "everyday," "public" world, the world of the anonymous mass (Heidegger calls the latter *"das Man,"* using as a substantive the German pronoun corresponding to "one" in phrases like "one wears . . . ," "one feels . . . ," etc.). It is a world in which man constantly hides beneath the mask of anonymity, silencing his anxiety by commonplace sententiousness and meaningless news-mongering. Heidegger's message seems to be that man should strive to lead a "genuine" life as much as possible, extricating himself from the mass which alienates him from himself. Thus freed, man can have essential experiences upon which his death casts a shadow of urgency.

The other outstanding exponent of German existentialism, Karl Jaspers, does not isolate the individual the way Heidegger does. One of the basic categories of *his* existentialism is "communication." "Nobody can be saved alone," he says; "there is no truth through which I could reach my goal in isolation." For Jaspers, too, "genuineness" and "being oneself" are ultimate goals; but these goals should be sought through communication, through self-expression, through the "loving struggle" with a partner, and, virtually at least, through the development of a community embracing all individual existences.

Jaspers is far less nihilistic than Heidegger. For Heidegger, existence is "thrown into" the inexorable, irresistible stream of Time; for Jaspers, ultimate reality transcends Time. "In every act performed out of primordial freedom," he says, "in every form of absolute consciousness, in every act of love, temporality, although emphasized rather than forgotten, is in fact transcended into eternity. Existential time as the appearance of absolute Being becomes, on the one hand, inexorable 'time as such,' and, on the other, the transcending of this time into eternity." This passage shows that Jaspers' version of existentialism represents far less complete rupture with the tradition of German philosophical idealism than Heidegger's one.

With all this, Jaspers, who is more "tender-minded" than Heidegger, is also more pessimistic. Heidegger, like Bertrand Russell, builds his philosophy on "a firm foundation of despair": since he expects nothing except annihilation, he cannot be disappointed. On the contrary, he is able to extract a sense of haughty, bitter, icy triumph from his contemplation of the finiteness of existence: just in so far as he does not "forget" death, man, a finite being, can achieve dignity and genuineness. In this way, he can succeed. For Jaspers, however, reality holds only failure in store for man. "The ultimate is failure." A genuine pessimist, Jaspers admits disappointment; he disdains Heidegger's stoical device of denying that he wants to have what cannot be had. Failure, he says, consists in not attaining or losing what one craves most, and all human striving is bounded by such failure. As a prophet of doom, Jaspers is far more specific than Heidegger. He wrote in 1932: "Should there be a possibility to destroy the foundations of human existence by technological means, there could hardly be any doubt that one day it would be done . . . Historical experience with man shows that the most dreadful things that are possible are perpetrated somewhere, at some time by someone."

For both Jaspers and Heidegger, man's situation achieves meaningfulness in the measure as it is confronted with its extreme possibilities, its limits. For Heidegger, the extreme possibility is death; for Jaspers, it is one of the "limit situations" (death, suffering, conflict). Both in their philosophy go to the limit and think under the highest pressure.

III. A Quest for the Absolute.

How can we understand the emergence of existentialist philosophies in Germany at a certain historical moment, between the two world wars?

It is obvious that there was something in the social, moral and intellectual situation of Germany between the two wars that prepared the soil for existentialist doctrines. To speak of the social factors first, we know that the war and the subsequent inflation permanently destroyed the economic basis of millions of middle-class families. To those affected, mere "existence" seemed, in fact, the quintessence of all problems; at the same time, they felt that traditional abstract doctrines were of no help in solving the problem of "existing."

Other experiences of the same generation also brought it to grips with "limit situations." Death, of course, had been a daily experience at the front, and many young Germans responded to this experience by developing a Heideggerian attitude long before Heidegger's book was published: they felt that the imminence of death heightened their sense of "existing." We know that after the war ended, flocks of young Germans found it simply impossible to go back to civilian life; they went wherever the spark of war still flickered in unruly Europe, to the Baltic, to Silesia, to the strifetorn industrial cities of Germany, in an attempt to perpetuate their "front experience" of communing, in "sacred comradeship," in the mystery of Death. Half illuminates, half mercenaries, these young Germans became a potential factor in the conservation and strengthening of the militarist spirit in Germany. And this spirit gained new recruits from year to year in growing boys who never experienced war but to whom their elders somehow transmitted the feeling that soldiering, bringing one in contact with death, heightened one's sense of existing. Militarism thus exercized a powerful lure away from the "triviality of everyday life."

There were other kinds of Germans too—those who hated war and wanted to build up a radically new world with new goals and values. But the nation was tired and workaday triviality soon reasserted itself. In the end, the Nazis profited, not only by the smoldering fires of militarism, but also by the frustrated gropings of abortive idealism. Their barked commands soon silenced all questioning.

Before they seized power, however, there had been much questioning and soul-searching. Was there a philosophy that could make sense of the radically new experiences of this generation? The official, academic philosophy of the pre-war years clearly was powerless to do this. A new philosophical approach was needed for intellectual orientation in a new, unstable world.

The predominant philosophy in Germany during the period immediately preceding the First World War had been neo-Kantianism. The outstanding characteristic of this school was a certain subdued restraint which may itself be understood as a reaction to the intellectual debauch of Hegelian philosophy. While the Hegelians had conceived philosophy as a "super-science" which is called upon to discover all essential facts about reality with the help of "dialectics," the neo-Kantians left the discovery and the explanation of the facts of the world to the various sciences. What philosophy could do, according to them, was merely to examine the methods and procedures of science and to marshal reasons for considering scientific findings as valid.

The same neo-Kantian approach was also applied to other cultural pursuits beside science. The neo-Kantian philosophy of law, for instance, examined the peculiar "validity" of legal findings, presupposing the existence and validity of the legal system within which they were delivered. Whether he was dealing with religion, or art, or any other field of human endeavor, the neo-Kantian philosopher contented himself with the rather secondary role of examining the peculiar kind of "validity" of an organized body of experience. He furnished a running commentary for the doings of the specialists who were in charge of the various cultural domains.

The mood underlying this kind of philosophy was that fundamentally, all was right with the world, since there were experts for everything who could not be wrong; or if they were, it would just be too bad, because no one could question their findings anyway. The neo-Kantian philosophy admirably expressed the average German's awe in the presence of every kind of expert and official. After the war, however, it was simply impossible to leave things at that. Authorities in every field had received too severe a jolt; a new philosophy was needed to replace the old beacon-lights which were swaying too dangerously with the heaving and crumbling of the ground to which they were fastened.

This situation gave Edmund Husserl's "phenomenological" school a chance to be listened to. Rebelling against neo-Kantianism, Husserl at the beginning of the century gave out the motto for philosophy to "get at the things themselves," to seek original rather than secondary knowledge. This original knowledge concerned "essential" laws—laws objective, eternal and immutable which were logical prior to, and independent of, empirical data. The claim that such laws existed and could be discovered was by no means extravagant, since the propositions of logic and mathematics are, in fact, "essential laws" in Husserl's sense. The question is, however, how far the domain of "essential laws" reaches. Is it confined to logic and mathematics? In that case, something, to be sure, would be safe from the danger of being sucked into the maelstrom of the general collapse, but far too little to give comfort to man in the sorry state of his affairs,—inasmuch as Ludwig Wittgenstein gave some very good reasons for assuming that logic and mathematics consisted of nothing but "tautologies," i. e., that they gave no real information about the world. What was needed, however, was information about the world, and about man, and, if possible, information of an "essential" nature, for the sake of certainty. Was phenomenology able to furnish it?

It had been understood from the beginning that no "essential laws" could be discovered concerning the physical world, and, in general, concerning the objects studied by the sciences. That is to say, phenomenology did not claim to be able to tell, prior to, and independently of, any experience, whether anything was either "necessary" or "impossible" in the realm of nature, apart from mathematical and logical necessities and impossibilities, which, however, are trivial. Phenomenology did, however, claim to discover "essential" laws concerning human attitudes. It proclaimed that, if man adopted any given attitude, certain things followed for him with ineluctable necessity: he committed himself to following through the inner logic of his attitude. It was, for instance, strictly "impossible" to see a color without seeing an extension. And the law expressing this impossibility was an "essential" law; in order to grasp it, it was necessary to conduct psychological experiments and to explore the actual behavior of human beings. It was sufficient to form a mental image of "color" and "extension."

Husserl developed a method for the discovery and isolation of similar "essential" laws concerning human attitudes and states of consciousness. He called this method the phenomenological *"epoché,"* a Greek word which means "abstention from judgment." The essence of the method was that the subject had to observe his own consciousness in an effort to find something that would remain as it is, no matter what would be true concerning the outside world. It is obvious that if there are essential laws concerning human states of consciousness, some such device is needed to discover them, since they have to be logically independent of judgments about the outside world.

During the post-war years, when phenomenology enjoyed a considerable vogue in Germany, its representatives were active in exploring all human attitudes for their "essential" elements. The general trend of this work was directed against all shades of subjectivism and relativism. The phenomenologists sought, for instance, to save values from their bondage to empirical psychology. Their point was that questions of value are questions of right, and that questions of right cannot logically depend on knowledge about how people actually behave. Does it not follow from this that the solution of questions of value must be based upon "essential" insights?

Such a bold assertion of absolute values was, of course, just the thing which a generation bewildered by the collapse of its values needed. And it cannot be denied that the phenomenological distinction between questions of fact and questions of right made sense. But how could simple human beings discover beyond doubt what was right,—that is, not what "right" was in general, but what the right thing to do was in their situation, here and now? Husserl's method could not help, because it was too abstract and detached. Clearly, *"epoché"* was something for philosophers only; it was unable to clear up practical situations. Other phenomenologists stressed the intuitive approach to values, but this avenue seemed to lead back to subjectivism, unless one was resolved to proclaim his own value intuitions as *the* objective truth about values. If one wanted to live by the principles of phenomenology, one needed, as a supplement to it, a dependable method of applying those principles to practical situations.

This was Heidegger's problem. His existentialism represents an attempt to make phenomenology vital. He wanted to lay bare, not the structure of this or that attitude, or of "pure consciousness" in general, but of vital interaction with the world. What Heidegger asserts about "existence," "anxiety," "care," etc., is meant as a set of "essential" laws—but essential laws of live situations, not of pale, abstract consciousness.

Was this the "supplement" to phenomenology that was needed to render it applicable to concrete questions of right? I do not think so. For the required addition was not, as a matter of fact, an analysis of human existence as such, but guidance as to how to make a reasonably objective estimate, in one's own situation, of what is right. And Heidegger's method made no contribution to this task. On the contrary, his radical individualism tended to obscure the objectivity of values which phenomenology sought to establish. The one absolute principle of behavior which Heidegger did proclaim was that of "genuineness," but his indications as to how to achieve it remained vague.

Jaspers reached existentialism by a different route, coming from a different tradition. His thinking is rooted in North German, Protestant and subjectivistic antecedants, contrasting with the brittle, South German and vaguely Catholic objectivism of the phenomenologist school. Jaspers' outlook is broader, more tolerant, more sympathetic than that of Heidegger; he wants to integrate in his system as many spiritual trends as possible, while Heidegger's aim is the "destruction" of the history of philosophy. But the final practical conclusion one may derive from Jaspers' philosophy also amounts to little more than the "realization of one's own potentialities." German existentialism failed to work out an objective theory of values. It forged no intellectual weapons to combat the moral anarchy which was an important factor in the rise of Nazism.

Or should we go even further than this, and say that German existentialism was essentially related to Nazism and positively contributed to it?

Heidegger's own behavior—he joined the Nazis and acted abominably towards Husserl—is apt to strengthen such a suspicion; Jaspers, on the other hand, firmly rejected Nazism. Moreover, our own description of the German post-war situation suggested a strong analogy between existentialism on the one hand, and certain Nazi and pre-Nazi attitudes on the other. It seems to me, however, that one can speak only of certain points of contact between Nazism and German existentialism, and not of an essential inner relatedness.

Let us consider some of these points of contact. Heidegger's theory of man's being "thrown into" the world is itself no Nazi tenet, but it is a nihilistic one and may be used in rationalizing one's yielding to Nazism. For if man is thrown into a fatal whirl of time and space, how can he reject wrongs which are firmly entrenched at the place and time where he had been "thrown"? Another point of contact is the dramatization of existence which is essential to both Heidegger's and Jaspers' theory. The thesis that life derives its meaning from death or from "limit situations" sounds like a glorification of militarism. We may also recall certain other aspects of Heidegger's theory: his depreciation of everyday routine, his contempt for the anonymous mass. All this combined easily with the romantic side of Nazism, its exaltation of dangerous and heroic living, its cult of a super-humanly bold and unscrupulous élite.

And yet, all these parallels are rather superficial. To be sure, a youth drunken with yearning for military glory may use the theory of "limit situations" as a rationalization of his attitude, but is this the real import of the theory? Should we not rather say that, precisely because "limit situations" are basic to existence, we need no extraordinary adventures to be confronted with them? And as for the élite of those who live genuinely, it certainly cannot be adequately represented by a political machine, built upon blackmail, demagoguery and terror. We must not forget that Heidegger is, first and foremost, an individualist. He sharply distinguishes "existence," and that means individual existence, as a unique mode of being, from all other modes of being, and especially that of mere things. Herein lies the germ of the recognition of man's essential dignity. This dignity is, I repeat, inherent in the individual as such. Heidegger says that existence is never "a case or instance of a species of existing things." In terms of existence, all humans have equal dignity. Heidegger, unfortunately, never explicitly drew these conclusions from his own theory, but they are inevitable. When Heidegger joined the Nazis, he betrayed his own philosophy.

Jaspers' case, while morally more simple, is more complicated on the level of theory. The danger of Jaspers' existentialism lies

301

in its too great inclusiveness. Everything has its niche in his system, including the romantic concepts of "people" and "race." He speaks of these under the heading of "passion towards Night" to which he neatly assigns its place in the scheme of things. But that place is a subordinate one. Control belongs to the "light" side of existence, to Reason. It is, to be sure, a Reason too much concerned with reconciling opposites and accomplishing virtuoso feats of intuition, but Reason nevertheless.

The criticism we have to make against German existentialism, then, is not that it represents a philosophical expression of Nazi attitudes, but that it does not push existential analysis far enough to make it applicable to the individual's situation here and now. What German existentialism gives us is still on the whole an abstract, formal analysis of existence as such, in spite of the existentialist language used which deprecates mere abstraction.

IV. *Existence and Action*

Of all European nations after the First World War, the French were the most knowing and the most bitter. To that generation it seemed impossible to believe in the existence of higher motives and ideal strivings in man. The assumption of unmitigated egoism and lack of sense of responsibility seemed axiomatic. Every one, it seemed, had to look out for himself. If mythical collective persons—such as the Country or Class or Humanity—claimed one's allegiance, one could be sure of being imposed upon. Sometimes it was impossible to remain aloof, since the myths were too powerful to permit the individual to resist their pressure. But the individual was able to *know*, at least, that he was being imposed upon. He also could deliberately choose to take advantage of the vogue of one or the other myth. Why not since there existed no valid moral law compelling one to condemn such behavior? Everything was in doubt, except that the individual "existed" and was anxious to exist. But this generation in France discovered that it was difficult for the individual to "exist" if no justification for his actions was possible. The problem was how to "exist" without the possibility of justifying one's existence in terms of higher laws or ideals.

Yes, there were concrete institutions to which the individual could anchor his existence—the State and the Church. Both were going concerns, not needful of any justification; what was needed was a constructive attitude whereby one could add to their substance. As Henri Massis said, the problem for man was to build, not to justify.

The epochal importance of the defeat of 1940 consists in the fact that it put an end to the unproblematic, automatic existence of these institutions. The French republican state ceased to exist, and a new, authoritarian state was put in its place with the help of the German invader. And the Church had to define anew its position towards the State. It was willing to cooperate with the new authoritarian regime which sharply rejected the anti-clerical traditions of the Third Republic; but it had to "justify" this decision, as the new state also was constantly obliged to "justify" itself against the charge of treason.

The net result of these changes was a bewilderment even greater than the one which had existed prior to 1940. Two great traditions which up to then at least had the support of two unquestionably existing institutions became utterly discredited. One was the tradition of the French Revolution, of republican "liberty, equality, and fraternity"; the Third Republic, the institution which embodied this tradition, succumbed in one short campaign, and who would want to build a country's future upon a foundation which proved so weak in a decisive trial? The other tradition which became discredited in 1940 was Catholic monarchism. It became discredited because it allied itself with collaborationism. Its visible exponent was Vichy.

No single body of belief remained intact after the hurricane of 1940. The mental and spiritual horizon of the young generation of France was marked by a nihilism more complete than ever. And yet, there was something new and positive in the situation. There was a task to be done, urgent, compelling, beyond the need for justification—resistance to the enemy had to be organized, the invader had to be thrown out of France. Practical certitude was complete, just as complete as theoretical uncertainty was.

This is how Albert Camus described this situation: "We had to confront (the crisis) with whatever values we could muster, that is to say with none, except for the consciousness of the absurdity in which we lived. Thus we had to go to war and face terror without consolation and certitude. We knew only that we could not yield to the brutes taking charge in the four corners of Europe. But in the position in which we found ourselves, we did not know how to justify this obligation. What is more, the most conscious among us realized that they were aware of no principle in whose name they could oppose terror and reject murder as a means." Camus concluded that his generation needed a philosophy which "can reconcile negative thought and the possibility of affirmative action."

It was Jean-Paul Sartre who, during the German occupation, formulated an existentialist doctrine which aimed to "reconcile negative thought with the possibility of affirmative action." Much in his principle work, *L' Etre et le Néant* (*Being and Nothingness*) is closely reminiscent of Heidegger. But Sartre's thinking is made of different stuff.

For him, the fundamental category from which everything else flows is not human existence, but Being as such, Being pure and simple, that which "is not even itself but simply is." And because he starts from such a "dense" concept of Being, the difficulty for him consists in accounting for such phenomena as human knowledge, consciousness and "existence." If there is nothing but that which is, there can be no knowledge and no consciousness, since knowledge and consciousness presuppose at least two different things—the known and the knower; conscience and that of which it is conscience. But there can be nothing but that which Is, since everything that is other than that which Is is not. It follows from this dilemma that knowledge, consciousness and existence can have their origin only in that which is not, that is to say, nothing.

Being, then, must be thought of as producing Nothingness. But this is absurd; nothingness cannot be produced; consequently, Sartre invents a new verb (following Heidegger's famous coinage, "*das Nichts nichtet*," "the Nihil nihilates"); "to nihilize" (*néantiser*). Being "nihilizes" itself. "The Being through which nothingness comes into the world must be its own nothingness." After this happens, the dull self-identity of "Being-in-itself" (which, as we have seen, is not even an identity but is beyond it) is at last transcended, and things, as we might say, begin to hum.

First, we learn that "nihilized" Being is freedom. It is also referred to as "consciousness" and "Being-for-itself." It is founded upon an "absolute act" of "nihilization." "The human being at first reposes in the midst of Being, and then tears itself away from it by a nihilizing withdrawal." The particular mode of being of man, his existence, is not founded in itself and substantial. It consists only in a "questioning" of the world.

For Heidegger, existence is finite but substantial; it is the source of all substantiality, and its proper goal is to achieve "being itself." For Sartre, however, human existence is merely "its own nothingness"; "there is no common measure between human existence and the *causi sui* which it would like to be," and hence "we can say that man perishes so that the *causa sui* may exist." Man cannot be himself, and he cannot know himself. The "ego" is transcendant, i. e., I can just as little know myself from within as I can any other being. Man always lives in "bad faith." He can only fail; the history of every man's life is the history of a failure."

So much for "negative thinking." Where, then, does "affirmative action" come in? Well, man can "engage himself" in the world; he can create "values." "In this world in which I engage myself, my actions scare up values like partridges; it is through my indignation that the anti-value 'baseness' is given to me, and the value 'greatness' is given to me through my admiration." Sartre vehemently denies any pre-existence or timeless validity of values. They are created by being affirmed.

"The existence of a value is derived from its being asserted, and not the other way 'round. It does not, therefore, reveal itself to intuitive contemplation which would then perceive it *as* a value . . . My freedom alone is the foundation of values and . . . nothing, nothing at all, justifies my adopting such and such values or standards of values." "In so far as I am a being for whom values exist, I am unjustifiable. And my freedom is anxiety to be the foundation without foundation of values."

Man is responsible for anything that happens to him; he "is responsible for himself and for the world." He "chooses" every situation in which he finds himself. This cannot be otherwise, for the very essence of man's existence is "freedom," that is, "the original projection of its own nothingness." Man cannot blame God or the world for anything that happens—neither for wars nor for social calamities which ruin his existence—because he has "chosen" everything himself. If he is dissatisfied with anything that happens, why, he can always commit suicide. And that's that.

As a metaphysical speculation, Sartre's book is interesting in spots. As a philosophy of existence, it is fundamentally worthless. It reduces all existential problems to a very abstract metaphysical level where nothing can happen and nothing matters. If man is essentially "free" and cannot be deprived of his freedom, existential problems concerning the defense of one's own freedom, or respect for another's freedom do not arise. I am the last to deny that man is "essentially" free, and I can see good sense in saying that he "chooses" his world in a way. But the existential question is how these general and abstract truths reflect themselves in concrete situations.

Nothing that Sartre says makes any difference to any situation, except in so far as he exalts the negative aspect of things and denies the objective validity of values. As a program of action, this is singularly unfruitful. One cannot put Sartre's doctrine into effect, because no action can contradict it. After all, I alone can create my values and it is silly to ask for any justification for what one is doing; so how could I be wrong?

Sometimes, reading Sartre's book, one has the distinct feeling that it is an elaborate hoax. Towards the end of the book, he himself gives himself away by saying that "the principle result of existential psychoanalysis must be to make us renounce serious-mindedness." I wonder whether the terrific vogue enjoyed by Sartre's existentialism is not due to the fact that it appeals to the subtle Gallic sense of humor. People, it seems, enter into the spirit of the game. But one can do that only if one does not take existence seriously.[1]

V. Pragmatism and Existentialism

As we see, both the German and the French variety of existentialism somehow fall short of their promise. Both claim to make man's situation transparent, to make it understandable. Both maintain that this can be done only by throwing away all "abstract" props and plunging into the situation as it affects man here and now. And yet, in both cases, the concrete situation seems to be left out in the cold. The German existentialists analyze the form of human existence or the abstract concept of "mattering-to-one"; Sartre's existentialism limits itself to the assertion of a completely negative, formless and spineless freedom.

Must we not conclude from this failure that the whole existentialist approach is intrinsically faulty, and that we must try another one if we want to get away from "abstraction" and to deal with the concrete situation of man?

Pragmatism might be suggested as such an alternative approach. I classified pragmatism above as one of the "abstract" philosophies, because in its analysis of the world it goes back to situationally neutral ultimate elements. But if we leave this aside for a moment, there is in pragmatism, e. g. in the formulation given it by Dewey, a trend away from abstraction and towards concreteness. Dewey raises a vigorous protest against

---

[1]Although space does not permit discussion of existentialist trends in French philosophy represented by other thinkers than Sartre, it should at least be mentioned that the existentialist approach is being used in a genuine and fruitful way by Christian thinkers such as Gabriel Marcel.

making concrete life subservient to hardened abstractions, rigid, absolute principles. He stresses the "experimental," non-dogmatic attitude which starts from the specific constellation prevailing at each moment. Thus, it seems that we have attained a position from which we can render justice to the specific, concrete content of each situation.

It is especially experimental science to which man can turn for the solution of his existential problems. Science can at least give him the guarantee of maximum success possible, since it does not do what man does when he does not adopt the scientific attitude—that is, obstruct the right course of action by clinging to antiquated, irrelevant beliefs and prejudices. Experimental science is the agency from which we can expect the solution of our existential problems.

I do not want to minimize the existential importance of the scientific approach. Experimental science involves, for one thing, a wonderfully balanced give-and-take between abstract formalisms on the one hand, and concrete situations on the other. But it seems to me that, in so far as human existence in its depth and its totality is concerned, the scientific approach has its limits.

To mention only one aspect of this problem: a really experimental attitude can be adopted only where we can *afford* to experiment, i. e., where we deal with material that is, broadly speaking, *expendable*. It is impossible to adopt a truly experimental attitude where the existence and the rights of human beings are involved Should we try to proceed in experimental fashion in ethical matters in earnest, the "existing" subject of our experiment would perish before we could experimentally find out what would be the most satisfactory path for him to follow.

I do not mean to reject a certain amount of experimentation in ethical matters; I merely want to point out that such experimentation is ethically acceptable only where it is not really "serious" experimentation, i. e., where it stops short of certain relevant possibilities. The ethical experimenter himself must be aware of certain limits; he must have tenderness for the subjects he is experimenting on; that is, he must act as a real scientific experimenter would not. That is, even when indulging in an experimental approach to ethical problems, we have to observe principles other than those of the experimental method.

These are the principles that existentialist philosophy would have to explore. In a way, these principles must be absolute and unchanging; we cannot declare them void merely to clear the road for some scientific experiment. But they cannot, on the other hand, be rigidly dogmatic,—not, at least, from the existentialist point of view. For it is essential to the existentialist approach to assume that abstract principles as such cannot be placed higher than the existence of the concrete individuals and groups for which they are claimed to be valid. Existence may indeed be given up under certain circumstances, but only for the sake of other existence, not for the sake of abstractions.

What we expect from the existentialist method is the working out of principles which are firm enough to circumscribe a universe of discourse with well-defined attributes of right and wrong, and flexible enough to allow the full unfolding of existence. Principles of this kind cannot be reduced to situationally neutral ultimate elements. This is why they can be worked out only by the existentialist method. Ultimate principles of action can be based only upon intelligent categories. Man can experiment with, and explore, what he does not understand. But he can freely refrain from certain actions only when he understands the reason why.

What we need, then, is a new kind of existentialism—one that shows us how we can go about securing intelligible ends, i. e., values. And although neither German nor French existentialism does this, these schools are important because they exemplify an approach that could help in solving this all-important task.

(This essay first appeared in "The Modern Review")

A LITTLE ANTHOLOGY
OF ITALIAN POETRY

edited by Renato Poggioli

The Montale poem has been translated by Maurice English, former head of the Italian Radio Desk, OWI; all the other poems by William Fense Weaver, now instructor in English at the University of Virginia.

INTRODUCTION

The presentation of foreign poetry to a new audience always involves running a risk and, more than that, causing the readers to do the same. This danger does not come entirely from the usual difficulties of translation: the disparity of means of expression, or the frequent lack of exact correspondences between two languages. Instead, the problem is the more serious one of establishing in some way the assumptions which are, within a given time and culture, the basis of a generation's poetic endeavor. It is easy enough to reconstruct what might be called the passive tradition of a literature, the tradition known from historic, concrete facts; but, on the other hand, it is almost impossible to give even a valid approximation of the active tradition—that fluid system of changing values, provisional ideals, that vague yet real condition of taste which acts as a kind of unwritten poetics. But, with all this elusiveness, this active tradition is a vitally important part of *avant-garde* literature in every American and European culture. So it is usual in presenting translations to expose the reader involuntarily to a deception, the deception of making him judge foreign poetry as if the poet's intellectual assumptions were the same as those that underlie the contemporary poetry of the reader's own language.

In other words, foreign contemporary poetry is read either in a void or within an esthetic framework which is different from the one in which the poetry was conceived. From any point of view, historical, critical, or informational, there can be no method of exposition which is more inexact or misleading. *Avant-garde* literature is not, as is commonly believed, something outside a tradition. In a certain sense, because it aims at reform or revolution, it is more conscious of the value of the tradition than the conventional literature, which is usually regarded as traditional *par excellence*.

For a writer or reader of *avant-garde* literature there is nothing more disorienting or disturbing than the experimental writing of another environment. But this disturbance is a splendid pretext and an effective stimulus for further experimentation. For this reason, the translated work of the German Rilke, of the French Valéry, of the Spanish Lorca, of the Russian Pasternak, are so exciting to the English or American writer. These foreign poets become examples instead of cases. Instead of being merely the objects of poetic research, their work is the stimulus of poetic action; thus they become true "beacons" in the Baudelaireian sense of the word. Reading them becomes more than the acquiring of critical material; it is an esthetic revelation and suggestion.

Thus, we may now present to the American literary public, in the fine translations of William Fense Weaver and Maurice English, four contemporary Italian poets, who belong to a literary culture known to all the civilized world in its remote past (in what we have called the passive tradition) and completely unknown in its active tradition, in the forms and beliefs of its present poetic ideal. Two of these poets belong to the older generation, and their names are not unknown outside of Italy. The first of them, Giuseppe Ungaretti, seems to have awakened greater interest in the Latin countries: Italy, France, and South America; while Eugenio Montale, the second poet, has aroused interest especially in English-speaking countries. The reason for this is easily understood: Ungaretti has performed with great originality a function within Italian poetry similar to that of Apollinaire or Valéry in French poetry, while Montale has more than once been defined as a kind of Italian T. S. Eliot.

They are being presented here precisely because these over-simplified parallels are not enough to define the significance of these poets. Moreover, this significance can be defined further by comparison between their poetry and the poetry of the new generation, represented here by two quite young men, Mario Luzi and Tommaso Giglio.

There is a kind of paradoxical association between the poetry of these two pairs of writers. While Ungaretti is the archetype of the mystic poet of illuminations and revelations, Montale is the poet of consciousness and understanding. Thus, in the former, we find the construction of a super-world not more divine, but more human, than the world of reality and daily life; and, in the work of the second poet, there is the unmasking either in microcosm or in macrocosm, of the skeleton of life. From such opposed positions their styles are derived: the musical, suggestive, harmonic style of Ungaretti; the broken, dissonant, strident style of Montale. And therein lies the paradox in the active tradition of contemporary Italian poetry: while the world of Luzi more closely resembles that of Ungaretti, he seems to have learned his lesson in style from Montale; and while Giglio's world is closer to that of Montale, his style shows the impact of Ungaretti.

In reality the esthetic inspiration of Ungaretti is tempered in Luzi by an interest in psychology, from which comes the discursive, syntactical character of his poetry and the justification of the use of some of the devices of Montale's dialectic. For the consciousness of cosmic tragedy in Montale's poetry (which is present even when he is writing of the "condition of man") Giglio has substituted the consciousness of a social tragedy, and from this comes a religious desire which has led him to prefer Ungaretti's oracular, prayer-like style. A further paradox is that Luzi seems more "poetic" than the "prosaic" Montale; Giglio, more "prosaic" than the "poetic" Ungaretti. This situation in itself can explain the agreement or compromises which are bringing about the formation of a new poetic tradition; it is an example, however, whose validity for the foreign reader is questionable. To the foreign reader, there remains the right and the obligation to search out in the poetry itself what he is supposed to find there. And to the interpreter there remains nothing to do except to give the reader the means necessary to a purely literal interpretation.

Let us begin with the work of Giuseppe Ungaretti. These twelve choruses are part of a work in progress which is entitled

La Terra Promessa. The title does not refer to the "promised land" of the ancient Hebrews, but to that land where a pagan hero is destined to arrive. It is the country of Aeneas, who became such a favorite of so many Christian readers, even those without classical or humanistic leanings. The city to be founded on this promised land is not Imperial Rome or Catholic Rome, but the City of Man. A little before the landing on the predestined shore, the hero is assailed by memories and visions, depicted in songs, or rather in these twelve choruses which according to the professed intention of the poet are descriptive of states of mind of the loving, abandoned, desolate suicide, Dido.

If Ungaretti's poem moves in the eternal atmosphere of fable and myth, the atmosphere of Eugenio Montale's *La Primavera Hitleriana* is that of current events, those tragic events that are the history of our time. The season is spring, the scene Florence, the moment is that of the Italian visit of the *Führer,* who rides through the streets of the cities accompanied by the *Duce* and their brown henchmen. It is almost hot enough to be summer; strange white insects die in the light of the street-lamps, while fireworks rise in the sky to celebrate the feast of San Giovanni, the legendary patron of the city. The grotesque meaning of that unholy holiday is symbolized by the forced closing of the shops: the toy-shops and the butcher-shops where, following the custom, the young goat is crowned with a garland as soon as it is killed. Angels of evil, demons of destruction, a swarm of threatening airplanes hover in the *Götterdämmerung* of the sunset, and dive, in a parade of Wagnerian monsters in the "mystical gulf" of the sky. The poem concludes with an appeal to a feminine figure and with a feeling of longing for the next coming of a new dawn of liberty, a tomorrow of peace, a life and a sky "without wings."

The motive that inspires Mario Luzi's *Quaderno Gotico* is, as the adjective of the title implies, the motive of mystic love, the eternal drama of the lover and the beloved, in the various phases of absence and presence, distance and nearness, hope and doubt. Or rather, its subject is that of love as an experience not only carnal, but spiritual also; and Luzi deliberates on the plane of poetry the favorite themes of the novels of Mauriac, an author on whom he has written an interesting critical essay. Nothing could be more different from the inspiration of Tommaso Giglio's *Temi per Una Sinfonia,* where the title reveals the attempt to find a voice for those human masses that do not yet have thought or word. Giglio's poetry, a true and proper jeremiad, is neither political nor propagandistic, neither social nor national. This is choral poetry, whose chorality is characteristic not so much of some forms of the ancient Greek lyric as of the drama.

There remains only to close with some bibliographical and biographical information. Giuseppe Ungaretti was born of Italian parents in Alexandria, Egypt, in 1888. He first showed his poetic bent during the World War I, with a volume in Italian, *Il Porto Sepolto* (1916) and a volume of verse in French, *La Guerre* (1919). His first important book, an extension of the two earlier volumes is *Allegria di Naufragi* (1919), issued in a definitive edition in 1932 under the title *Allegria*. His other important books are *Sentimento del Tempo*, published in 1933 and, revised, in 1936; and *Il Dolore* (1947), collecting all the excellent poems of the last ten years which had appeared in magazines. To these works may be added his *Translations* (1936) and minor poems, *Poesie Disperse*, published in 1946.

Eugenio Montale, born at Genoa in 1896, began his career with *Ossi di Seppia*, the important editions of which are the first (1925) and the third (1931). *La Casa dei Doganieri*, in 1932, was only an advance notice of the more important *Occasioni* of 1939. His latest book, small but of great importance, is *Finisterre* (1943).

The most significant titles of the work of Mario Luzi, born in Florence in 1914, are *La Barca* (1935), *Avvento Notturno* (1940) and *Un Brindisi* (1946). Tommaso Giglio, born in Naples in 1923, has not yet published a collection of his work, although his merit is already recognized through poems published in magazines.

All of the poems translated here first appeared during 1946 in the same magazine, *Inventario,* in Florence: *La Terra Promessa* and *La Primavera Hitleriana* in Number III-IV, *Quaderno Gotico* in Number I, and *Temi per Una Sinfonia* in Number II.

THE PROMISED LAND

Giuseppe Ungaretti

1

The shadow disappearing,
In a distance of years,
When grief did not wound,
You hear the then childish
Breast swell, longed for,
And your alarmed eye
Unveil uncautious fire of April
From a perfumed cheek.

Scorn, diligent specter
That makes time inert
And its fury known at length,
—Leave the bitten heart!

2

The evening is prolonged
By a suspended fire
And a shudder in the grass little by little
Seems to reunite the infinite with fate.

Then unperceived, a moonlike echo
Was born and was fused with the shiver of the water.
I don't know what was more alive,
The grumbling up to the drunken stream
Or the expectant echo that was tenderly silent.

3

Now the wind has become silent.
Silent also is the sea;
All is quiet; but I cry out
The cry, alone, of my heart,
Cry of love, cry of shame
Of my heart that burns
Since I watched you and you looked at me
And I am nothing any more but a weak thing.

I cry and my heart is afire without peace
Since the time when I have become only
A thing in ruins and abandoned.

4

Only I have in my spirit hidden wounds,
Wooded equators, on swamps
Brumal clots of vapors where
There rages the desire,
In sleep, never to have been born.

5

As yet unweaned, but infants
Whose impatience increase too hastily,
We were transported by anxiety, along sleep
Toward what other, elsewhere?
It took on color and the aroma began to sprinkle
Those first-fruits
So that, through tender tricks
Disclosing itself surprised in the light,
It offered its true richness only
Later, when we were already maddened in our vigils.

6

All its griefs mystery has lost,
Accustomed crown to long life,
And changing in itself,
It concedes the bile of remorses in drops.

7

In the darkness, silent
You walk in fields empty of any wheat;
No more do you wait for anyone, proud at your side.

8

From my face to yours your secret comes;
Your dear features are repeated in mine;
Our eyes contain nothing else
And, in despair, our love ephemeral
Eternal shudders in the sails of a delay.

9

No more am I attracted by the wandering landscapes
Of the sea, nor by the searing
Pallor of dawn upon these leaves or those.

Nor do I fight any longer with the heavy stone,
Past night that on my eyes I bear.

Images, what use are they
To me, who is forgotten?

10
Do you not hear the plane-tree's
Leaf, do you not hear it suddenly creaking
As it falls along the river over the flints?

I will embellish my decline, tonight;
They will see, joined to the dry leaves,
A roseate glow.

11
And restless
Since their space offered
To our intimate fires a cloud's refuge,
Cherishing each other,
Our ingenuous twin
Spirits were awakened, already in flight.

12
In a squall there opened, in the dark, a harbor
Supposed to be safe.
It was a starry gulf
And its heaven seemed unchangeable:
But now, how changed it is!

THE HITLER SPRING

Eugenio Montale

The dense white cloud of the mayflies crazily
whirls round the pallid street lamps and over the parapets,
spreads on the ground a blanket on which the foot
grates as on sprinkled sugar; the looming summer now
releases the nightfrosts which it was holding
in the secret caves of the dead season.
in the gardens of Maiano where the sandpits stop.

And soon over the street an infernal messenger passes in flight;
the murderers salute; a mystical gulf, fired
and beflagged with swastikas has taken and swallowed us;
the shopwindows, humble and inoffensive, are closed
the armed—they also—
with cannon and toys of war;
that butcher has struck who dresses with flowers and berries
the muzzles of the slaughtered goats,
the ritual of the mild hangmen, once innocent of blood,
is changed to a spastic dance of shattering wings,
the mayflies' tiny deaths whiten the piers' edge
and the water continues to eat at
the shoreline, and no one is any more blameless.

All for nothing, then?—and the roman candles
at San Giovanni, which gradually
blanched the horizon, and the pledges and the long farewells
strong as a baptism, in the sorrowful expectation
of the horde (but a bud striped the air, distilling
on the ice and on the rivers of your country
the messengers of Tobias, the seven, the seeds
of the future) and the heliotrope born
of your hands—all burnt, sucked dry
by a pollen that cries like fire
and is winged with ice and salt.
                              O this ulcered
spring will still be festival if it can freeze again
in death that death! Observe once more
up yonder, Clizia, your destiny, you

preserved though changed by a love which does not change
until the blind sun you carry in you
blinds itself in that other and confounds itself
in Him, for all. Perhaps the sirens and the bells
which salute the monsters in the night
at their witch's sabbath are already confounded
with the sound which unloosed from heaven descends and
    conquers—
with the breath of a dawn which may yet reappear
tomorrow, white but without wings
of terror, to the parched arroyos of the south.

GOTHIC NOTEBOOK

Mario Luzi

I

The high, the dark flame falls over you,
figure as yet unknown,
for such a long time wished for
beyond that veil of years and seasons
that a god perhaps is girding himself to cut through.

The intact delight, the painful anxiety
of existing burns both of us equally
to ashes. But when the music is silent
between our unknown faces
a wind rises, laden with offerings.

Like two opaque stars in their slow vigil
in which a planet intimately revives
the luminous night-time spirit
now we rise sharpened,
fevered by an endless future.
Thus in the vehement spirit breathes and flutters
a desire that is close to alarm,
a hope like to fear;
but the eyes look further, there enters
into the blood the more fruitful breath of the earth.

Assumed into the cold measure of statues,
everything that seemed perfect till now,
is set free and is alive again, the light
vibrates, the fruitful banks tremble
and augural cities hum.

The faithful image no longer seems to have color
and I rise and hover, tormenting myself
to make of me a Mario unattainable
by my self, in the incessant existence
a fire that his ardor regenerates.

319

II

Ah you do not stay inert in your heaven
and the street is peopled again with alarms
since your imminence breathes, enclosed
by the silence of clear walls
and by windows that gaze at winter.
To walk is to meet you, to live
is to progress to you, all is fire and fear.
And how many times near to unveiling you
have I trembled because of a sudden face
behind the folds of an ancient portal
in the half-shadow, or at the head of the stairs.

III

Once more the stars of love cross
clear over our cloudy heads
there where we sit unknowing
on opposite banks. And it appears natural
never to have seen you or heard you
and to gaze at you in an ancient light.

Desire or regret? Desire
and regret, a lone bitter fever.
An astral wine radiated in the crystal,
a melted sunlight that you gulped
and you stared at the blindness of the landscape.

IV

The branches sway, the sky invokes
the moon. A living desire breathes
from the starry shadow, the air sports
on the field. What presence stirs?

A palpable breath has passed
among the trees, a wandering burst essence
turns round, caressing the hair;
in the portico a music reposes.
Ah this obscure joy is due to you,
the secret makes you more alive, the wakeful
wind in the briar is you, you are here
on the grass in this lucid ferment.

V

Now wakened in the lucid flow
of the live, airy day on the slopes,
rise finally in the sun, victorious personage,
incorrupt body, you who were a fire
too long repressed within me.
How many times have I seen you and doubted,
uncertain whether it was you or spring
tired out by insinuating itself among the plants.

But when after a dream and after a nightmare
I saw you in the incandescent morning
with your hand benumbed upon your forehead,
weeping the tears of your existence,
there was no more deception, it was you yourself,
lost in the labyrinth, you could not come out of it again
and you wept your predestined weeping.
There was (wherever it came from) a full suffering
impassive, mute, without trembling,
that moved in you fear, in me piety
and a pure desire to give myself.
So in me you remained at length;
thus when the day has fallen beyond the mountains
the vision of the sun stays on within the soul.

And behold, now I *felt* my own suffering:
how many boundaries I had crossed over,
the hedges that had protected me,
pride in existence and indifference to it,
nothing subsisted any more; under the sky,
intact the mysteries were rekindled.

VI

The sky vibrates, the full hyacinth falls
among the dark walls, the air blows
through my clothes, a cloud pervades me,
what insidious presence breathes?

A rare dizziness has passed
over my forehead, behold, a living fire rains
fused with the quiet and animate shadow,
an invisible essence stirs itself.

Ah it is you who have nimbly grazed the sky
of evening. Thus if a figure
disappears in a doorway, there spreads a chill
of death and a lucid fear.

You have passed from there where the swallow
hurls itself on the road, a hermit foot
breaks the veil of light over the pavement,
summons the darkness, fades away in the hearing.

VII

There was a living expectance that radiated
in you fear and trembling and in me
the palpable delight of going in
among the trees, of drinking at the fountains.
The dazzle of the wandering waters, the sky,
the quiet shadows in the animated air,
even the wind moved in me a smile.

It was the same fever that estranges us
rapidly from the dead and misdirects us
while they remain alone among the torches
in the monstrous labor of excavating for themselves
a path among the rocks of shadow, weary
and intent on penetrating to the very bottom.
You see their pointed profile, nearby
the emaciated hands are at rest.

VIII

The glance of a humid star falls
on the meadow, the sharp tempest breathes
among the animated trees, a puff of air shaves
the paths, a restless perfume rages.

A fleeting frown has passed
over the grass, a green exploded clearness
vibrates in the brief and undulant wind,
the swift air slides and settles.

It is you, the waiting was not vain.
You have come even here where the rain
smokes the plants and goes away,
a quiet echo sleeps in the gallery.

Ah but the anguish within me is not finished!
While heaven delays and does not change
you are still the nightmare, you are perished
in a place in the soul and lost.

IX

Shudder (from wherever it sprang) whirlpool
that rose in me again, mute, insistent,
and alternated dizziness and pity
at existing, and often moved me to weeping.
When toward the extreme of the fever
the nightmare had already escaped into a dream
and a fixed apparition, suddenly
it was you, you breathed here, present.
You have passed by the rare rain, the live
heavens, fragile beneath the cold lightning,
you have thrown yourself down here like the swallow. . .
quickly you were confused with the color
of the spirit. Thus after a pure,
a spring-like, long waiting
there appears on the threshold a vivid
figure that extinguishes itself in a room.

X

Often in dark sleep, without images,
I was assailed by the anguish of a closed
intimate obscure possibility
and the yet undecided fate
of a sun that was to have ripened me.
In the most live, the most pure part of the dream
if I looked for you there was disclosed to me
the interior of an unknown sadness,
a secret landscape in which faded
you, nothingness, the upright and wakened shadow,

You were reborn more hopeless and more lonely,
surprised, you dared no longer to flee
the horror of finding yourself live and true
and you wept your irreparable tears
the weeping that was your due.

But when in an immobile rejoicing
I saw you transfix the morning
with two humid stars upon your eyelids,
ah the trip into Hades was fulfilled,
I had arrived, I could abandon myself.

XI

Only an unsteady gust has extinguished
the weak dazzle, a sharp moon mows
the illuminated wind, a pure fire
is ingrained in the unquiet shadows.

Again a long day dies elsewhere
from your forehead, again through the vain
spaces the confident star moves
to seek you in the clear tomorrow.

Another night rises and does not raise
your shadow on the plain, another empty
night whistles among the briars and gets up
to depict you more live and remote.

And desire flies to crown
in you a rich season, the light
of a fleeting augury disappears
among the trees and leads me to you again.

XII

Ah that time is a dazzle from afar, from the eternal frost,
the hours freely given rose again to heaven,
one into another, days are mirrored into days,
trees shifted happily in the faithful wind;
at evening the highest star seals your joy,
hope, always fulfilled, always was reborn.
You did not meet me, you resided in your grace.
Whenever I turned myself to you, your shadow was distant
drawn by a light caduceus among the torpid flowers
among the subtle flames of the berries and the briars.

XIII

After the thunder and rain, in a slope
of the moon, sad from an eternal greeting,
there was opened to me the force of the gardens,
the blue origins of the night.

On the clouded pinnacles there was undone
the blue of the recurring stars
and a face took the empty place at the windows
unharmed by its diurnal exile.

And the sound of your step bit again
into the quiet of the heavenly embankment
while, content with the obol, the boat
tried again the torpid current.

There where between two banks melted
the last wandering rose, almost like a dead day
before the darkness, the pity
of incessant life annulled you.

XIV

Where you were not how much peace: the sky
among the ripe trees gathered
the white offering of the roads,
was relit in the darkness of the fountains,
the rich marrow of honey
tempered the anguish of the passers-by
and beauty shone
disappeared subdivided among the roads
shining in the wind-swept silence.

Neither memory, nor image, nor dream.
The face of the absent was a mirror
reflected by the first opaque star
and you were not even in it, you had fallen
outside of existence;
the whiteness afflicted the cross-roads,
and it was not evening,
it was the white truth, listless,
in the depth of my tumult, unperceived.

THEMES FOR A SYMPHONY

Tommaso Giglio

I

To unite men with heaven
the desperate outburst of hands
stretched out against the air is not enough.

The outcry of looks into the blue,
the anguish of ecstatic mouths that beseech,
are weak to conquer space,
to attain the heart of the stars.

To unite men with heaven
heaven must be joined to earth,
the outburst of hands must be cut,
the beseeching mouths must be smothered.

Today we have to destroy, to confuse
heaven with earth, sea and river,
silence with the shout of torrents.

Nothing transforms vile nature
like blood and sorrow: when earth
is changed into a mortuary
the weak embrace of life
will have smothered death.

II

If you walk along a land
that does not bear the traces of sorrow
and laughs in a tranquil sunlight,

and you hear all around the calm voice
of men who have not suffered
who raise their arms to heaven
to bless their own riches,

if you are men and you do not know
the fever of feeling yourselves lost
in a world that does not stop to look,

and if you have never seen with terror
the swelling of blood in the veins
when your life, more bitter, is darkened
or the flesh falls ill without remedy,

if you are hungry and find bread,
if you are thirsty and find water,
if you walk along roads
that do not know the cry of anguish
that the world transmits to its sons,

if you have not learned
that the weak life of men
is a bread leavened with tears,
I tell you that you are walking
on the livid sands of a desert
blown by the breathing of death.

III
No one is alone in the world
because the world is like a desert
that drags the sands of life
towards the waters of an oasis.

No one is distant from us,
even if he lives in remote lands:
all the roads of the earth
lead in our direction.

No man is different from the others,
because our root is grief:
we are sound and silence,
blood and dust.

Even when no one replies
to our insistent call,
to our weak outburst,
we are not alone in this solitude.

IV
No thing can be loved, you know,
when our voice is discordant with others
and all music is ruined in a mournful
lament of breathless instruments.

No thing can be dear to us, nothing can live,
when on a worn-out hinge, without pause,
the joints of the earth are creaking
and making of every gesture a mean renunciation.

Tomorrow we can regret nothing
of this surf that dins on shores, on rocks,
against consumed houses,
like a weeping of things that cannot resist.

We can regret nothing of this life that is breaking to bits.

V

Everyone walks disturbed, apart,
on this worn-out earth of exiles
waiting for fabulous departures.

An old bronze bell resounds
against the walls of the houses
vainly calling together
men who cannot reply.

Life is consumed too hastily
to let us leave a regret
and now the days seem only
a broken flight of remorses.

From our windows the horizon is seen
as the point in which heaven precipitates
collapsing into marine abysses.

Here, no thing has the strength to resist.

Women curse the days without bread
and sons spit on the tombs of fathers.

VI

Thus, without love and without hate,
pierced by sound and by silence,
we learn to confuse
the boundaries of good and evil.

On this road that is divided
between purgatory and hell
a people suffers without sadness
laughs without joy.

On this world without memory
the guilty judges the innocent,
the victim sacrifices the executioner,
the scaffold is changed into altar.

Life careens blinded
among the abysses of the foul and fair:
we look for sin in the temple
we perceive salvation in the mud.

Thus, after centuries and centuries,
we have unlearned how to suffer:
what is the use of sorrow
when joy has no sense?

Without love and without hate,
without quiet and without anguish,
a people learns that hope
begins out of despair.

TWO STORIES

Jack Jones

ALL ABOUT PERCIVAL'S FATHER

OUR PERCIVAL was three and a half years old, twenty-two and one-fourth years younger than herself, his mother sometimes said, seeing something amusing in her preciseness, and transmitting this amusement to him with little difficulty. She began to introduce new ways into their play, all of which had a quality that was rather strange. The following incident may serve to characterize the trend. The porch of the house in which they lived, a white two-story apartment structure whose other tenants were in no instance under forty years of age, was four feet from the ground, about a foot higher than Percival. It was the custom for his mother to swing him over the railing, like a pendulum, sometimes lowering him to the ground and letting him drop from a height that did not usually exceed a foot. He had never yet jumped from a place higher than he himself on the ground. On this afternoon, when he climbed on the railing holding his mother's shoulder, she pushed him off. The landing was not bad, and he remained in the position he had reached as the momentum ceased, knees bent and hands on the sandy grass, until, certain that the next motion would proceed from within him, he turned his head, deflecting from the young royal palm in passing, and found his mother's face, from which the contortion of laughter was just about to relax. "Wasn't that fun?" He behaved quietly for the rest of the day, but in the afternoon of the next, feeling something change within him acceptably, he was already smiling as he climbed the rail and saw her hand dart toward him. Within ten minutes it was a routine, and one upon which it was he, not she, who insisted. One curious derivation should be mentioned. As it was no longer possible for his mother to catch him off guard at the rail, so whatever she might have intended, when approaching any height, of steps or a street curb, he would attempt to drop behind her, with a suspecting smile. Then there was the affair of the balloons. Percival was born during the rubber shortage (there is no intention to imply any connection between these facts—it was a defect in the material, not a lack of the same.) Balloons were no longer around; Percival had not had any experience with them. One morning his mother returned from marketing with a box of them, colored with the war drabness. She blew up several for him, and returning an hour later, found all three intact, having been treated with a reverence and caution which in one of so tender an age was rather comic, though also, to be sure, touching. She told him how to blow up balloons, and it was not long before he was doing so. One of the balloons had reached the size which to the initiated eye would seem the largest advisable, and she encouraged him to keep on blowing. The explosion left him with a few shreds of rubber scattered by the blast, one of which was shot into his mother's mouth. She spat it out, but did not resume the attitude which had been a preparation for laughter. The incident involving the scissors should neither be overlooked. From the apartment above, with the windows of theirs also open, sometimes came, besides sounds of other interest, curses and obscenities, which Percival's mother would listen to, telling him to be quiet. Percival had a tendency to repeat some of these overheard words, indifferently, in spite of having been warned by his mother not to do so, perhaps because she did not wish the persons above to realize that they were overheard and deprive her of moments which could not fail to brighten up any day. Finally she threatened to cut his tongue off, unless. About a week later, he used one of the words with intention to impress a goldfish. She procured the scissors and pinned him down on the couch, compelling him to open his mouth. As he did not really believe she could do without his tongue, he felt the snip of warm steel with a cry and lunged away, feeling in his mouth. His fingers were stained with blood. With what embarrassment, it may be imagined, did she explain that she had only meant to frighten him.

At seven the next morning, they were standing behind the house, in the service yard, while she was washing some sheets. A sanitation truck drove up, and began to remove the garbage pails from the buildings on the block. He ran over to watch them work, moving with them until they reached his building, where his mother was standing. He began to play with an empty garbage can beside her. She lifted him into it. He was not quite able to get out. The Negroes having emptied every other can, began to climb back into the truck. "Stop! Take this." They looked at her obliquely. She pulled her dress above her knee. All the Negroes looked away, but not at each other. She removed a bill from her stocking and gave it to the one in charge, smiling as if to white men. "I want to get rid of him, he's no good to me." The Negroes began to laugh, whether just after or just before Percival began to cry was not certain. "She wants to get rid of him," the tallest Negro said (not the one in charge, who was slowly folding the five dollars). "She wants to get rid of him," another Negro said (not the one in charge, who was just looking up). She whispered into the latter's ear; her lips touched his lobe and he flinched. "Yes, mam. Thank you, mam," he said. They lifted the can containing Percival and placed it upon the truck. Abandoning the rest of the route, they drove rapidly under the postcard airscape, two hours after a Florida dawn. Percival was trying to upset the can. They replaced the top, hammering it tightly into place, and stuck a few holes with a screwdriver. At the city dump, they rolled the can off, and returned to public duties.

About the can were piled the rotten rinds of oranges, grapefruit, tangerines and bananas. The dump was on a lot two hundred yards square. With his head Percival butted the lid of the can off before noon; lying with his head outside, he went to sleep. When he awoke it was late afternoon, and he crawled all the way out. He ate part of an orange he found lying near. He sat propped against the can, watching the cats and the rats looking for each other, tense maneuvers in three dimensions through piles of decay. In deepest twilight, across the field, their blue coupe stopped under a street lamp. A flashlight gasped, advancing erratically. About forty-five minutes later he was dazzled, and heard his mother's voice. "Percival, Percival!" she said. "Those men made a horrible mistake!"

IN THE AFTERNOON'S MAIL
AT DARK GARDENS

DEAR YANKEL—It rained and stopped (but no sun), rained and stopped (but no sun) all afternoon, and of course this made me think of you! Here people never use umbrellas because they wear bathing suits all the time. You go inside a bank and all the employees, from the president to but excepting the janitor (Negroes can't or don't wear them) are in these suits, which are also uniforms of the institution. The men don't wear tops. This is the same in every business in this town, though in some they wear, instead of uniforms, any suit they like. Not all people on the streets wear suits, four out of five. After dark, of course, no one wears one—even in Florida, it's too cold. The biggest department store has a swimming pool built into the middle of the ground floor—when you buy one buck's worth up, the clerk gives you a green counter, which admits you to the pool.

After two weeks' looking, I went to a rental agent. He had his bare feet on the desk with his toes folded; he wore a sport jacket and was pulling at the hair on his chest between the lapels. He asked me to sit down, smiling a little at my dress (I wasn't wearing a bathing suit that day), and explained that the situation was very bad even though half of the expected "seasonal visitors" (what they call tourists now, exactly like calling a prostitute a lady of the evening) had not yet arrived. The Chamber of Commerce had discontinued all advertising, and now ignored all requests for information. It was inevitable that a great number of people would this year be frozen out, "no pun intended!" He had nothing listed. Unfortunately too, there was a long waiting list, I would be somewhere in the three hundreds. "It would be very difficult, but I might just possibly be able to find you personally a place, outside the usual business channels." I said that would be very kind of him. He asked if I was married. "Maybe you and I could do a little house-warming in your new place." I said perhaps we could. He was looking a little past my head as I said it, and then his gaze seemed to harden. I waited a minute, but as he didn't move or say anything, I looked around to see what was interesting. There was a studio couch over in the corner shoved against the wall. I got up and went out. Some men don't know when to stop.

Old people come here from all parts of the U. S. to die in the sun. I don't know what the mortality rate is here; if they keep it, it must be in a locked file. You see ambulances every day; there are 120 of them in Sun City. Dying people in motorized chairs roll slowly down the morning-shadowed sidewalks. You look out of the trolley which sometimes brushes aside branches of the palm trees, and see them on the streets too, driving with a terrible care; one good bump would be the end of them. The two types here (tourists and invalids, they can't really be told apart) sit on the blue benches—there are 7,000 of these lining the sidewalks, perpendicular to the streets—and fasten their gaze on you from a block away up to the moment you pass the bench, then look panic-stricken for some other object to bearably occupy their sight. The ones that can walk have given this place its name, by which it is known among those who came only once, "The City of the Walking Dead." I found some local literature that described this designation as "jocular." On Sundays they mob the churches, on the edge of hysteria, so that the police reserves and sometimes the fire department have to be called up. Whenever I return to my apartment I find come-to-Christ leaflets under the door, though I've never caught anyone distributing. I have to empty my wastebasket twice a day.

I have seen three men drop dead. The first time a week after I came; I was hurrying along with a bag of tangerines (they are hard to get because most of them are shipped to Northern markets, and the price jacked) when he fell in front of me. I tripped over him and fell too. (I never did find the twelfth tangerine.) Then only three days later I was waiting for a trolley car, when it stopped and the door opened a man dropped out, like from a closet in the movies, and fell to the street on his face. I guess I should have tried to catch him, but I dodged instead. You know, all this passing away is bad for business, it gives the survivors who see the corpse an "existential" twist, makes them wonder if they will be alive tomorrow. So three or four years ago, Elizabeth Lou told me (more about her later) they made the doctors forbid anyone on the verge to leave his dwelling.

This didn't always work; they couldn't force anyone to stay inside if he didn't want to, so now they have a regulation that the doctor reports dangerous cases to the police. The police detail an ambulance to follow him around, moving about six feet behind, inching along. When he drops, the internes get him to the stretcher and into the ambulance before hardly anybody knows what's going on. When you see an ambulance moving along the sidewalk that way, you're naturally curious to know

who hasn't got long to live, and in a crowd it's hard to tell. I
was watching one the other day and picked a certain man; in
order to be sure I had to follow for a while, until he was in isolation. Then an idea; I followed him all morning, while he had
lunch (I remember thinking that shrimp couldn't be too good
for him), and after that until four o'clock in the afternoon, six
times up and down Central Boulevard, I thought he would never
die! When he put his hand to his face and stopped, I got close,
grabbed him as he fell and let him to the ground. The internes
appeared on both sides of me. "Oh the poor man!" I said, "You'll
take care of him?" An interne said it was too late and was told
to shut up by the other. They had the door of the ambulance
closed before I could rise from my knees. I didn't look at the
calling card until I was in the telephone booth. I called the number and got the superintendent. "Mr. Walter Du Bois is dead.
I would like to rent the vacancy." "Oh. Yeah. Well, you got
to rent for six months." "Oh, I know that!" Then I asked if
there were any Jews in his place. "Certainly not." What do
you think we're running, a synagogue?" "You can't be too
careful." He said "not with kikes you can't and we got along
so well he didn't even ask me about the children or dogs. I said
that I would be right over with the check.

It was a pretty little two-room apartment, of course I would
have taken anything. At the first sight of his apalling face, I
saw that he was in love with me. He said that he had phoned
the hospital and Du Bois was dead all right—I think he believed
I hadn't waited to make sure and wanted to reassure me. "Welcome to the Jacaranda, not often honored by such lovely girls!"
I said he was a tease, and went upstairs. "I'll have the junk out
of here by tomorrow," he promised. I handed him the check
and over his shoulder I saw a book lying open on the bed, half-
finished. I wondered if Du Bois had got to the big sex scene.
Something about the jacket color bothered me. Then I saw
that it was Jim's book. I couldn't move for a minute or two, and
he kept prodding me in the shoulder with my check, not trying
to recall me so much as to demonstrate his amazement. I nearly
confessed about being a Jew. But after a while, I informed him
that I had come to the resort for my nerves. He treated me as
if he were my brother; as a matter of fact, I began to rather like
him No, I don't! God damn him!

10 a.m. Friday

Elizabeth Lou. She lives with her mother in the other apartment on my floor; her mother might be an atheist for all she's

ever said to me, but once I dreamed that I got up in the middle of the night and caught her sticking leaflets under my door. Elizabeth works at the Chamber of Commerce, at the information desk. She says she has made three thousand dollars on the side this year, for (illegal) apartment tips. But she hates the job and next month she is going to leave the South for New York. I said that it would be cold, and she said that was one of her wildest dreams—to be really cold. She seems to know everything about this city; I never met anyone who was more in the know—not so much about the personalities (although when we were having lunch she mentioned that the girl behind me had made a deal the previous night to become the mistress of the chief of police) as the trends, the development of the organizations. It was she who told me about the censorship, not that it is a secret—it is just never mentioned by the press or any organization, though occasionally by individuals. Sun City advertises itself as having the lowest amount of rainfall in the U. S. and gives out a figure that is actually below that of any other large city. The figure is faked—it is published by the C. of C. after the other returns are in. (There isn't any weather bureau.) E. says that Sun City does have one of the lowest rainfalls, but that there are at least two other places in Florida alone superior in this respect. The weather prediction in the papers is the same every day, "Fair and Warm." However, in the summer they do print stuff about the heat and hurricanes. The trouble with all this, is people come down here and expect rain two or three times in six months, and it rains about once a week. (If the sun breaks through the overcast sky for a minute or two, it goes down in the records as a sunny day, even though these records are only for the private information of the officials.) It isn't so bad, so they don't get sore, but they write home about it. The censorship covers all outgoing mail and excises all references to bad weather in the city. According to Elizabeth, the clerks don't have time to read the letters to see if the weather under discussion is that of New York or Sun City; they just run through quick looking for two words, rain and cold, and black-out that sentence. They can do this because there is a local ordinance saying they can (I looked it up. It gives them authority to remove all "scurrilous matter" from the mails), and the mail is not collected by the U. S. but by the "City Post Corporation," and then turned over to the government mail agent. I believe this the only place in the U. S. where the mail is under control of the locals. E. says that's all they do, just the weather, but in certain instances the clerks can be bribed to monkey around or pass over information, and advises me to post "special" letters out of town. I guess this is a "special" letter. Incidentally, anyone who wants to mention the censorship down here, does so by referring to "the weather bureau."

Last week I went to Palm Theater which is, as it does not deny, the biggest and best in Sun City and in Florida outside of Miami. All the shows are held here; professional tennis, bathing beauty contests, etc. I was passing by and glanced at the notices outside; they said in light green "The Poetry of Conflict" on a white background, nothing else. So I went in. With such an arty come-on I didn't expect many people, but there were a lot. It turned out to be a fish show. There was a tank running the length of the stage out of sight on both sides, about three times the height of a man and probably a little wider than that. It was all lit up so that you could see everything. They used colored lighting and music; some really lovely effects. The fish were put in at stage right, behind the curtain, then after the lecturer was through with them, a net operated by machinery fitting to the bottom and both sides, swept from one end to the other, clearing the tank completely in a second. Then the net went back, and other fish came on. The lecturer was young, with a yellow vandyke; he looked as if he might be down from the North. The lecture was deep and technical—I know a little about fish from zoology in college, but I could hardly follow him. He was using the scientific (Latin) nomenclature, and didn't employ one 'popularization.' This impressed me; I thought, all these fish-lovers know a thing or two and I looked around to see if they were the same you see on the street. They were, but few of them were paying the slightest attention—not watching the fish or even listening to the alternate music. Some of them seemed to be taking notes with paper and pencil. I forgot to mention that at the beginning of the show an old bitch in the front row was taken to the stage and introduced as a representative of the League for the Overcoming of Indifference to Non-Humans. The manager who introduced her, wearing a white shirt open at the neck, and black trousers, said something about charges of mistreating the fish. After half an hour of the lecture the net swept all the fish off in the middle of a sentence. The lecturer didn't finish the sentence. The manager went smiling to the stage and everybody began to perk up. "I give you in solitary splendor, carcharodon carcharias," the manager said. "In solitary splendor." A shark swam into the tank and the manager glanced down, grinning obscenely through his fingers. "Everything is over tonight. I thank you." The LOIN-H representative got up with her shoulders moving, covered her giggling mouth with a handkerchief, and walked up the center aisle, with her dead-pan friend following her looking from side to side as everyone in the place began to laugh. (Except me.) The ushers showed them out, and opened the door to the betting room. Some of the fish fights were duels, some were free-for-alls with the survivor paying off. I didn't win any of my bets, but I met the lecturer coming back from the teller's with a wad.

It was very hard to worm out of Elizabeth what follows: I think if she weren't leaving, she wouldn't have told me. Again, this is not a secret, but it is underground, like sex used to be. The founders of the city are unknown, but they also founded the custom, which has been followed to the present day, of annually sacrificing a Negro boy. The procedure E. says, has been changed in many particulars since then. They once dropped him to a "carcharodon carcharias" in the open bay; now it's an octopus in the tank of the Palm Theater. And about ten years ago they started giving the boy a knife. Not that this made any difference; the boy has never survived. The only witnesses of what goes on are the technicians and the members of the special committee designated by the city council. No matter what friends you have, it is very difficult to get in. Elizabeth says the last three times she has pulled every wire she could think of, but she never had a chance. The date is kept secret; during that week (in summer, after the tourists have gone) the city is terribly overwrought; people telling each other in whispers the latest rumor about *The Octopus and the Pickaninny*. To let them know that it is all over, the council declares a day of mourning (this means that the public buildings, the theaters, and the bars are closed, but everything else is open). E. says that it used to be a day of celebration; they changed this suddenly in 1928—she never found out why. I asked her how they got the boy. She said they used to just take the one that struck their fancy, but now they give the parents of the boy five thousand dollars, if he will volunteer. There's even a certain amount of competition. The age limits are 10-12 and they have to be "presentable," presumably to the octopus. A week before the "contest" the boy is taken in charge by the committee and instructed in the use of the knife; the octopus' weak points are explained, and he gains an idea of the creature's psychology. There is also some attempt to fortify him with the grandeur of the event. Before he goes to the tank, for the first time in his life he shakes hands with white men. I said, "What happens if he kills the thing? Just for a change, I mean." She said she didn't know, that had never happened yet; but very likely they would put in another octopus.

In August when you said that you would tell me everything, I refused to promise you the same, and I could feel your thought, "How many things she has concealed from me!" But even though you don't love me now, you would never dare tell me this. (We have always agreed that happiness and illusion, unhappiness and reality, are complements; but it sometimes happens that happiness and reality are joined for moments, of which there are altogether perhaps a few hours in any one life.) You told me a few years ago that one of these moments occurred when you saw me two blocks away as I was going toward the bus and caught me just before the door closed. It was when you were waiting for me to come off the bus, you said. I lied that that was one of my moments too. Do you want to know what the reality was, at this moment you said was the most trustful in your life? I was looking at you as a camera, a sharp impression into which no memories entered. I don't mean that I felt nothing. I was very pleased. But then, I thought you looked rather like an exhausted horse, and I did not care for the dried spittle in one corner of your mouth, or for other repulsive associations which I cannot bring myself to mention. Your face was as stupid as it could not have been if you had not been happy. How it hurt me to write this! Now that I have, I do not want your reaction. Your letters make me unhappy. I have to open everything from you, but I beg you not to write to me. I have never loved you so much!

339

LITTLE ANTHOLOGY
OF FRENCH POETRY

translated by Lloyd Alexander

SIX POEMS

Rene Char

MEDALLION

Waters of green lightning which sound the ecstacy of the beloved face, waters stitched with old crimes, amorphous waters, waters pillaged by an approaching consecration. . . Even though he had to bear the reproaches of his eliminated memory, with his lips the gardener greets the absolute love of autumn.

Identical wisdom, you who compose the future without believing in discouraging weight, let him feel the spark of journey vibrating in his body.

SO THAT NOTHING MAY BE CHANGED

1
Take my hands and climb the black ladder, oh Devoted; the voluptuousness of our seeds smoke and cities are iron and distant voices.
2
Our desire took from the sea its hot robe before swimming on its breast.
3
In the flower of your voice, flights of birds drive away the care of drought.

4

When scarred sands, issuing from the slow carts of the earth shall become guideposts, then calmness shall approach our closed space.

5

Fragments tear me. And torture stands upright.

6

The sky is no longer so yellow, nor the sun so blue. The furtive star of rain appears. Brother, faithful flint, your yoke is split. Understanding has sprung from your shoulders.

7

Beauty, I go to meet you in the solitude of the cold. Your lamp is pink; the wind glitters. The threshold of evening is worn away.

8

I, captive, have chosen the ivy's slowness in an assault against the stone of eternity.

9

"I love you" repeats the wind to all it makes alive.

I love you and you live in me.

YOUTH

Far from the ambush of tiles and the alms of calvaries, you give yourself birth, hostages of birds, fountains. The midden of man, made from the nausea of his ashes, of man wrestling with his vindictive providence, is not enough to dishearten you.

Eulogy, we have accepted one another.

"If I had been mute as the stone step faithful to the sun and which ignores its ivy-stitched wound, if I had been a child as the white tree which welcomes the fears of bees, if the hills had lived till summer, if the lightning had opened its gate to me, if your nights had pardoned me. . . . ."

A glance, an orchard of stars, heather and solitude are separate from you! The song ends the exile. A rippling breeze of lambs brings back new life.

ANNIVERSARY

Now that you have joined a springtime without frost to the mists of a massacre already starting the journey of its ashes, reap the harvest collected on the dubious horizon, and restore it to the hopes which surrounded it at birth.

May the day hold you to the anvil of its white fury!

Your mouth cries out the extinction of your breath. Your hot half-open filters spring out to liberty.

Nothing but the soul of a season separates your approach from the almond of innocence.

DUTY

The child whom, at nightfall, winter cautiously dropped from the moon's chariot, once within the fragrant house, cast his eyes upon the hearth of molten metal. Behind the narrow burnt-out window, ardent space held him completely captive. Breast bent toward the warmth, his young hands sealed by a flight of the dried leaves of well-being, the child spelled out the reverie of the icy sky:

"Mouth, my confident, what do you see?"

"Locust, I see a poor mushroom with a heart of stone, a friend of death. Its poison is so old you could turn it into a song."

"Mistress, where do my lines go?"

"Beauty, your place is marked on the park bench where the heart has its crown."

"Am I the present of love?

In the constellation of the Pleiades, in the wind from an adolescent river, the impatient Minotaur awoke.

GRAVITY

If he breathes he thinks of the hollow
In the tender confident clay
Where his hands of evening spread your body.

The laurel exhausts him,
Privation strengthens him.

And you, monotonous absent woman,
Spinner of saltpeter,
Behind immobile layers
An ageless ladder lifts your veil!

342

You go naked, starred with splinters,
Secret, warm, available,
Attached to the indolent earth
But still the intimate of man abrupt in his prison.

To bite you days grow larger,
More arid and invincible than clouds ripped apart in the heart
of bone.

FIVE SKETCHES

Henri Michaux

I THE PEACEFUL MAN

STRETCHING his hands out of the bed, Plume was amazed at not finding the wall. "Well," he thought, "the ants must have eaten it . . ." and went back to sleep.

A little while later his wife took hold of him and shook him: "Look, you lazy bum," she said, "while you were so busy sleeping someone's come and stolen our house." And indeed, an unbroken sky stretched all about them.

"Bah! The thing's already done," he thought.

A little while later he heard a noise. A train was bearing down on them at top speed. "If it's in that much of a hurry," he thought, "it will surely get where it's going before we do." And he went back to sleep.

Then he was awakened by the cold. He was drenched with blood. Several pieces of his wife were lying nearby. "With blood," he thought, "always flow all sorts of discomforts. I would have been very happy if the train hadn't gone past. But, since it's passed already. . . ." And he went back to sleep.

"See here," said the judge, "how do you explain the fact that your wife was so badly wounded, cut into eight pieces while you who were beside her were unable to make one move to prevent it, without even noticing it. There's the mystery. The whole case hangs on that."

"Things being what they are," thought Plume, "I certainly can't help her now." And he went back to sleep.

"The execution will take place tomorrow. Accused, have you anything to say for yourself?"

"Excuse me," he said, "I haven't been following the case." And he went back to sleep.

II PLUME AT THE RESTAURANT

Plume was dining in the restaurant when the maître-d'hotel came up, looked at him severely and said in a low, mysterious voice, "What you have on your plate is *not* mentioned on the menu."

Plume excused himself immediately:

"It so happens," he said, "I was in a hurry. I was in a hurry. I did not take the trouble of consulting the menu. I asked for a chop, offhandedly, thinking that perhaps there might be some, or if not, that one could easily be found somewhere in the vicinity. Nevertheless, I was ready to order anything else if no chops were to be found. Without appearing particularly surprised, the waiter went off and a little while later brought this back to me and here it is. . . .

"Naturally, I shall pay the stipulated price. It's a fine cut, I don't deny that. I shall pay the price without a moment's hesitation. If I had known I would have willingly chosen some other meat or simply an egg. In any case, I'm not hungry any more. I shall pay the check immediately."

However, the maître-d'hotel does not budge. Plume feels terribly put out. After a few moments he raises his eyes. . . . Hmm! Now the manager of the restaurant is standing in front of him.

Plume excused himself immediately:

"I did not know," he said, "that chops were not included on the menu. I did not look because I have very poor eyesight and had not brought my pince-nez with me—and besides, reading always pains me terribly. I asked for the first thing that came into my mind rather to leave it free for other matters than by personal taste. The waiter, who was undoubtedly preoccupied, did not pursue the question any further and I—quite put out—began to eat. In any case, I shall pay you personally now that you are here."

However, the manager of the restaurant does not budge. Plume feels more and more put out. Just as he holds out a banknote toward the manager he sees the sleeve of a uniform. A police officer is before him.

Plume excused himself immediately:

"This is the way it happened. He went in there for a minute's rest. Suddenly someone shouts at him at the top of his voice, 'What will Monsieur have . . . ?' 'Oh . . . a beer,' he said. 'And then . . . ?' shouts the waiter angrily; then, rather to get rid of him than for any other reason, 'Oh well, a chop!' "

He thought no more about it when they brought it to him on the plate. Then, good heavens, since it was there in front of him. . . .

"Look, it would be very kind of you to settle the matter. Here . . ."

And he holds out a 100-franc note to him. Hearing steps retreating he thought himself already free. But now the commissioner of police is standing in front of him.

Plume excused himself immediately:

"He had an appointment with a friend. He had looked vainly for him all morning. Then, knowing that his friend always passed this street on the way back from the office, went in and took a table near the window. Since the wait might possibly be long and since he did not want to give the appearance of shirking expense, he ordered a chop. Just to have something in front of him. He never thought for an instant of eating it. But once it was in front of him, mechanically, without giving a second thought to what he was doing, he began to eat."

You must understand that nothing in the world could induce him to go into a restaurant. He only dines at home. This is a rule. Here it is a question of pure distraction, such as might happen to any nervous person, nothing more than a passing unconsciousness.

But the commissioner had called the chief of police on the phone:

"Look here," he told Plume, handing him the receiver, "explain yourself once and for all. It is your only chance for salvation."

And a policeman shoved him brutally.

"You better watch your step, see?"

As the firemen were entering the restaurant, the manager said to him:

"Look at the loss to my business. A catastrophe!" And he pointed around the restaurant from which all the customers had hurriedly left.

The Secret Police told him:

"We warn you, it's going to be hot. You'd better confess the whole truth. This isn't our first job, you can believe that. When things start to take a turn like that it means it's serious."

However, a great, boorish policeman somewhere above his shoulder told him:

"Listen, there's nothing I can do about it. Orders is orders. If you don't talk into that phone I'll knock your block off, get it? Confess! You been warned. If I don't hear you I'll knock your block off."

III PLUME TAKES A TRIP

Plume can not say that he is especially well taken care of on a trip. Some people walk all over him without a word of warning, others calmly wipe their hands on his coat. He has finally grown used to it. He prefers to travel with modesty and as long as it is possible, he will do so.

If they ill-temperedly serve a root on his plate, a big root:

"Go on, eat it. What are you waiting for?"

"Oh, of course. Right away. There."

He does not care to bring trouble upon himself needlessly.

And if they refuse him a bed at night:

"What! You didn't come so far just to sleep, did you? Go on, get your trunk and the rest of your things, this is the best time of the day for walking."

"Yes, yes, of course. Certainly. It was only in fun. Oh yes, only . . . only a joke."

And he turns away, back into the dark night.

And if they throw him off the train:

"Ah! So you think we heated up this engine and hitched eight cars onto it just to carry a young man of your age, in perfect health, who can be perfectly useful here, who has absolutely no need of going anywhere—and for that we dug tunnels, blew up tons of rock with dynamite and laid hundreds of miles of track in all sorts of weather, without counting continual inspection of the line for fear of sabotage, and all that for. . . ."

"Of course, of course. I understand perfectly. I got on, oh, just to have a look around. That's all. Simply curiosity. A thousand thanks."

And he goes back to the road with his baggage.

If, in Rome, he asks to see the Coliseum:

"Ah, no! It's already in bad shape. And then you want to go and touch it, lean on it, sit on it . . . that's why there's nothing but ruins everywhere. It taught us a lesson, a hard lesson, but from now on—no more, finished."

"Of course, of course! It was . . . I only wanted to ask you for a post card, or a photograph . . . if maybe. . . ."

And he leaves the city without having seen a thing.

If, on the steamer, the purser suddenly points his finger at him and says:

"What's that man doing here? I can see there isn't much discipline down there. Send him back into the coal hole. The second watch just rang."

347

He goes off whistling and Plume breaks his back working all through the crossing.

But he says nothing, he does not complain. He thinks of the unfortunate ones who can not travel at all, while *he* travels, he travels continually.

IV THE NIGHT OF THE BULGARIANS

We were on our way back and had taken the wrong train. And we were in with a whole pile of Bulgarians muttering God knows what among themselves, always squirming around, and we decided to get it over with in a hurry. We took out our revolvers and fired. We shot quickly because we didn't trust them. It was better to get them out of the way first thing. They all looked surprised, but Bulgarians . . . you mustn't trust them.

"A lot of passengers get on at the next station," the brakeman said. "Take your seats over there with the rest of them" (he points to the corpses) "so you won't take up more than one compartment. Now there's absolutely no reason why *you* and *they* should have separate compartments."

And he looks at them severely.

"Yes, yes, we'll go! Right away! Of course! Right away!"

And they quickly sit down next to the corpses and bolster them up.

It is not too easy. Seven dead men and three living. You sink down between the cold bodies and the heads of these "sleepers" are always bending to one side. They drop against the necks of the three young men like urns carried on the shoulder, touching the cheek, the beards stiff and suddenly beginning to grow with redoubled speed.

The whole night to pass. Then we shall try to be off early in the morning. Perhaps the brakeman will have forgotten. The main thing is to stay quiet. Try not to attract his attention. Stay squeezed together, just as he said. Show good will. In the morning we can sneak away. Before reaching the border the train usually slows down. Escape will be that much easier, further on we can cross the forest with a guide.

And so they encouraged each other to be patient.

In the train the dead are much more shaken up than the living. Speed disturbs them. They can't stay quiet an instant, they bend and slip to one side, they become more and more restless and nonsensical, they can't stand any more.

One must be firm with them and not let go for a second; flatten them against the backs of the seats, one on the left, one on the right and crush down on them—but their head is the one that takes the bumps.

The most important thing is to hold them tightly.

"Could one of you gentlemen make room for this lady here?"

Impossible to refuse. Plume takes one dead man on his lap (he has still another at his right) and the old lady sits down at his left. Now the old lady has gone to sleep and her head nods. Her head and the head of the corpse touch. But only the old lady's head awakens and she says that the other one is quite cold and she is afraid.

But they all quickly tell her that it's terribly cold in the compartment.

All she has to do is touch. Hands stretch out toward her, cold hands. Perhaps it would be better for her to go into a warmer compartment. She gets up. Then she comes back with the conductor. The conductor wants to see if the heating is working normally. The lady tells him:

"Just touch those hands."

But everyone shouts:

"No, no, it's because we haven't moved. Our fingers have gone to sleep, it's nothing. We're all warm enough here. We're perspiring, here—feel this forehead. You perspire at one part of the body and you're cold at another. Going for a while without moving does it, it's nothing more than that."

"Let the ones who are cold cover their faces with newspaper," Plume says. "That keeps you warm." The others understand. Soon all the corpses are capped in newspapers, in white, crinkling hoods.

It is much more convenient. They can be recognized immediately in spite of the darkness. Besides, there will be no risk of the old lady touching any more cold faces.

However, a girl gets on. Her bags are set in the corridor. She makes no attempt to sit down, a very reserved girl, modesty and fatigue weigh upon her eyelids. She asks for nothing. But a place must be made for her. They absolutely insist on it; then they think of disposing of the corpses, getting rid of them a few at a time. But, all things considered, it would be better to try and get them out right away, one after the other because the thing can be hidden from the old lady but with two or three strangers it would become rather difficult.

Cautiously they lower the wide window and the operation begins. They shove them out as far as the waist, once there they can be swung clear. But the knees must be well folded up so that they don't catch on anything—for as long as they remain hanging like that their heads give light taps on the window—exactly as though (they wanted) to come in.

All right! Courage! Soon we can breathe in peace again. One more corpse and that will be the end. But the cold air that has blown in wakens the old lady.

And hearing something stirring, the conductor returns, out of conscience and affection of gallantry, to see—even though he knows perfectly well there is not—if there is a seat for the young lady in the corridor.

"Certainly! Certainly!" they all shout.

"That's funny," the conductor says, "I would have sworn. . ."

"It is funny," says the look of the old lady as well, but sleep postpones all questions.

If only the girl will sleep now! True, one corpse can be explained more easily than five. But it would be best to avoid any questions. When you are questioned it is easy to become confused. Contradiction and misdemeanor appear from all sides. It is always preferable not to travel with a corpse. Especially when he has been killed by a revolver bullet, since the spilled blood makes him look quite badly.

But since the girl in her great prudence does not wish to sleep before they do—and after all, it's a long night and no station before 4:30, they are not excessively worried. So yielding to fatigue, they sleep.

Suddenly Plume notices it is 4:15 and he wakes up Pon . . . and they are in complete agreement. Worrying about nothing else but the next stop and the implacable daylight which will reveal all, they quickly throw the corpse out of the window. But no sooner are they wiping off their foreheads than they feel the dead man at their feet. Then wasn't he the one they threw out? But there would be time for questions later! They seize the corpse and threw him into the night. Oof!

How good life is for the living. How jolly this compartment is! They rouse their friend. Here, we're coming into D——. They wake the two women.

"Wake up, we'll soon be there. Was everything all right? An excellent train, isn't it? Did you get a good night's sleep at least?"

And they help down the old lady, then the girl. The girl looks at them without a word. They stand there. They don't know what to do, as though they had ended everything.

The brakeman appears and says:

"All right, get a move on. Get down and bring your witnesses with you!"

"But we don't have any witnesses," they say.

"Well," the brakeman says, "if you want a witness, you can count on me. Wait a second at the other side of the station, in front of the ticket windows. I'll be right back. Here's a pass for you. I'll be back in a second. Wait for me."

They arrive and once there, flee . . . flee.

Oh, to be alive now! Oh, to live at last!

V THE TEARING OFF OF HEADS

They only wanted to pull his hair. They didn't want to hurt him. Suddenly they tore his head off. Surely it had been put on badly. It shouldn't have come off like that. Something was surely missing.

When the head is no longer on the shoulders it is embarrassing. You have to give it to someone. But you must wash it because it stains the hands of whoever you give it to. It had to be washed. Because whoever gets it—his hands already starting to be bathed in blood—begins to be suspicious and look around him like someone expecting information.

Bah! We found it in the garden. . . . We found it with a lot of others. . . . We picked it out because it seemed to be the freshest. If he'd rather have another one . . . we could go and see. But keep that one while waiting, anyhow. . . .

And they go off, followed by a look which says neither yes nor no, a fixed stare.

If we went to look on the other side of the pond. You can find any number of things in a pond. Maybe a drowned person would do the trick.

In a pond you'd think you could find anything you'd want. They come back quickly, they come back breathless.

Where to find heads all ready to give away? Where to find them without too much fuss?

"I have a first cousin. But we have the same face—the same head, you might say. No one would ever believe I found it by chance."

"I . . . I have a friend named Pierre. But he's strong enough not to let it be taken away from him like that."

"Bah! We'll see. The other one came off so easily."

So they follow their idea and arrive at Pierre's. They drop a handkerchief. Pierre bends over. Laughing, as if to lift him up, they pull back on his hair. The head is torn off.

Pierre's wife enters, furious . . . Drunkard, now he's gone and upset the wine again. He can't even drink it any more, he has to spill it all over the place . . . and he can't even get up off the floor.

And she goes off, looking for something to clean up with. They hold her by the hair. The head comes off in their hands. A furious head, dangling from long strands of hair.

A big dog rushes in, barking loudly. They kick him and the head falls off.

Now they have three of them. Three is a lucky number. And there is a certain amount of choice. None of these heads are really alike. No. A man, a woman and a dog.

And they go off again, back to the one who has a head already and they find him waiting.

They put the bouquet of heads in his lap. The man's head on the left, near the first head, the dog's head and the long-haired woman's head on the other side. Then he waits.

He stares at them with a look that says neither yes nor no.

"Oh, these—we found them in a friend's house. They were there in the house. . . . Anybody could have come in and taken them. There weren't any more. We took what there was. Another time we'll have better luck. After all, it was merely luck. Fortunately there isn't a shortage of heads. Still, it's pretty late. Finding them in the dark. Taking time to clean them, especially the ones that were in the mud. But we'll try. . . after all, we couldn't have brought back a tumbril full of them. Of course . . . We'll go back. . . . Maybe some others have just fallen down now. We'll go and see. . . ."

And they go off, followed by a look which says neither yes or no, followed by a fixed stare.

"Oh, here! No! Go on! Take my head. Go back with it, he won't recognize it. He doesn't even look. You can tell him . . . here, when I was going out I butted into something. It's a head, isn't it? I'm giving it to you. And that'll be enough for today, won't it?"

"But you're all I have left."

"Come on, come on, no squeamishness. Take it. Come on, pull, pull hard. Harder!"

"No. You see it doesn't work. This is our punishment. Go ahead, try mine. Pull! Pull!"

352

But the heads do not come off. Real assassin's heads.

They don't know what to do any more, they go and come, back and forth, followed by a waiting, expectant look, a fixed stare.

At last they lose themselves in the night and it is a great comfort for them; for them and for their conscience. Tomorrow they will start off again in some direction which they will follow as long as they can. They will try to rebuild their life. It is quite difficult. But they will try. They will try not to think about all that any more, to live as before, as everyone else.

SIX POEMS

Paul Eluard

FOR EXAMPLE

Has it not been forever
That days have been without love
Each dawn impardonable
Each caress ugly
And every laugh a curse

I hear myself and you hear me
Howl like a lost dog
Against our solitude
Our love has more need
Of love than grass of rain

It must be a mirror.

RING OF PEACE

I have passed the gates of coldness
The gates of my bitterness
To come and kiss your lips

City reduced to the size of our room
Where the absurd tide of evil
Leaves a reassuring foam

Ring of peace I have only you
You teach me again what
A human being is when I despair

Of knowing whether I have likenesses.

DAWN

The sun which races over the world
I am as sure of it as you
The sun brings the earth into the world

‚A smile above the nights
On the bared face
Of a sleeping woman dreaming of dawn

The great mystery of pleasure
This strange tournament of mists
Which takes heaven and earth from us

But leaves us one for the other
Made one for the other forever
O you whom I tear from oblivion

O you I wanted happy.

A BODY

On this side it is summer
Music from the cage of birds
The language of the birds' palace
The river of the sorceress
Whose current burns between my hands

Is she dark
With hard flesh
Marked in blue
Hard golden with force
A tulip the evening
Of grapes' caresses

Is she white
Tender russet and orange
Whom warmth weakens
Clear grass inert pearl
A whole timid beach
Fallen from a sky of cotton

No game distracts us
Our weapons have little space
This is a lovely cloudless summer
The heavy duty of summer.

THE AGE OF LIFE
to René Char

I

Morning of winter morning of summer
Lips closed and roses ripe

Tearing expanse where sight draws us
Where the sea is in flight where the beach is entire

Summer evening collected in the voice of thunder
The plain burns and dies and is reborn in the night

Winter evening exhaled by implacable ice
The naked forest is flooded with dead leaves

Scale of the seasons insensible and living
Scale of the seasons balanced by age

II

We have been eight years old we have been fifteen
We have aged and blackened dawn and life

The men and women whom we did not love
We never thought of they cast no shadow

But we have aged the chasm has peopled itself
We have reproduced a future of adults

III

And yet this tiny mirror
To see laughing two eyes eye to eye
And the nose nothing else
The tip of an ear and the time for pouting
This limitless mirror
In which we made one with the universe

This tiny mirror where one
Of a thousand virgins played with us
A thousand definite promises

IV

We confused the colors
Of softness of extremity

All were useless
And we what good were we

All were grains of sand
Impalpable in the wind

All were sparks
Beneath a parasol of flame

Are we the men and women
Of these children that we were

The wind is led astray
Light is confused

A nothing holds us motionless
Reflecting in the black

V

The toys and games have changed to tools
To work to capital to care
Now we must hide to simulate a childhood
We are forbidden to laugh without reason

On the curve of day the sun of death
Weaves a thick window of well dressed beauties
We have but two hands we have but a single head
For we have learned to count and to reduce

Clouds of health mists of rejoicing
Midway from all murmurs of pleasure
Springtime diminishes winter is tolerable
How many more nights to dream of innocence

VI

Of innocence and strength upon the springboards
Of hope and confidence

Of strength and weakness my massive friend
Violent and subtle
Just and living long

As long as I
Since we were young
In such different seasons

But young as one is not
Searching all the roads
For traces of our duration

We shall not be a hundred years forever

And hope one day will go as lightning
Making the stricken harvests rise
Making the lead of our disasters shine

Old age is yesterday already

VII

And despite the stones
With the faces of men
We shall laugh again

And despite the hearts
Knotted and mortal
We live on hope

Nothing reduces us
To sleeping dreamlessly
To tolerating shadow

On the hour is neither
Doubt nor suspicion
Of a similar hour

Forever on the earth
All moves and sings
Changes and takes pleasure.

THE WORK OF THE PAINTER
to Picasso

I

Surround this lemon with a formless white of egg
Enrobe this white of egg with azure supple and fine
The straight black line comes from you in vain
Dawn is behind your painting

And the innumerable walls crumble
Behind your picture and you eyes staring
Like a blindman like a madman
You raise a high sword toward the void

One hand why not a second hand
Why not the mouth naked as a feather
Why not a smile and why not tears
Around the canvas where the small nails dance

Here is the day of others leave their luck to shadows
And with a single stroke renounce the eyelids

II

You raised a high sword
Like a banner to contrary wind
You raised your look against the shadow and the wind
Of confounding shadows
You would not share
There is nothing to expect from nothing
The stone will not fall on you
Nor the flattering eulogy

Hard scorner advance renouncing
Pleasure is born in the breast of your denial
Art could have been a grimace
You reduced it to a door

Open through which life enters

III

And the conventional image of a grape
Placed on the carpet
The conventional image of a sword
Raised toward the void an exclamation mark
Mark of stupor and stupidity
Who then can reproach me for it

Who then can reproach you the immemorial
Pose of all men prey to shadows
The others are of shadow but the others bear
A burden heavy as your own
You are a point of the shadow star
Which determines light

The ones who speak of shadow do not make us laugh
In the underworld of death
Those who believe in disaster and who charm their death
By a thousand and one vanities without one thorn
But we bear our sack of coal
To the fire which consumes us

IV

All starts with images
Said the madmen brothers of nothing
But I bind with images
All the dawns in daylight

I have the best conscience
Of our desires they are gentle
Soft and violent as a scythe
In tender blushing grass

Today we want to eat
Together or even play and laugh
Today I'd like to go
To the U.S.S.R. or simply rest

With my bride's heart
With the power to do well
And hope strong as a sheaf
Of hands bound about a kiss

V

Picasso my demented friend
My wise friend beyond all limit
There is nothing on our earth
Purer than your name

I love to say it and I love to say
That all your deeds are signed
For from that point men
Are justified in their greatness

￼And their greatness is different
Their greatness is all alike
It holds itself on the pavement
It holds itself on their desires

VI

Always it is a question of alga
Of hair of ground
A question of sincere friends
With a fever of ripe fruit

Of the old dead of young flowers
In incorruptible bouquets
And life gives all its heart
And death gives all its secret

A question of sincere friends
Across the parent ages
The everyday creation
In the indifferent greeting

VII

Curtain there is no curtain
Only a few steps to mount
Only a few steps to build
Without fatigue without care
Work will become a pleasure
We never doubted it we know well
That suffering is in excess and we want
New texts and canvas virgin after love

Eyes like anvils
Sight like the horizon
Hands on the threshold of knowledge
Like biscuits dipped in wine

And the sole goal of being first everywhere
Day shared caress without degree
Dear comrade to you to be the first
Last in the world in a first world.

FOUR PIECES FROM "LIBERTE GRANDE"

Julien Gracq

COLD WIND OF THE NIGHT

I waited for her in the evening, in the hunting lodge near the Riviere Mort. Fir-trees in the perilous night wind shook with a rustling of shrouds and a crackling of flames. The black night was lined with frost, as an evening suit with white satin—outside, *twisted* hands raced everywhere across the snow. The walls were great somber curtains and from the snowy steppes of white table linen, like fires from frozen pools rose the mystic light of candles. I was king of a people of blue forests, like a whole procession with banners motionless on the shore of a lake of ice. A cyclone of black thoughts, motionless as watered silk, at times trembled on the ceiling of the cavern. In evening dress, leaning on the mantlepiece and handling a revolver in a theatrical gesture, to pass the time I questioned the green and sleeping water of antique mirrors; at times a gust of wind stronger than the others clouded it with sweat fine as that on the carafes, but I emerged anew, spectral and stiff as a bridegroom on the photographic plate of a cameraman half hidden in a maelstrom of green plants. Oh hollow hours of the night, as one travelling on the light pneumatic bones of an express train—but suddenly she was there, seated upright in her long white garments.

STOWAWAY

At times I was carried past the inordinate shores of a glorious city, spread to the wind by its thousand masts, crying in the air as an extinct geyser its cries of clotted stone, a high pyramid of walls covered with a silky patina where, in the streets of evening, *like a mirror above an iceberg in the sea, the noble crystal of sonorous air was caught,* and far beyond the ramparts calm trumpets endlessly protected a mysterious solemnity—a seaport washed by winds and devastated by a sea into which rapid suns plunged red, and there, lying at the foot of a pier, on

363

the swell of surging waves curled by a single gust of driving wind—on my shoulders towers and golden domes smoking with the sun's dust in a dissipated blue, bent beneath the yoke of a sultry day—fascinated by a briny dream of solar spray, and on my back the enormous bubbles of secular tortoise shells, the corridors of crime of these million honeycombs, deserted squares around statues of glory and specters of broad daylight, porches of blind palaces plumed black by the shadowy creaking of banners like a man screaming at high noon—the city which was inhaled with me in the overflowing mirror of evening sank into the sea with a hissing of hot embers, and split the water with a breast monstrous under its canvas columns, on a swell of clamors and silences, under the mist of living light and the ardent bush of its flags.

THE TRUMPET OF AIDA

Great secret landscapes, intimate as dreams, endlessly spun and volatilized about her, like the light incense of clouds on the incandescent peak of a mountain. Her coming was like the face of light of a forest seen from a tower, like sunlight dissipated by mists on a rainy shore, like fortifying trumpet calls across widened squares of morning. With her, I sometimes dreamed of a barbarian horseman with pointed helmet, astride his dwarf poney as on a straight, stiff church chair, small and alone, trotting like a mechanical toy across the Mongolian steppes—and other times of some old Bulgarian emperor, like a parchment reliquary entering Saint Sophia for thanksgiving, while the bone-colored pavements of Byzantium sink beneath the grass of centuries and the superhuman orgasm of trumpets tetanizes the setting sun.

FURNISHED ROOM

In the somber light—of the especially sinister hue which, on a torrid August afternoon, drawn blinds filter into a death room—on walls painted with this translucent glaze, viscid to see and hard as glass to touch, which tapestries the walls of stalactite caverns, a light sheet of water, soundless as the water on slate slabs of public urinals, trembling, shimmering, soft as silk. The rivulets, running together in the half-light in the left-hand corner of the room, feed, before trickling away, a tiny bed of watercress. On the right, in an enormous lightning-proof Faraday cage thrown negligently over the arm of a curule chair, as if just back from a morning walk, the bloody toga of Caesar, recognizable by its museum tag and the *sui generis* look of the particularly authentic rents. A two-toned rustic Swiss cuckoo clock, striking half and quarter hours in the fishbowl silence. On the mantlepiece, victims of some premeditated show of evidence, in the midst of a profusion of *much* too sumptuous bibelots, an open packet of tobacco and the confirmation photograph (heavy cardboard, clipped corners, gilt-edged, specifically prepared for Catholic families, with the photographer's signature) of President Sadi-Carnot. In the shadows at the rear of the room, a freight car, on a track spotted with daisies and umbelliferae, exudes through its half-open door the sparkle of a Sèvres porcelain table service and a lovely set of tiny liqueur glasses.

FIVE POEMS

Jacques Prevert

THE LAUNDRY

Oh the terrible and surprising smell of meat
rotting
it is summer yet the leaves of the trees in the garden
fall and split as if it were autumn. . .
this smell comes from the pavilion
where Monsieur Edmond lives
head of the family
head of the office
it is wash day
and it is the smell of the family
and the head of the family
the head of the office
in his pavillion in the capital city of the canton
walks back and forth before the family washtub
and repeats his favorite formula
Dirty linen should be washed at home
and the whole family clucks with horror
and shame
and shudders and brushes and rubs and brushes
the cat would like to leave
all this makes him sick at heart
sick at his little house-cat's heart
but the door is padlocked
so the poor little cat pukes up
the poor little piece of heart
he ate the night before
old billfolds float in the water of the washtub
and scapularies . . . jock-straps. . .
night caps . . . policeman's caps. . .
insurance policies . . . bankbooks. . .
love letters asking for money
anonymous letters asking for love
a rosette of the Legion of Honor

an old piece of cotton ear-plug
ribbons
cassocks
circus tights
a wedding gown
a fig leaf
a nurse's blouse
the corset of a hussar officer
diapers
plaster pants
skin pants. . .
suddenly there are long sobs
and the little cat puts his paws over his ears
so as not to hear this sound
because he loves the daughter
and she is the one who is crying
she is the one they're after
the daughter of the house
she is naked . . . she cries . . . she weeps
and with a blow from the scrubbing-brush
to her head
the father brings the girl back to reason
the daughter of the house has a stain
and the whole family ducks her
and ducks her again
she bleeds
she screams
but she won't tell the name. . .
and the father screams too
Let none of this leave the house
let all this stay strictly between us
says the mother
and the sons the cousins the mosquitoes
shout too
and the parrot on his perch
also repeats
Let none of this leave the house
honor of the family
honor of the father
honor of the son
honor of the parrot Holy Ghost
the daughter is pregnant
the new-born child must not
leave the house

no one knows the name of the father
in the name of the father and of the son
in the name of the parrot already named Holy Ghost
let none of this leave here. . .
with a supernatural expression on her face
the old grandmother sitting on the edge of the tub
weaves a crown of artificial
immortelles for the natural child. . .
and the daughter is trampled
the bare-footed family
tramples and tramples and tramples
it is the family grape-harvest
the harvest of honor
and the daughter of the house dies
at the bottom. . .
on the surface soap bubbles
break
white bubbles
livid bubbles
color of the child of Mary. . .
and on a piece of soap a crab-louse
saves itself and its little ones
the clock strikes half past one
and the head of the family and the office
puts his headpiece on his head
and goes out
crosses the square in the capital city of the canton
returns the salute of his assistant-head
who salutes him. . .
the head of the family's feet are red
but the shoes are well polished
it is better to be envied than pitied. . .

FOR YOU MY LOVE

I went to the bird market
   And bought birds
      For you
      my love
I went to the flower market
   And bought flowers
      For you
      my love

I went to the iron market
And bought chains
Heavy chains
For you
my love
And then I went to the slave market
And looked for you
But I didn't find you
my love

SUNDAY

Between the rows of trees on Avenue des Gobelins
A marble statue leads me by the hand
Today is Sunday and the movies are full
The birds in the branches watch the humans
And the statue kisses me but no one sees us
Except a blind child who points his finger at us.

HOMECOMING

A Breton is returning to his native land
After having a pretty hard time of things
He walks up and down in front of the factories at Douarnenez
He doesn't recognize anyone
No one recognizes him
He is very sad
He goes into a restaurant to eat crêpes
But he can't eat any
Something keeps them from going down
He pays
He goes out
He lights a cigarette
But he can't smoke it.
There is something
Something in his head
Something bad
He is sadder and sadder
And suddenly he begins to remember:
When he was little someone told him
"You'll end up on the scaffold"

And during all these years
He never dared do anything
Not even cross the street
Not even go to sea
Nothing absolutely nothing.
He remembers.
The one who predicted it all was Uncle Grésillard
Uncle Grésillard who brought bad luck to everybody
the bastard!
And the Breton thinks of his sister
Working at Vaugirard
And his brother killed in the war
Thinks of all the things he has seen
All the things he has done
Sadness presses against him
He tries once more
To light a cigarette
But he doesn't feel like smoking
Then he decides to go see Uncle Grésillard
He goes there
He opens the door
The uncle doesn't recognize him
But he recognizes the uncle
And he says
"Bonjour Uncle Grésillard"
And then he wrings Uncle Grésillard's neck
And he ends up on the scaffold at Quimper
After having eaten two dozen crêpes
And smoked a cigarette.

FIRST DAY

White sheets in a closet
Red sheets in a bed
A child in its mother
The mother in pain
The father in the hallway
The hallway in the house
The house in the city
The city in the night
Death in a cry
And the child in life.

TWO STORIES

Paul Goodman

LITTLE BERT, or THE INTERVENTION

HIS SISTER Lucy clambered across the stony wall to pick buttercups with longer stems, altho nailed on the apple-tree was the sign "Beware of the Bull." She was 13 and wore a dress of color faded nearly white, and she had formal curls that hung on her shoulders. From out his hiding place, the bull sauntered in her direction, indecisive, like a drunken man on Ninth Avenue. The little boy opened his mouth past his ears and screamed "Help." The outcry made Lucy freeze in fright, but their companion, the farmboy Dan in his overalls, jumped on the stones, took her by the hand, and led her back across—while a flush of admiration and gratitude colored the little boy's cheeks, and a pang of envy smote him between the eyes.

Then sitting near the well that had a hood and a windlass, Lucy was braiding the daisies and long-stemmed buttercups into a garland. She wove daisies into a starry circlet and placed it on Bert's hair where it tickled with embarrassment. Dan watched her with big eyes of desire his thighs trembling to his embarrassment.

The grown-up boy and girl walked behind the house and did not reappear at once. Little Bert became fearful and suspicious. His anxiety grew. Sauntering near, as if indecisively, he peered round the corner of the white house, and the two were kissing in the shade. Silently he slipped his arms between them, round her waist. In this way he intervened; he effected a rescue; he shared in the secrecy.

With terrible violent spite Dan twisted Bert's arm behind his back. The tears and sweat started into Bert's face but he would not cry out. But Lucy said, "Let him go, you're hurting him."

Dan was confused and abashed. "He didn't hurt me," said little
Bert.

Trembling in every joint and his fingers fumbling, Dan
turned aside to pee. The trembling communicated itself to Bert
and he watched him with open mouth and also with terrible envy.

2

Auntie Dora, the guardian of the children for their visit at
the farm, was at the piano composing *The Lucille Waltz*. Childless as yet, and ultimately childless thru several marriages, she
was considered excellent with children because loving and firm,
or sentimental and cruel, or perversely lascivious and guiltily
vindictive. The piano, of a kind heard no more, was equipped
with a special peddle that allowed the upper register to twang
like a guitar.

The Lucille Waltz was complete and, however it was, Auntie
Dora furiously began to upbraid and beat the girl about her head
and shoulders, while Bert cowered behind the wicker chair. "A
child is beaten, not I—" What! it was Lucy that was being
beaten—whether Bert himself had told Dora about the kissing, or
that she had heard about the charge of the bull.

But in the city, Papa had gone away in vain, because Mama
saw Mr. Gericke.

The little boy cried out, "Don't hit her any more!" Dora
had picked up an iron poker, and Bert thought, "She can't *mean*
to hit her with that and hurt her forever." He stepped between,
intervening, and hid behind his forearm and cried, "You're bad,
Auntie Dora. You made *The Lucille Waltz* and you hit Lucy."

But Papa's sister brought down the poker on his arm, then
dropped him and slapped his head from side to side. There was
an unfillable void in his wail.

He implored, "Don't hit me any more. You meant it."

3

His sore eyes covered with a gritty dust the flirtatious smiles
and the flowers of the field. This dust lies there opaque between
the eyes and its objects, intervening, rescuing us from the vividness of what is *meant*.

Little Bert's forearm was as if breaking with fatigue as
he masturbated, offering himself the day's images unmeant.
They made threats about his naughtiness, but he willed not to
take them seriously.

He wailed at midnight, just to make it impossible for the others to sleep.

In the morning they were shouting in the next room about money and the crying child. Narrowing to a pointed grin the wide quadrilateral mouth of pain, Bert stretched his happy grin taut from ear to ear.

Auntie Dora came in and at once opened the drawers to pack the clothes. Lucy's movements were unwilling. The boy was not unwilling to return home, to surprise Mama. He did not like the milk warm from the cow.

So they made preparations to go. But now they were going indeed—away from the serious theatre where alone the flowers sprang alive. The horse was harnessed to the trap. The sobbing child stretched out his arms in longing. Auntie Dora sat stiff and their hostess was thin-lipped, but the farm-boy helped with the valises with the dumb willingness of the baffled. The fat behind of the horse was the type of all things that hold back. Nevertheless they moved off.

Bert and Lucy silently stretched their necks to see back—in unison, but he could not touch her.

Bert was going back to the city.

Going to intervene, with a new insincere purposiveness.

So a man unwillingly (but why then does he do it?) boards the train that takes him from the place that promises a little comfort.

But to see the flowers in a little comfort.

His arms are lifted high: when will they come pounding down?

I cannot take your troubles seriously, as if they were meant; why do you tell them to me?

Many the lovers I have brought together; then intervened like a physician watching the fever-chart—watching the progress of it like the figures on a fever-chart.

TERRY FLEMING, or ARE YOU PLANNING A UNIVERSE?

1

MOTHER TOLD TERRY that his father was dead. But when he grew old enough to read and to ferret in the trunk, he found newspaper clippings that his father was in jail. He was excited. His father was not dead but alive, not nothing but a person, not nowhere but in a place. He was angry with his mother anyway, now he was angry with her because she tried to hide his living father. She kept secrets from him, he kept his secret from her; but he had the advantage, because he knew.

His father and his father's plight seemed wonderfully interesting to Terry and he bragged to his mates in school. "*My* father is in a tremendous jail. It goes on more'n fifty miles. It's far away." His schoolmates were doubtful how to take this novelty. Those to whom the word *jail* meant something vaguely guilty and frightening were stirred to awe and envy, because what is guilty is forbidden and what is forbidden is delightful without limits. The thought of this ecstasy communicated itself from them to Terry. He radiated privilege.

He bragged to his teacher Miss Agostine that his father was in the great jail. She started and Terry was convinced that there was something unbelievable. So he insisted, to enjoy the reaction again and again. But when she showed signs of pity, he felt contempt and anger and said, "What do you know about jails, you old maid?"

To preserve his little glory he made a devaluating judgment of them all.

His schoolmates, fortified by information from home, conspired to take him down a peg, and at the corner after lunch they greeted him with the outcry, "Your daddy's a jailbird."

But Terry said serenely, "What do *you* know about jails? My daddy's alive. My daddy's alive and in jail. Even my Mom tried to keep it secret from me, but I found it out by reading. It's in the papers. He's not nowhere. Yeow! *My* daddy's alive, he's in jail."

2

Terry's father, Dick Fleming, was inured. Whether in fear or perverse hope, he could not foresee any extraordinary punishment that they could inflict on him that would not be indifferent, indifferently sad, to him. When he first reached this condition, his attitude was exasperating to the prison authorities; it seemed to be insolent, defiant and provocative, a show of force to be met with new force. But there was no increment of reaction on his part and even a superficial observer could see that his expression was not a judgment of them nor of his relation to them, but of a certain relation to himself. To create such an inward-turning relation was the purpose of their reformatory, and therefore usually they now let him be.

374

Punished, or let be in his cage, Dick Fleming left no anger. He had achieved a control of his feelings that prevented the fruitless anger from rising and disturbing the pleasure of surcease from pain. The worst pain would be to repeat the process of bursting with anger and swallowing the anger. Of turning four colors: red, black, white and purple: for there is the red anger of boiling anger, the black anger of settled wrath, the white anger of blazing fury, and the purple anger of suppressed rage.

The expense of soul in repeating this fruitless process was too exhausting to endure. Dick was preoccupied with avoiding the pain of the rising of the instinctive reaction of anger, and he was inured to the hurt, usual or extraordinary, that they inflicted on him. He did not fear anything but the obliterating fury itself, that would obliterate first himself.

But when he slept, he dreamed of the fire. We others dream of the fire with its features and colors and licking its objects: houses burning, explosions, and bolts of electricity. But the fire that Dick dreamed of was more like the dark fire of physics, an invisible mass not even hot because it touches no objects—the fire itself, filling a space, where nothing else can be, except that occasionally there is a white flash and annihilation because of some flaw in the perfect destructiveness.

3

"My father is a king," thought Terry. "Enemies have locked him in jail. They have cruel guards and use heavy stone and iron to keep him unknown. But his dignity shines.

"They gave me to a gypsy. My real mother is dead."

Terry was too prudent to brag to his schoolmates that his father was this important person. But his knowledge of it enabled him sometimes to withdraw from stupid competitions with a distant smile. But the secret of it isolated him from his friends and he had no other confidants.

Terry did not let on to the woman he housed with that he knew she was a gypsy.

"Also, my father has a daughter, my older sister," thought Terry. "She is beautiful and she has let-down hair. She is not in jail, but she has a way of getting in to see our father. She works on the outside with our party. She is the one I must get in touch with, to know what to do next."

But it was not the case that Terry met his sister on any corner, altho he had a suspicion that certain persons, by their dignity, belonged to their party; but he was too prudent to be forward. Instead, what he recognized clearly, by their pretended dignity and their cruelty, were the enemies. He learned to mark how they usurped privileges and were abusing them. The enemies did not aim any special attacks at Terry himself because he kept his secret too well, that it was *his* father who was the king. Terry saw that most of the kids were ignorant sheep who did not know what was going on, and they were the most abused.

Sometimes he was buoyed up by hope. At other times, especially in the anxious dark before sleep, Terry felt that the enemy regime was becoming the accepted order of things: the king was literally rotting away in jail and it was too late to rescue him. The world was closing in and there was no way of making a break-through, even if he met his sister.

Most of the day he was neither elated nor anxious but masturbated with dogged courage.

4

Are *you* planning a Universe? Are you thinking of creating a *Universe*? Here are some *do's* and *don'ts* to bear in mind. If you follow these simple suggestions you will have a better chance of being content with your Universe.

Don't have any "chosen people." The fancied advantages of such an arrangement are found to be far less than the complications that arise.

Do have a good supply of material on hand, so that at the last moment you don't have to skimp on whole realms of being.

Don't try to settle everything beforehand, but *do* have a reserve for unforeseen changes, so that you don't end up stuck with an undesirable scheme and hating it.

Do show a little pity.

If you're planning a Universe. If you're thinking of creating a Universe.

Do show a little pity.

Don't hide your face too completely, because you might as well get some satisfaction out of your handiwork.

Do give the souls a little substance along with their necessary flexibility, or they will become complicated to the point of monotony.

Don't have any "chosen people."

If you follow these simple suggestions, you will have a better chance of being content with your Universe.

Do try to keep it clear what is nature and what is violence.

Don't hurry, putting in a week's work and thinking you can have something to be proud of.

But *do* let yourself go, according to your whim. Remember that it's your show from the beginning to the end.

But *don't* have any "chosen people."

And *do* show a little pity.

If you're planning a Universe. If you're thinking of creating a Universe. Here are some *do's* and *dont's*. Follow these simple suggestions and you will have a better chance of being content with your Universe.

Don't forget?

THE NEXT ARMISTICE
AFTER THE NEXT

(Tentative sketch for a radio-play, pantomime, ballet, dance-drama, oratorio, song-cycle, free-verse epic, or a public declamation designed to win first place in the Manatoma Highschool Forensic Contest.)

Irwin Kroening

At exactly 2 P. M., Eastern
Standard Time, the second Thursday of that
Month, the names were fixed upon official
Documents, the photographs were taken:
Marshal Lyons frowning at the vanquished,
General Atwood smiling for reporters.
The word was detonated in a formal
Corner of the ether. Concussions rattled
Table-radios on all the continents
And set up tremors in the farthest bowels.
Factorywhistles were tied down, their hoarsened
Agony shutting in the cities like a
Wall: sirens were cranked into arrogant
Hysterics, and beneath that frenzied air
Triumphal ten-year holidays were given
Generously to faithful workers. Careful
Not to soil their virgin arms or blouses
Patriotic girls leaned out of windows
And blew promiscuous kisses to the Hour,
While common councils quickly ordered all the
Country's vital institutions: beauty-
Shops and fishmarkets, all-night waitingrooms
And churches, the drugstore and the brothel, the power-

Plant and shooting-gallery, the zoo and broker's
Office closed, gilded public statues
Protected with the best barbwire, good bulbs
Removed from streetlamps, benches from the parks,
Waterhydrants more securely bolted
Down, drinkingfountains camouflaged,
Garbagecans and trashcontainers sealed,
Sewers barricaded, buildings sandbagged,
Pedestrians and motors off the streets
And welltrained riot squads on certain corners
To welcome home the Republic's conquering armies.

      HUP! two three four
      HUP! two three four

Some folks thought the boys might be unpleasant,
A trifle restless as they disembarked,
Wearing last month's valor on their khaki
And this month's grievance on their faces,
To shake the unemployed but servile hands of
Memory, hug their old frustrations, say
Hello to smiling and familiar faces
Of all the neighborhood anxieties,
Lie down once more with their faithful and flatbreasted
Doubts, while in darkness freighttrains fled
Across the loveless countryside to carry
Shining goods of peace to bloodied houses
Of the rich, where the poor were fed the careless
Scraps from tables, scolded for their manners
And punished for an old uncleverness,
Then taught new tricks of Hate with kindness or a
Leash.
      Some folks thought the boys' return
Might mean a little trouble in the cities.

      HUP! two three four
      HUP! two three four

      It had been a good war
      As far as wars go
The President's own son had been wounded in action
Three new poets and one novelist had come to light,
      whose works the critics unanimously agreed

would form an imperishable part of the mighty
edifice that was American literature

The Motion Picture Industry had given its unstinted
support to the Government, providing numerous
stars for pinup pictures and barrackroom entertainment; produced important civilian films
to maintain political misinformation and hatred
of the Enemy at a standardized level; educa-
tional films for the Army to demonstrate the
newest technics of murder and the oldest discomforts of syphilis in Technicolor and Three
Dimensions

The universities had furnished men whose heads were
stuffed with all the highly specialized knowledge
necessary to understand the Enemy's language,
review His history, evaluate His culture, undermine His morale, annihilate His forces, expro-
priate His wealth and occupy His land with the
correct approach to efficient military control
and limit reconstruction

Television, Inc. had helped to sell over four billion
dollars worth of warbonds

Mrs. Munz's boy, in the next block, had lost an eye

The Secretary of the Interior's daughter had joined
the Women's Auxiliary and was lauded for her
creditable work in improving the old method
of dehydrating potatoes

Thirtyseven outstanding scientific discoveries had
been made by international scientists: these
were in the fields of chemistry, aviation,
ballistics, metallurgy, electronics, meteor-
ology, nuclear physics, psychiatry and plastic
surgery

Mrs. Romano, whose husband operates the fruitstand
next to the railroad depot, had been given the
honor of speaking to a nationwide audience
over the radio, after eight of her ten soldier
sons had been blown up by the same landmine

The usual amount of declarations, manifestoes, principles, conferences, terms, charters, official
statements and denials had made their way to
front pages of the newspapers: the usual amount
of serious decisions had stayed off

Strikes, permanently outlawed, had broken out in only
    a few backward areas, where production was in-
    significant and obsolete methods of subduing
    the workers were still in effect
Many medals for distinguished service had been post-
    humously awarded the families of men who had
    gone down with their ships, ignited oiltanks
    with their burning bodies, saved the lives of
    superior officers, informed authorities which
    comrades were spreading subversive propaganda
    among the troops, wiped out an Enemy civilian
    population of 500,000 and those who had de-
    liberately exposed themselves to Enemy fire
    so that tacticians could measure the rate of
    expendibility for the storming of an abandoned
    fillingstation or the seizure of a polluted
    reservoir
The nation's symphony orchestras had fearlessly played
    Mussorgsky, Tchiakowsky and Stravinsky right
    back in the Enemy's teeth, as well as contributed
    many members to the Army Espionage Service, who
    were able to cunningly exploit the Enemy's love
    of music
Many artists had contributed fine posters
All parties of the Left had fought vigorously in the
    underground, denouncing each other in the most
    unequivocal terms as multi-bolsheviks, permanent
    revolutionists, fascists, totalitarians, centrists,
    liberals, adventurists, formalists, chauvinists,
    absolutists, negativists, pacifists, terrorists,
    bureaucrats, dilettantes, moralists, schoolboys
    and lunatics, thus precipitating some exciting
    street skirmishes and several obscure debates
    that were promoted as carefully as prizefights
    by the editors of little magazines for their
    gullible audiences, who knew better than to be
    taken in by anything except their own intellec-
    tual snobbishness, and at last forcing the
    Government to shoot a few rebels who were in-
    discreet enough to bring their personal quarrels
    out into public places
The intelligensia had suddenly remembered man's Primor-
    dial Fall, or turned to subtle new dialectics of

the Irrational which philosophy had just brought
forth, read Malthus as well as Kroger's new
Unzuverlässigkeit psychology in cheap paperbound
editions, and decided once more that life's
deepest values were tragic
The nation's civilian masses had cultivated victory
gardens, saved wastepaper and fats, turned in
old sodawater bottlecaps, collected used telephone slugs, endured poor transportation, strin-
gent foodrationing, high livingcosts, long working-
hours, low wages and loss of all democratic
privileges while believing, for the most part,
everything that was told them by their rulers
with no more than the usual amount of unspoken
resentment or the usual amount of apathetic pride
The International Anarctic Council in Charge of Deter-
mining and Controlling all Illegal Implements of
Modern Warfare had functioned with a remarkable
degree of efficiency, failing only once to enforce strict sanctions when the Enemy had tried
to make use of the banned atomic bomb and completely destroyed three of His own cities through
inexpert technical management
The peace measures had been harsh, altruistic and
secret
It had been a good war

HUP! two three four
HUP! two three four

(ballad)
O spread the news to Mother
And tell her all is well;
Her boy was killed battle
But he didn't go to Hell.

He went where all good heroes go;
I think she ought to know;
I mean six feet below the earth
And not the U.S.O.

He died to save his dear coun-tree
From the awful Mongol's boot;
O spread the news to Mother—
Who else will give a hoot?

382

HUP! two three four
HUP! two three four

When the first contingent was ready to march down the gang-plank the situation, let me tell you, was tense. Picture, if you can, this huge milling crowd of mothers, fathers, brothers, sisters, wives and sweethearts, whose waving of handkerchiefs and cries of joy were gradually inhibited by a growing awareness of the boys' own apathy as they, lining rails of the ship ten, twelve high with complete negation of gesture or facial mobility, only gazed down silently into this ebullient aggregation of humanity who had come to welcome them back to glorious American soil, eyes giving not a sign of recognition or delight; I say picture, if you can, the ultimate consternation of these good people on the dock. What anguish must have wrung their hearts; What frantic questions must have beat at the gates of their lips! Were these avenging faces looking down upon them the faces of their own beloved sons and brothers and husbands and lovers? Were these the stalwart youths who had risked life and limb so that all the world might be purged of that godless and barbaric tyranny of the Mongol hordes? Many were inclined to answer these questions, and others of their ilk, in the negative as the sullen strangers began slowly to file off the boat, whilst the small cordon of police and military officials grew rapidly uneasy. And now what was the reaction of the civilian crowd? Many drew back cringing, afraid to speak a word, afraid to cry out the name that had only a few minutes before been so gladsome on their tongues. Women fainted. Children went into convulsions. Strong men paled. How can one find words, as the khakied sons were almost upon the mob, to describe patrolman Flannigan's tightened grip on his ineffectual billy, the pathetic whistle to the lips of government agent Meyer, Colonel Randall's impotent gesture of authority? In Washington wires were paralyzed; the President and his cabinet sat starkly waiting around a White House table, cigars dead in their mouths. Wall Street held its breath; bankers and industrialists cowered underground in their bomb-proof chambers. Physicians, college professors, lawyers, labor leaders, priests and dentists began feverishly to abjure their loyalty to capitalism, announced their espousal of the Collective State, a cause for which all admitted they had been covertly working right along. The existence of our Republic had reached a terrible crisis, and many were the oaken hearts that cracked under this greatest of all dishonors to the Flag. Was this the fruit of

that long hard struggle in which so many had sacrificed the very
joy of breathing a freer air in a freer land, of watching that
evening sun go down? Was this the reward for those of us who
had given so unsparingly of our time and our money? O America, shame.

> HUP! two three four
> HUP! two three four

The first one on the dock was only two years
Older than the former Peace: a child,
Whose childish cruelties had since been used
For larger ends than corner catcalls: who looked
About suspiciously, taller, clumsier
Than all the statesmen's unkept promises,
And showed where humiliation hid itself
Behind the conqueror's tic, and where the rooted
Apprehensions of his fellow had come
To bud and stand upon his face like flowers.

> HUP! two three four
> HUP! two three four

The others were behind him, pushed him forward,
Wading through fatigue like water: the heavy-
Bearded and the hollow-eyed, the chronic
Frowners and the easy weepers: keeping
Close to anonymity as if
It were a sheltering tank advancing on a
Land where public nightmares prowled the streets.
Their State-conditioned reflex, meant to take
The place of Love's still held them in formation.
They stared about the crowd and squared their shoulders;
They shuffled down the gangplank and were dumb.

> HUP! two three four
> HUP! two three four

All could see Injustice stand before them,
Comfortably upholstered, smoothly geared
And highly powered, tricked out with fancy gadgets,
Lavished with the most expensive metals
And painted shrewdly as a chorus girl.

384

The Mayor sat in it, mumbling to his committee,
Smiling uneasily, ready to give away
The City's genuine gilt-edge cardboard key.

     HUP! two three four
     HUP! two three four

They stared. It was their country, their dishonor.
But all were tired. Anger had slipped away
From them in rubbled towns like blood and bowels
And conscience. Although the tallest buildings looked
Indifferent, the crowd was waiting like a laurel
And home was any word without an accent.
        They hesitated. All at once the first one's
Mouth fell open in awareness. Slowly
He was drawn in wonder through the ranks
To where the reception committee sat dismayed.
He stood before them gazing solemnly
Until a mounted policeman moved his way.
He only shook his head, grinned and swallowed,
Stepping out of suspicion as if it were
His uniform.
          'Gosh,' he said. 'Gosh,
I never thought I'd ever get to see
The latest Cadillac.'
         The cheering started.
The President silently lit a fresh cigar, gazed at his
     cabinet and permitted a faint smile to cross his
     lips before he blew out the match
Financiers appeared in their clubs again as if by magic
The Stock Market climbed
The middleclass repudiated everything it had said in the
     last twentyfour hours with a series of nationwide
     editorials on the advantages of a free enterprise
     economy
Department stores lit up their windows; petshops resumed
     a thriving business
Seventy of the Enemy's finest scientists were imported
     on the next transoceanic clipper to begin immediate
     research on new military weapons
Tentative plans were made in Congress for inexpensive
     work projects and government agencies of relief
There was some dancing in the streets

HUP! two three four
HUP! two three four

It had been a good war
And the next one
Would be even a bigger and better one

(Song)

Keep smiling, keep smiling,
It's everybody's Peace;
Keep smiling, keep smiling,
Although they starve in Greece—
We've won some brand-new islands;
We're saving for a frigidaire—
Keep smiling, keep smiling,
The brave deserve the fair!

TWO ESSAYS FOR
MY PHILOSOPHY PROFESSOR

Irwin Kroening

I. Truth

I HAVENT been able to sleep well the last several mornings, worrying about the rent, which is a month overdue and no one ready to hand me forty dollars, so while I was in between sleep and actual wide-awake worrying several definitions of truth have flowered in my head: these I shall now write down before I forget them or somebody else thinks of the same definitions, though I admit the former is more probable. At any rate here's one: *truth is a peg on which we hang the conscience before committing evil, like War.* I suppose none of these definitions will sound very profound, but you must remember that I didn't spend a lot of time deliberately thinking them up; they sort of thought themselves up at four o'clock in the morning while I was lying in the dark trying not to think about something else, like the rent. It's surprising what crazy things will fulminate in a man's head at that hour, especially when he's trying to keep his mind a blank. Here's another one: *truth is the brass monkey we keep locked in the greening cage of our desires.* Reading it over now I see that this one doesn't make much sense, but if you're a mystic and keep in mind how these things evolved you might find a great deal of significance in number two. I think I'm something of a mystic myself, particularly when I'm eating lightly and worrying about the rent, and as a mystic it's my duty to say that truth is everything under the sun. Absolutely everything, far or near, up or down, left or right, all of it is truth. To a rational mind that's a pretty untidy statement. If you talk to a Marxist (you must force yourself) he will concede that only the following is true: matter exists and can be acted upon. This is a rather innocent gnome, but a surprising amount of damage has resulted from its application, I'm thinking of a friend of mine who was taken to the outskirts of Detroit a number of years ago and beaten to unconsciousness by a group of socialists for his trotsky-ist activities in helping the CIO organize the automobile workers for the stalinists. So if you're a mystic and attempt to define truth, be careful to whom you define it. That brings us to solip-sism. I can't go into solipsism myself without feeling a bit nostalgic, because I seriously came across the word for the first time reading Santayana. I began to read Santayana when I was nineteen years old, flat on my back in a hospital bed with my gut laid open by an emergency appendectomy and a number of rub-ber tubes stuck into me at odd places, so all the Old Adam could drain from my system. After the operation they wheeled me into a ward filled with factory workers who had been disabled by industrial accidents ranging all the way from the trivial to the common-place. Outside of the few who were maimed for life these workers were a pretty rowdy crew, for they figured they were having a vacation on the company's time and money, an illusion the company did its best to sustain. The only other per-son in the ward besides myself who stayed outside their circle of horseplay was a man dying of cancer of the mouth. I didn't mind him at all; as a matter of fact I studied him with a great deal of morbid enjoyment. The whole lower half of his face was eaten away and wrapped in white bandages. Mind you, I'm not saying that watching a man die of cancer of the mouth brings you any closer to a conception of truth. I can't even say that it gives you a sense of values. What I mean is at this time I felt I wanted to be left alone, so I could drain in peace. I didn't like the factory workers. They were too loud and rough and they swore. Their grammar was poor. I didn't like the internes either, for the same reasons. I liked the dying man because he was quiet, except for the little groaning he did during the night when the morphine wore off. He stayed in his corner minding his own business, which consisted of reading the baseball scores in the early edition of the evening paper and dying, and I stayed in my corner minding my own business, which consisted of read-ing Santayana and draining. I read part of *The Life of Reason* and the whole of *The Last Puritan*. Oliver, in the latter book, is the darling of all fiction heroes. It takes a philosopher to beat the novelist and playwright at their own games. Plato had one of the most striking figures in all Greek literature: an ugly man who deserted his wife and children to wander around the city asking people embarrassing questions about themselves until they tired of him and allowed him to die a tragic and noble death. Nietzsche also invented a remarkable fellow—one, it's true, who never actually appeared on the stage himself, but who had a well-known character actor, conventionally made up as a prophet, standing in the spotlight and giving a long song and dance about him: 'So alien are ye in your souls to what is great, that to you Superman would be *frightful* in his goodness!' It's too bad Nietzsche didn't pull Zarathustra off into the wings and bring Superman out on the boards to speak to us in his own words, even if it was only Nietzsche himself wearing the comic mask. That might have spared the world two petty and vulgar concepts of the Superman: the German version, appearing in World War II, and the American version, appearing in our funny-papers. It's hard so say which concept has done the most harm to the youth of both nations. Anyway, Oliver is my favorite uptodate hero: a sensitive young man who was a serious student of philosophy and heir to unmentionable millions of dollars. Not having to worry about where he could get forty dollars in a hurry to pay a month's back rent, his definitions of truth were untainted by compromises with the landlord and the grocer, by the anxieties of finding and keeping a good job, or by the humility of having to use the bedpan during visiting hours in the ward. I think that during those months I spent in the hospital (peritonitis requires a lot of draining) I *became* Oliver, and the rowdier the factory workers behaved the deeper I buried my nose in the book. I was remote from everything, including the cramped penurious life with my parents in a suburban bungalow; my mind asked itself all the dark tortured questions that Oliver's mind asked itself, and luxuriously ignored all the answers: many of the nurses remarked on the abstract look I had in my eyes when they performed certain tasks for me. Later, struggling out of my critical illness into the normal American state of poor health and pruriency, I realized that several of the nurses were even prettier than I had formerly assumed, and Oliver became a separate entity, retreating lost and pale into a forest of print. The man with cancer of the mouth died after I left the hospital, an action I don't know to this day was considerate or inconsiderate. I had already decided by the time I returned to the suburbs that I had fallen in love with the prettiest nurse in the ward, so clumsily made a date with her some agonized weeks later. The event was facilitated by the money, the secondhand Ford roadster and the company of a friend, for whom I had to jeopardize my love with a vulgar request for another nurse. It was a pathetic evening and I never saw my girl again. Several years later on a New Year's Eve I tried to make up for it by getting another friend to drive me into the city past the nurse's home, where I leaped out of the moving car and thought, drunkenly and poetically, to storm the barricades of love, manned by two perfectly composed nuns, who responded to my shouts of 'I love her, I tell you, I love her!' and 'I intend to see her again at once!' with indulgent smiles and a firm stance in the doorway until my friend came to pull me away. She had probably finished training and was living in another city. Even on that impassioned night I couldn't remember her face any more. But I do remember what Santayana said about truth in one of those books I read, lying in the hospital ward where she used to come every day and touch me with her cool hands. He said: 'Truth is a terrible thing. It is much darker, much sadder, much more ignoble, much more inhuman and ironical than most of us are willing to admit, or even able to suspect.' I suppose that statement fits in somewhat with my *third* definition of truth, which also flowered in my head at four o'clock in the morning. My third definition goes like this: *truth is something you can't occupy yourself with for a very long time without feeling down in the mouth, and when you try to look through the middle of it there's nothing on the other side.* I admit that this third definition isn't quite as electric as the first two. The reason for that is because it was the last one, and I was either falling back into sound sleep or getting definitely awake to put everything else out of my head for some good solid worrying about that forty dollars' rent. At any rate, until I can borrow some more money from my friends or my family, this is all I have to say about truth for the present.

II. *What I Think About Logic And So On*

MAN is particularly ingenious when it comes to inventing instruments for his selfdestruction, everybody knows that, and next to War, which is the most spectacular if not the most efficient of these instruments, I've decided to place Logic. I came to that decision the other night, after I watched a Truax Field soldier stagger out the door of a nearby tavern to lean his head against the fender of a parked automobile and vomit with much sorrow and indignation over his place in the contemporary world. They use the War to kill your body, and they defend the necessity of

War with Logic, which they use to kill your spirit. Some people may be amused by my employment of the words 'body' and 'spirit', the display of a dualistic bias now unfashionable in a good many quarters, but you must remember that I'm being literary (the chief qualification of a philosopher) and in order to oppose the subjects 'War' and 'Logic' in the previous sentence with a like number of direct objects, I've split the human complex into two parts, hence forming the dichotomy as well as a symmetrical phrase. I suppose many philosophical concepts have arisen out of smaller exigencies of rhetoric. Schopenhauer had some interesting things to say about Logic in his *Art of Controversy*. I have this essay in the Little Blue Book No. 98, pocket-size, edited by Haldeman-Julius. As a matter of fact, I have several dozen of these Little Blue Books, all bequeathed to me by an uncle of mine, who subsequently went blind. They cover quite a diversified field, with titles extending all the way from *A Handbook of Commercial Law, The Moorish Civilization in Spain* to *A New Light on Witchcraft, Mathematical Curiosities* and *The Child's Sexual Life*. In his younger days my uncle read all of these books with a great thirst for knowledge, as they say. The fact that he's now blind and sits in a damp basement, a sort of unapprized neo-Platonist, weaving baskets and waiting for the essence of Science to descend upon the heads of men (something like the tongueflamed Holy Ghost) to direct all human energy into peaceful orderly progress towards a better sort of world, is neither a disparagement nor a commendation of the Haldeman-Julius publications. Another one of my uncles has never stuck his nose inside a Blue Book, or even carried one around in his pocket, and his eyesight is perfectly good. As a matter of fact, this other uncle of mine is an Atheist, except when he goes for walks. That's to say, he's a man very fond of taking long walks out into the country, where now and then he finds it convenient to spread God thin over the natural landscape in order to increase his enjoyment of it. But though he uses God externally, like salad-dressing, he never makes the mistake of taking God *internally*— that is, into his heart—a place my uncle feels it a highly private one, reserved for only himself and his fellow humans. Some people have reproached my uncle for this, telling him he can't have goodness in his heart unless he has God there too, and his reply is the obvious sort of sophistry we can expect from a man who has spent the better part of his life avoiding hard work by becoming a successful athlete in his youth: many of the people who profess to have God in their hearts reason that consequently He can't exist in anyone else's; therefore we have such evils as flabby stomach muscles, capitalism, racial injustice, intemperance and improper breathing in our Western civilization. I have several uncles besides these two, all of them interesting. I mention this fact not to confound, but simply as an observation on the multifariousness of human nature. Anyway, Schopenhauer says in his *Art of Controversy* (I can't quote because I've misplaced the book) that when two people use logical form, or dialectic, to defend their own point of view against the other person's, truth itself is only incidental to the business. Now what does that mean? I'm writing these words during the most depressing part of a Sunday afternoon, when it's difficult to spin thoughts at the end of my spinal column like a sideshow juggler. All I can keep thinking is that outside the window there's a very pleasant October day in which a lot of butchering is going on some place in the world and truth seems to be mighty incidental there too, brother, mighty incidental. Of course, we know what kind of a man Schopenhauer was. He was a pessimist. He was a man who spent the latter years of his life dining every day at the same table at the same hour from the same kind of food in a black crooked solitude. George Bernard Shaw says a pessimist is 'a man who thinks everybody as nasty as himself and hates them for it.' Can we say then that an optimist is a man who thinks everybody as well off as himself, and loves only *himself* for it, ignoring nine-tenths of mankind. Sure. Sure, we can say it. We can say anything we please, and at this point I'd like to exhort all the governments and peoples of the world not to be frightened of the Word, written or spoken. The only thing to be frightened of is yourselves and one another. There's no need to cringe at what you see in the newspapers and the treaties and the manifestoes and the subversive pamphlets, or in the textbooks and encyclopedias, the poems and novels of the great masters. Don't cower in the lecturehall or the churchpew or the movie or the theatre or before the radio speaker or out on the street corner around the soapbox speaker. Get it into your heads that listening and talking and reading and writing are the mildest forms of physical exertion. Get it into your heads that a word can't shoot a gun, throw a grenade, direct a flamethrower, stab you in the back or rape. If you feel a little uneasy after perusing a line of Shakespeare or a draftboard notification relax, shut your eyes for a minute, or get up and walk around, take a drink of water. It's only words. What do you think a notice of dispossession is? A life sentence for murder?

A love song? Words. That's all. They can't hurt you. But when you get that drink of water don't look into the mirror if you can help it. That person looking back at you is the one who should chill your heart. He and the one grinning behind him. Or don't you see them? O. K. I got my induction papers not so long ago, but when I went down there and they put the rubber tube to my chest they heard death politely sniggering in one of the auricles, so they let me go. That was all right. There are other things besides a War that can destroy, and it'll be an even chance whether they use them on me or I use them on myself. The thing to remember is that it's not *what's* being used, but *who* uses it that's important. You and me. That's what I mean about Logic. It's the same whether it's dealing with all the funny innocent little things like cats with ten tails and the alphabet and God in the classroom, or with the exploitation of a race and poverty and murder and revolution in the snarling outside world. The Logic itself can't hurt you, but the men who are using it can. You can maim yourself with it, if you feel that way about life. You can shut yourself away from the world with it, never touch another woman, take another drink; smear your head with dung and lay yourself down on a bed of spikes. You can use Logic to help you bomb the Capitol or deface a picture of Christ. You can use it to build a new society or pull out the last props of an old and rotting one. You can use it in a business deal or a seduction. It's simply words again, and with skilled murderers over crowding the market nowadays, any young fellow with a talent for words can do pretty well for himself. Knowing the right people helps too.

FIVE POEMS

Hubert Creekmore

THE BIRTH OF OSIRIS

In no month of no year shall the child be born
　In no bed of no inn or no house.
Sunny heaven's hostess enveloped the seed
Of the earth-god and Ra has damned it within
　To be born in no month of no year.

Win, magic lover, oh Thoth, from the moon
　Unknown time, novel time for this birth.
Twenty seconds compounded from each winning game
Will increase to redeem this dark-prisoned child
　From my winter solstice of womb.

On a day lost at drafts from the moon's hoard of time,
　When the child had thrust up its head
In the heat of the blazing loins of the sky,
All the fields rose alive with green, with goods,
　With the spring of Osiris to earth.

Bright Osiris, your fingers pour multiple gifts
　But they fail, for your birth was accursed
Because earth had invaded heaven. Oh lost,
Long-forgotten Osiris, bringer of grain
　And of health, your rites are decayed.

On a day of some year shall a child be born
　In a home or a stable or inn.
His conception, Osiris, will be your reverse:
Holy commerce will flow from above and pierce,
　Not receive, as your mother did, earth.

So the maleness of heaven will lodge within her
    Whose mate will not curse but be blest
That his wife should distribute to men the divine.
Thus the God condescends to scatter his seed
    Through one woman to all stoic earth.

THE BIRTH OF ATTIS

Father Almond, ripe with passion,
Thrust by Nana in her bosom,
Virgin Nana on the plains
Stripped of leaves, your creation

(Save this goddess' faint confusion
That the seed of pomegranate,
Rival of your early bloom,
May have bred—yet a virgin!)

Father Almond, your conception
Guarding here your greening children,
Elder son of all your race,
Attis, god of vegetation,

Keeps the swelling blooms of Phrygian
Highlands fresh in their succession
Through the summer through the years
Flawed by only condemnation

(Since his mother was of heaven—
Matriarchic, vain petition—
And his father of the earth,
Once again despoiling fountains)

Such as comes to sons of maidens
Who conceive in isolation:
Virginal to die, perhaps,
Yet for love and resurrection.

ADONIS DELIVERED—Method I

        Sundered the myrrh tree
        Lies with its limbs split

All its leaves pant, quiver
At this unbotanical labor

Greet her, Adonis
Mother who bore you
Sweetly her breast kiss

Fibrous and wrenched thighs
Womb into bark changed

Pity the incest
Sequel that flesh bear
Such transformation

Cry on her, who lewdly
Incited your fantastic birthday

You, Aphrodite
Meddler of love's life
Maker and wrecker
Fuddler of all sex
Mother of half-men
Daughter of sea foam
Lover, abductor
Would-be seducer

Of Adonis, go, you have
Deluded the world with your worship

Smyrna, be thankful
Forests on Meles
Sheltered your shame. You
Fared somewhat better

Than the other souls under
Those psychopathetic ancients

Calling themselves gods.

396

MOBILE PERPETUUM

In gold green days of childhood, he
    Belabored kiddy-cars.
On all tricycles piston knees
    Pumped far too slow. He was
Too rushed to see the leafing trees.

And Congress took a breath and spoke

No hands, he rode upon two wheels
    And pedalled with a fury.
His soul cried out for automobiles;
    His soul was made of hurry,
And never stole what lovers steal.

And Congress rhetoricked in halls

Transecting air in a silver plane,
    He felt his life breathe union
Where all was moving—all earth's pain
    Below the cloud's confusion:
For clouds, wing-pierced, were misty slain.

And Congress spat and spluttered laws

When pall-bearers bore, too slowly paced,
    His coffin to its grave,
And fretful whir of motors raced
    Within, all said, "Alive
As much as ever, and as waste."

And Congress said, "We represent. . ."

TROPICAL LANE

    Leaves, porcelain shining
    Laminate medallions,
        Lapping in wind,

Fuzz of mail cascading
In the air, let
   The flowers through

The sheath—the dark, the green,
The deep of branches. Let
   The brightness pierce:

Shameless, clustered flowers,
Unpetticoated by
   The missionary,

Abandoned, wagging colors,
Absurdly dangling stamens,
   Greedy petals.

Fat and plop to earth
Falls a silk white ball,
   White sea-urchin,

Monstrous mass of stamens!
(Oh blush and turn aside.)
   Rosy anthers

Pouring pollen dust
The air with life.
   (Beware, fear

This atmosphere of life.)
Man, guilty creature,
   Sings of flowers,

Swollen, flagrant symbols.
He can't be but must
   Imagine beauty.

398

"CONGRATULATIONS BILL"

Hubert Creekmore

WHEN THE DOOR SLAMMED, Mrs. Thornhill popped her head out of the kitchen to see who it was. A spoon, steaming from the soup kettle, projected from her grip on the edge of the kitchen door. She squinted through the dim room toward the hall.

"Who is it at the front, Papa?" she called, coming through the dining room. No one answered her. She walked around the table where three places were set beneath the green and orange mottled glass chandelier. At the wide entrance to the living room she recognized the figure.

"Why, hello, dear," she said. "I didn't expect you home tonight. What's up?"

"Hello, Ma," said Ellie. She threw her hat on a table in the living room after inspecting herself in the hall mirror by the hat racks. "Nothing's up. I just swapped duty with one of the girls. I'll have to work tomorrow and stay on till five."

"Why'd you do that?"

"I wanted to see George Haverford's new movie tomorrow with Anna. She has to get home early most evenings, you know, and we can't go after I get off so late." She fell back in a chair and sprawled her legs.

"Where you going to meet Anna?"

"Canal and Dauphine about five-thirty."

Ellie pressed the slippers off her heels and left them lying by her chair. In another of the overstuffed cerise and yellow plush chairs sat her father, reading the baseball news. He had neither spoken nor looked up when she came in. When he finished the baseball news, he would begin reading it again. Alec, a brother, lay stretched on the sofa, reading the remainder of the paper. He had grunted a greeting, and got little more than a look from her.

"How's the hospital?" asked Mrs. Thornhill cheerfully.

"Christ, if I don't get out of that place soon I'll go crazy!" exclaimed Ellie. "Smells and groans and dead men and guts —ugh!"

"Well, you asked for it," said Alec, rustling the paper.

"And I can take it, if I have to," said Ellie. "But I don't want to. And I'm not going to, much longer. I'm getting out of it the quickest way I can, let me tell you."

"But I thought you wanted to be a nurse, and help suffering people," said Mrs. Thornhill. "You used to talk about the nobility and courage of—"

"Oh, Ma, don't be silly."

"She wanted to meet a nice doctor," said Alec.

"Shut up." She scanned the assortment of decorations along the walls —figured net curtains, tropical plants, hanging baskets, colored panes in the windows, an aquarium, a carved oak what-not with ten-cent store trinkets.

"Your sidekick Anna says Dr. Stern is hot stuff," the brother went on, turning the pages of the paper with pretentious suavity.

"Listen here, you little pup," burst out Ellie, "even if you are nineteen years old, I'll pop your ears wide open if you go around eavesdropping on what we say, or telling anything you hear. Now shut up."

"O. K."

"Children," soothed Mrs. Thornhill, "please, can't you be pleasant when you're home together? What would the neighbors say if they heard you? How can your father read about who's going to win the pennant this year? Who's ahead, Papa?"

"Don't bother me. I'm tired," he said in a muffled voice.

Mrs. Thornhill looked at him a moment as if he were almost there, and turned to Ellie. She brushed back her rat-colored hair with the hand holding the kitchen spoon.

"Going out dating tonight, dear?"

"Yes. Bill Reiner's coming over."

"He's a nice boy." She folded her hands in serene contemplation, as a smile brought a silly gleam over her face. "How much salary does he get?"

Ellie's head slowly turned toward her mother with a very strange expression on it. Her mother colored under the muddy skin, flapped the spoon against her stomach and moved toward the dining-room door. Ellie took out a cigarette and began to light up.

"Oh, I guess I was—just hoping a little—" laughed Mrs. Thornhill. "He is such a nice boy."

"He's a lousy date, that's all I can say," snapped Ellie.

"I better put dinner on," said Mrs. Thornhill. "It's either ready or burned up."

"I guess you'd like a lover like a beautiful movie actor, maybe," simpered Alec.

"Yes, I would," said Ellie, "if he was man enough. Some of 'em aren't men at all, I hear."

"I guess you wouldn't mind having the powerful arms of George Haverford twined around you in a soul-throbbing kiss, would you?"

"No, I wouldn't."

"Well, why don't you run out to Bayou La Manche and grab him?"

"What do you mean?"

"Ain't you seen the papers?"

He tossed them at her. As she grabbed wildly, they spread over the floor, and she scooped them together, sorting the pages to read the movie section. A movie company from Hollywood had come to Louisiana to spend a week making location shots for a historical picture in which George Haverford would be starred. They had already been working for four days in secret so as not to be bothered with curiosity seekers and hoped to finish the most difficult work the following day. When the shooting was done, there was to be a party at the Blue Hawaiian Room before they departed for Hollywood.

Ellie's heart sailed right out of her body. This was her greatest love and if he was to be in the Blue Hawaiian Room tomorrow night she must make Bill take her even if she had to leave her job. No one had ever thrilled her as much as George Haverford. No man ever would touch the same depths physically or spiritually that George Haverford touched by his shadow presence. Just to see him at a distance would fulfill her life.

She sat dreaming over the three-column picture of his face at the top of the page. She did not hear her mother call her to dinner. She did not hear her brother say, "What was that I heard last night on the porch? Something you said to Eddie. Sounded like you said, 'I didn't want to say anything till I was sure but now that I am sure, I'm afraid. . . ' What you sure of that scares you?"

She stayed searching the newsprint eyes of the actor. The soup-slurping of her father never broke upon her dream.

2

Her tongue slopped over his, lobbled the tip, and eased through his lips as she closed her mouth wetly against his bristly skin. Before withdrawing from him completely she contracted the muscles in her mouth in a variety of ways. When she drew back, the iron chains of the porch swing creaked with her movement. He opened his eyes and took a deep breath like a movie hero.

"Gee, Ellie, I'm a frazzle," he said in a low intense voice. He wiped his mouth furtively on the back of his sleeve. "Even if I was broke I'd find some way to take you to the Blue Hawaiian Room tomorrow, and to that guy's picture at the Saenger, too. Gosh, you leave me weak!"

"Me, too," she said settling herself against his chest.

"Hell, I don't do nothing. You know your stuff. It just gets a man down."

"I know one time it got me down," she said, with an emphatic slowness. "Two times . . . three times. And I ain't quite got up yet, either."

Her right foot touched the floor in rhythm, as the swing moved monotonously in the milky night. The tall oleander bushes by the fence cut off the street lights and the spill of automobile headlights, but moonlight made a streak at the edge of the porch and tinged the darkness. They had been sitting there a long time since her family went to bed, and he had thought of getting through tonight without a reference to "that time." His skin prickled.

For over a month now she had insisted on dragging up the incident every time they were together. Each time it became more and more serious to her, as if the whole thing hadn't been her idea in the first place. He hadn't suggested drinking absinthe in the French Quarter till three in the morning, had he? It wasn't his idea to go out to Lake Ponchartrain afterward and go swimming naked, was it? It wasn't his idea—well, after all, a girl gets a lot of ideas working in a hospital, he supposed.

He looked at her, but her eyes were piercing through the black trees at the street corner. It was probably best to say nothing. He patted her shoulder. She responded immediately.

"I been afraid ever since that time, Bill. I didn't want to say anything till I was sure."

It couldn't have been summer with such cold air about. His hand floated from her shoulder to the back of the swing. The skin on his chest became extraordinarily sensitive.

"You—know what I mean, don't you, Bill?" she asked.

"No."

"I think you're lying."

"I think you are too." His voice shook as he said it. There was a shock in his words like sudden thunder.

She sat up erectly and indignantly.

"You know perfectly well what we did and you know what could happen. I've been watching and it's happened. And it's your fault. I think you ought to feel more responsibility." As she talked she became more upset and tears began to ooze from her eyes, which she blotted with a square of coarse lace.

"You know, Ellie, there's no love between us," he said. "We're not the two for each other. I want to sell my insurance and you want to nurse your sick people. There's no sense in us getting married just because you've got a—got caught. You work in a hospital. You know them doctors over there. All you gotta do is get one of 'em to fix you up. Whatta you want to tie yourself to me for?"

Ellie still wept, but very quietly, as movie actresses did when they nobly faced a great sorrow. She leaned her head back on the swing, and spoke with moody courage.

"I'd thought you'd have more honor than that—wanting me to do such a thing. I'd 'ave thought you'd have more love for your own child than that. I don't mind the disgrace myself. But I'll lose my job unless I marry. I hate to see our child grow up with the whole neighborhood talking about it."

"What a hell of a marriage it would be, Ellie," Bill said. "We've got nothing but kisses and hugging. My God, don't you want more out of marriage than the ceremony? What kind of a life could we lead together?"

"I don't care, Bill. I don't care about that. You got to be realistic about it. The ceremony is what counts in the long run. Being married is something in itself."

She moved to the end of the swing, letting the momentum die swiftly against the drag of Bill's feet. He sat, hands crossed helplessly in his lap, head hung down, cursing himself for getting mixed up with Ellie, wondering where a life with her would bring him, remembering that somebody in the office had said that marriage always helped a fellow in his business, settled him down, won civic respect, and so on. Ellie stood up decisively.

"Well, Bill, it's all right, if you feel that way," she said. "I'll face it alone. I'm not afraid. I won't even tell anyone it was you."

He twisted his fingers together until they were white and hurt like frozen flesh. "I feel like a dog," he muttered. He knew he was dying in a familiar way, but he knew a man could die only once. "All right, I'll—help," he said. "We'll get married."

3

Fastening her uniform the next morning, Ellie felt like breaking out into some kind of chant of joy. A sense of freedom kept welling up inside her. She couldn't wait to tell Anna that afternoon when they went to the movies. Married to Bill, she wouldn't have to worry about working or money or anything any more. She wouldn't have to put on a stiff white uniform and go about sticking thermometers into pasty people's mouths and washing their grainy backs and legs and carrying out bed pans and listening to and seeing and smelling death and holding her stomach down with coca-cola all day long. Sure, after the wedding, she would have to fake a mis-carriage. But then she could lie in bed and drink bourbon and coke and smell perfumes and wear lace negligees and go to the movies—

"Yes, ma'am," she said efficiently and lifelessly when she heard her name called at the end of the corridor. She snatched up her cap and began pinning it in her hair.

"Go up to 4-D right away," said the floor nurse, standing before her. "Serious case and quite a mess."

"O. K." said Ellie and hurried away, adjusting her clothes as she went.

4-D must contain someone very important, since it was a suite of two rooms which almost never had a patient. She quietly opened the door of the sitting room and went in. Four men with very abject countenances were sitting there. They wore bright suits, of a sporting type, with and without neckties. Two were bald, two were Jewish, and one of each pair was biting his fingernails. They barely glanced at Ellie as she came in, but looked through the door to the bedroom as she entered it. One of them groaned, "Oh God, what'll we do!"

An oxygen mask covered the face of the patient. The man's body was bare to the hips, the chest crushed, bruised and torn. There were four men in this room too, one of whom was working over the wounds. The graduate nurse stayed, almost like a trained police dog, always at the left and to the rear of one of the doctors. All were very grave, staring at the bed, stroking their chins, shaking their heads. The man at the oxygen mask looked up with apprehension. Everyone halted a moment, until he nodded faintly. Ellie recognized Dr. Sternholtz, the greatest internal surgeon in the south.

"Take that out," said a low voice. "Bring a needle with one CC of adrenalin."

It was Dr. Henderson, the south's best bone surgeon. Ellie took the bundle of soiled linen and went to find an orderly. There was little change in either room when she returned. She handed the needle to Dr. Sternholtz and soaked a piece of cotton in alcohol with which she rubbed a spot on one arm of the patient. The doctor had just pierced the skin when the man at the oxygen mask lifted it from the face.

"Sorry, doctor," he said. "It's no use." He began to assemble his apparatus.

Ellie's eyes wandered slowly and casually to the face of the dead man, while the doctors made a few final examinations and pronounced him dead. Seeing now for the first time the real face of George Haverford, and that dead, she felt as if she were turning into iron threads that revolved rapidly in a hot bright light.

The odors of the slopjars and the alcohol came to her. The doctors drew up the sheet and went into the other room. She heard the four friends come in from the sitting room. One asked what would Trans-American Pictures do without dear George; and one, what would he do without his dear, dear friend; and one, how could his wife be consoled now that dear George was gone; and one, where was he going to find another forehead and nose to photograph like George's. They stood two on each side of the bed and turned back a foot of the sheet and looked at him.

"Gosh," said one, "ain't it a miracle for the fans the camera crane didn't fall on his face?"

Having finished some details of the death certificate, the doctors re-entered the room. Dr. Henderson spoke softly to the bereaved men from Hollywood.

"If you will come to my office I will have one of my associates help you and do what he can about the necessary arrangements."

"Thanks," said one of them. "Come on, fellows."

They went out ahead of Dr. Henderson. Dr. Sternholtz turned to Ellie and said, "Nurse. . . . Nurse. . . . "

She quivered as she turned toward him. "Yes, doctor."

"Get this room cleaned up. Have the maid and the orderly do it in the best possible manner. You know the importance of

405

making an impression on these people."

"Yes, sir."

"The undertaker will come in about two hours, I'd say. These men may come back with him." He lowered his voice. "We must keep the room locked, and say nothing of it about the wards. We don't want any curious mobs and all that."

"Yes, sir."

He went out through the sitting room and into the hall, closing the door after him. She stood very quietly now. She had watched him slowly breathing his last, had watched him stop, just as in his movie "Flight to the Tropics." She stood now in the room with his body, alone, as Gloria Tempest had, before she threw herself on him and wept. She had cried a lot at that movie and she felt like crying now, but somehow it seemed odd, because she had never really known George Haverford the way Gloria had. He had been the thing that all the men she had ever known, intimately, had never been to her. And yet she had never even touched him except to rub a piece of cotton on his arm.

There was a heavy stillness in the room that even the street traffic never broke. She walked to the edge of the mattress and reached for the corner of the sheet. No one could come in except through the living room door. Why shouldn't she. . .

She remembered the time in "Saints in Love" when he sat on a mountain top in Italy overlooking a moonlit bay and held Alice Manners in his arms and said, "Man tells me I shouldn't do this and God tells me I shouldn't do it, but something in me cries, 'Do it, do it, do it, even if you lose your soul!' " And then he kissed her lips, her chin, her throat, her collarbones, her breast —just the top part because the censor cut the film right there. But Ellie knew what was going on.

Her hand lay pleasantly on the warm cup between George Haverford's shoulder and chest. With a faint smile, she looked at his face. She never would have thought she'd even have touched him in her life. She drew her fingers over his features and ran them through his dark hair. That's the way Alice Manners did in "Saints in Love"—she ran her fingers through his hair, just like that. "I love you so much that no matter what the world may do or say it can never destroy my love," was what she said.

Ellie sat on the bed. The body slumped a little toward her, the handsome face turning like a tired sleeping boy. She ran her hands down the strong arms, leaned over and threw them flopping around her back, clutched her fingers in the hair and kissed him.

Goosepimples burst out all over her, and with a low whimper she leaped up. She looked with a frown of horror at the grotesque figure sprawled on the bed. Perhaps she had soiled her uniform. She recoiled exactly as Gloria Tempest did when she thought he was a savage, in "Southern Cross." The way they tortured him in that picture, the way they whipped him, beat him across the chest, bringing oozes of blood in broad streaks looking like his chest today when she came into the room, making her want to protect him, pity him, love him. . .

She caught the sheet again, and whipped the cover back. She gasped at her recklessness, but dreams of movies flooded her head and she saw herself urged to surrender to George Haverford, the trapped and noble savage who was to die because he loved a white woman. The scene went on and on at lightning pace, a rapid concentrate of many other movies, tore at her inner life until suddenly she was again kissing not only the mouth, but the shoulders, the neck, the collarbones, the wrist. . .

4

The heat, that afternoon, bristled up from the pavements while Ellie and Anna walked toward the theater where George Haverford's last picture was playing. As they came near, the crowd grew thicker and more feminine and more ill-tempered. Women who couldn't get past them quickly enough knocked them aside with their elbows. About the box office there was a great wild-eyed panic that trailed off into a queue around the corner, suggesting a giant spermatazoön. Newsboys went throught the crowds, calling "George Haverford killed in local accident!" and sold papers on every side.

With unusual poise and satisfaction, Ellie walked to the end of the line to wait. Anna, tagging along behind, tugged at her girdle, smeared her face with powder, and looked at her curiously.

"You ain't acting like yourself today, Ellie," she said.

Ellie shrugged a shoulder slightly under her chin, like Gloria Tempest, and said, with her eyelashes drooping, "Well, how would you act if you had kissed—" she whispered the rest in Anna's ear.

Anna shrieked thinly and stared. The women behind pushed her savagely to make her close up the line.

"I was on duty in the room where he died."

"You mean—you mean—" Anna stammered breathlessly. "He *asked* you to kiss him before he died—to make him happy?"

"No. When everyone had left." Ellie told briefly what she had done.

Anna trembled and gave an enraptured sigh. "Oh, Ellie!"

"I'll tell you all the details tonight, but you mustn't say a word to anyone else, or they might put me in jail."

"Oh, I won't! It'll be a sacred trust between us—and him."

The line moved faster and in a short while the two girls bought tickets and hurried through the long passage of brown-orange marble columns.

"Oh, I forgot to tell you something else," said Ellie with a giggle, at the head of the aisle. "I'm going to marry Bill Reiner. He asked me last night."

"And all that with George Haverford this morning too!" Anna sighed as they descended into the dark cavern of the auditorium. "Gosh, some people have all the luck."

"Don't I, though?"

THREE POEMS

Elliott Coleman

A DAY ON AN ISLAND

Though the briar rose simmer on the air,
Though the honeysuckle wine and whiten,
Though the broom, dead and ghosted, blow bare,
Though all the shores lighten

With illusion, and the darning needle hover,
A blue dash between sentences
Of rose and dead thorn, though the sea cover
Its quarrel with the shoals, these

Are not islanded. The sea is all around,
And straight to Portugal I point my finger.
The company enlarges on this ground.
All land comes to linger,

A long kiss at the horizon where the guns bite,
And the last aloneness broken at the dark
Where the returning, glittering passion stuns the flight,
And the wing leaves no mark.

IN CENTRAL PARK

Now while the water shatters
Its glassy veins, and night
Is gone as if forever,
It is right

As the sun breasts the winter
And a swan stills the lake,
To review night matters
For the sake

Of what light discovers
To see if we can see,
In all the anxious bother,
A unity.

The swan's sharp feather
Furrows the gold.
The blue world above hers
Is still cold.

Well, sometime after dinner—
Where the warm talk ran
Of heroes on a tanker,
And the time of man,

Of burning alive, and the bitter
Adjustment of each cell.
And then, of a one-cell-sinner
—paramecium's hell.

Of a capillary tube of water:
"Observed to swim straight."
Experimental data,
Heaven's gate—

I tore the night like a letter
Recounting the death of a son
And of a father and of a mother and of a
        daughter,
And had some fun.

Dark, where the dead love lowers.
The swan burns upon the lake.
These the resplendent hours
Give and take.

ELLIOTT COLEMAN

WHAT WAKENS

Lost upon the mountain
Spirits glimmer by,
Beautiful as action
Stares the zero sky.

In such and such an ocean
Actors fail their parts
And dying planets fountain
The cold flame on their hearts.

What wakens, O what wakens,
What activating stain,
What loosens and what fastens,
What storms and sings in pain.

What diamond bright dactyl
Stays the heaving night,
Falls down and breathes the idol
To sibilance and light.

Pure of will it cannot
Abash itself in death.
Lips to the rose filled faggot
Breath to burning breath.

THE DEATH OF A FATHER

O. Klausner

IN THE WAR WINTER of 1944, Americans in Europe were being killed or about to be killed; and at home, what seemed to those in Europe not to matter, others were finishing their lives and dying. It is true, that for most of those at home, the enemy was being killed by our soldiers there, and this was a worthy and satisfying activity for us here, and a necessary one in the nature of war, and a great punishment of an enemy that killed from other considerations as well. Yet amid the causes and the motives, there was one fact our soldier accepted with regret, that of his own death.

We sometimes think that this fact is of no importance after all our victories and accomplishments in the war, particularly if the soldier has survived and now has taken his place in the line of those waiting for an ordinary death. Yet for him who felt this regret, there was no more important feeling, though this proves that there was a true sense in which the war was not his, that his participation was an act of reason, not of that necessity in which the value of the individual, even for himself, is for a while completely forgotten in a great cause.

One who felt this regret was Otto, an American soldier in Europe on the particular date who, in all the dying of young life, was lost between life and death. He expected at any moment to be killed; and when he was not killed, still he did not expect to live. In not expecting to live and not being dead, he was, in a way, already dead in his own mind. He had, that is, given himself up for lost, an achievement for a young man who was still alive. Yet for one who knew a great purpose in the war, and could name many others, it was not to be expected that he should give up his life before he was dead.

He was given his life again, when he heard that his father was dying, and in the very war, he would be sent home to watch his

412

father die. He did not believe that for the sake of an old man dying his own young life would be given back to him, but he felt a new need to live. He felt, even from where he was, his father's impending end as his own ending, though his own will had been freed years before by his own purpose in his own life. If the source of his life, his father and his ruler until Otto became a man, were to die, his own life would die with it. That is how he sensed it unaware, and wanted at the very moment to hurry, saving himself to save his father and himself. Then consciously he knew that he would live to die his own death at the end of his own life, or the death to which he had been sent.

Is it possible, we may assume Otto to be thinking, for these were his thoughts, that the army is in awe of a father's dying, and his death, that its own high authority over me, his son, is derivative of him? Is it that my father's death is a high moral scene more important than the war? Let us answer him that it is the origin of all absolute authority ending, and the son should be there. For he must be there, and others relative to the father should yield all individual and independent power derived from him over all the children. Everyone in the whole family acquired and descended must know the origin of his being and see his own life in the death of the father. And the high authority, the army, gives up Otto the son, for it knows its origin in the father; but not for Otto but for the idea of the father in which it is.

This idea of the father he had to honor in his own father; but fathers honoring one another would be the peace of the world, he thought in amused sorrow. If he did this honor, then his mother was honored too in the same honor; for it is not in vain, that it is said, honor thy father and mother, for thy mother is thy father's wife and the right honor is to honor her as if she were he. But she is not, for the power of the father is not benign as the nourishment of Otto as an infant with the body of his mother. If he was tolerant to let Otto live and then sometimes kind that he had let him live, his will was yet absolute. Not as the arms of his mother cradling Otto, his father's strength was by his right arm, at full length in the space of the world, where he would keep Otto to his will or his purpose even more than he kept the infant's mother to his need. To what was docile he added his will, on what was weak he put his strength, and what was yet purposeless in an unknown world he led to his own purpose.

In sending Otto to his death, what his father had not done for the sake of the mother, the army was using the power of the father. For is not war, asked Otto of himself, the sending of sons to their death? No doubt the fathers have another purpose too in their own enmity. This death to which he had been sent was not even his to fear, for his life was not his. Like a child, not knowing, he faced death simply as nothing, as if he did not yet know who he was or what he was doing. For he had given up his identity and was again Otto the son. His yet young and once independent life had this indignity of not being his. For he could not be himself without fearing for himself, and fearing fear he gave himself up. There was no fear so, and docile he would have died.

That was Otto toward his own death when feeling only what was in him as a son toward his father. But when seeing an American dead, he saw himself dead there, and looked away from it, and then from the remembered image, and then from himself. For it was not to see this image of himself that he had given himself up. For it was for this more than else that he could not be until it. And knowing this, the army saw to it that there were few American dead to be seen for long; and answering the manner of the child's wish for the death of others, they merely disappeared. They were and then were not, remaining, no doubt, as they were dead-alive elsewhere, or nowhere or anywhere, but just so long as they were not there dead.

As for the enemy dead, they remained where they were, dead bodies only, not he. They were, in the cold, dolls only if whole, or horrors at most, but not he. If in the way, they were pushed away, or if unsightly, put just out of sight, but they were there where they were, and there left. If Otto was mean, he hated them, wished them dead as they were dead, triumphed over them that they were dead and he not. If they were boys and he was sad, he could pity them, leave them untouched, mourn for them a moment in his own small sorrow of the moment. But they were they, those whom he could kill as he was loosed to kill, those whom he could see dead without seeing himself so instead.

Otto, as we see, was in an odd and a bad way. The other soldiers shared the sorrow of his father's death with him, though this was not yet a final fact, and consoled him with the idea of his own life, that he would have that anyway. They would have envied him his going home but would not, in their own minds even, have taken his place. However he may have found the situation unbelievable, and he could not believe it, everyone else accepted it as inevitable. Since Otto had not wished it, and who is there who would wish it now, he had a certain right to be chosen, if there was any advantage in the choice.

He knew, though he did not permit himself to feel it, that he wanted to go home. Wanting to go home meant almost to wish his father to die. He had to keep the two apart and they were in fact inseparable. It was clear to him, however, that the wish alone had no power. Yet it was immoral and before his own death he had remained pure, perhaps from fear of retribution or from the fear that he would assume some responsibility for it. A wish, if it were ineffective, was a crime that had been frustrated, but was still punishable. He held in now the opportunity to indulge in any imagined pleasure, or comfort, or sleep. This was not as before when he did not have a real hope and therefore feared the indulgence as a danger to his sense of reality. Now it was a superstition of another kind. He was afraid to wish for what he knew he wanted. Wishing it might put on him the responsibility for his father; but this would have an effect the very opposite of the one in the theory of the real power of the wish. Otto felt, though he did not know it, that as all his wishes had been proved ineffective when he was a child, this time too wishing what was so would change the fact, his father would get well and he would not go home. He was afraid to associate his wish with a natural force and we see that he still believed that to wish something is not to get it. He would not tamper with nature. He might, by obtruding his wish even to confirm the process, upset the delicate balance of forces now in his favor.

Having given him up even as an object of envy, his fellow soldiers saw in him another advantage. He could carry home the latest sight and impression and news of them to their families. He would communicate the assurance of sight and touch that they were still alive in a real place from which he had just come. He would be their representative; more than that, be them, prove that they too could go home when the time came. As their emissary, he took their letters for a personal delivery. He thought this an important rôle to play, but it was only another intervention before his own independent purpose to go home for himself alone.

Carrying thus all the desires of his fellows to go home and he was now on his way home for them, his mind would have remained behind, but then merely accompanied his body. Though it was evil to want to go home, he made this progress toward admitting the wish, that he left the time as he left the place he was in before, and entered the present though not the one that connected with the future at home. There was this change in his sense of time that he felt that he was in the present and the world was immediately present to him. He was out of the indefinite, which had been between a discontinued past and an unknown future that might never become present at all. He was in an abstracted present, all of immediacy. It was a pure present with no history and committed him to no future. Being the special time of the wonderful world of sight, he experienced it wholly as a sight of the world. The world was his to look at in this time, and he felt all of it in great landscapes, vistas and panoramas. All was safely and simultaneously there and around him. Tolerantly, patienty, he viewed the whole of a world now become contemporaneous with him.

In this mood his wish escaped into consciousness. For intervals, when he looked with interest at the world, he felt an invisible smile, the one he had projected into the winter landscape, on his face and throughout his body. Awakened in his smile were his pleasure, his comfort, and his sleep; his wife, his chair and his bed; three in one and he in all three. They were his home, but not the home to which he was returning, where his father lay in bed and his mother sat in a chair beside him. The two images of home, congruent and superimposed, like two complementary colors, vanished into the unconscious as by a formula of magic.

The waiting and the traveling, before he was home, was long enough for him to be enraged that he did not get home sooner to his dying father. But the army, once having given him his moral priority, his order of liberation, left it to him, as his own time with what means he could persuade, to reach his father's bed. He observed the great transporting movement across a continent and ocean that were organized by great nations for war and which he diverted to his use, to his superior purpose. He learned to do this as he went, and sometimes waited for days before he could fit himself to a particular movement in his direction.

These days of waiting generated a time of their own, definite as was his direction of going, during which, as in one town in the rear, he was detached from everything but the tendency of the local event. This event had no outer reference, no dramatic disposition by which it could be related to corresponding moments in other times. It was circular with the days, almost with the hours, and some special mathematics would have to be invented to fit it into the universal time, and some new philosophy to include it in the universal meaning, unless this has already been achieved and this understanding has not yet associated itself with the common perception.

The periods were and had to be limited enough to hold only one phase of living. A freer or a longer time would have drawn into itself the full potentiality of Otto's life. Under the circumstances, he could be a provincial for a day or a week in the safety of a place that was tranquil in its own internal motion. Entered in its orbit, held in its molecular system, he felt he was in an unrelated and non-significant algebraic point on a graph, or that no point for his position could be found.

This was, of course, an error. The town was in the route of the great movement, but a rare point, significant for a moment now and then, and then again only an ideal one. For this reason there was the possibility of remaining there forever if he could avoid or hide from the significant moment when a passage was made through the town; or if he did encounter it, absorb it unknowingly; or if he knew it, let it last its time, and then reenter deliberately the rolling circle of the private time.

At the very first coincidence of the great movement with what was after all a local spiral that had in a week perceptibly increased its orbit, Otto continued his journey across the continent in his particular direction. His sense of control in the swift motion after the lost time aligned itself with the designated goal of reaching home before his father's death. The urgency paced itself by the speed of his travel, and when this was high his purpose was a geographic line being traversed between his past and his future. This future was really his past life, so that he was, it appeared to him, meeting it head on, as if he were ahead of it and he were going back to it where it was in the past. The physical sense of leaving the continent behind in its own time confused his sense of direction and he imagined that just before he arrived home he would have to turn around and back his body into the situation.

He crossed the ocean slowly and violently through a storm. The preservation of himself in the enclosed life of the ship against the uncontrolled power of wind and wave threw him to the end of his time in life. Sick of the sea to the point of not wanting to live, he asserted that if there was any further time for him, it would be all his. He smiled thinking that he need not now worry about his father. His own life had been liberated in order to save his father, but would he lose it before it was of use to anyone?

He was still at sea when he got well, but he had lost the meaning of the crossing. His weak and tentative assurance had all his care and attention. At this level he was indifferent to time as in a happy moment of childhood when everything is present at once that has any use or meaning. He did not associate himself with the dramatic approach of the ship to America, though, by now on the tenth day, everyone watched for the shore, and there was a feeling that the whole past movement was to terminate in the discovery of a new land, or rather, what was more dramatic, in the confirmation that the land was still there.

Otto landed fixed in his own right to live. He was weary, dirty, subdued and unhappy. His desires and hopes did not anticipate their realization by appearing with any vividness. Indeed they were not there at all for him to observe or feel, so he doubted them altogether. Immediacy was there, bright and definite, but, in referring it to the real world and his particular circumstance, he was vague. The transition to this time and the transfer to this place gave no fixity to his location. He expected no change or awakening, he did not doubt his identity or purpose, but he did not truly believe. He remembered what he saw and felt like certain impalpable dream images that one remembers but cannot keep even in their own space. He would have to wait until the social assurance and his own effort would dominate his mind into a state of belief. The army and the war had dissociated him to the point where he could no longer believe, though he did not doubt that he could take a definite position in a definitely appearing world.

His wife, his chair, his bed, that is his home, were there when he looked, on his arrival, and to these he gave a passionate though a nominal greeting. Before having any further of them, he went into the absolute privacy of his bath, washing himself with a totality and a thoroughness he had never so deliberately thought of in all his life. It was with a serious almost a solemn attention that he cleaned his body, feeling the baptismal purity of the water. He extended his body into the deep, hot bath in full length to his neck in delicious immersion, but suspending himself floating just below the surface. Then doubling his legs to allow for his head, he bowed in altogether for a breathless instant. Then except for nose and eyes and mouth, he stayed underwater in the maternal deep for minutes of oblivion. Drawing in for a last time the inlets of outer life, he remained submerged until it was not to be endured. Then he gasped forth into the air for a quick and smiling birth. He let the water run out as he lay there still. He watched it recede, subside in the tub, evacuate through the drain, washing him up as it ebbed away.

Languid and limp he rose to his feet for a cold annointing shower. First he soaped the recesses and crevices, the hirsute and the surfaces, fingering, rubbing, reaching behind and below, to the right from the left and downward. Under the stream, the water washed away the froth, as he offered his body to the pressure over and against him. He twisted, bent, turned, lifted his arms and opened his legs, keeping himself in a continual whirl, illustrating in undeliberated ceremonial, the dance of the shower, a modern orgy.

Otto dried, and powdered himself as if for an ancient festival. He put on a dressing gown and slippers, clothes of his past that he had rarely worn, but which now represented the important sense of being in his own home for himself. Returning to the living room where his wife awaited him, he did not yet feel familiar with himself, nor in embracing her, did he find himself there. He noted his mind as aloof and absent, hovering above him and Ruth as in the clear consciousness of a dream. This was not new to him and he understood also that in time he would have no reason to stand off and say: "This is so" as if it were like such a dream of which one said while dreaming "This is a dream." He knew this from before, but he could not help abstaining from the deep fulfillment of his wish, for it was, after all, not a dream. With Ruth in his arms in the great chair or in the vast bed, with the light dim or in the total dark, his mind, seeing by its own light of wonder, remained all awake, as his body enacted the wish which is thought to be in the intermediate state of passion. Functioning with the precision of an automatic act, and with the feeling of observing a performed one, Otto tried to enter the passion, as on awakening he might try to reenter a dream. It was all effort, and it would be a long time yet before he would establish his identity in his passion, abandoning himself to its depth without fear of drowning.

At least his day and night in his own home, before he went to see his father, reassured him of himself, put his army past definitely behind him. Europe was on the other side of an ocean which he might again cross, but for the time it was the place from which he had come. All the contradictory lines of space and time are finally absorbed by the one historical line. The geometry of Otto's past was one where every line of space is finally parallel to the time line or in it, which is the same. The forward point of this line moved into the future of Otto's wish, to which he had become determined and of which he was now assured. Though his ego could say no more than, "This is not a dream, this is real, your wish is being fulfilled," so tentative was as yet his total identification with his present life, his will was ready to assert his purpose even against his father.

On his way to the parental house he remembered, without feeling, the communication of his father's impending end as his own ending. His imminent confrontation with his father made him think of the actual sight of the American dead. He saw the difference. One was the sight of himself dead, and the other an apparent loss of the source of his life, his origin. The last, if he were really independent of his origin, need be only a nominal loss. The paternal authority had indeed been for many years, even before the war, purely nominal, if not altogether denied. Otto's submission to the army, which is the realization of that authority in absolute form and seriousness, would not make him automatically subject to his father again. Even if with his father this was the original submission, and therefore perhaps easier, even more natural, could it again be maintained? What was the purpose of his homecoming? From the circumstances, he knew that it was to take his father's place; there was no one else who could. But this would be when his father died. While he was merely dying, Otto's position would be tentative or expectant, certainly not simple. Before the end, Otto could only help to save his father. Would he, as on his first impulse, really be trying thereby to save himself as well? He no longer felt this. His own being was independent and secure. He had no more need of his father than he had of his mother, now that he had a wife. In himself he felt a need to show that his submission to the army was for a purpose beyond the army, the external reason for the war, and the best way to do this could well be his denial of his father as authority. He was in suppressed revolt against the army, as were all the American soldiers, and submitted only for the war. To deny his father, to regard him as just another man, to treat the dying as he did the term of the war, to give no true submission, this seemed to him necessary. He would not die with his father, nor in saving him, save himself. At most, he would offer him a helping hand.

This preparation of his attitude, limiting his willingness to be of use to his father, was reasonable for him. The evolution of Otto's ego to this point of independence, at the first choice of freedom, was made possible by the full execution of the absolute authority of the army in sending him to his death with the full consent of his father. Yet for the sake of his father, and by the luck that Otto was still alive, he was now home. He, it would seem, owed his life to his father again, as when he had been born. Was his life then his, or was it his father's again? He felt in answer to this that the order of event was in reverse, that by whatever sequence he was now home, the authority could be used only once. As an infant, the tolerance of his father had let him live, but later he had sent Otto to his death. It was one act; a man has but one life. He was liberated from his father, even if the army usurped the authority again. Otto had given his life, and by luck he was still alive. This he owed to no one, it was the one chance in the million. Hereafter, his docility would be without his consent, he was a free man.

The first effect of Otto's presence on his father was one of pride. He was a returned son, a warrior, big and powerful and miraculously there over the large bed in the small room. Otto's smile was broad enough to ripple like a wave into the surrounding space and on the faces of his parents. He kept the initiating impulse of the smile discharging its radiating ripple for a full scene, and until he saw that his father had been fully charged and was smiling quite by himself. But not quite sure, he let him smile alone by not smiling himself. Otto's radiance had been transmitted and the glowing smile on his father's face sought to keep the room bright in the illusion of its own force. Otto smiled its reinforcement when the glow seemed to be going out, but otherwise subsided into the solemn expression of his photos on the walls and into the chair beside the bed.

His father was propped up by all the pillows of the house into a position between sitting and lying, being unable to do either. He was an old man but men have lived longer. He was small, smaller than he seemed to Otto who, as he looked at him from memory, saw him attenuating as a dream coming into the focus of the conscious mind, with the diffused areas, the secondary elaboration, disappearing. The mass of him had vanished; even his forehead that extended into the bald curvature of the skull could only etch four thin lines of skin over the eyes, for there was nothing more to gather. The hands showed big as if in a foreshortening, with the body lost under the comforter of the large bed. Later when he slept with his mouth open, his head hung backward from the thin neck and his eyes were half open.

These were blue, bright with smiling now, but with a dim look for everything that was immediately to his hand.

Yet Otto's mother from the couch, where a comforter showed that it was her bed, saw the father and the son as alike and said so, thinking to confirm her husband's pride and somehow also her son's. Perhaps she was seeing the situation reversed as when Otto was a boy and small as compared to his father, and looking more like him every day. But now it was his father who was small and growing smaller every day. "You look exactly alike," she said, "I could mistake you one for the other," and she was no doubt trying to, and perhaps, in the reverse, was succeeding. His father was embarrassed but pleased, saying, "Not now when I am old and dying." To this she quickly added, "You are a young man and soon you will be well." Otto felt a quick horror, tried to look at himself as if he were outside himself, and could admit only, "I am almost as bald as you." Neither would admit this, and it was not quite true, but his mother made her own comparison definite. "The eyes, the expression, even the smile are exactly the same." As father and son looked at each other smiling, they felt that this was true, and that it meant only a consciousness of self.

From his picture on the wall, Otto saw nothing of his father in himself. Instead, he saw himself there over a body that was still eager, a face that had lost belief, if not all hope. His eyes were held open wider than simply for wonder and looking rather too hard at what he was seeing. He had that unavailing hope for something after everything was done, as if he had come when it was over or had not understood. His parents looked with him at his pictures, noting that he now had more weight, apparent strength and a smile. It was his mother again who inquired, "Why don't you ever smile in a picture?" and his father who answered, "He had no reason for smiling." "But he is smiling now," insisted his mother. "Nor do I have any reason now," said Otto with a smile. "But you are home now," said his mother. "But I may go back again," said Otto. "Soon?" asked his mother in terror. "No," answered Otto without reassuring her.

"Tell me about the war, Otto!" demanded his father. "But there is nothing to tell," said Otto. "You know all there is to know as well as I. You get killed, or you don't get killed; and if you live, you still expect to die. I was almost killed a hundred times." "But you killed the enemy," added his father. "Yes," Otto agreed, "or he killed you." His mother shook her head as he looked at her, warning that talk of death was not good for his father. Otto continued enumerating and elaborating the times he had almost been killed, needing to prove in quantity his moral ground. Having been before death himself so often, he required his father to die willingly at the end of his life. In elaborating how he had done it, he showed what he expected of others who were merely ending their lives. Without saying just this, he said as much, but it was not enough. He could not prove his ground for independence and indifference. His mother spoke of her suffering and distraction while he was away, wishing for his return so deeply that she saw him in every similar looking soldier and according to traits that were his no longer. From what she said, he knew that his life was only a part of hers to her. His life or his death had no value of meaning that was not hers. Her suffering was the true suffering; the war was suffered by her and other mothers, and it was hers by right. The loss of a son by a mother was the whole meaning of the war. To this he was at first witty and then severe. He was witty in answering that she made unnecessary that he should suffer, since she did it for him, that he had not known it could be done. He was severe in asserting that his life had a value for him that was unrelated to her; that it was he and not she who had been to the war. His father thought of the war as something to win and the fighting as only a minimum part of it. Everyone shared in the purpose, each one doing what he could without order of value. We were all fighting, even if some individuals were more important than others. The unknown soldiers, of whom his son was one, might be less important than a general, but without them the war could not be won. Otto felt that his father was disappointed in him as a soldier, that he would have much preferred his being one of the important ones, if even less than a general, but at least more than he was. He repudiated his father's right to expect him to be anything more than he was. Further, he asserted that the war had a moral meaning only for those who were killed in it or who were placed in the open to die. The important point was not who won the war but who died in winning it. This point of view meant nothing to his father, who, with right, was thinking only about his own life and impending end.

So, when his mother left the room, he told Otto what he already knew, that he was dying, that he had only so long to live, but that he wanted to go on living and that he would use all his power in the effort. He warned Otto not to tell his mother how serious was the case or even what it was. Then he asked Otto to

leave him alone to sleep, the excitement of the visit having worn
him out. Otto joined his mother, who told him that his father
had not long to live, and that this should be kept from him
because, as it was, without knowing his ailment, he was afraid
to die. This was the effect of the argument, that both of them
thought him strong enough to accept his father's death. He
showed them that he could, proving to himself too that he could.
The old man dying at the end of his life had no immediate appeal
to him. His own life was young and if he were to die now, it
would be in another way. His own was too definitely a case of
not yet having lived out his life. He felt the confirmation of his
own right to live, now that he was free of the violent threat to his
life. He held himself aloof from acting as if he were dying with
his father. He thought of it smiply; even saying it so, that each
man died in his time and that he would not think of death until
he himself was dying. This was not the way his mother wanted
to interpret his attitude; she saw in him an opportunity for herself. She tried to overwhelm him with her sorrow so that she
could then conform his behaviour to that of her own desire.

Her lamentation was first self-pity for Otto's father, and then
there was helplessness, and she wept. Why had it happened to
her? There were so many others to whom it could have happened first, older men and men more evil. She was being punished, the Lord was punishing her, what had she done? But if
they were punishing her, why was he dying and leaving her
alone after having been with her all these years? If there were
only something to do, but she could do nothing, there was nothing
to do, unless Otto could do something. Thank God he was home
and would do something if there was anything to do, if only he
wanted to do it for his father who was dying, who wanted to
live, who was afraid to die. He was not old, it was a pity that
he should die so soon. He had done everything for them, worked all his life, lived for others, did not think of himself. If he
lived, he would still live for others, he was so good. But it was
hard for her; she had not the strength; she was weak and sick
herself; she too was old and weary and needed rest. He did
not let her sit or sleep, for he could not rest and did not let her
rest. He was not used to lying in bed all the time; and what he
used to do, she now had to do; he never gave her a moment's
rest. But if he were to die, it would be worse for her. She
would not be able to live without him. Yet she did not want to
die, she was not ready for that, she had not lived enough. And
thank God he was still alive, perhaps he would not die after all.

He wanted to live, he would not die, he was better as he was than dead.

She was silent now and in the silence, for Otto said nothing, she listened and he listened with her and heard nothing. She, in great fear of the quiet surface stilled of event by their very attentiveness, could not endure it. From holding her breath with open mouth and wide eyes, she left her son, and was ready to scream and weep again out of the prepared grimace. He moved into a position for looking after her and saw her wake his father to see if he were still alive, asking if he were awake, of which there was no sign, for he was asleep or dead, and this was her doubt. He woke out of his sleep and seeing only her, slept again, but she would not let him sleep, fearing that he would die in his sleep and she would not know he was dead. She would have him awake and alive, not asleep or dead; awake he was still alive, asleep he might be dead. She would be in doubt if he were silent as if dead, asleep as if dead. To have to think that perhaps he is dead was an uncertainty worse than having him dead. If she assumed that he was alive when he might not be, she would be indifferent to his death, for she might laugh at the very moment. If she assumed him dead when he was alive, she might be wishing him dead, leaving him for dead, weeping for him that he was alive. She had to know one or the other, not in error to mourn for the living or laugh at the dead. Sure that he was alive, she returned to Otto to prepare some food for him, but from time to time left her son to see if his father was still breathing.

He finally awakened, and as if by the illusory powers of his dream, commanded the presence of his wife to determine if he were indeed as he was; as if he were not yet used to being so, and in a voice so faint that Otto, not attuned to such attentiveness, did not hear it. He heard the conversation between them as his mother said that Otto was still in the house and eating, and his father asking for his dinner, so he knew that his mother had not gone to him on her own impulse of fearful doubt. Again and again the command was given, but it remained inaudible to Otto. He suspected that his father was lowering his voice almost to the bare wish, to test its power, and that it was to the intimation of this wish that his mother was responding. Until he went back to his father's room himself, he further reasoned that the calling of his mother was a device to establish continuous fixity by the frequency of the moving image. That is, not being able to keep his mother there, he thought his father was attempting to keep her coming in so often, that it would appear that she was really there. Yet when Otto joined him, he did not cease from setting her into this continuous motion of service to him. Otto thought that there would be an end to this sooner, if he helped his mother in satisfying his father's needs. It did not have this effect. Instead, his father seemed to expand the scope of his operation with the increase of his forces. Otto did one little service for him after another, until he found them conceived particularly for him. He had thought to serve the immediate indispensable need and in doing this was impressed with all that had to be done, that his father could no longer do for himself. It appeared that more than one person was necessary to do all this. It was much more than had ever been asked of Otto and as soon as he suspected the plan, more than he was willing to do. In a short time, he found that he was being asked to do more even than he could do and have any time left.

His father explained that he was not used to confinement in bed, he so active a man all his life and now ill for the first time. From this it was evident that he was attempting to continue his activity by means of others. In itself, a simple act, distributed into parts for several people, to meet his need, might still be called his in a certain sense without delusion. He might say that he took his drug when it had been given him, since there was some part of the act that did remain his. Yet when he said that he had shaved when someone had shaved him, though it did not seem important, there was a confusion between the command and the performance. Otto reacted to this as to an officer's command, and the officer being his father, he refused to act. This identification of the command with the act, the wish with the fulfillment, needed differentiation and Otto differentiated it to zero. The immediate result was curious. As if not believing that his wish was not absolute, his father ordered him rapidly several times differently. The barrage of command remained as ineffective as one. Otto hoped that this would distinguish the real world from the dream world for his father. He further thought to himself that the rulers, the commanders of the real world, were also living in the dream world and that it was time they learned. But, as with his father, it was a dream from which they could not awaken. Thinking of it thus, Otto saw his father, propped up as he was on the pillows, as a king in bed, an absolute ruler for whom there is no transition from sleeping to waking. Rather, as if to continue the dream with which he has just awakened, he commands from his bed while awake even greater powers. The tyrant in bed, who was now his father, with his pure executive will, was set back like an infant in its absolute rule by Otto. Otto denied his father the illusion of omnipotence, or at least its realization in ruling him. This interrupted for awhile the play of power, his mother even coming to rest. It was a development; a proof that Otto did not need, that he was not acting on his father's will but on his own. He did not move, nor did his mother for a while, and his father sat in bed quite alone with his wish. Then his mother, like an attendant genius, stood up in a general offering of helpfulness, but it was an offer and not a response to the wish, so Otto's father had her sit down again.

In a great determination, as if to perform some extraordinary act with his own body beyond any normal power and without Otto, he uncovered himself with a well deliberated turn of the comforter. As an indiscreet observer of an exhibition, Otto looked away and then back to stare at the bare remainder of his father. He maintained the sight as remembered childhood shame and fear and envy, and his fear of the dead, appeared and disappeared as old and irrelevant pressures breathed out in a sigh or a smile. He felt pity for what he saw and for the purpose of the revelatory act, at which his father rested. It was to be the first move of an independent performance of the first social achievement of man, that of evacuating in a different place from where he lay. Getting out of bed alone was for him a complex action, which he had analyzed into simple movements to be executed in sequence, leaving him thus in unusual and interrupted postures, clumsy and transitional, yet designed as points of rest. A master of patience and analytic thought was necessary for this reversal of continuity to sequence, a masterful ego of a father demonstrating his will before his son. It took him five minutes to reach the bathroom, walking the ten steps one at a time rather than one after another and taking a separate deep supporting breath for each step. He even pushed the door behind him and Otto was made to feel the greatness of the will and its absoluteness, its separateness and finality in relation to him. The will that would prove its absoluteness, when doubted, with its personal power, had subdued Otto without reservation in the past, not doubting its authority and right. The demonstration confirmed Otto in his independence as against his father, and instead of the pity, he felt determined in his indifference, and to leave that power in its own limit and economy; to do what it could without using other power, at least not his. He heard his father's alarm as part of his idea, for it was in his mind as he imagined diminution unto death that he would observe abstractly, and he went slowly into the bathroom to see his father dying. From the appearance, his father might have been, as he was panting with little breath, unable to swallow the air. He was seated on the bowl, but insecurely trying to hold himself in the center of his quivering. This was all of his motion, not much beyond his very surface, and if it had been free would have turned in a dizzy circle of all the little tangents of motion to that surface. Seated as he was, he would have fallen, so Otto held him in place and gradually stilled the quiver. There remained only the little breath, but this too lengthened its rhythm, and in a while his father was ready to return to bed. He stood up and held Otto's arm, and weighing nothing against it, and tiny next to him, he went step by step the ten steps, each one a separate breathless event between a deep though tentative breath and a sighing exhalation. At the bed he sat down to rest. He was not humiliated by his dependence on his son, his situation had been too tragic, but he still wanted only the minimum of offered help. All Otto had done had been to steady him on the seat of the bowl, but he had taken the arm himself. Not like a child nor a woman, yet something horribly of both, incestuous, a dying body violated, was the touch of the flesh. Instead of being humiliated by his dependency, he used it as a new basis for his authority and ordered his son to get the doctor, and his wife into her servile activity to and from him. Perhaps it was not a new basis, thought Otto, but the new condition in its infantile extreme for the old authority. The attitude of this had not changed, though it was now based on its opposite. The despot had no excess of tolerance now; he disposed of his forces for his personal need and use, for the defense of his life, the very state itself. But the doctor did not immediately come, he having said that he could not, and Otto felt that there was nothing to do but wait. The mother, however, pleaded with him to go again, agitating herself into a state of emergency, so that in refusing he explained that it was not her life that was to be saved. After her lamentation, he was certain of this and that she was merely evading the responsibility for his father's life, remaining alert to any effectivity of a possible wish for his death. As if to repudiate his son, to leave him with this very responsibility and no means to liberate himself from it, his father ordered her to get the doctor. Otto went again, this time to nullify this purpose, for he knew that there was no need to go, to deny his father the pleasure of blaming him for his death in any way, or to allow him the peace, or the strength, or the resignation of righteousness. It would remain the life that had been lived to the end in its own way, and Otto would give it no strength to die, though he would do what seemed necessary to let it go on living.

Unhurried, the doctor arrived in his own time, from others no doubt dying and afraid to die. He was unperturbed by this common end, seeing it as a terminating event perhaps, but evidently as the end of every man. Techniques of postponing and impercepting the event, which he was applying now, were all that he had to give, not the life freed of the invading inorganic chemistry. But he too abstracted himself from the event, denied the responsibility even for what he was doing. Before all of them he said: "I will not be responsible. You are a dying man and I can do nothing for you. In doing what I do, you might die at any moment, and you will blame me. You should be in a hospital, where, if you die, everything will have been done for you. I have other men whom I can help and I should give give my time to them." Otto had looked to him for the reasonable attitude, for a proper indifference, unconcern as a man, but not a rejection which showed a concern of his guilt as a doctor. Otto did not accept his father as dead, only as dying; but the doctor who could not help him, gave him up as dead. He discussed it with the man later alone, and assured him that he would not be blamed for his father's death; but wondered why, if the doctor did everything he could, he should have this concern. It was because people wanted to live forever and always blamed someone when they died. Yes, the dead were dead and did not blame anyone, but those who wanted them to live would blame him. He preferred to treat those who would live. A dying man should go to a place where people died, and where he cannot make a scene. There he is not abandoned, he can be seen during the hours of visit, and every known device is used to keep him alive and at ease until he is dead. Besides, he would be observed by those who might any day find a way to make him live; he might be the very first one on whom it is done.

From this talk Otto made a summary from his own point of view. His father's life was his own even when he was dying. The responsibility for it being his alone, he would dispose of it according to his own need and desire; Otto not interfering even if he could, for he did not want to. As long as his father wanted to stay at home, or until he was no longer able to choose, there he would remain. If for some reason he should want to be in the hospital, whether or not he saw in it an opportunity for life or for greater comfort, or for the sake of oblivion, he would be sent there. It would, however, be his choice only until his treatment did not require a hospital, or the house turned into one. Then there would be no choice and he would leave the house. He could spend his last days in his own home with his wife and his friends and his son with no authority but his own, ruling and ordering whatever he could; or he could submit to the doctors for whatever hope or comfort they had for him in their hospital, where there was always a little hope and a last comfort. There he would be with others like himself, which would be better than with those who would be more and more unlike him, even if he could get them to live as if only for him.

In presenting the alternatives to his father, Otto showed no preference for either one, exceeding the doctor in neutrality. He saw that it did not seem enough to him who was to make the choice. As a son, it would seem that he should have a personal concern to choose what was best and to recommend it, to be pleased at least with whatever his father chose. He was too scrupulous in leaving it to his father, too exact in limiting his own right, too correct in recognizing his father's independence. His mother saw this too and turned to him to say: "What shall we do?" His father said it also: "I know all that, but what do you think I should do?" seeing no difference between the mother's we and his I. He would want to decide and then share the responsibility for what he had done, the blame, if there was that. He went even further, he would let himself be persuaded by his son to decide in a certain way, so that he could be the judge now and later without having all the responsibility. Otto would not advise or persuade; the one who ordered others would decide for himself. Any other way was as evil as ordering others to do your purpose and imagining that you were doing it yourself, and afterwards that you had done it yourself. Those who did not decide by and from and only for themselves were not equal to themselves. It was more than enough of Otto to present the alternatives. "I do not see it as something for us to do, but something for you to do. I cannot decide for you what you want nor can the three of us. It is only you who can decide that." "We will decide without you," said his father, asserting his power to do so, "we do not need you." Very soon then he did decide to go to the hospital, for it was on a high hill where he hoped to breathe easier, hoped also to return from there with the full breath of life.

430

His adjustment to the hospital was compulsory; once there his subjection to the authority was automatic and inescapable. The possibility of living, though it continued in his mind in a still imaginable future in which he would be well, appeared in the environment of helplessness and dependency inapplicable immediately. He became involved in the series of tests that were made of him, interested in their general meaning and their individual interpretation of the state of his body. His interest in these measurements and analysis of him was at first passively optimistic, as he waited for the results, confident that something new and important, mysterious and magical, yet simple and delightful would come out of it all. This phase lasted a long time, dropping him into the long intervals between the hopeful offer of an excretion and its evaluation. During these intervals of unworried belief in the confirmation of patted pride and caressed patience, he lived out the greatest part of his remaining time. It was not an active waiting in which one is impatient of the time, but the peaceful relief at the postponement of a worry, of a fatal issue. It was a triumph in infantile flattery to agree to so high an evaluation of excretion. But all fluids and matters that left him or circulated within him were read for his fate, and all pressures and inner noises were felt and listened to for signs and symbols of the inchoate language. The elaborate probing, touching, hearing and tapping in known and even new ways was a game of curiosity that he joyfully played, feeling that now at last the deep and secret meaning of him was being read. During this time it was enough to be in the hands of the doctors to feel safe, even saved. In this transfer of responsibility to them, it was with indifference that he observed the men in the many beds around him who, he learned, were ill as he was. Mostly as old as he or older, they revealed to Otto on his first visit, all that he could not see directly of his father. It was evident that all of them were dying and he wondered at his father's indifference to this fact, for he was himself not indifferent. He could not look at them without the idea of death, which they expressed in a range of Goyesque images. His own equanimity was an effort here and he felt that there was no moral order among the ways of dying. Rather he felt that here was the way he would die after a while. He imagined himself diminished to that last endurance of life, worn away to the inanimate structure with the look of being almost alive, or living but not alive, as if the breath of life was all there was and it could not animate what remained of the flesh. Looking at his father now among the other old men there

431

to die, he felt an identity with him, not as merely between them alone, but as to another who was a man and was ending as he would end. He was able to pity himself in pitying his father, which was more than he could do before with only a simple relation to him. He listened to his father's purpose in being there, that of studying the treatment so he could use it for himself when he left, and saw from his understanding of the army how the long intervals were their own purpose; that they, when added together, were all there was to being there; that in time, that would be all there was left of his father's life, when no new meaning to it would be given, and that this not given when most needed, immediately, would be of less interest and finally unnecessary. In this way, he would die willingly in the long waiting rhythm without needing to know, or if he did know at the very end, it would be with the feeling that he had waited so long and was ready for it. The dying around him, for one or another died every day, did not at first affect him during the lulling rhythm, though he could be amused with the idea of old men foregathering to die; unknown to one another in life, meeting for death. They had the same fate but it was not in common; each one died alone as each knew about the others without knowingly knowing his own. Those who died a little longer made friends among the dying as among the living and missed the dead as the promise of their own life. It was not possible to be alone with the others around, and Otto's father entered the community of dying men, the last, and acquired its oral tradition which was passed on from one to another, for no group of a moment lived long enough as a unit to be known as a generation. It was a tradition of mutiny to the authority, bribery for the full attention of the system to keep it to its purpose, methods of protest and threat, and the use of the main resource, that of the outside power that one could still command. This was in addition to their spontaneous mutual aid, as one of them often helped Otto's father to the toilet, and he in turn offered bits of fruit that Otto's mother brought him. More for this purpose and that he had not lost his status with her, she brought things to him and then took them home when he found them of no use. He used Otto only to make him known as a son to his new friends in his first good will in his new life.

As his friends died, he became more active in his own life; as nothing was done for him, his fear of death returned. It was no longer enough to give parts of himself for deep analysis of his fate. He had now to know it and to determine it himself. As his right, he put himself in authority, attempting by his own plan not only to reject or accept phases of the treatment, but on his own judgment to modify all of it on the basis of the evidence of his symptoms. He used superficial alternatives to the treatments he had learned from the men of medicine, and demanded that his excretions be analyzed for him for his own interpretation. He seemed even to improve and announced the alleviation of symptom. In this attempt to convert the hospital into his own home, he had the support of the other men. He required his wife to bring him his own food and bedclothes, and to come at hours when she could not get in. He ordered his son to inquire about his ailment for theoretical confirmation of the self-treatment, and to obtain drugs for him different from those being administered. Taking over in this way, he remembered duties to others, his unfinished acts outside, and had Otto do them for him. Again, everyone he knew was doing his will, and the illusion of self-activity became so real that he spoke of it all as what he was doing. He overcame all the defense of the system with his own organization and was face to face with the head doctor, with the alternative, which was his real power but which he could not use, of leaving for his own home and turning it into a hospital. Before the high authority of the head doctor he was submissive, the achievement had been to find him, to get to him. Once with him, he stated that he wanted to live and not merely to wait until he was dead. He wanted something done; he himself wanted to do something. He was sure that his will to live had a value toward living and that it should be used instead of leaving him passively in bed like an infant. He asserted the right, on the basis of his understanding and the experience of himself, to supervise his own treatment, for his own perception was more sensitive to the tendencies of his ailment. Further, he demanded to know what they were doing to him and why. All this was granted to him and he submitted to an examination with the pleasure of purposeful exposure.

It seemed that there was a chance, for the next day the doctor returned with it; an offer of ten years more of life if, by the removal of his testes, the glandular economy of his system were reorganized on a new basis. Certain irritants, it was hoped, would then not be formed and a stasis in the dying in the particular direction might set in. In this way several had lived another ten years. It was not a cure, the doctor was scientific to say, it was a slowing down almost to a halt of the dying. Also it was uncertain; several had not lived. He was taking a chance, but he had nothing to lose anyway, for he was an old man and had no further use of his testes. A couple of ugly, hanging, globular glands, his appearance would be neater without them. Their removal would be simple and safe, without his knowing; there was nothing to fear and no one would know of it. It was a hope, what they could do for him, and what he could do for them for the others. His change of life was to be soon anyway; there would be no loss; he would go on living as before; he would not miss them. It was up to him, only he could say, and only he need know.

It was something to think of, but Otto's father could not do it alone. He needed the consent of his wife and his son. His testes were now important only to them. He was not really dead as a man and his wife might still need him as one. It was up to her to give up her sexual life with him. He wanted to live but not alone, uncertain that he wanted to without the nominal relations. His son, too, must consent, for he wanted to remain a father. If Otto did not consent, it would be a refusal to save his father. It was a major symbolic operation, and those whose symbol he was, would have to give him up, so that he could live. It was the affect on them that was the issue. Would they permit the breaking of their idol, the castration of Priapus?

Otto's mother consented without thought, as to the only thing that could be done; at once, without relating it to herself as to the effect on her life to come, or to the meaning it could have to her unconscious past as a fulfillment. As she waited with Otto's father at his bed for Otto's consent, in the ward where other sons were visiting the other fathers, she showed in her face the hope that he would be like what she thought they were. Otto saw those sons and in responding to his mother's expression, he wished too to be like them. He was sure he had no reason to be different from them, nor any right. For awhile it appeared to him that it was as against them that he was acting and took on the guilt. As against them, he had no rights, did he have any against his father? As he heard what his father wanted to do, he smiled that he should be told about it, and that his consent should in any way be necessary. His parents treated the subject as if it were a natural one with no meaning not in the immediate reference, as if it were the loss of a finger. Treated thus in their words, not in their eyes, Otto too remained neutral as he heard. His mother's look, and the other sons who looked at him from time to time, pressed him to go as far as he could go, and he saw that he could go further than his neutrality. Giving in to his father's wish was to give in to his own, they were the same. He said, "If I were you, I should do it." He did not mean this, for how could he be his father? He could not assume his father's responsibility; the way of the father is not the way of the son. For himself he doubted that he would give up his own power as a man just to live, even with his wife's consent. He meant that he would accept the shame, that if his wish were fulfilled, he still would not fear its power; he was independent of whatever his father would do even in letting Otto have his way. But what did he mean in saying, "If I were you?" He meant only that his father was no more a man than he, but if he were less, Otto would not mind being more; indeed he was really more than his father. If he were as weak, he would do what there was to do. This is then what Otto knew that he meant, "If I were what you are, I would do what you want to do, but I am not what you are and what I would do I do not know, or if I did, I would not say." His father felt this and said without a sense of deliverance, "That is what I wanted to hear." Otto had not consented, but had not remained altogether neutral; he had not refused him yet had denied him. Saying that he knew what his father would do, being what he was, his father could now do it. Otto was now superior, but in this remained neutral, inactive and indifferent.

What should have been a great drama of the castrated Priapus was a trivial event in the death of a father. The primitive and secret symbolism was impressive for the living but not for the dying. Authority relative to life submitted all its pride not to die, was willing to be nothing in order to live. Otto's father was given a neater appearance but it did not help. Yet he believed almost to the moment of his death that he would live. During the period of waiting to know if he would live, he slept more than he was awake. Often he did not know who was with him, though it appeared that he always knew who he was and for what he was waiting. He waited for death as if for life, but when he died, he knew it just before. Before he knew, but as if to test his power for the last time with his death, he had someone call his son to him. Otto, understanding the purpose did not go. If even when his father was no longer a man even in his death, he remained his father in his arbitrary authority, and this proved the failure of his father's submission, Otto would remain the son opposed to that authority. A day later his father died, and a minute before he left a message for Otto and his mother that he was dying, that they should be told when he died. A little while later Otto and his mother were there; he had died just before they would have seen him die. Otto felt as he had when he first heard that his father was dying, as if something had undermined him. Then it had been as if it were about to happen, now it had happened. Then, as he realized that his father was still alive, he wept a little and went in his direction. Now that he knew that his father was dead, he felt a deep fear and did not know where to go, but finally ran to his mother. She would have made her lamentation to the world, but she had been given an opiate. Otto sat with her for an hour, smoothing her hand as she wept, feeling with her that they were alone. As the structure of his life resettled on a new base, his unconscious taking notice of the new fact, the doctor took him aside. He wanted to make an autopsy, to find out what had been going on inside Otto's father all this time. Otto smiled to know that they had not known, that they as well as his father had been struggling with an unknown power. He could not give his consent to the doctor, knowing too that it meant that he would die like his father. It was not his body, it was the body of his father and he should have been asked for his consent before he died. As for the final disposal, his father had arranged that, so Otto had merely to attend the burial. He saw his father lowered into a narrow grave, such as Otto had dug for himself in the war. He knew that he too would be dead in one soon, and as nothing had happened to his father that would not happen to him, he felt no pity for the particular man.

On the way home and at home, Ruth did not speak to him, and when she did, it was to tell him that he was pitiless. She kept away from him and he thought that she too had no understanding of him, that she gave him no right to be independent of his father. His own return from the dead had not with her given him any special right to live, though it was his very life that she had wanted for her own. Now he felt that she did not want him, that in achieving his independence, he would be quite alone. In his profound self-pity, he saw no good reason to live, and he went to sleep in his loneliness to dream. He dreamt a scene in a large empty room with only a bed in which his father is dying and his mother, Ruth and he are standing by the bed, they on either side and Otto in front of it. In another scene, Otto is at a table with his mother and Ruth. He hears from them that his father died two hours before. Otto lays his head on the table to cry. Ruth interprets the crying as for his father. She says: He did not know. The women do not cry; it is as if they had wept their share before.

At last Otto wept for his father, for in his dream his father died again and Otto wept for him. For Otto this was as with the enemy dead; he triumphed over them that they were dead. In the case of his father, it was a triumph to weep for him, for now Ruth could not say he was pitiless. He had wished his father dead a second time so that he could weep for him. This weeping is not a true weeping; in the classic dream in which a son wishes his father dead, he weeps in order to conceal the wish from himself. In Otto's dream the weeping has a purpose, to show Ruth that he is not pitiless. The dream is then an actor's performance in which Otto shows Ruth that he can weep for his father. So the weeping is false; it is not for the father but before Ruth. Yet the weeping is also true, for did not Otto feel alone in the world with his mother for an hour after his father died? He was sorry for himself and might have wept in his loneliness. Why did he dream, if it were not because he was lonely, that Ruth did not understand him and thought him pitiless? Therefore he was weeping for himself in the dream, though it appeared that he was weeping for his father. It is a dream of loneliness and self-pity; and because Otto feels so, he wishes his father dead though he is dead. As with the enemy dead, he could mourn for him in his own small sorrow of the moment.

SEVEN POEMS

Julian Orde

ALL NIGHT AWAKE

The growing up morning is rising round my house
       Like tall white women.
The beginning clock puts trees; birds begin.
       But I am yesterday
Wearing a lost coat, left over, merely
       Dragged on the wheels
Across into morningtime with resisting heels,
       Sick and bombarded
With the signs of arrival to stay of a day; unguarded.
       I crossed this corridor
Wanting to watch my cheated nerves; explore.
       I saw grey girls
Endlessly opening doors in silence and tears.
       Going away
In a light was the King of Fright, his crown and shadow.
       You may ask:
What tune or geometry resolved this unnatural task?
       The thin fingers
Strangling down on the bounding ball of wings?
       Or the pooled window
Gathering bundles of trees and preparing for morrow?
       What tune or geometry
Was finally lined by a lover of order, discovery?
       I can only repeat:
I felt the slow the quick of the world's and the heart's beat,
       The loud the soft
Of the snow squeak underfoot and the snow in a drift,
       The soft the sharp

That is cats, the low the high view of my toe and eye,
    The turning two ways
Of a planet, the alternately hissing and stilling of stars.
    My body divided,
Slid away from the bones with a snarl with a bag of wool,
    Spun through the gate,
Went spinning an angry thread round an empty estate
    And never came back.
My window has gathered the morning into its lake.
    I am left hollow.
My window is putting up trees and preparing for morrow.

THE UPWARD RAIN

Dropped, let fall with a sigh, the clouds have released rain;
The brown earth hisses and swarms up the silver branches,
Green climbs to the sky till the clouds are swelling with flowers.

Splashed come the fruit and the bees and the waves of the tree;
Flashing wet metal, there is sudden arrival of dragonflies,
Held in the air by their rigid and quivering wings like church
    windows.

Such a meeting of water and lovers of water I see!
Such communion of flower and cloud and the waves of the tree!

ON LOOKING OUT

A mushroom morning and a day for kites,
And the ricksha boys bickering in China,
And myself in the middle of the middle ring,
(But everyone else thinks they are);
And a skyscape just arrived, with quite
Its best and unrepeatable design, a
Water-land built solid out of nothing,
And beautiful as my imagined China.

THE KIND SOFA

Edward Rigg and Emmeline
Swam on a sofa which became
Their closest friend,

439

Yielding, kind,
Providing their whole needs for one
Striped, buttoned hour.
To the hanging moon
Of Edward's face she could not explain
How he set free her convict mind
To visions flashed off a knife blade,
To astonishing landscapes slitted
Through dungeon walls.
She could not tell him how she lay
Smiling to find herself pelted with white
Paper boxes, dropped deliberately
From some sensational height.

JUSTICE

A theatrical agent got lost among acrobats,
His glasses fell off as he swung from the high trapeze.
Miss La Rue in her Pimlico front and back
Smiled through the pins as she walked on her knees
Round the flounces of Violet Beauchamp's second-act frock.
And Septimus Rorke, still touring the Isles of Si Pong
(With no contract)—looked up to the sky full of trees
And crackled a laugh as though he were young,
Or happy, or talented, or not wearing stays.
The agent had carved up the world into "Seconds",
"Stout Character", "Elderly Blondes". He never returned
Photographs. He was cruel to midgets. He fell, screaming,
                among sea-lions.

THE SIX JULYS OF 1947

Such a summer! Till the last December-heart melted away,
And the newspaper woman sat steaming out on her box in
                Kingsway,
(Wet as a rag for months she'd been) and down side streets
The heat barred your way.

Everyone went on the tops of buses, (up there you go fastest,)
You get entangled in trees and the leaves come swimming against
                the glass,

440

And the drivers repay the lost minutes down Muswell Hill
        Broadway,
Diving down; fearing nobody.

It was so warm for so long; you could lift your arms in summer,
Or walk home slowly, thinking, with the dark as soft as a flower,
And the moon as green as an opal and the town quiet as a breath
That shows a man's alive.

It came like a gift, like good news, like a kind of forgiveness;
At first we could not accept; only the worst reassures us.
And then we gave in, and the summer swept over us, reaping
Bruised grain, poorly sown.

THE CHANGING WIND

Past my window runs a tree,
All the leaves are in my room,
A shiver of water passes over.
There is no stillness ever again.
I saw the table break in three,
I saw the walls cascading down,
I saw the hard hair of my lover
Drift out upon the flowing green.
I saw the clove dark enemy
Stare from the bed where I had lain,
I saw my face in hers to be.
There is no stillness ever again.

Sun and wind had come for me—
What is my house but a flight of wings?
A flight of leaves, a flutter of rain,
A sidelong slipping of light in rings?

And now a scream possesses me—
Too high to hear, yet can I hear it;
And now transfixed upon a pain,
Too thin to feel yet must I bear it—
This scream, this pain, they are not mine,
Water and air is all I am,
A tree has shaken the staircase down—
Then what has rustled and entered in?

I knew the other ones had come.
I knew my heart was theirs to claim.
I felt the millions in my room.
There is no being alone again.

THREE STORIES

Liz Jacobson

SEE, I AM READING A LETTER FROM A SOLDIER

OH PLEASE GET OUT, ladies; please get out. You spoil it for me, sitting there in front of me, eating your ice-cream and cake, and looking at me vaguely with your middle-aged eyes.

Oh I know this is a public place, an inexpensive restaurant serving sandwiches, ice-cream, cold drinks and things like that; a cheap, gaudy place with painted walls, garish juke-boxes, and cozy, low-built booths; a large place with a shining marble floor (cracked here and there) and long brown counters; a popular place with lots of waitresses and tables. I know you have every right to be here. Still I want you to be away from here. We just don't go well together right now. A hundred differences separate us; twenty-five long years divide us. You ladies read your letters in World War I. I am reading them now.

See, just two tables away from you, I am reading a letter with the emblem of the United States Army engraved on each page.

See, this letter comes a long way; from a different country, from another continent. It's censored. It's cut up a little. And it's not very long. A flyer wrote it to me; a bombardier, whose arms can bend and retract as if they were made of some marvelously pliable substance instead of stubborn flesh and blood; whose eyes change speedily from one shade of grey to another shade of grey every time he looks at you, and whose mind is set on one thing, to make his plane when he is sitting in it and searching the earth for target points, a fierce, avenging angel.

But you are not concerned about this letter, are you ladies? (Let me call you Mrs. George Jones and Mrs. Harry Kraus) You sit there, dressed in red skirt and yellow print dress, eating large spoonfuls of ice-cream and munching small chunks of cake. You sit there smiling at each other while the trimmings on your hats cast their bright shadows on your sagging cheeks. You sit there with your stomachs sticking out and legs crossed in that dainty movie manner. And you sit there talking intimately to one another. What makes me think that you should be interested in this letter? What in the world could this letter, which is not even well written, mean to you?

No, ladies, this letter is not interesting. This bombardier who sent the letter to me from "somewhere in England," is not a great letter writer by a long shot. And his grammar is a little off. For instance, he writes: "Your letters will reach me regardless of where I am." This is probably wrong. He should have written, I believe, "Regardless of where I am, your letters will reach me." In another place, he says: "I think more of you than you think." Wrong again, I am afraid. I suppose it should read: "I think more of you than you realize." And there are other mistakes. But somehow I don't mind them. Somehow I know that I must not forget that he is average, like your son, like my brother, like thousands of other soldiers who have gone through many schools but still cling stubbornly to the unwritten grammar they have learned from mother and dad in Vermont and in Kentucky.

This is good, isn't it? The way I talk about grammar as if that could be interesting to anyone and least of all to you. But obviously it's not. You are still eating your ice-cream and cake, I see; almost half done now. You are still shaking those fancy plastic earrings as you talk to each other, and you are still crossing your legs, which I see are considerably swollen around the ankles and heavily veined across the instep. You are still smoking your cigarettes, just starting on a new one. And you are still casting looks now and then at the chair on which you have piled your packages.

But why am I worried about what you are doing? Why am I cataloguing you like this, watching your antics as if you were putting on some kind of act here? What are you to me, and what am I to you? We are just passersby, I suppose. You stopped here to have yourselves a time; I stopped here for a sandwich on my way to work. And my reading a letter from a soldier at a table not far from you is nothing spectacular. But somehow there is a link between us. Somehow I feel you know me and I know you and and indefinable anger comes over me and makes me frown. I know there is something wrong about it, something terribly unfair. Nevertheless, I continue to nurture this antagonism against you; filling myself up with it as if it were a seven-course dinner; spreading it all over myself until I feel as if I were ten people instead of one, strong, wild and reckless, and ready to throw myself into a fight to the finish.

Yes, ladies, I am carrying on like this while at the same time I keep reading my letter, looking at certain sentences again, to see if I had understood them properly at first, to look if I can't find some additional message somewhere on the first page or on the second one. Oh I am really happy about the letter, about every word in it, about the beginning and the ending. But I have not been calmed. I still hold it against you.

Well, what have I got against you, what am I blaming you for? I am afraid to say it. I cannot even say it, not knowing how to say it. Still I line up a hundred sins against you, place them all over your face and hands, as if they were black marks that would show you off for having muffed the First World War, for having caused the depression, and most of all, for the present catastrophe, for the burning of Rome again; for the soaking of the earth with the rich young red blood of our young men.

This is my unreasonable anger against you. But as it isn't quite true, I cool off. Yes, ladies, this wrath against you vanishes quickly as if it were a thick sandwich in a war worker's lunchbox, once the worker begins eating it; as if it were a shovelful of coal thrown into the furnace on a cold winter day. Yes, Mrs. Jones and Mrs. Kraus, this silly anger against you is now gone and forgotten. I'll start reading this letter, from the flyer I saw only one evening, over again.

What, the anger is coming back. I am afraid you would not think any too well of me if you knew how I met this soldier. It was a pick-up ladies, nothing more formal than that; the same kind of pick-up you have heard so many people talk about in whispers. I was eating a sandwich, just as I am doing now, in a similar kind of joint, when this ordinary-looking soldier came in, examined the place cursorily, and then sat down next to me.

Did anything like that happen to you in World War I, ladies, did it? It doesn't seem possible to look at you now, with your sagging muscles, your squinting eyes, your thin, gray-streaked hair, your dented cheeks (heavily rouged), and your flat-looking lips.

God, this is vile. Forgive me, ladies, please forgive me. This is unkind. This is not right. This is awful. I am probably doing it because I am not pleased with my conduct, because I know very well I am no heroine, but a cheap so-and-so. Yes, ladies, I am blaming you for my sins, I admit. I am the culprit, not you. You are not guilty, you are not to blame.

No, ladies, you are not to blame for the way you look, flaccid, and unimpassioned, or for the way you dress, in spite of the grotesque earrings, or for the way you act. Neither are you responsible for the things that have happened in the world at large. You never sat in at the big councils of state. You never made any deals at the conferences of ambassadors and attaches. You did not give birth to Hitler, or raise him. You did not sell guns to Franco.

No, you are not to blame. You are just two middle-aged housewives; two ordinary human beings; two swallows in a summer long; a small part of a dot on the population charts —nothing more. I absolve you then from guilt, even as Tolstoy did, I believe, when he too could not find an answer to the same awful question in his thousand-page book, *War and Peace,* deciding at last that neither Napoleon, nor fate, nor some of the other big figures, nor the people as a whole, were to blame for the terrible death of a million men that winter of 1812. Oh yes, ladies, I too absolve you from all guilt, even though I cannot quite spit out the last drops of hatred that still circulate in my veins; making me shake, and making me feel pathologically pessimistic as I look at this letter and ask myself: "How many more?"

"How many more?" What a silly question to pop right now, isn't it, ladies? I've got this one; why worry about more letters? I've got this one, and I waited for it six weeks. I've got this one and it came yesterday and I've not stopped reading it. Oh yes, why worry about others?

What is it, ladies; did I see you wink? Did I hear you snicker: "She thinks he is a hero, a Galahad, plunging into the forest in search of the Holy Grail."

Oh pardon me, ladies, Mrs. Jones and Mrs. Kraus, you don't talk like that; you don't know much about Galahad, Guinevere, King Arthur, the Lady of the Lake, Queen Bellicent, and Excalibur. You didn't care to read about that old stuff. You read instead "True Episodes" and "Deep Secrets." Lancelot and Guinevere are total strangers to you—but not to me.

No, ladies, they are not strangers to me, not those warrior knights who sat around king Arthur's table so many centuries ago. I could recognize each one of them, I think (not that I expect to see them) by the twists of their mouths; by the sheen on their hair; by the length of their strides; by the motion of their hands.

This knowledge of those long-forgotten days, you would say, ladies, makes me romantic. You believe that? You are sure of that? Well, you are wrong, dead wrong. I have another nature to me, a hard-boiled one, a cynical one, just as nearly everyone of my time does, both those who saw a lot of books, and those who didn't. For it was easy to learn things with the radio going all day, from a thousand teachers who taught us daily.

There was Walter Winchell: "flash, flash, flash, I have been told by a certain party that. . ."

There was Louella Parsons: "A little birdie tells me that a certain beautiful movie star is about to. . ."

There was Rudy Vallee: "My time is your time. . ."

There was Bing Crosby: "TADADADADADADA. . . "

There was Ripley: "This is really true, this extraordinary occurrence, believe it or not."

There was Franklin Delano Roosevelt: "My friends, two-thirds of the nation are ruled by the one third of the nation who have made themselves. . ."

And oh, there were other things beside the radio that gave us hundreds of pointers. There was the WPA with its unreliable shovels on which you could not lean; there were the Youth Camps, where the boys were sure of three meals a day; there were the movies, where Greta Garbo and Joan Crawford afforded us a lot of romance and pleasure; and oh, there were the libraries, new ones, large ones, roomy ones, with tall windows and glittering chandeliers. Here we could read (and kill time too) Percy Bysshe Shelley: "Spirit of Beauty, thou dost consecrate . . . ," or all about the growth of the C.I.O., or all about getting a job where you could advance, and even a score of novels.

Oh yes, ladies, even without "books" in our large cities, we still could find books all around us. It was easy to pick up the facts of life, the whole truth about life. It was easy to be "smart," and to know things. And we made use of this knowledge. We lived. We were not lovers of solitude as the generation of Byron was. We did not wish to be left alone. We wanted to be with the crowds, at the baseball game, at the football game, at the concert hall. We were mixers, we were extroverts, the majority of us. We believed in living.

We certainly believed in living. We believed in jazz. We believed in burning the candles and the gas. We believed in the noise of the night. We believed in the smell of the beer joint. We believed in the flight of the airplane. We believed in the beauty of the sun. We believed in the open road.

Oh, we believed in living—but not in dying. No, ladies, we did not believe in dying at all, if we could help it. We liked life, every moment of it, from the minute we were born, it seemed. And it was well that we felt like that. Maybe we had some warning of what was coming. Maybe we had some secret message about the way things would turn out. Maybe a small voice urged us to go faster and faster because there was not much time left for us.

Yes, ladies, it was well that we believed in living with a capital L. For suddenly we heard that death was coming to pay us a special call, to look us over and see whom he wanted first. We saw him clearly as we listened to the professor lecture on history as early as the summer of 1939; as we lounged in the living room and dialed the radio to pick up a part of the speech of our favorite news commentator; as we glanced hurriedly at the front page headlines.

So death was coming to us, we laughed as we danced to a new song on the juke-box. So what, so what, so what? Suddenly we began to believe in death with the same intensity as we believed in life, even though we were sure that many of us would die, in one way or another, on land, or sea, or in midair. Even if we would die, we would not be lost, we knew; not this time. We knew that others would come after us, bury our bones, or our legs, or our arms, or whatever was left or us, and fight on to restore life to young men of the world.

There, ladies, you are lighting another cigarette. Well, cigarettes are fine. I'll try one too. Yes, I think I'll do that, smoke a cigarette and let the puff of smoke curl itself—all over my table while I turn this letter of mine over again, play with it for a while longer. Maybe if I do that, I'll be able to remember some things I managed to pick up about my soldier during those five hours (from seven in the evening until one in the morning) I was with him.

Did he walk with a long stride or a short one? He walked with a medium kind of stride, I believe. What did his nose look

like? I don't quite remember, I am afraid. I think it was inconspicuous. Was he tall? No, not exactly, some five feet eight or
so. He was, I guess, just average; nothing more than that; pretty
nice, pleasant, but that's all.

That's all I can remember about him and that isn't much,
is it, ladies? It's very little and I know it only too well. And
as I read the ending of the letter again—"From One Who . . . . ."
(you fill that in)—I am not sure that this is the real McCoy, the
honest-to-goodness business. I have my doubts, but I don't care
to think about them. All I know is, that he is a soldier; a soldier
with a "pair of wings"; a flyer who sits in a pit and looks down
intently as if he must see the inside of the earth, a bombardier
who will not be still even when he sits next to you and says nothing. This is about all I know, and as I touch the letter again,
it seems as if my heart sticks out of me as if it were a gun in a
woman's purse.

But what is this, ladies? You are putting on your lipstick;
you are finished; you are leaving? Oh, I don't want you to go
now. You're no longer strangers to me; no longer outsiders. You
are now closely related to me; deeply involved with me in this
episode, as everybody is. This letter is not just my letter; not
just my personal property, but yours too, Mrs. Jones and Mrs.
Kraus. It's everybody's letter, badly written perhaps with
innumerable grammatical errors, but still everybody's letter. It's
the unknown letter, which all of us must answer.

THE LITTLE THIEF

I have a definite distaste for starting this piece. I'm calling
it a blind-alley type of thing, and other derogatory names. This
is very unusual for me. Ordinarily, the minute something that
barely resembles a story touches me lightly on the shoulder and
calls out: "See what you can do with me on that toy typewriter
of yours," I immediately get busy, get involved to the point of
complete identification with it, and can't stop until it's all done,
good or bad.

This is different. This has been going on in me like a shrill
telephone, ringing away insistently. It has been doing this for
five or six months. But I have not answered. I have not written
a line all this time. And even now, even now as I'm punching
away at the keys of this same typewriter of mine, I cannot get

going in a regular, orthodox fashion, if you know what I mean. Instead, I'm beating about aimlessly with a vague hope that it will die on me before long.

It's not dying. It's not petering out. On the contrary, it's now making its way into me; making me give in gracefully. It's making me see clearly this odd-looking colored kid, by the name of Wallace, who worked with me at the time in a two-by-four department store—he, as an all around little helper, sweeping floors, dusting shelves, wrapping packages, and I, as the temporary typist addressing envelopes for some special sale—as the main characters of this so-called story.

There were other people involved; the boss, the other sales-girl, the two plain-clothes men, and people outside who do not figure directly but who still are very important, as you know.

But Wallace stands alone in this just the same. There are people like that, adolescents like that. You can never think of them as being part of a crowd, as having anyone closely or even distantly related to them.

That's how Wallace struck me the minute I saw him; although his mother, a thin, quiet-looking thing, very dark, and very young—about thirty at the most—was the one who came to ask for the job for Wallace in the first place. She even came with him for the first interview. But, in spite of all that, Wallace still seemed alone. He looked as if he had been born alone, grew up alone, and undoubtedly would die alone.

And that's how he looks to me now as he is peeking in my bedroom window. His face is pressed against the window-pane; and his muffled-looking, round, brown eyes seem so much darker than his skin, which is dark enough, that it makes me wonder a little how that can be.

It's quite late now, close to twelve o'clock; a minute or so before midnight. I was just getting ready to go to bed when I saw his face in the window and walked over closer to see if I were right.

Yes, he's there. I can see him fairly well. There is a round, full moon—clear and white. The sky itself is also clear—a deep solid, flawless blue that makes you think the whole world has finally found the perfect answer to everything.

As I said, there is a lovely white moon moving around the sky at a very deliberate and stately pace. Still Wallace's face seemed framed in a solid dark background. This does make it hard to see clearly—to see his vase-shaped face, his unaccountably high forehead, and his pointed head which rises above his forehead like an ill-chosen ornament on a woman's hat.

It's really difficult to see him clearly, in spite of the cream-like moonlight. Still you can get a pretty good idea of his general outlines, of his undeveloped, adolescent (pre-adolescent, I would say) body, with its thin shoulders, thin neck and thin arms. And you can see, very easily, the way his gray jacket falls over his shoulders and reaches way down to his knees.

I look at him like this, and the same doubt creeps into my blood again. Was he seventeen as he claimed he was, or was he twelve as he looked; still looks? But he insisted he was seventeen, I remember. He had to show me his birth certificate to make me believe him. I remained unconvinced, though. I couldn't doubt that other something in me to that extent. It seemed more logical to doubt Wallace. And to look at him, no one else would believe him either. Everyone who saw him would ask him how old he was. When he said he was seventeen, they felt someone was lying. As they were not given to lying, it was obvious who was. Who would.

And yet it wasn't easy to doubt Wallace. He was the kid with the quick, "Yes ma'am, I'll go for coffee for you right away; yes ma'am, I'll bring you a package of cigarettes; yes ma'am, I'll run right out to the drug store and bring you an afternoon paper; yes ma'am, yes ma'am," open-arm response.

Just the same, as I'm looking at Wallace now, who is peeking in my bedroom window, I still doubt the irrefutable evidence of his birth certificate. It makes me want to swear again that he is no more than twelve. But I can't be sure. After all a birth certificate is something quite unalterable as far as I know.

Wallace is still standing in the window. His face looks a little different now than I remembered it. He looks very solemn now; not exactly solemn either; but rather quiet, ever so quiet. I wonder when the change took place, since after all, he is still a kid even if he is all of seventeen as he says he is. To tell the truth, there is no noticeable or obvious change in him outside of that somberness. His chin still looks round and child-like. His cheeks are still pretty much puffed out. But there is a change. There is a flatness to his face, not all over it which makes it even more odd, but in spots, particularly around the mouth, around the eyes, and in the middle of his forehead above his nose, where it wrinkles so deeply now.

That's about all. Otherwise he looks just about the same. And he certainly hasn't gotten taller.

What, he's ducked? He's gone. I can't see him at all now. I keep looking and looking at the window, thinking he's sure to come right back. But he hasn't. And I'm beginning to wonder; maybe he won't come back. Maybe he'll decide it's quite useless to do that, quite futile to look in at somebody's window, by day or by night? Maybe he'll let things go the way they are, and just walk straight ahead, straight down the road? Maybe that will be his next course?

Still I keep staring at the window the way you do, you know, when you start seeing somebody's face in windows and in other places. But there is no sign of Wallace. The moon is still wandering around as innocently as it did before, and the sky looks just as blue.

As it's really very pleasant outside, I keep looking out of the window. Finally I tell myself that Wallace will not come back. And suddenly I decide I want to find him. Really I do. I want to find him as one human being wants to find another. I want to run after him through all the awful streets, the raucous and thief-infested streets where I imagine Wallace is hanging out at the moment, and look for him there. I have something to tell him.

Well, supposing I do find him, as I may very well do? What is this thing that I want so much to tell him? I could tell him that I was personally sorry. Will that be enough? What earthly good will my personal regrets do him? Even if I do succeed in giving him this little pat on his shoulder; if it should be any help to him; could I do it without remembering my own share in this stark episode in his young life?

Hardly. I could not, for instance, tell him frankly to his face; to his, "Yes ma'am I'll run right out and get you a package of cigarettes," face, that I too used to hide my purse from him as soon as I learned that he had broken open the boss's desk and had stolen thirty-three dollars and forty-three cents from it. You just can't do that. But that's the way I acted, just as anyone would, I presume, once one learned that he was the little monster who could smile at you one minute and the next one, when your back was turned, break a lock and steal money.

Could I tell this twelve-year-old kid, I mean seventeen-year-old kid, how uneasy I was when he came back to work after he gave back the money and was released from jail? I couldn't even look him straight in the face. I didn't ask any special favors after that. I was very uneasy and uncomfortable after that, to tell the truth. So was the other girl, Adeline, who sold the underwear, the aprons, the housecoats, and what-not in this place. She would tell me to keep an eye on her purse, and I would tell her to keep an eye on mine. The two of us watched him until we almost bored a hole in his back.

When the boss finally fired him after a few weeks of this tense atmosphere, admitting that he also was uneasy about Wallace even though he didn't want him to go to reform school, the two of us, that is Adeline and myself, were ever so much relieved.

"Gee, I'm glad they let him go; it gave me goose pimples to be with him in the same place all day long," Adeline said.

I nodded. I agreed. And I imagined what else he could do with the same little knife of his he used to pry open the cash drawer in the boss's desk. I felt safe again too.

Then the week after he left, I discovered something that upset me again; that made me realize that I wasn't safe after all. The mere fact that Wallace was gone didn't change things. Wallace had spent about half of the day packing merchandise. Maybe he had time left to kill. He had used this time, it developed, when the new boy, who was very tall and energetic, stacked up a row of boxes all ready for packing, for something at that. Wallace had used the stolen time to draw pictures on the backs of the boxes.

Wallace used his time, when no one was looking, to draw all kinds of pictures, mostly of handsome young colored fellows with large, smiling eyes, and beautifully shaped heads; of tall gangly fellows, all well built, all well proportioned, all carrying canes all set to stroll down tree-shaded streets; of smiling dazzling young colored adolescents who seemed to be growing right before your eyes on the backs of the cardboard boxes; of gay fellows who were humming flirtatious songs with their red, sensuous lips and admiring all the girls they saw; of guys, in fact, who saw everything and got everything.

That was what Wallace did when no one was looking—drew pictures. That was what this little thief did when our backs were turned. Did this make a difference? Yes, to me. I wouldn't know about anyone else. I wasn't afraid of Wallace any more. I felt altogether differently toward him. I felt as if I wanted to do something for him that was beyond me. But then, of course, I didn't do anything.

There you are, at the window again, Wallace. You've come back for a second, I see. And you are smoking a cigarette now, the way you used to do all the time you worked in the store. You said, you remember when I told you you were too young to smoke so much, that you had been smoking for three years already. You are smoking hard again, I see.

Oh, you've ducked again. You have gone, for good now, I believe. You have vanished again. Maybe you've broken somebody's cash drawer again and are in reform school now at that? Or maybe you have been paroled and are working again someplace, sweeping the floors, packing packages, licking stamps? Or maybe you are walking around the streets with fellows much older, much taller than you are, much wiser in other things than you are? And then again, and then again, maybe you are drawing pictures again on some pieces of paper that float around in such abundance on the dirty streets on which you walk day and night?

Well, that's that. I'm walking away from the window. The moon is still there. But it's dark yet. There's still half a night left before it will get real light.

I'm going to sleep. I might as well. I don't think I care to finish this story. It is a blind-alley kind of thing after all; and I never should have started it. I think I'll tear it up.

A REAL DOLLAR BILL

It was exactly twelve o'clock when all this happened The sun was shining lavishly over the doorway of the burlesque show; over the life-size and gorgeous legs of the burlesque queen on the poster in front of the entrance of the theatre; over the lower half of the show window of the second-hand store on the right side of the amusement place; over the top of the iron fence of the cathedral across the street; and over the crack in the sidewalk next to the mailbox.

There it lay in front of the mailbox in which she had just dropped a letter. There it lay, crumpled and unrecognizable, half-folded up, and green against the grayness of the sidewalk. There it lay expecting her to pick it up immediately.

A heterogeneous crowd was passing by the pawn-shop-filled street. Young girls were looking into mirrors hanging invitingly in the store windows. Old women walked by heavily, their coats still buttoned, their hats askew, and their packages about to slip out from under their fat arms. Some young men were pressing their faces against the show window, admiring the display of cameras. And other people walked by, aimlessly, it seemed; not knowing where they were, or where they were going, to judge from the look on their faces.

Elma looked down at the crumpled object before her. She didn't feel herself doing it, but she knew she was; and she knew people were watching her.

She didn't want to be watched. But she was there in front of the dollar bill and she couldn't do anything else but look at it. All she could do at the moment was look. Her sense of sight had spread itself all over her.

She could see everything. She could see in front of her and above her; on the right side and on the left side.

She could see the north corner and the south corner; the east corner and the west corner.

She could see the line-up of men walking furtively into the burlesque house, the girls hanging their legs coquettishly over the stools in the beer joint next to the burlesque place.

She could see the color of the quiet October sky and the faded look of the red brick of the cathedral.

And she could see the dollar bill in front of her. She bent down to pick it up.

A hatless, brown-eyed man with a button-shaped nose and a depressingly receding hairline, called out to her, even as he was walking hurriedly past her: "Let's spend it together."

She heard him. And she heard herself answering the youngish looking man with the funny nose: "Sure, let's."

He gave her an enigmatic look and walked on. She could talk then as well as she could see, Elma thought, watching the man walk away without being able to do anything about it. She could talk, but she could see more.

She could see the hundreds of cars parked on the abandoned-looking side street facing the corner. She could see the hundreds of cars driving by slowly, impatiently, as they were hindered by the heavy traffic from picking up all the speed they could. And she could see herself at different ages: when she could reach her father's pockets; when she was small and thin and somewhat stooped and hollow-chested and sat and worked feverishly on an arithmetic test in the seventh grade. She could see herself trying to learn a dance step for the class operetta and not catching on readily—when she rang the bell of her girl-friend's house for her first sixteen-year-old party, when she hurried up to the fourth floor of the large city daily and offered some dark-visaged man a poem she had written in praise of a high-school athlete. She could see all the looks, the smiles, the grimaces and the sneers of her aunts, uncles, girl-friends and boy-friends, and others.

She picked up the dollar bill, and wanted to move on. But she remained on the same spot; her right foot still slightly bent and her left one stretched out a little, ready to run.

Elma slipped the dollar bill into her pocket, instead of into her purse. She wanted to start moving, but somehow her muscles were slow in picking up the right signals for this purpose.

"It's a dollar bill, a real dollar bill," Elma crowed to herself half apologetically and half involuntarily.

She wanted to examine the bill thoroughly for some reason. She pulled it out of her pocket and started turning it over. It had all the four "ones" on it; one in each corner. It had innumerable symbols, scrolls, markings; all kinds of embelishments she had never noticed before. But then she had not looked at a dollar bill before as she did now. Now each curlicue added to its value, to its intrinsic worth.

The sun was still shining on the big poster in front of the burlesque place; concentrating on it. The sky was still quietly blue, and the downtown crowd was still moving at the same steady pace towards the main street. She could start walking now, she was sure. She felt herself straightening out without being told by anyone to do it.

She had never felt so straight. She looked up. And she thought that someone in that quietly blue sky was waving to her; was telling her that she was "lucky."

Elma began walking. A fairly strong wind was now pulling at her skirt. It came on suddenly. But she didn't pay any attention to it. She only knew that the sun was warming her face, her hands, her hair; and that she was at the next corner in no time at all.

An acquaintance suddenly loomed before her. It seemed to Elma, who saw him instantly, that he had come there purposely to share this strange experience with her. She wanted to say hello to him. But she couldn't bring it out as collectedly as that. She giggled instead, and called out rather loudly: "I found a dollar bill." Then she looked closely at him to see if he had understood her substitute greeting.

"You don't say," the cynical fellow with the light blue eyes (small ones) and the thick black hair grinned at her, "You can buy me a drink."

The suggestion sounded good to Elma and she moved toward him as if she was all set to cross the street with him to the nearest drinking spot to comply with his request.

The well-built man with the small blue eyes and the thick black hair was a little taken aback at her stride. Quickly, he mumbled: "Not now. Got to go to a meeting."

"Tomorrow then," Elma said, not quite knowing what she meant by that. "Okay?"

"Okay," the tall, well-built man answered and hurried off.

Elma saw him merge with the crowd. She didn't mind the rebuff. She remembered his wide smile when she told him that she had found a dollar bill. She believed that he too was impressed with what had happened to her. That was all that mattered; that was all that counted, that for once, she, who had never won a great prize, never been head of anything, had at last been singled out.

Still feeling tall and straight and beautiful, she turned down the street, the one behind the big hotel. Half-way down, she recognized a girl friend called Kay coming in her direction. Elma had avoided Kay for some time now, having found little in common with her.

But now Kay seemed the one girl she wanted to talk to.

"Kay," Elma called out from some distance, "I just found a dollar bill."

"That's fine," Kay answered casually.

"Isn't it, though! Isn't it, though?" Elma gushed.

A café sign over the side door of the large hotel caught Elma's eye. Suddenly, she wanted to go in there, sit in the darkened booth, sip something cool, and talk and laugh. She proposed the idea to Kay. Kay said she was sorry, she couldn't make it just then, she had to go and find a hat, for a "special date" that very night.

"Let's make it for tomorrow then?" Elma pressed her point. It seemed necessary for her to do this if she wanted to hold Kay's friendship.

Kay answered that she was "busy" the next day also, and the luncheon date was left hanging in the air.

Elma nodded some sort of goodbye, and started walking down the street again. It didn't seem to put her out too much that Kay had not gone with her for the drink. She decided she didn't want to talk to Kay after all; she didn't want to sit in the darkened room either. She wanted to keep walking as she had so far, in the same swaying exultation. And she still wanted to tell herself that on this particular October day; at this odd moment; at this lunch hour; she had been touched by a magic wand in a sense. She still wanted to chant: "I found a dollar bill; what do you think of that?"

She walked on and before long saw the many windows, the large center door of the gray stone building in which she worked. She had reached the corner in record time, it seemed. And as she looked around more specifically now, she saw that the sun had disappeared behind some black clouds; and that a fairly strong wind had risen. The purse which she held under her arm seemed to make her feel uncomfortable. She changed it to her other one. And as she did this, she began noticing other changes taking place within her.

She no longer walked so straight, she thought. She was stooping a little. Again her hands didn't seem to know what to do with themselves. Again some of her hair fell over her eyes. And she seemed to hear herself saying in an awful voice, as if she were testifying against herself at a sensational murder trial, convicting herself, much to the surprise of a whole courtroom of people: "It's not so much to find a dollar bill, not very much really; certainly not enough to act like this."

"No, come to think of it," Elma told herself, as she entered the lobby of the building, "a dollar bill is not a Rockefeller fortune by a long shot; and finding it didn't make me Lady Luck's favorite daughter. It was okay, sure; but not important enough to put oneself into such a state of ecstacy."

Her talk became harsher and harsher and like a gust of rain: the words fell on her body and took away all the warmth it still had. She tried to argue with herself that it wasn't the money that had made her feel hilarious, that it was just the coincidence of finding a dollar bill in such a place.

Her protest had no chance of success against the larger array of solid facts. Something was wrong, she finally admitted to herself. She told herself that other people also are elated at finding a dollar bill. But, she pointed out grimly: "They don't carry on like this."

The elevator came at last. Elma got in with the other people who had been waiting in the lobby. From the corner into which she was hedged in, Elma listened to the small talk of the other passengers.

"They were the 'other' people," she told herself.

Yes, they were the other people, she thought, who certainly would laugh heartily about finding a dollar bill in broad daylight, in the middle of a busy street; who would be delighted with it, sure. But that would be about all they would think of it. They would not imagine that a great fortune had befallen them. No siree, not they.

They would take it in their stride, but not she. She never did.

There was more room now in the elevator as most of the passengers had gotten off. Elma put her hand in her coat pocket and felt the dollar bill. It was still the same dollar bill all right. She touched it lightly, as one would a newly made wound that could not stand much pressure; as one would a love letter that one still valued in vain; as one would a tear in a special party dress that one hoped to fix somehow.

"A penny for your thoughts," the friendly, synthetically red-haired elevator girl called out.

"Oh," Elma answered, " it's my floor, isn't it? Thanks, Jane," and got out.

Oh, quick comprehension; oh sunshiny vividness; oh bright knowledge; oh deep penetration; oh instinctive awareness; oh flying moment when all parts of the body do nothing but look, look, look.

Oh clean washed window through which, Elma thought, she could see right into all the houses on all the long streets of the thickly populated, sprawly city in which she lived.

Oh bitter knowledge; oh painful penetration; oh grim comprehension; oh savage clarity; oh long moment when all parts of the body—the head, the heart, the ears, the lips, do nothing but stay quiet.

Oh shaded window, through which nothing may be seen, not so much as a child's shadow in the house next door.

SIX POEMS

Richard Wilbur

FOLK-TUNE

When Bunyan swung his whopping axe
The forests strummed as one loud lute,
The timber crashed beside his foot
And sprung up stretching in his tracks.

He had an ox, but his was blue.
The flower in his buttonhole
Was brighter than a parasol.
He's gone. Tom Swift has vanished too,

Who worked at none but wit's expense,
Putting dirigibles together
Out in the yard, in the quiet weather,
Whistling behind Tom Sawyer's fence.

Now when the darkness in my street
Nibbles the last and crusty crumbs
Of sound, and all the city numbs
And goes to sleep upon its feet,

I listen hard to hear its dreams:
John Henry is our nightmare friend
Whose shoulders roll without an end,
Whose veins pump, pump and burst their seams,

Whose sledge is smashing at the rock
And makes the sickly city toss
And half awake in sighs of loss
Until the screaming of the clock.

John Henry's hammer and his will
Are here and ringing out our wrong;
I hear him driving all night long
To beat the leisured snarling drill.

A SIMPLIFICATION

Those great rough ranters, Branns
And catarrhal Colonels, who hurled
Terrible taunts at the vault, ripped down Jesus' banns
And widowed the world

With Inquisitorial thunder, dammed—
Up Biblical damnations, were
The last with tongues to topple heaven; they hammed
Jahweh away and here

We are. The decorous god
Simply withdrew. If you hear
A good round rhetoric anywhere give me the nod.
I'd like to hear

Bryan lying and quoting sic
Transit nux vomica. These foetal—
Voiced people lack eloquence to blow a sick
Maggot off a dead beetle.

FIRST SNOW IN ALSACE

The snow came down last night like moths
Burned on the moon; it fell till dawn,
Covered the town with simple cloths.

Absolute snow lies rumpled on
What shellbursts scattered and deranged,
Entangled railings, crevassed lawn.

As if it did not know they'd changed,
Snow smoothly clasps the roofs of homes
Fear-gutted, trustless and estranged.

The ration-stacks are milky domes;
Across the ammunition pile
The snow has climbed in sparkling combs.

You think: beyond the town a mile
Or two, this snowfall fills the eyes
Of soldiers dead a little while.

Persons and persons in disguise,
Walking the new air white and fine,
Trade glances quick with shared surprise.

At childrens' windows, heaped, benign,
As always, winter smiles the most,
And frost makes marvellous designs.

The night-guard coming from his post
Ten first-snows back in thought, walks slow
And warms him with a boyish boast:

He was the first to see the snow.

A DUTCH COURTYARD

What wholly blameless fun
To stand and look at pictures. Ah, they are
Immune to us. This courtyard may appear
To be consumed with sun,

Most mortally to burn,
Yet it is quite beyond the reach of eyes
Or thoughts, this place and moment oxidize;
This girl will never turn,

Cry what you dare, but smiles
Tirelessly toward the seated cavalier,
Who will not proffer you his pot of beer;
And your most lavish wiles

Can never turn this chair
To proper uses, nor your guile evict
These tenants. What surprising strict
Propriety! In despair,

462

Consumed with greedy ire,
Old Andrew Mellon glowered at this Dutch
Courtyard, until it bothered him so much
He bought the thing entire.

L'ETOILE

(*Degas*: 1876)
A rushing music, seizing on her dance,
Now lifts it from her, blind into the light;
And blind the dancer, tiptoe on the boards
Reaches a moment toward her dance's flight.

Even as she aspires in loudening shine
The music pales and sweetens, sinks away;
And past her arabesque in shadow show
The fixt feet of the maître de ballet.

So she will turn and walk through metal halls
To where some ancient woman will unmesh
Her small strict shape, and yawns will turn her face
Into a little wilderness of flesh.

THE WALGH-VOGEL

More pleasurable to look than feed upon,
Hence unconserved in dodo-runs, the round,
Unfeathered, melancholy, more than fifty pound
Dodo is gone,

Who when incarnate wore two token wings
And dined on rocks to mock at mockeries.
Empowered now by absence, blessed with tireless ease,
It soars and sings

Elated in our skies, wherever seen.
Absolute retractility allows
Its wings be wavy wide as heaven; silence endows
Its hoots serene

With airy spleenlessness all my unhear.
Alive the dodo strove for lack of point,
Extinct won superfluity, and can disjoint
To joy our fear.

Dive, dodo, on the earth you left forlorn,
Sit vastly on the branches of our trees,
And chant us grandly all improbabilities.

THE PETITION

Philip Siekewitz

OUR COUNTRY has many laws, but none is so rigidly obeyed as
that one pertaining to familial occupation. Because of this I became a tight-rope walker, like my father, like his father before
him, and like all my ancestors as far back as the state can trace
them. Oh, it is considered a very good occupation, as good as
any one I might have chosen had I the chance. You see, the chief
amusement to the people of my country is watching circuses,
particularly circuses with tight-rope walkers. That being so, the
heralding of a new tight-rope walker, as my birth surely was,
was somewhat of a great event, considered highly even in the
élite circles of the country.

I will not bother you about my early training. It was all very
hard work, but I enjoyed it, and in my youth even truly believed
that I had chosen this calling of my own free will, so happily was
I pursuing the teachings of my father. And too, so well was I
learning that I soon became the pride of my family, and since my
family was considered, by all the people, by the judges and teachers, by society itself, to be the very peer of entertainers, I had
late in my youth a wide and popular name as the up and coming
tight-rope walker. I was very proud and haughty in those days,
and treated people on the streets like animals, but since they
knew it was I, they merely shrugged their shoulders and let me
pass. In my country it matters not so much what you do to others,
to their persons, as what you do for the benefit of all. So the people let me pass on the streets without jibing back at me or striking me, for they knew that one day I would certainly entertain
them very well. It is all the result of the particular law of
familial occupation and not to be considered an inherently snobbish or degrading trait of the people. Since the law was thought
to be precisely set down, the people adhered to it greatly, and
since hardly anything could be done to challenge the validity of

465

the law, for how would you argue against such a universal law, the people consequently believed that nothing that one did was as of equal consequence as who it was that did it. This all resulted in a very rigid social structure, but from observation I had noticed, even in my youth, that most of my acquaintances were as happy in their occupations as I was in mine. Who then, even if he had a mind to, could doubt the truthfulness of the law which produced such happiness?

Thus, at my performances in the circus, the people forgot my rudeness and haughtiness as they enjoyed the exhibition of my familial occupation. In very quick time, due to my quick mind and fine sense of balance, of even better sense of entertainment, I became not only one of the best tight-rope walkers in the country, not only admired but even liked a little. And not only with my occupation was that so. It could be said, even if one was a scoundrel, a falsifier, if he were adept and respected in his profession, all else was forgiven. Even in the courts of law, I understand, this is adhered to, as the law of familial occupation sways the judges in favor of the defendant, or against him, as the case may be, and in many cases resulted in mercy or even acquittal. No one ever questioned this judicial practice, for, like the heavy rains or the tornadoes, or the numbing cold, all men were born equally under its influence, and one might as well question the injustice of the natural phenomena as question the inequality of this law.

Naturally, as a result of this law, there came into being many subsidiary laws, derived from this one; namely, three important ones, the hierarchy of position, the statement of payments, and finally, the possibility of going from one occupation to another. As for the first, those decisions were left much to the desires of the people, and rightly so, for hierarchy implies social order which in turn implies social conduct, and throughout the past ages of my country it has been gradually found that while laws could be set up governing social behavior, such laws must not come into conflict with preferences or beliefs or ideas. This being the case, the preference of the people for tight-rope walkers, for instance, made me quite a figure in the social whirl of our country, admired and respected by all. As for the second subsidiary law, that was something else, for who can argue with the fact that a tight-rope walker is not as necessary as a justice, for example, or as a minor state official, or even as a lowly engineer or a court clerk. While we entertained the people, we were not strictly necessary, while even a street-cleaner was necessary for the health of the nation, or the ringer of bells in the courts was necessary for the smooth functioning of the state. So while my father and I were fêted in many high places, my family lived in hovels on the outskirts of the town, and sometimes hardly had enough to eat, so that we all greatly looked forward to the affairs in our honor, and even sometimes brought back home with us enough food wrapped under our cloaks so that we looked like greatly-warted human frogs, to last us for the entire week. As for the third law, the possibility of going from one occupation to another, you can readily see that if that were allowed too freely the whole order of familial occupation would crumble. But however, in a few cases, the justices would decide that, say, a second degree baker could become a first degree baker, or a major official of the lowest category could be elevated to a minor official of a higher category. This third law was not really a law but merely a wish of the judges involved, but what swayed them to say yes in one case and no in another was a matter of much dispute, and for these cases lawyers were a necessity, for they were the only ones who had the training to decide about the wishes of the judges. Indeed these cases were the only ones which employed lawyers in the courts, the others being foregone conclusions, so to speak, so much so, that lawyers were not even trained to practice these other cases before the courts.

Despite the rigidity of these laws, there are always some who do not agree with them, would not agree to any law for that matter. So they would question the system of hierarchy, and be laughed at by the judges, for these involved the mysterious reasons of human nature, and the judges were not fools enough to try to change that. So they would question the law of payment and sometimes bring cases involving it before the judges. But the judges would also laugh at them, for how can you hope to maintain a social structure without differential payments for various functions, persons being not alike. And was it not the function of the law to maintain the state in equilibrium, not tipping it very far this way or the other way and some judges even said not tip it at all. These latter were the hard judges, shunned by all litigants, while those holding the former opinions were the soft judges, who now and then allowed the tipping of the state, but not too much, they would say, and to them the lawyers tried to have their clients steered. However, all the judges were as one and unbending in their interpretation of the law of familial occupation, for there the state could hardly be tipped at all without being upset altogether. And it is only very rarely that a case is brought before the court involving it, for the litigant must henceforth be assumed to be an outcast, for who would want to upset the state and still be a part of it. Needless to say, these cases were never won, but what made such cases be brought up was a matter of great conjecture. Statistics have been compiled to show which occupations bred the most such dissenters, as they were called, and which the least, and even the reasons advanced in court for such seemingly insane tactics. In this matter the tight-rope walkers have a very high regard in the eyes of the court, being the least of all in the number of such cases, hardly any in fact. But as one wit once remarked, it might well be because we are all killed before we think of bringing such cases before the courts. That might be so.

You might well ask if there were not, now and then, some grumblings about such hardness and solidification of the laws of our country. And here the judges would explain, in cases involving perhaps such a point, that this structure was not of the moment, but had been prepared gradually, many centuries ago, in the history of our country. And since the country was indeed great and prosperous, how could one say that its laws were not beneficial. If the people were happy one day, was that not the fruit of the law. If they were sad the next, was that not in their inherent nature as human beings, to be incapable of happiness every day and every night of their lives. The judges answered in many circumstances that the litigant should mend his own ways if he were dissatisfied, instead of coming to the courts for sympathy. For on the average, they would continue, and this was their telling point, the laws were bound to be suitable in most instances, among the majority of the people, and, it being absurdly impossible to please everyone all the time, the laws were, of their very mathematical nature, the best of all probable laws. In cross moods, one judge would cry out that it is bad enough trying to estimate the greatest probability of exactness of the laws without acting as nursemaids to many people. But nevertheless, there were grumblings now and then, but minor and few. Sometimes, to illustrate, I could see that some persons, only a few, would not applaud my performances at the circus, though the majority did so. And sometimes my father could be heard to grumble of our poverty of food and clothing and shelter, but only a few times, for he was happy at his work and that is what mostly mattered to him. A judge would say that, under the law, he was on the average happier than sad, and thus the law was just.

That my father was happy in what he was doing I was thankful for, for one day he tipped too far and fell to his death from a tight-rope, landing in the open pits before the spectators with a clack heard booming, hissing round and round the tented circus.

I was very sad that evening and cried a great deal, though my family told me it was what was to be expected, as his father had been killed the same way, as his father before him, and what better way to die, as die we all must, than in doing what we are best fitted and most happy to do. But logic cannot cure grief, nor reasons only explain misery, and as I cried, I grew angry and asked "Why should he have died, for such a one slip. We all make slips, and if a butcher makes a slip, or a transporter, is he killed? Even a judge is not beheaded for a misjudgment. Should my father be executed for one error, should he be different than others, is that the meaning of the law, of an equal nature for all of us? From this grief and these questions, I evolved the idea of a safety device, a net, underneath the tight-rope, so that if I, or my children, or all tight-rope walkers ages after, fell, we need not be killed by only one error. It was a very good device, but I was in fear of showing it at first, even to my family. When, from pride and anxiety, I did show it to them, they cried in horror, as I knew they would, telling me this was some devil's scheme, some outsider's device to wreck my profession and their livelihood. "Who would understand it," they shouted, "what purpose would it serve in benefitting the state? For true, it might benefit me in a short period, but societies are not short-lived," they said, "so destroy it, and be content that you are at least a tight-rope walker and not an outcast, without a profession, a beggar, a dog after the leavings of the people."

But the more they talked, the more convinced I became of my own righteousness, and one day, I resolved to take the case before the state, in response to the least of their arguments. I therefore went to the secretary of the recorder of familial occupations and told him of an improvement of my position. He was surprised, for such a request had never come before him in his lifetime, though he remembered his father telling him once about such a category of case as mine. Besides, whom could he go to, there was no official whose task it was to look into improvements and pass upon them. Such things were not even thought about, improvements coming from the judicial bench, not from whims and fancies of the people. But as it was his duty to refer requests to one official or another, he had to do something, it being against the rules of his office to dispose of any case himself. He told me to wait a few days and the matter would be called to the attention of the proper official. I frettingly went home and waited. The days telescoped themselves into weeks, and months, but one day, after my family had forgotten about it, after even I had almost forgotten about it, I was summoned to the district official in charge of inconveniencies. I really should not have been surprised, for knowing the state as I did, I should have known I would be called, but in due time. It is an excellent system, everything being worked out, but sometimes procedures take a little while.

This higher official, surprisingly enough, knew nothing of what I wanted, and more strange, did not want to know. He merely asked me to make a statement, in writing, of any inconveniences I had encountered, without, however (on this point he was adamant), mentioning what I had in mind to do about it. He would pass it on to the proper channels relating to my profession. This I did, but however, dropping the hint, now and then, of a net. Again I went home and listened to the questions of my family. They were proud of themselves in heading me off in this way, hoping that I would get tired of the whole matter and drop it before long. They argued with me, saying if it takes so long, months not weeks, merely to ask for a telling of my idea, how long would it take, years not months, before a final decision would be made. "Discontinue it," they said, "before you too forget about the whole matter and are discouraged by false hopes too much." They talked so long and with so much knowledge that I finally gave in, and went to the district official to tell him not to press the matter any farther than he had already and to give me back my statement. He was greatly surprised and asked me if I did not know enough about the state to know that once a matter is brought forth by any person it no longer belongs to that person exclusively, but in part also to the state, and now in my case it was almost entirely out of my hands. However I remonstrated so much with him, that he finally condescended to let me make another statement refuting in whole the first and asking for both statements to be returned to me. Perhaps, as he put it, the one can catch up with the other, and if the latter outweighs the former in the eyes of that particular official, I would get both back. On my leaving he chastised me loudly for bothering the state over my personal matters when I did not know of their exact nature myself. Who was I, he went on, that I should bother such busy officials with such minor matters.

During this time I was at the height of my career. With my father dead, I alone could and did hold up my family's name, and if I may say so, I was considered a better performer than my father, even adding little tricks with which to amuse the spectators at the circus. I was admired by the people, given great rounds of applause many times, and invited to holiday fêtes many times, for which my family was thankful, they having enough to eat most of the time as a result. During one of these parties, a man whom I did not know told me he had heard that I had a petition about an inconvenience before the state. This reference to something I had forgotten from someone I did not know shocked me very much. Before I could question this man he disappeared and even though all night long and many parties afterwards I tried to find him, I could not. He might have been a messenger from the judges, for shortly after, in a few weeks, about one year after my father's death, I was summoned to the major official in charge of inconveniences. My family and myself were very eager to know whether one statement had caught up with the other, and this for the most part interested me more than the ruling upon the original petition, for I had begun to lose interest in my plea for a net, so confident was I in my ability as a performer upon the tight-rope.

This official informed me that the matter had been taken up by his board and that they found my inconveniences based upon some sound principles, though in general the logic was false, but for the sake of these few sound principles he would refer it to those judges who determine whether such inconveniences are valid or not according whether it will benefit the people as a whole as well as myself if they were eliminated. When I told him of my other statement which requested this one back, he said he had not heard of it, and since I cannot submit any requests to him, but all requests must come from officials subordinate to him, he had naught else to do but to pass on his approval of my petition. Again I told him I would like the whole matter dropped and to this he answered, very angrily, how dare I presume to waste the time of busy men by denying the relevancy of my petition. At least, he went on, be good enough to acknowledge the correct few principles I did propose, and furthermore, how could I question the decision of men like him who were trained to look into such matters, and knew more than I about the correctness of what I had said in my petition. As I left he called after me, as from a mountain, that it was entirely out of my hands now and belonged exclusively to the officials concerned, and I should not bother them with untimely and insulting requests.

After these interviews my family and I hoped that the case would be dropped by the judges themselves or else denied entirely, for then at least I would know where I stood. It might be thought by outsiders to the country that such requests on my part from the law were of no consequence, but that is not so. Persons who petition the courts are looked upon by the other people as aliens for even questioning the law, and even if the courts decide the case in their favor, the very thought of some people questioning the validity of the laws was enough to make such persons seem dangerous to the orderliness of the state. For if one person could argue a case well and win it, by discovering some little-known significant phrase in the law, others could do the same, and since the judges were impartial in their interpretation of the law, absolutely just and righteous, and were well understood to be governed by what was inherent in the law, there could be no telling where such stretchings of the law would lead to. True, the state should not suffer by any such decision favorable to the litigant, but since the whole body of the law was not known to the common people, many said not even to the judges, how could one tell how far the state had been tipped already. A little discovery of a new meaning could tip it too far, toppling it over, and how would the people fare then, ignorant, in the dark, not knowing by which laws they were governed and accordingly how best to conduct themselves. Based on such fears by the people, my family kept my secret, for its discovery might easily ruin my reputation as a performer and their livelihood. Such thoughts even kept me from marriage a little while, but after one year had gone by and nothing more was heard, I did get married, hoping that at least the case had been dropped or at worst the paper was misplaced, though I knew that that hardly ever, if ever, happened.

Nor did either of these possibilities happen. Quite a while after my marriage, at the height of my career, I was summoned one day to the chambers of the secretary of the presiding judge who was then in charge of interpreting the laws. The judges, I later learned, rotated positions upon the benches, from one court to another, so that they could not be too set in their judgments upon one phase of the law, and also so that they could learn more about other sides of the law, though never did I hear of any one judge who did live long enough to rotate through all the courts and thus know all about the law. However, by this system, the difficulty of having such a large body of laws was handled very well, and very few litigants indeed questioned the capability of any one judge attending their case. This secretary told me that I had the choice of picking the day for my court hearing. also the time and the place. Since I did not know the judge then and there presiding, nor did he know me, this action was deemed by all students of the law as another indication of the utmost fairness of our judicial procedure. He told me he would make the necessary arrangements after I had done this.

When I told my wife of this, she immediately began to speculate on when and where. What time is the best? In the morning, when the judge is perhaps still tired after a gruelling night before, though I could not be sure what he had done the night before? Or perhaps it would be better if he were fresh after a good night's rest? In the afternoon, when he would see clearly the aspects of my case in the light of a bright sun, or in the evening, when a calm and reasoned, though perhaps tired, judgment, would prevail? And of the place? In his chamber, where he would have the advantage over me, there under the protection of centuries of legal codes decided upon and obeyed? Or in my house, where naturally I would have the advantage, but then would not the judge think it presumptuous of me to issue him there, and even think that the petition was written carelessly, so to speak, and not worthy of the legality of the court building? Or yet again in some neutral chamber, where I should call the judge and immediately put him on the defensive towards me, but yet too I would have to bear to that place and would be somewhat at a disadvantage but yet equally so as the judge?

My family, my mother and sisters and my wife argued the whole week back and forth, thinking up fine points of which I never thought and, I suppose, the judge never thought. But yet it seemed of such momentous consequence, these pickings of time and place. If they were not so, why should they be in the legal procedure of the state? Indeed the secretary had told me that often cases were decided in the judges' minds by just these selections, either for or against the plaintiff. Finally, we, or rather my wife, decided on high noon, under the glaring sun, at the home of a cousin of mine who was a shoemaker, and who had a much finer house therefore, and who was delighted to have the honor of a judge being at his house, though only for business to be sure. This information I transmitted to the secretary, and was told I would hear from him about the disposition of the judge, and thus settle the whole affair definitely.

In one week I was summoned again, though why I did not know, it all seemed settled. But in affairs of law one must be exact in all procedures so there should be no recourse later, after a decision has been rendered, to any excuses as to the incorrectness of these procedures. According to the secretary it seemed that my petition was considered very important to the judge who had been rotated to this particular bench, and in such cases, it was of a necessity that all the superior judges of the country would have to sit and judge. And since it was absolutely im-

possible for me, an outsider, to know of the convenient times of
these very busy men, they themselves would set the date and
place of the hearing. My family, upon hearing this, cried a little,
remembering all the work and thought that had been done, but
were glad that it would be more correct, and in my favor perhaps,
that the petition would so be handled.

In a few weeks, I was told, by the secretary coming in person
to our humble house, which in itself was very unusual and somewhat of an honor, the time and place of the hearing. My family
and I were very much relieved, for after years of waiting it would
be decided yes or no whether I could so save my life by having a
net under the tight-rope. My wife remarked how I seemed to
have forgotten the purpose of the whole suit and in that she was
nearly right. The net lay dusty and corroded in the shed back
of our house, and should I be able to use it, I would have to
make a new one, this one being so full of large holes it could
hardly be called a net at all. We were all excited the day I left.
My family gave me a bag full of pork for sustenance for my
ordeal. My wife gave me advice, warnings and urgings. Full of
hope and their appeals to reason and to the fates, I left my home
for the courthouse where the hearing was to be held.

I was to see the secretary first to be ushered in, but his office
had been moved, no one knew when or where, probably in the
building somewhere, they told me, and before I could locate him
in another smaller office stuck in the basement of the building, I
was already one-half hour late. He was very angry and accepted
no excuses but showed me to the judges' chamber, into which I
was led. This room was very small, with a lowered section in
front, where stood a hard rough table and many hard rough
stools. In front of these, higher up, overlooking it, were placed
large, cushioned chairs, only a few, but they crowded the room.
Above was a low ceiling, so that when we came in from the dark
hallway into this bright, windowed room, we must stoop, so as to
not knock our heads against the beams of the ceiling. The secretary knew of this, of course, and did stoop, but I did not, and
received a jolt on the forehead that stunned me for a moment, so
that the secretary had to hold me up, saying at the same time, as
if in consolation, that so many litigants do this. Since the floor
sloped down to where the hard benches stood, which evidently
were the seats of the judges, they themselves had no such difficulty when they came in through the door in front. The room
was also empty, and when I remarked about this to the secretary,
he informed me that since the judges set the time, they have
every right to be late, and since they had to come from distant

cases to this one, and I only from my house here, there was no reason I should be late, but every reason they should be. "Indeed," he said, "sometimes they were even a day or two late, but that was to be expected under the trying circumstances."

I waited a good half-day, during which time I was alone in the room, the secretary having left me to attend to his other business. I began to nervously eat all the food my family left me, not enjoying it at all. I rubbed the bump on my forehead, slouched in the cushioned chair until I was tired of that, walked to and from each of the walls in the room, thinking, thinking all the time. Towards evening, I noticed the front door slowly open and the judges walk in, their backs towards me, and sit down, still with their backs towards me. In an instant, I recognized the utmost fairness of th's procedure. They could not see me, in my slovenly attire, my hands greasy with lard, and the leavings all about me in disorder, and thus prejudge me, with resultant unfairness towards my petition. Also I was unable to recognize them, and so not do them any harm if the decision was against me. I remember I had heard once that, long ago in the history of our country, many of the judges, being old men, were assaulted and sometimes killed by angry litigants, and this turning of the backs was a result.

They seemed to me to be all small men, some even bent and disfigured, some having beards which waved back and forth as they turned their heads and talked to each other. They had no papers with them that I could see, but some had knives and pieces of wood upon which they whittled after a while, others had stringed balls which they swung back and forth sometimes, and still others merely sat with their hands upon their chins or foreheads, and nodded their heads every so often. Out of curiosity I began to count them, but the stools were so arranged, some were in front of others, some were higher or lower, the whole arrangement was askew, so that I got a different number for each count. One would have to be a sage to even count the judges, much less guess their wish.

"Do you have a lawyer with you?" one of them asked, I could not tell which one, for the room was getting darker with the disappearing sun, and the sound so vibrated back and forth between the warm walls that it was even difficult to tell it came from within the room.

"No," I replied, and could give no reason, for I had never thought about my case as being one to redress a wrong, as I thought lawyers were for, but merely to further expand a right, for which purpose only the arguments in the petition were necessary.

At my answer I could see them huddling together and whispering among themselves. Had I said the wrong thing? While on the one hand I should have had a lawyer to instruct me in the ways of the court, I could see that now, on the other hand, the fact of my not having one must show that I believed in the correctness of my arguments, so much so that a lawyer was unnecessary to explain them, and to invent excuses for their mere presence.

One of the judges began to speak, interrupting my thoughts, "The lower magistrates have gone over your petition many times, and though the arguments in it are entirely false, and the logic is in error, there is a phrase here and there which admits perhaps of some decision, and since it effects, as you are well aware, the basic laws of the country; namely the laws of familial occupation, of payments, of hierarchy, of change," (here he recited some one hundred-odd laws, of which I was unaware, but surprised and somewhat elated that I had touched upon all of them in my petition) "we therefore have decided, only through the goodness of the judge for this rotation, to have a hearing upon your petition."

By this time the room had grown quite dark, and all I could see was a vague outline of the judges and their bench and stools.

"First of all we deny your petition in the full, but certain parts are to be remarked upon. We can see your point of view, but unfortunately for you, that is not all we can see. Your family is well-known to us, we have seen them many times in the circus. We were there at your father's death, and since the petition was presented shortly after, we perceive that was the underlying cause of it. On that count alone it is unworthy to be admitted as a document of state, its selfish outlook and individual character should not be dealt with in these courts."

Though I was chagrined and angry, I knew my saying anything would make it worse, and besides, I was suddenly becoming very sleepy, because of, or not, my full meal, or the bump on my forehead, or the gradual warming up and darkening of the room. Under these conditions I still had enough sense to know I could not be sure what I was saying, so I said nothing.

"Under the law of familial occupation you are a tight-rope walker, and the question is, whether the occupation of yours is a tight-rope walker with a net or without a net. This involves an interpretation of the true meaning of the law. The law clearly does not mention a net, and does not recognize either with or without specifically, but since it does not mention a net, we presume it means tight-rope walker without a net. That is the second point upon which we have based our decision. Thirdly, however, since you were born a plain tight-rope walker, you yourself have presumed to add something to your occupation which was not there before, thus asking us to sanction a change in an occupation, and this comes under a different heading. Since you add something, namely a net, and not subtract, that, we may add, is in your favor. But since you also subtract from the possibilities of your death, as you so state in your petition, this factor balances the former, and thus on the whole, still leaves us as judging against your petition. However, again, since we have never seen your net, we do not know whether it is efficacious or not, and we presume you do not know that either, never having tried it, so we have decided on this point that the net is therefore hypothetical in its advantage, however real an object it may be."

By this time I was dozing off now and then, and could only catch a word here and there, as when the voice of the judge would suddenly rise, or when the other judges would add a loud "yes" or "no," and once, in the midst of dozing off, my head was thrown back by the sharp sound of the bounce of a ball, as if the judge could see me in the dark, not paying attention, and warning me.

"At this point, we were about to throw the case out as having no consequence, involving an illusion, a net the efficiency of which we have no proof. But again, it must have some consequence, or we would not have considered it for so long. Its consequences rest therefore in this matter, whether or not an effort, mind you an effort, can be made to add refinement to an occupation without being unfair to other occupations in which no effort has been made by those persons engaged in those occupations. In other words, whether it is fair for you, as a tight-rope walker, to petition us to allow you to change your work so as to lengthen your life, and presumably make it happier, without our being able to change other people's lives, without their having made the effort to do so. This might have been the question if the net could be demonstrated to work, and had it been so, our decision would be "no," you cannot ask for an advantage to yourself without thus lowering, in a relative way, the position of all other occupations to which people were born. But since we do not know if the net works, the petition has some acknowledgement in our minds in that the possibility of its working ought to be set against the possibility of your slipping and killing yourself early in life, of fulfilling your life at an early date or at a later date, as chance may have it."

I was sleeping by this time, yet hearing the words, so that they seemed to float above me, and enter slowly, one at a time, through my ears, one into my right ear, another into my left, swinging about my head from ear to ear, touching my nose so it tickled and I sneezed, dropping upon my eyelids and they tickled and they opened, revealing the words become objects, altogether like little robed, bearded elfins, poking whittled sticks at me and bouncing stringed balls on me.

"Therefore, if we balance the one possibility against the other, the probability of your elevating your birth occupation above that of other occupations should be the same as before the petition was considered. Therefore, after much arguing and thinking, oh, it has not been easy, our wives having scolded us for not eating on time with them, for not sleeping on time with them, for not paying due care to our babies, for innumerable other minor, though necessary, household duties, after so many tribulations that are given to us as fathers, we have decided to let the mathematical probability work out. Since we do not know when you will fall or not fall, we will give you the use of the net, whether it works or not none of us know, but you will not know when this net will be there. In some performances, during some time, it will be there, and at others it will not, the being there and the not being there being equal. We have entrusted the secret of its timing to one of the court officials attending the circuses. In this way, no one can say you have been exceeding the boundaries of your occupation, and yet say that we have not judged fairly in dealing with only a question of possibility, not actuality, as would have been the case had the net been shown to work."

I do not know when I become fast asleep, but I awoke the next morning in the big chair in the empty room. As I walked home, I tried to remember the phrases and the sentences of the judgment, particularly towards the last, but all they seemed to do was to float up to me and then flee away. All I could remember was a cough here, and a slithering sound of wood being chopped there, or a ball bouncing, or a clapping of hands. Try as I would, I could not tell my wife and family what the decision was, so that they thought I was a fool, a weak stupid dolt, to have fallen asleep at my trial. What could I answer, I could not even tell myself how it was I fell asleep as even try to tell them. My wife scolded me and urged me to go to the secretary and find out. "No use wasting so many years and not know the result of them," she said. She prodded me so much that I went. I was ashamed to admit the fact to the secretary, and dodged from one question to another, saying I was not sure of this fine point or that fine point, but he seemed to understand, for he told me, interrupting me, that many litigants, in fact, nearly all litigants, fall asleep in the court and have to be told their decisions. In fact, I was the first to so come back to him, though his father had told him of one such occurrence in his lifetime. But most are too ashamed of themselves to appear before the secretary to ask about it, and so they never appear and seemingly forget about the whole case. It seems that the judges have thought about this often, and they believe that the reason for all this falling asleep is that the people are so nervous, in such a distraught state, so afraid of the judges that keeping awake is too much for them, so they fall asleep and dream of having looked the judges in the back, so to speak, all the time. The secretary is the only one who can tell them the decisions, "which really is a pity," he said, "for it is all a simple matter," and he produced the papers from his desk and gave me the particulars of only the final decision to read there, for I could not take the papers out, all records now belonging to the state, but since I was an interested party I could see them at any time. This was very fair of the officials, I thought.

When I went back to my house and told my wife of the judges' decision, she was taken aback by the matter much more so than I was, much more so than I thought she would be. "What kind of judgment is that; it is neither here nor there?" she asked. She berated me, "What foolish arguments you must have put forth." She admonished me, "You were better off before, at least you knew what fate you had. Now what does a slip from the rope mean? Anxious waiting during the fall, fearing it would be your last, but not knowing. What a fate!"

She was right. At first the decision had seemed to me to be a victory, but upon longer contemplation I began to glimpse the life ahead of me. How could I know what day, what fall, would be my last? At least before, I knew, the moment I fell that that would be the end of me, but now, but now, how many times would that be repeated, what was the probability. Probability was a word the judges used, I could remember that much, but of the sentences, the particular phrases, the whole logic I tried and tried to recall and could not. Oh, I could reconstruct the logic that I thought they used in my case, that was easy enough to do, but how did I know if the judges reasoned and thought as I did. Of course, we all knew the laws of the land somewhat, but they must have known them better than I or they would not be judges. I cursed myself for falling asleep, as if it would have made any difference had I been awake. I felt I would have to accept the decision as just without knowing precisely why, and gradually, the only thing I thought about, wanted most eagerly to learn, was whether my interpretation of the law was right in the eyes of the judges, whether my logic was their logic. That was the difference had I been awake. But then, the secretary had informed me that nearly all, if not all, the litigants before the judges fell asleep, and most did not even know what their decision was, so wondered all their lives not only why it was but what it was in the first place. What a fearful life.

The very next day, when I appeared at the circus for rehearsal, the carpenters were already making a net and putting it up. Where they received the instructions I knew, but where the specifications of the net I could only guess. I might have talked in my sleep before the judges about the specifications, for in no other way could I so account for it. That evening, the carpenters, working hard, had finished the net and had stretched it on the ground between the guy wires. It seems the arrangement was, that at given moments, the net would be raised along the poles, above the ground, and thus, catching me should I fall at that moment, break my fall and bounce me back into life again. And at other times the net would not be raised, and should I fall then, my fate would be as my father's, and as his father's had been. The times were of course secret, known only to the judges and to whomsoever would raise and lower the net. That evening, as I went out to the circus rings, I even thought that one of the judges would take it upon himself to raise and lower the net, so important a bearing had it in my case, they would not having dared trust anyone else. Coming out to the ring, I saw a child, scarcely a youth, standing by one of the poles. He was the only one there, so he must be the one regulating the net, but such a frail creature in so important a position! During the next few nights, he was the only one around the pole, so more and more I thought it probable that he was the regulator of my death, but then I could never be sure, for I would never look down from the rope, for fear of losing my balance, to see when the net was off the ground or on the ground and who did the pulling. Oh, it was probably he, but such an unworldly fellow for such a significant task. Sometimes, when I was on the middle of the rope, and thinking "Is the net up or down? Suppose I slip now, at this time?" it would even seem to me, in that fretful condition, that the youth could be one of the judges themselves. For after all, I had not seen their faces, and could only guess what they looked like. Some had beards, others had not, and these latter could be mere youths, whose fathers had died, leaving them to be judges in their place. Of course they all knew the law equally well, that being the nature of the judges.

During the first few weeks of the net-period, as I called it, I often wondered what the people seeing the circus thought about the net. I could never tell, for I could never get up enough courage to ask them, hence they never told me. After a few years I no longer wondered about this question, but often asked myself when is my slip coming. I was getting old, old for a tight-rope walker, that is, and during these days I often thought about the fall, the possibility of the net being raised. At this time I had my first child, a son, whom I would soon begin to teach my profession. Not knowing which day would be my last, for at my age the mortality of tight-rope walkers is very high. I began to teach my little boy right in his crib to balance himself and the other fundamentals of tight-rope walking. I also began to invent procedures to follow and things to say, hoping somehow that by so doing and so saying I would insure the net being raised. Mere superstition, I know, but I would still enter the ring, for example, and walk around always the same way, and say, "Good evening," to the youth, now already a young man, responsible for the net. I do not see now how that could have been effective, but in those days I wanted so to live that I thought any signs I might make would greatly help.

I would even try to guess the time of the net raising, oh, by logical reasoning, as a working out of a formula between the date and the time of the net raising, or the days after my court decision and the time of net raising. I invented arithmetic and geometric progressions, and even used exponential curves to try to arrive at some formula. After all, the judges must have given some formula to the young man handling the net. It surely was not at his own discretion that he raised and lowered the net. That absolutely must not be the case, they being the law, not he. There must be some mathematical law which expressed it all. Only in that way, I thought, would it be fair to me.

My wife even nagged me, day after day, to try to get the secret of the net from the young man pulling it up and down. At first I revolted at the idea. "Such cheating, think of the punishment that would follow," I told her. "The punishment would come only if you were discovered," she said, and tearfully begging, "perhaps the youth can be bribed to pull the net up when he sees you falling. Then we could all live happily for a long time." Several times she so implored me that I resolved to approach the youth on this question, but at the last moment my

481

courage would fail me. I was ashamed of myself that I lacked
the courage, perhaps more so that I even entertained such an
idea. Those nights I would be afraid to come home to my wife
and admit my cowardice; that she could understand, but my
shame, never. Sometimes I would sleep in the circus tent so as
to escape her wrath. Sometimes, on my tight-rope, it seemed to
me that my fate swayed from my wife on one side to the youth
of the net on the other.

All this worrying about my fall, this nervousness, had its
result inevitably, for one night, a few months later, before a
distinguished and intelligent audience, I slipped from the tight-
rope and began to fall through space towards the earth below.
You can imagine my condition of mind. I began to hurriedly
review formulae, in a twinkling of an eye, and see if any favored
me, so to speak. I began to repeat favored phrases, hoping in
some way that they may affect the man working the net below.
Later on, on recounting, I even thought I had shouted bribes to
the man below, but of that I am hazy. As I tumbled around and
around falling, the walls and the roof of the tents turned my
eyes, and my mind began to see judges' chambers, transformed
the spectators into judges, and here I was getting dizzier and
dizzier and falling asleep and not knowing what they said about
me nor why, and trying to grasp a word here, with outstretched
arms, clawing fingers, as I fell through space, reaching for support, and finally landing upon the raised net, bouncing me up
and down, up and down, so that the people swam in the tented
sea, and I breathed easier, and swimming gaily in the net, tried
to remember what formula it was I evoked that was responsible
for this saving of my life. As I stepped off the net, I thought,
should I thank the man, he might have raised the net from the
goodness of his heart. But remembering the efficiency of the
state, I thought, who is he that the judges knew he would never
do that, but work only by formula. Surely he must be one of
them. This I am almost convinced of.

It was only after a few minutes that I realized that the
applause which usually greets me was absent this time. They
were probably shocked by my fall, I thought, or perhaps chagrined that I should fall and therefore not applaud a failure. At
least they should do something, but here they sat, immobile and
unsmiling, or unblinking as far as I could see. After a few minutes of uneasy waiting, as I was leaving the rings of the circus,
one among them stood up and addressed me, "Who are you to
have put up a net?"

What right had he to speak about my affairs?

"Who are you to take it upon yourself to do this, without asking us?"

And why should I ask them, it was my life?

"Are we not a part of the circus, as well as you! Do we not applaud at your successes, as well as weep at your misfortunes?"

True, true, I had to admit. But who is this man that he presumes to judge me? As if in answer, another one arose from the crowd and began to speak, looking like the first, and from my distance, as far as I could tell, having a faint resemblance to my father. But all this is nonesense.

"Do we not decide what you are and who you are? If we took a dislike to tight-rope walkers, would you be here?"

True, true, but what has that got to do with trying to lengthen my life, for your benefit also, as well as mine, so that I may live longer to entertain you more.

And as if in answer, he spoke, "Can not our voices be heard to decide whether you should live longer or not so that you could entertain us more or not?"

But it was all done to benefit you. It was with you in mind that I went before the judges, that I asked for a change, that I conceived the net, to bounce me back into life again, to entertain you more. It was for better happiness for all of us, so that we can have a little more freedom from our own cares, and enjoy our circuses the longer.

And again, as if in answer, "We blame you and castigate you for presuming to speak for us before the judges. Perhaps we might have agreed to your idea of a net, but now we must all abide by your rules, whether we like it or not. Have we not the right to be angry with you to have forced us to watch you use the net?"

I had never thought about it that way, but I could see his point of view.

And yet a third one got up, from the other side of the tent, and demanded of me. "What right have you to have tried to change laws which govern us all? What right have you to have put yourself before us, so that now we must live by your rules alone? Do you also presume to know the true meaning of the law?"

I bowed my head, not in shame, but more in fear of what they were saying. As I walked out the circus, I turned a few times to look at the silence of the crowd. And each time I so did, they would all rise at once, as if they were puppets, and shout after me, with hatred, "This is what he has given us, we who have honored him!" And with scorn, "Tight-rope walker who wants to be a judge!" And with fear, "Who knows but perhaps you are only the first who wants to be a judge but was not born one!" And in shame, "What right have we to change it, this state which we did not make?"

My wife cried over the matter the whole night, alternately fearful for me of what was to become of me, and hateful of me over what was to become of her. The next day I went to see the circus manager. He told me that, obviously since the people would not pay to come to the circus were I to perform and use the net, he could not hire me. Of course, I had to have the net, that was in the law now, and for either he, had he wanted to, or I to try to change that law would require more years than were left in our lives, if it could be done at all. "But how could I live, have a livelihood, feed my family, be again a member of the community at least?" He was very sympathetic to me, but all he could offer was that, since he could not prevent my doing my familial occupation, he couldn't pay me, but he could have me as a performing guest in the circus, and perhaps a person or two would throw me money if they so desired. "Was I to depend on that, not knowing where I stood from one day to the next, living only with the wishes of the people?" He shrugged, "We are all under the law, at least you can be sure of that."

There is another alternative and one I often think about these days. There are other countries in the world, of which I know nothing, but surely I could do something there, a fresh start at even being a tight-rope walker again, or perhaps some other profession, a carpenter, or even, I thought sarcastically, a judge. But if I did this, I would of a certainty be an outcast from my own country and people, alone in a strange and fearful land, unknown to the rulers of the land, and not knowing even the laws under which I would live. It is a hard decision to make.

Sometimes, I wail to myself, in anguish, "If I only were like an animal again, not to be faced with such an alternative as this."

ARGONAUTICA

George Seferis

And for the soul,
if it is to know itself
it is into the soul ᜑ
that it must look.

The stranger and the enemy, we have seen him in the mirror.
They were good lads, the comrades who did not grumble
because of weariness or because of thirst or because of the
      freezing.
They had the manner of trees and the manner of waves
that accept the wind and the rain,
accept the night and the sun,
and in the midst of change they do not change.
They used to sweat at the oar with downcast eyes,
breathing rhythmically together,
and their blood flushed up to a subordinate skin.
There were times when they sang, again with downcast eyes,
when we passed the desert island with the Arabian figs,
towards the setting of the sun, beyond the cape of dogs
that howled at us.
If it is to know itself, they used to say,
it is into the soul it must look, they used to say.
And the oars beat on the golden path of the sea
in the middle of sunset.
Many the capes we passed, many the islands, the sea
which leads to the other sea, sea-gulls and seals.
There were times when unfortunate women with lamentations
cried out for their children gone,
and others with desperate faces looked for great Alexander
and glory buried in the depth of Asia.
Our anchorages were shores steeped in the perfume of night,

among the singing of birds, waters that left on the hands
the recollection of a great good fortune.
But there was never an end to the journeys.
Their souls became one with the oars and the rowlocks,
with the severity of the figure head at the prow
with the curling wake of the rudder,
with the water that flecked their faces.
One after another the comrades died
with their downcast eyes. Their oars
indicate the place where they sleep on the shore.
There is none to remember them, and the word is Justice.

Translated by Rex Warner

THE DECOY

Robert Payne

FOR SOME time the man over the machine-gun had been asleep.
It was late in the evening, an hour or so after sunset, and there
was no light except the dim stars. Over the Finnish lakes the
moon would rise later, throwing down a hard white road over the
reeds—a road so white that the man over the machine-gun would
be forced to open his eyes.

He was dreaming now, though occasionally in his dreams he
was conscious of the larch forest and the broad lake. One arm
was thrown forward over the cold barrel of the gun, the other
hung uselessly at his side. As he slept, the hollows under his eyes
grew darker, and the stars grew brighter; he dreamed of the
Himalayas.

The moonlight rose over the larches and pines, and blinded
him with its intense unremitting light, a full moon so blinding
that there seemed to be no shadows at all.

"The moonlight," he moaned, shading his hands with his eyes,
and at that moment his pale face had the look of a man caught in
the search-lights. His face was covered with a soft down, innocent and tender like the face of a lover. He was twenty-three,
and he possessed the look of a man who is accustomed to doing
his simple duty. He was wakeful now, living on that borderland
where sleep is an enemy to be destroyed, and there were no
weapons except human patience and persistence. "Sleep," he
said. No one had seen him sleeping. The patrol had passed some
hours ago and was not likely to return before dawn.

He waited, gazing steadily at the lake, wondering at the
glitter of wildfowl among the reeds, and the whiteness of the full
moon. There came a time, long before midnight, when his eyelids seemed to stick together with glue, and he would have fallen
asleep again but for the presence of night-birds flying up under
his feet. It was as though the white earth was carpeted with

487

black birds, which flew in dead silence across the stretch of pines, wheeling above him like leaves in a whirling wind. At first he paid no attention to the birds. The faint rustle of their black feathers passed unheard, and he did not hear the croak of the ravens as they flew out over the lake, and he did not even look up to trace the dark pattern they cut in the canopy of the stars. They frightened him, the weaving curves of their mad flight spun into his brain: but the dream had left him heavy and morose, and he was more frightened by the larches and the pines.

In the moonlight mirages appeared—hedgerows neatly laid out, gardens with running streams, an old cemetery surrounded with graceful wax-like branches of elms. The burning moonlight fell on his face from the blue immensity of the powdered heavens. He heard voices, and closed his eyes. When he opened them again, the mirages had vanished; and the moon which had numbed his mind until it was a frozen shadow of itself, seemed now to be racing faster and faster among the clouds in intoxicated flight, and there were blue rings round the moon.

He fell asleep again, but only for a few seconds. When he awoke, a white mist was arising through the pines, and he saw only dimness and this pale vapor rising through the level fog-bank; and this pale vapor, whiter than the mist, lifted itself up and stood motionless like an exhalation from the lake. He remembered then his childhood, when landscapes were equally vast and silent. Was he returning to his childhood? The pines were now invisible, the reeds and the wildfowl could no longer be heard, and he felt sick with apprehension at the thought that he was falling into a white pit of mist—a pit which would lead him back to his own childhood.

The sharp images of his childhood came clear to him now, Tubingen-am-Neckar, his mother walking along the willows, the warmth of summer, the rye blazing gold in the fields. And the little church, where the poet Hoelderlin had prayed, and the rocky cliffs, and the sweet pulpy taste of the vines. He could still see these things, still listen to the swish of his mother's skirts and smell the cool tablecloth on Sunday mornings, and the servant Leni who was so plump that her melon breasts would jump up from her bodice, and the sweet cool water coming through the forest, and the German earth. He tried not to think of these things but as the mist rose higher, revealing the roots of trees and hiding their leaves, he sank back into his childhood, and at the same time he drew his helmet still further over his eyes, and gazed only at the starlight shining on the blue metal of the gun-barrel.

"My childhood," he said aloud with a groan, and then ,inexplicably, his thoughts returned to the moment three days previously when, after a heavy night of gunfire in the Karelian marshes, he had been summoned to the adjutant's white tent hidden in the snows.

In the tent it was like home. There were German voices, German faces. There were people who walked like Germans, with a haunted look in their eyes, in polished boots, with small guns hanging at their waists and there, at the back of the tent, stretched out, lay the new flag of Germany.

In the fur-lined tent the air was thick and warm with aromatic smoke—tobacco-smoke. It took him some moments to adjust himself, his ears still dinned by the gunfire of the late afternoon, and his eyes still blinded by the sulphurous yellow flashes. The adjutant was talking in a clipped voice, crystal-clear, and his long narrow face shone in the faint blue acetylene flame hanging overhead.

The boy saluted smartly, kicking the heels of his snow-covered boots together, his hand rigidly at the salute.

"Karl Christiaan, to report, sir."

The adjutant looked down at him from his immense height. He spoke in a voice that was clear and at the same time soft, a voice which was weary beyond endurance.

"Exactly. I have ordered you to take part in a special mission—a very dangerous mission. I may add that there is very little likelihood that you will come out alive."

The eyes, pale-blue, were searching into him. They were eyes which were accustomed to command, and they were so pale that they were almost white, and there were no markings in them. It was like gazing up at a pale autumn sky, when the rain has fallen and left the sky clear of dust.

"Yes, sir."

Once more the boy clicked his heels.

"You are to go round the lake towards Iisooma. It doesn't matter how you get there, but you must get there. Once you are there, it doesn't matter very much what you do. The important thing is that the enemy should see you and know that you belong to the *Feldherr,* and that you should remain where you are. You will take a machine-gun and occasionally, but only occasionally, fire off a few rounds. You must be seen with your field-gun at the edge of the lake near Iisooma, and at irregular intervals you will fire a burst—it doesn't matter in the least whether you fire it at the lake or at the wildfowl. The enemy is silent. We, too, are silent. The important thing is that you should make a noise and attract their attention. You will almost inevitably be killed. You are to stay there for the longest time possible.

The boy nodded and stepped back. Instinctively his right hand leapt to his forehead in salute.

"There is still more. You will be given a chart. On this chart you will find exactly where you are to stay. You must stay there for at least seven days, unless the enemy captures all the villages round the lake. I can tell you that it is extremely improbable that the army will capture these villages in less than seven days."

"Yes, sir."

"Furthermore, and this is my last order, you will not attempt to communicate with the army in any way until the expiration of seven days. You will take sufficient food, and you may also take benzedrine tablets to keep awake, but it is not in the least necessary that you should keep awake. You will, as I have said, almost inevitably be killed, and therefore when you leave here, I shall salute you and you shall not salute me in return. You will leave at nineteen hours thirty-five. You have exactly half an hour to prepare for the journey."

The boy nodded and stepped back. Once again his right hand leapt to his forehead in salute.

"You have disobeyed orders," the adjutant smiled, and the boy was surprised to see those pure blue eyes light with pain.

"I will give you the chart in the next five minutes. Meanwhile I shall introduce you to the Staff captain and the S.S. guards in the tent."

The boy had not noticed them before. All his attention was concentrated on the adjutant, who wore the medal of the Iron Cross hanging down from his collar, and the blue and white ribbon of the *Pour le Merite* hanging on the lapel of his coat. His gloved hand was slipped into the coat a little below the ribbons. Suddenly the officer smiled, took him by the shoulder and led him to the place in the corner of the tent where the two remaining officers were smoking, their elbows on the table. A servant, a young and extremely handsome private with curly blond hair, entered the tent a few moments later.

"I want you to meet—" but the adjutant for some reason had forgotten the names of the two officers, one in field-grey, the other in silver and black; and his hand went to his forehead, he mumbled something, and it was some time before he could regain his composure. He had been disturbed by the heavy strafing, and the subsequent bombing of the late afternoon, and though the place was silent now, he was suffering from amnesia. The others looked on, their faces blue in the light of the acetylene lamp, and smiled condescendingly.

"Staff-captain Lowenstein," the adjutant said at last, with a flicker of triumph at the corner of his lips. "And Group-captain of the S.S. Von Drakensberg."

The boy bowed low from the waist. Von Drakensberg smiled at him, and Lowenstein lit a cigarette from the pulpy remnants of the previous one. The boy noticed that their hands were shaking.

"*Schnapps!*" the adjutant nodded in the direction of the servant, and a few minutes later, while the cloud of tobacco smoke cleared, the table was laid, the bottles of *schnapps* were opened and the boy was invited to join the small company.

Lowenstein was talking in a soft southern drawl.

"How old are you? Eh, can't you hear me? I asked you how old you were?"

In spite of the repetition, and the surly expression on Lowenstein's face, the voice was pleasant.

"I am sorry, sir. Twenty-three."

"Let me see. That means you were born after the conclusion of the last war."

"Yes, sir."

"May I ask where you were born?"

"Tübingen-am-Neckar, sir. The birthplace of the poet Friedrich Hoelderlin."

"I didn't ask you where Hoelderlin was born," the officer said, but he smiled, and though the boy flushed red, and looked with a profoundly guilty look at the table, the officer patted his gloved hand which lay rigidly on the table.

"And what did you do then—I mean, after you were born?"

"I stayed in Tübingen."

"You never left it?"

"No, sir, except for a visit to Munich and the Starnberger See."

"It's extraordinary!" the officer said, looking down at his hands. "The man hasn't left Germany at all! Quite extraordinary! A young provincial from Tübingen-am-Neckar!"

The boy smiled to himself. It was very warm in the tent, and he had long ago forgotten the duties he had been ordered to perform beside the lake. The *schnapps* warmed his spirits, and the conversation of the two men leaning forward, with expressions of

491

deep concern, pleased him. For the first time the senior officers were paying attention to him.

Von Drakensberg snubbed out a cigar, and said sharply: "Tell me, Karl Christiaan, why did you join the army? You are a German?"

"Yes, sir."

"And yet your name is not German?"

"No. Danish. My grandfather was a Dane."

Von Drakensberg smiled, lifted up his chin, and exactly like a cat he began to rub the taut flesh under his chin with his knuckles.

"One other question. Are you in love with a girl?"

The boy waited for a while before answering, in a strangely weak voice: "Yes, sir."

"That's all we wanted to know," Lowenstein said with a comforting smile. "It is clear that you joined the war because you loved your country and the girl, and you wanted to protect them from the enemy."

The boy nodded. There was a finality in Lowenstein's gestures which suggested that the conversation would not be resumed; there was beer on the table, lamb cutlets, knives, forks and even salt-cellars. It was over a year since he had sat at a table with a tablecloth.

The conversation became desultory, Von Drakensberg, the senior officer, spoke of the early days of the war, days of triumph which were already passing into forgetfulness. He had been everywhere. He had spoken many times with the *Führer,* and every time he mentioned the name of the *Führer,* he would incline his head a little to one side: it was a gesture of reverence, and also of interrogation, for if the others did not make some gesture in return, he would silently accuse them of lack of faith in the leader.

He told a story of the early days of the invasion of Poland. It was shortly before the occupation of Cracow. Then, a lieutenant in the S.S., he had driven a tank in an armoured column which had got lost among the rye-fields. It was a hot day, for the weather in Poland had never been better. The scent of rye, the willows bordering the road, the green-scummed lakes and the distant villages with their painted blue walls, had filled him with pleasure. He wore a flower on his helmet; in front of him there was mile upon mile of deserted road, with resinous pine-forests low among the hills, and somewhere there was a clean milky river in which he had bathed. The airplanes flew overhead. The sky was clear. It was one of those days which are entirely without excitement, and yet the knowledge that he was obeying the *Führer* and taking part in the campaign filled him with extraordinary pleasure.

"I need not tell you that such days are rare, and perhaps they will never return. But this day was not entirely pleasurable. The morning, yes—the bright early mornings, with frost on the ground, and then the cloudless sky. This was exactly what I had imagined in my student days, except for one thing—there was no enemy. The *Luftwaffe* had, of course, made it extremely difficult for the enemy to come near us. The villages had, of course, been bombed, and we would occasionally pass them, and sometimes on the horizon we would see small straggling columns of the enemy. The divisional general would order one of the tanks to pursue them, but these stragglers were clever—they hid in the forests, and sometimes they laid mines, and sometimes our tanks did not return. The luck of war! But this happened very rarely, and we had methods of squeezing the rabble out of the hills."

He paused, took another swill of *schnapps* and smiled at the blond servant who was standing by his side. Then he continued:

"This is how the day passed—no excitement, the pleasant tingling of the sun on our faces, an occasional bathe and the thought of all the triumphs ahead. A soldier is not a sentimental person, but he has excellent opportunities for studying scenery: and there was much that we found *convenable* in those early days in southern Poland. But it happened one evening that we were ambushed just outside a small village. We sent a scout car ahead, and it had returned with the information that the village had been deserted some hours previously; there was no sign of any living man, and yet the village had not been bombed. It was dusk when we entered the village. We stopped for a little in the hope of finding a few of those damned Polish girls, but they had all gone and we proceeded in the direction of Cracow. It was now dark—and as we left the village we were caught in heavy crossfire from guns hidden on the banks of a sunken lane. The first three tanks were set on fire, my own included. I jumped out and made a dash for the bank; but already our own guns had silenced those small mountain guns. We then returned to the village. Perhaps ten minutes had passed since the opening of the attack, but what was extraordinary was that the villagers had returned to the village, and it became clear that they had been in hiding, and when they heard the mountain guns open out, they had assumed we were all destroyed. We were not destroyed. On the contrary we were out for destruction, and I ordered that the whole male population should be taken out into the field, made to dig their own graves and be shot. As for the women—."

Once again he paused and drank *schnapps*. As soon as he had drunk the *schnapps*, Lowenstein leaned forward and filled his glass. The adjutant remained silent, trembling a little, his face turned slightly away so that the blue trembling light of the acetylene lamp fell on his eyes.

"Well, we can guess what happened to the women," Lowenstein answered with a half-smile.

"Perhaps you can," the Staff-captain answered. "But you must remember that these were the early days of the war, and much has happened since then. We have developed techniques which may be better now, but you must understand that in the early days we behaved with—shall I say?—a kind of spontaneous delight in life. The girls were almost all small and full-bosomed. The best of them we kept ourselves. We made them drink with us, naked, at the table, and we pretended that their husbands and lovers would return the next day. We said we had come to liberate Poland, and we had the greatest respect for Polish women. I think some of them even believed this. There was a Jewish girl with golden hair—extraordinary to see Jewish girls with golden hair—and I shared her with another lieutenant. We knew it would be dangerous to go on further that night, and we stayed in the inns and in their own houses, on the rush-floors or in those beds in which there were at least four great pillows. We drank and sang, and meanwhile we made the girls drink and sing, and sometimes we would disappear with them, and it was good to have real girls again. Some of them tried to escape, but they were brought back and whipped. One tried to commit suicide in a well: we simply threw a rock down the well to make it more certain. Early in the morning, tired and unwashed, we debated what to do with them. They were naked, and I must say, we were not altogether dressed as though on parade. It was Staff-lieutenant Schickmann who had the astoundingly brilliant idea of allowing each tank to take one or two girls. There we were in the early morning, two of us on the roof of each tank, and each of us had a naked Polish girl in his arms. Delightful! The freshness of the air! The young bodies! Their flesh very cold and firm, and their hair in the wind! A really magistral spectacle!"

He sipped the *schnapps* and looked solemnly at the boy, and then at Lowenstein. He looked as pleased as a child who has just found a toy. And he continued, in the same unaffected and perfectly natural tones, occasionally laughing to himself, occasionally looking slyly at the adjutant who remained unmoved, with his eyes fixed on his wrist-watch.

"A capital spectacle, is it not?" Von Drakensberg continued. "We wore our heavy overcoats, because the air was cold and damp, though the sun would soon shine; and of course many things can be committed under the secrecy of an overcoat. I remember there was a milky-white mist, and I was telling her of all the beautiful things I would buy for her in Cracow. And so we went along, very slowly, with the hedges on either side of us, singing and playing about with the Polish girls, and then at a given signal from the leader we each took up one Polish girl and threw her with all our strength in front of the tank. There was a moment when the air was filled with screaming, and a moment later there was the perfectly satisfying sound of their bones being broken under the treads. It was really capital! Only one escaped, and we shot her down as she climbed through the hedges. It was amazing to see the little red berries of blood appearing on her white flesh. There she was, caught up in the hedge, with a silly smile on her face, and as we passed we each fired at her. Capital spectacle!"

He had come to the end of his story, and he was more thirsty than ever. It occurred to the boy from the expressions of Lowenstein and the adjutant that the story had been told many times before, and was now being told for his benefit.

"Wasn't it a capital story?" Von Drakensberg said kindly, gazing with a sad expression at the boy's face.

The boy bowed his head. There was no need for him to answer the question, for at that moment the adjutant motioned him towards a map, where the village of Iisooma was marked with a red circle. Beside the map lay provisions for seven days, an unsheathed dagger and a requisition for ammunition.

"You have five minutes left," the adjutant said, gazing steadily at his watch. "Is there anything you would like to do in the remaining five minutes?"

"I would like to write a letter to my mother."

"Certainly."

Pen and paper were brought for him, and he began to write slowly and with immense difficulty the date and then the words: "*Liebe Mutter.*" All his love, all his sympathy and understanding, all his memories of his childhood home—all these struggled to express themselves, and at the same time he was conscious that there was nothing worth saying. "*Liebe.*" As he wrote,

495

chipping the words from his own breast-bone, the trite phrases that came to him, he knew that they were all unnecessary: he knew that he would die: he knew that nothing would be left of him. He had wanted, ever since he left the theological school to join the army, to put on paper all the sensations, all the bewilderment of war; but there had been no time to write, and even if he had written, how can one describe the long days of marching through the snow, the graves, the guerrillas, the gruelling torments which are unrecognisable except to those who have experienced them?

"My dear Mother, I am going on a dangerous mission, but be sure that I will return. I think of you, the orchard, little Leni, the river. I beg you, Mother, to lay a wreath on the grave of the poet Hoelderlin for me, because we were born on the same birthday. Dear Mother! Karl Christiaan, your son, sends you his love."

That was all. He handed it to the adjutant, who glanced at it swiftly, hardly seeing what was written, and then carefully folded the letter and placed it in the breast pocket of his coat.

"Your mother will receive this letter."

"Thank you, sir."

Von Drakensberg stood up and threw out his hand.

"I wish you good luck," he said simply, and as the boy lifted the light machine-gun to his shoulder, he added: "Wildfowl, eh? You can do some good shooting tonight."

Then he must have left them—he could not remember now. He remembered only that he had walked out in the snow with the adjutant, past the guards who stiffened to attention, and the adjutant was still talking, and he heard the adjutant saying: "That's all, and God be with you. I know you will do your duty like a good German soldier."

That was all, and that was nearly three days ago. He was no longer listening to Von Drakensberg's story, he was no longer looking at the flickering blue flames of the acetylene lamp. The air was clear, and there was a great brush of starlight sweeping across the heavens. It was all over now, the tramp through the forest, the waiting and the silence. Though it was midnight, and the moon was directly overhead, the birds were awake, and the quick scurry of their wings in the ice-cold air was pleasant after the long silence of his dreams. He gazed out over the lake, pointing his machine-gun idly on the opposite shore, following the flight of the gulls, and occasionally he would let off a burst of a few rounds, and he was delighted at the echoes reverberating over the lake and the sudden scurry of the fowl.

As it became colder, and the night passed, he thought more often of Von Drakensberg's story. Von Drakensberg had told the story so well that he had seen, almost as if he had been there, the village girls lifted naked on to the tanks, he had seen them struggling under the warm coats and he had seen them being thrown into the air. He had not seen what happened afterwards, because whenever he thought of it, his mind shut tight like a clamp and there was only emptiness and a feeling of horror. Why had they done this? Why had they been doing things like this ever since the beginning of the war? Why had nobody prevented them? His own hands were clean, but he had done nothing to stop them. He saw the officers and the women huddled on the rush-floor of a Polish cottage, he saw the officers holding them up on the tank, he heard the screams and the sudden silences—and always he knew that the final horror was missing. And he thought: "Did the country which has produced Goethe and Hoelderlin deserve to die? Yes, it deserved to die."

He thought in this way quite mechanically and abstractly, as he would think of a problem in ballistics. He knew that in the early morning, an hour or so before the grey dawn, the mind was a wanton and refused to behave its necessary laws. He had hoped, when he was young, to become a poet. He remembered now his last conversation with the adjutant as they came across the snow.

"You are young and strong. It is a task which is worthy of you." A short pause. The adjutant seemed to be bowed under the weight of his helmet. "You understand that it is possible that at the end of seven days we shall have gone?"

"Yes, sir."

"I have not told you, but it is probable that we shall soon be retreating under the orders of the High Command."

"Yes, sir."

"But you will not retreat?"

Again, the short pause.

"You have no wife?"

"No."

"Only your mother?"

"Yes, sir."

"It is a pity. It would be better if Germany had more children like you."

That was all. He looked down at the boy in field grey under the heavy white cape, with the snow-shoes and hand-grenades and knives hanging from his belt, and the light portable machine-gun on his shoulder. This too was camouflaged and covered with a white cowl. They faced one another in the desert of snow, the adjutant looking down at the fine thin face of the boy, and the boy looking up with an expression of bewilderment as the adjutant said: "God be with you" and stood rigidly at the salute. The boy saw the grey light of the afternoon held in the crook of the adjutant's arm as he stood at the salute, and then, while tears fell in two streams down his face, he turned to go.

He slept for a while. He was surprised when dawn came. He felt hungry, and at the same time he felt sad that so much time had passed in sleeping. The dawn made everything look unreal. There were no longer any stars, and the thick clouds were spread over the sky. But soon stealthy fingers of light pushed down through the clouds, and slowly, slowly, the lake turned from black to pale blue.

In a sudden exaltation he fired a burst from the machine-gun.

What was surprising was the way the colors came out of the lake: the long stretches of blue, the brown shadows, the white ripples where a wildfowl ripped the surface with its wings. The small green buds of the larches, too, were curiously unexpected. Stranger than any of these was the colour of the tree-trunks. He had thought they were black, but they were silvery grey with splashes of brown moss, and there were spaces between the branches through which he could see a pure unclouded sky.

He got up and walked down to the lake, still wearing the white fur-lined cape. It was a clear wintry day, with the tumultuous clouds high up. He had never seen the sky so high. The cool air beat against his face, warming him, and when he returned from the lake he felt hungry, but it was a clean hunger, not the hunger which comes after long hours of marching.

He opened the tin of butter and then unhooked the aluminum frying-pan from his heavy knapsack, and gathered a little armful of dry grass from the forest. At first, when he lit it, there was no flame. Small puffs of black smoke arose, choking him, but afterwards there was a thin green flame, and this he shielded carefully from the wind, and all the while he was looking at the tumbling wildfowl. Sometimes they would tower up to the clouds, lonely and ominous in their high-ranging flight, but more often they would fly low, skimming the reeds with the tips of their wings.

"The birds," he said. In childhood he had only to summon the name of a thing, and it would instantly appear to him, and it would possess a freshness than that it never possessed at any other time. And now, as he said the word "birds," he saw still whiter birds above still greener lakes, and he was no longer gazing over a lake in Finland, but at the hot heat-haze of August rising over the Starnberger See.

"The birds," he said again, and watched them flying in undulating flight from one edge of the lake to the other. "The birds have a freedom which is denied to us. They fly where they will, and all the roads of the air are open to them." And it seemed to him, then, that each bird was flying over a white road in the sky, a road which could be faintly discerned, which was permanent, which was eternally safe for those strange voyagers of the sky.

He opened a tin of eggs, put butter in the pan and breaking the eggs on the rim, watched them spill out, bubbling and warm-smelling, shooting up little sizzling sparks of yellow. The butter had no sooner entered the pan than it turned liquid and green. And now the warm smell of eggs, the woodsmoke, the little gay sparks and the sight of the wildfowl pleased him with a kind of detached pleasure, and it was almost as though he was contemplating something perfectly beautiful, which he no longer desired.

The eggs tasted good, and long after he had finished them, a white transparent smoke rose from the blackened pan. He lay back against a larch. The distant pines were golden now. He could see for miles. He could see the pebbles along the shores of the lake, bright blue, perfectly round and glistening. He could see the yellow beaks of the birds and the low blue hills in the distance, and the dark shadows of the reeds, and all the silvery magnificence of the lake. And yet he was perfectly detached from the scene. It pleased him, but he had no desire to possess its beauty. He thought he heard firing. It was a long way away, muffled by the snow and by the sound of distant marching. And then he said aloud: "I must catch some fish."

The lake was clear, and it was not too cold. He threw off his white cape and slowly unlaced his boots. After rolling off his trousers he began to wade out until the water was up to his thighs. No, the water was not cold, although he sucked in his breath at the first contact with it. In a little while it was pleasantly warm, tingling, and he enjoyed the luxuriance of wading about, splashing in the sunlight. He plucked one of the bluish green reeds near the bank, pulling it from the roots, and he was surprised to find how white the roots were, and how succulent. Sometimes he heard an otter gnawing the deadwood on the shore, or the scamper of a water-rat, but he never saw them. He saw the sun, the lake, the high clouds and the birds: and sometimes he thought he saw the glitter of steel on the further bank. The sun climbed higher. He unloosened his short great-coat, returned to the bank, undressed completely and waded out until the water was under his chin. A wildfowl dived close to the strange white creature, and he knew that he could have caught its wings. He bathed and dived, and occasionally looked back at the blue un-hooded machine-gun along the shore. The clouds were opening, and in the blue sky there was promise of a golden sun.

He returned regretfully to the bank, fired a few more bursts from the machine-gun and warmed himself over the now blazing fire. For a while, wearing only a great-coat, he lay there, look-ing up at the clouds, waiting for the moment when the sun would appear. When the sun appeared, he would swim again.

He was laughing like a madman or like someone intoxicated whittling a branch with his knife and gazing at its sticky white flesh underneath. He wished he could have come to Finland in peace-time. He had no quarrel with the Russians, or even with the Finns. He had seen them, a few Russian prisoners, and the Finns had all looked at him as though he had been a stranger. But it didn't matter now. He was alone, the sun was coming through the hole in the clouds, the smell of wood-smoke was in-toxicating, and in the great fur-lined cape he felt perfectly warm.

Once more he began to wade among the reeds, waving his stick in the clear water. Immediately the fishes began to rise from the mud—rose-molded fishes which resembled trout, and dark silvery fishes which resembled fat eels, with copper eyes and transparent waving fins. He put his hand in the water and felt them nibbling his flesh; and it was pleasant to watch them gliding in and out among the white stems of the reeds. He crouched low, watching them. A trout was rubbing itself on his ankles, its little black lips moving, the grey fins flickering, the delicate rose-moled skin curiously soft when he touched it. He could see the gills moving, and the little heaving of the belly, and the way the tail curved gently in the current, and the blue shadow which it left at the bottom of the pool. It seemed a pity to take the fish out of the water, but he was feeling hungry again, and soon he had lifted it up, watching it with an amused pitying expression as it thrashed its tail.

He was afraid then, not because he hated killing it, but be-cause he was disturbing the serenity of the lake. He pressed hard a little behind the gills, but as soon as he released his pressure

500

the tail swung desperately from side to side, the small mouth opened, revealing pink teeth, and there were two little hooks which came from its mouth and trembled violently. It was already bleeding, the skin was torn; and as he returned to the bank he gazed steadily, with the same expression of bemused pity, at that soft thing which no longer possessed any freedom.

He cut it up slowly, put more butter in the pan and gazed tenderly at the red flesh and the bones which were whiter than cool stones. The flesh turned a warm brown, and though there was an indefinable bitterness in its taste, he was pleased, and yet at the same time he decided that he would take no more fish from the lake until his rations were exhausted. He opened a tin without looking at the label. It was marmalade, and this pleased him. He wished there were potatoes, perhaps a veal cutlet, but he was satisfied with his meal. Once more he let off a burst from the machine-gun, and he was delighted by the sudden scurry of wildfowl and the crackling echoes among the hills.

After eating the fish there was nothing to do. The sun came out shortly afterwards, and he sunbathed, lying on the fur of his cape. He was strong, but his skin was as white and delicate as a girl's, and he had lost flesh during the campaign. Soon he fell asleep.

The strong sun burnt into his shoulders and down the whole length of his back, but he slept on, deep in the dreamless sleep which is not of exhaustion but of pure content. He was conscious of the sun, of the warmth, of the reeds, of the wildfowl soaring over the lake; but these images only slipped into his brain to remind him of his presence in Finland. They were not dreams. He did not think of Von Drakensberg or even of the adjutant. All these problems had been solved. He had solved them many hours ago, in a spirit of perfect detachment, and he knew that there remained for him on this earth nothing further to do. And if he was killed while he was sleeping, he would have no regret, and he would understand as clearly as he understood the sweeping flight of the wildfowl that this also was necessary. And so he slept during the long afternoon, naked on the fur, basking in the warmth of the earth and not dreaming.

When he awoke it was pitch dark. The fire was out. The wind was rustling the reeds and freshening the lake. There were no clouds, and the stars were shining clear and bright in the heavens. He felt miserably cold, but he was warm again when he had slipped the fur round his shoulders. He began to light the fire, shielding it with his body, and when at last the wet twigs began to crackle and puffs of black smoke arose, he huddled comfortably over the fire and prepared to open some more of his rations.

He remembered how at dawn the roads were pink crystals of water-melon flesh, and how the sun fell on the clouds and spread a faint diffused light on the blue lake; but in this darkness it was difficult to recall the past, even the past of a few hours before, and it was with the greatest difficulty imaginable that he began to summon out of the days events the memory of the rose-moled trout. Thereafter his memories arose more quickly. He could remember how the blue acetylene flame lit up Von Drakensberg's cheek, and he could remember the pale face of the adjutant. He could remember so many things now—his home, the red cliffs of the Neckar, the cemetery where the poet Hoelderlin lay buried Huddled over the fire, he breathed the smell of wood-smoke, and of sardines. He had never known the air so pure. It was spring, the little moist buds of the larches glittering in the red flames from the fire. He could feel the sap rising, and the coming of spring.

"How good it is," he murmured, and it occurred to him that soon there would be no more Germans left on the earth to enjoy the spectacle of spring. And he had no regret. He began to eat, but no longer enjoying the taste of his food; and there came to him a great weariness as of a man who has accomplished all that he intended to accomplish on earth. His white coat, the golden flames of the fire, the waving reeds—all these entered his consciousness and into his weariness, which was beyond sleep. Beyond sleep.

Then, for the second time that day he began to think of his childhood. A cold wind was blowing across the lake, and he took the pickaxe and began to cut down a tree. He had not enough energy to cut it deeply, but he enjoyed seeing the chips flying, bright gold and curled in the light of the flames. He heard footsteps. Some habit of continual reflection and obedience made him turn uneasily at the sound, but he could not tell from which direction they came. He said: "They are coming. I ought to be dressed." But he kept on chipping the tree with only the white fur-lined coat to protect him from the cold, and sometimes, because it was not buttoned, the coat would fly apart, and the gold light of the flames flickered and licked his body in the dark.

Now, though no moon rose, a bright mist lay over the water, and once again he saw the spires and cliffs of vapor rising from the level fog-bank. The mist cast a deep shadow and was almost tangible, whiter now than the cloud-covered sky; and through the mist the wildfowl sometimes appeared unexpectedly, screaming so stridently that sometimes they could not be heard. And still he kept chipping like flakes out of the larch trees.

He looked at the machine-gun which lay like a black rod across the mist, faintly visible in the light of the small flames. It had always been so splendidly kept: sights oiled and barrel gleaming, and it seemed to him that this squat blue-black object in the snow with its three legs, its round muzzle and perforated barrel was also something he had seen in his childhood dreams. He stopped hacking at the tree with the pickaxe and returned to the gun, let off another burst and waited for the last echoes to die out before he lit a cigarette. Then he folded the white cape more tightly around him, and staring straight ahead, listened to the approaching footsteps.

"They are coming," he said again. "They are always coming. There is nothing I can do to prevent them. They are furies. They are avenging angels." And for a short while he thought of the girls thrown naked from the tanks.

They were coming nearer and nearer, and they would never cease coming. A twig broke. The pickaxe glinted in the gold flames, and once more he began to be hungry. The mist was as thick as cheese-cloth, completely hiding the stars. They were coming nearer, and yet when he turned slowly round, with the expression of a child who hears at night a noise which he does not fear, they were still invisible.

"I am here," he said.

He heard the footsteps again. They were coming nearer, and he heard them as distinctly as he heard in childhood the footsteps of his mother in the oak-lined corridor. He knew that he would never be able to forget these footsteps, and he thought of the stories she told him from Grimm's *Maerchen* and of the three bears. It was curious to be lying there, drowsy by the side of the Finnish lake. Suddenly startled by a broken twig, he opened his eyes wide and saw coming towards him from the direction of the forest three bears exactly like the bears in the fable—there was mother bear, there was father bear, and there was little bear, a little stunted bear which kept running and hopping beside the two larger bears. He jumped up. In the starlight it was difficult to see clearly, and besides there was a mist as thick as cheese-cloth all over the forest. He smiled. He could almost have touched them, and already they were so near that he could smell their warm fur. "The three bears," he murmured, and he looked quickly at the fire to make sure that there was something for them to eat.

But the bears did not move. They stood there looking at him, tenderly and compassionately, and sometimes they would whisper together and point to the fire, or perhaps they were pointing at the machine-gun and the small aluminum cups. The little bear kept hopping on one leg.

"Come, there is nothing to be afraid of," the boy said, gazing sadly into the dark shadows of the forest. "Father Bear, Mother Bear, Little Bear, I have known you ever since I was a child—."

He said nothing more. When the Russian soldiers threw themselves upon him they were surprised because he was smiling when their bayonets descended. They stayed only for a few moments. As he fell to the ground his great-coat opened wide, and they saw him lying there naked in the snow, his white skin golden in the light of the flames, and on his lips, from which blood welled endlessly, the smile remained like the print of his own footsteps in the snow, a smile which reflected the starlight and the pines and the scales of the rose-moled trout in the snow.

from THE SOLITUDES

F. T. Prince

Proud wild and idle childhood,
Luxurious mild childhood
Still casts a backward glow or floating pallor
On the virginity that emerges, the new life
Mysterious as the sea
Towards which you turn your face, brow mouth and blood
And white and unused skin, the form of youth itself
That takes our longing most and wrings it most
Because it is unmixed
With other things than human life and which
We call experience; and where you stand,
Your head bent and your eyes
That follow down and stare
As with a dreaming stare on that taut breath,
The burnished tarnished surface, rich
Stretched like a rustling mirror, haunts the air
Flutters the glowing gulf,
Supple and subtle, full of stirrings,
And the impatient flood of calm,
To suffer but the mirrored softness, burns
And longs to melt its shores.

                              Your youth is like the sea
That rubs on its rough case
Beneath the gazes of a sky
The rival of that velvet face,
And the uneasy airy glitter, the slow glow
And then the massive flash
That answers irresistibly
Begins and sobs and woos

Mirrors and writhes and rocks itself and sighs
And strives to glut itself with light:
The noon that climbs the air
Troubles, makes more than ever now excessive
Rubbed and ruffled, thumbed,
Outrageously more beautiful
The burning young tumescent sea.
—And I too bruise my peace
With joys and torments, I too feel increase
The thirst, the burning touch, the sea of love
That opens the dread doors, and with the sense
Of the unknown, unknowable,
And naked and impossible,
What would be beautiful
That I have never done,

It comes back, yes it comes
Through the offended wondering air,
The dream and care for what is far, the tender fire
Still quivering in its hope-desire, a smile
That hides within the thought or the eyes.
The sky is lovely as a prayer
That makes a path from heaven to earth,
And, stripped of all delight, yet my desire
As with the dream sees and denies
And drifts and faints and tries to rise
As if it were a smile or a sob.
Being itself a thing of hope, it makes a world
Of a luminous sea-richness where we see
The stained wall of the tenement is as pure
And proud as the dressed palace,
And the sea bathes in a breath of love
                                    that dies
And lives and dies and floats under the noon—
Serenely-restlessly-illumined gulf
Of changing and unchanging skies.
It fades and then it gleams
With the immobile golden wounds of dreams,
Chains veils veins, silken skeins,

And we are cradled in its breath, taste when it glows
Finite angelic sweetness
Of our thirst that comes and goes

As from the hollow of some sky,
And listen, how it sings
'It can do anything but rest'
And flutters and unfolds itself and springs
Deserting where it nests,
And battered by the brightness
Of sea-noons and sea-wings,
What if it fears that all these precious things
Are merely wishes? We shall wish them yet,
AND let the exhilarated wild and noble sorrows
FLASH through the solitudes! like the cliff-swallows
Swoop out and cut and glide, chafe joy and scud and skim
Twittering drunkenly in flight
That delicious scurrying music! dart upright
Climb, totter, drop incontinently
Grazing the low trough of the sea
Sea-spumed of a pure space
                                        white golden glow
Still purer and more bare, more wild and rare
Along the bare beach of the world. . .

But destitute and impotent and amorous
Of an impossibility
A sweetness and a passion
Held naked to the breast, the collocation
Of glory and the impossible
That we should love and have our will,
The being in love is one with loneliness:
And while the noon dreams overhead
The sea that moves in you and me
Begins and re-begins
And melts and blazes, mirrors restlessly
And gnaws and undermines the world
Built only on a perishing breath
And shudders and despoils itself and gleams
From that torn luminous envelope.
Unclothed of everything but love
It tumbles with a hiss
That travels slowly on a level shore
Seething the milk of nakedness, and mocks
Half tenderly, half bitterly
The lost auroral solitude
That glimmered to our minds.

And the sky opens
Like a fan its vaulted violet height, unfolding
A wide and wingless cradle for that happiness
Which longs to melt in the impossible.

THE MORTGAGED HEART

Carson McCullers

The dead demand a double vision. A furthered zone,
Ghostly decision of apportionment. For the dead can claim
The lover's senses, the mortgaged heart.

Watch twice the orchard blossoms in gray rain
And to the cold rose skies bring twin surprise
Endure each summons once, and once again
Experience multiplied by two—the duty recognized.
Instruct the quivering spirit, instant nerve
To schizophrenic master serve.
Or like a homeless doppelganger
Blind love might wander.

The mortgage of the dead is known.
Prepare the cherished wreath, the garland door.
But the secluded ash, the humble bone—
Do the dead know?

When we are lost what image tells?
Nothing resembles nothing. Yet nothing
Is not blank. It is configured Hell:
Of noticed clocks on winter afternoons, malignant stars,
Demanding furniture. All unrelated
And with air between.

The terror. Is it of Space, of Time?
Or the joined trickery of both conceptions?
To the lost, transfixed among the self-inflicted ruins,
All that is non-air (if this indeed is not deception)
Is agony immobilized. While Time,
The endless idiot, runs screaming round the world.

3) If you have friends who are on the edge of élite taste try to push them up to where they belong. Indirection is best for this. Don't be compulsive or snobbish. Just leave the good books around where they can pick them up by curiosity. Or hand out for Christmas presents a few subscriptions to a good Little Magazine.

4) By all means, support the Little Magazines. How many are you subscribing to now? By helping the Little Magazines you provide a place where the serious writer can publish free from the censorship of convention imposed in the commercial magazines. And you help support the effort of the consecrated editors who are working concretely for the ideal with very little chance of personal reward.

Think up your own variations and additions. And keep at it over the years. Rome was not built in a day, or by one man and his brother.

And while we are building our élite we might try to help keep Europe from losing hers. Remember that whatever we do here bad or good gets copied. There are plenty of smart little grubs in Europe just waiting to reproduce things like *Life* and *The Readers Digest* and *Forever Amber* if they think they can get rich doing it. It will be harder to do it there than it was here —because of the traditions of good taste—but it could happen.

How can we counteract that tendency? For one thing, by taking a cue from the British and trying to export a little of the *good* side of our culture. Do you know about the British Council? If you don't, you should. It is an organization financed by the British Government to promote British culture abroad. Fortunately it is in the hands of the right sort of people and the culture it exposes abroad is of the best. It has libraries in all the principal foreign countries and sends good writers and artists abroad for lectures, exhibitions and concerts. A few years ago, just after the War, the American USIBA had a number of Information Libraries operating in Europe, but they have been allowed to run down and die out. What is the result? The only American "culture" which the average European can now see is not representative of our best tendencies—*Life, Readers Digest,* Hollywood movies and translations of bestsellers. Our serious culture—the Little Magazines and the good books—hardly permeate Europe, because the profit in importing them is not great enough to overcome the exchange obstacles. A reader in England

510

or France cannot simply order an American book or magazine by mail at will. Far from it. He is forbidden to send out of the country any of his nation's horde of dollars, even in picayune amounts. Nor are most European bookstores allowed to import American publications, except medical and scientific texts. But the forces of darkness get around these bans by setting up European companies to publish European editions of American trash. What pays always finds a way.

There is no greater need now than for a European magazine devoted to serious American culture. There is such a pent-up hunger for a magazine of the kind that I think it might soon become self-supporting. But it needs a push to get started. How would it work? It would have to be printed in a European "soft-currency" country, not England, to get around the dollar bans. To pay writers and editors here at home in dollars it might be possible to obtain an exchange fund through the State Department. This has already been done for the benefit of certain American publications which have a recognized political propaganda mission. The editing ought to be done from the States, probably by a committee made up from the editors of existing Little Magazines, plus advisers to cover the fields of film, music and art. A system of guest editors might make for catholicity. At first, the magazine should be largely of the reprint type, picking up material from the Little Magazines, but *using it whole, as written, un-digested, un-capsulated, un-castrated* and not so doctored that an article about athletes foot is indistinguishable in style and treatment from one on how to conduct a symphony! There could be supplementary letters on the arts, and illustrations from films and gallery shows, to round out the picture. Later it might attract specially commissioned material. Its whole aim would be to show Europe the serious side of our artistic and intellectual activity. After the English language edition got running it might be possible to add translated editions in the European languages. Be it noted that a magazine of this type is already published by our Military Government in the American Zone of Germany. It accomplishes something but suffers from much too tame editing.

Now I'm sure that almost everyone who reads the above suggestion will think it a good idea. But how many will do anything toward making it a reality? Certainly no agency of the government is going to attend to it. If Congress balks at radio propaganda think how it would yawp at pure art! The initiative will have to come from private groups. Why could not one of the great Foundations—the Rockefeller, the Carnegie, or the Mellon, for example—sponsor such a magazine? I have no personal stake in the matter, and no desire whatsoever to put a finger in the pie, but I do know from a year spent in Europe that such a publication is urgently needed. So let's have some action on it. Try writing to some of the Foundations. If they hear enough about the idea they are likely to give it an investigation. They move slowly, but when they move they push some weight.

It has not been possible to include in this number of *New Directions* very substantial selections of the new writing in Europe because so much interesting domestic work had been received. As it was, it was necessary to postpone half-a-dozen American pieces until *New Directions XI,* to appear within the year, barring upsets. To present the new European writing properly we are preparing supplementary anthologies of translations, one devoted to each of the principal countries. The German volume is being assembled by Edouard Roditi and Alexander Koval in Berlin. The Italian volume is in the very capable hands of Elio Vittorini in Milan. The French collection will be chosen through suggestions from several advisers in Paris. For England there is no need to edit a new volume inasmuch as two excellent collections already exist: John Lehmann's *New Writing* and *Orpheus* anthologies, and Wrey Gardiner's *New Road* annuals. All three collections are distributed in America by New Directions and may be ordered from our catalog, which is free on request.

Reader, if you have gotten this far, you are indeed indulgent and patient; you deserve some reward. What better than to spare you my "in closing" remarks?

J. Laughlin